Fragile Mountains

Fragile Mountains

MK Limbu

A novel about life, love, death and rebellion in the eastern hills of Nepal.

Vajra Publications
Jyatha, Kathmandu, Nepal

Fragile Mountains

Second Edition Published in 2005 by
Vajra Publications
Jyatha, Thamel, P.O. Box: 21779, Kathmandu, Nepal
Tel/Fax: 977-1-4220562, e-mail: bidur_la@mos.com.np
www.vajrabooks.com.np

First Edition Published by Trafford, Canada, 2005

Distributed by
Vajra Book Shop
Jyatha, Thamel, P.O. Box: 21779, Kathmandu, Nepal
Tel/Fax: 977-1-4220562, e-mail: bidur_la@mos.com.np
www.vajrabooks.com.np

© 2005 MK Limbu

All rights reserved. No part of this publication may be reproduced, stored in a retrieval system, or transmitted, in any form or by any means, electronic, mechanical, photocopying, recording, or otherwise, without the written prior permission of the author.

Cover photos by Kumar Ale

ISBN No. 99946-644-5-X

Printed in Nepal

In memory of my grandmother
who lived and died in ignorance.

I also dedicate this novel to the following:

- My *father* and *mother* who grew up in the eastern hills of Nepal and who instructed me on their lives in that remote corner of the world,

- My loving wife *Sarita* who spent a part of her childhood there and who has been such a great support to me through all these years, and

- My daughters *Natasha* and *Rojisha* and son *Mishek*, all of who have brought such joy into our lives and who will never get to see the life described in this novel.

Contents

1. *Part 1* – Life is a River — 9
2. *Part 2* – Acts of Destiny — 153
3. *Part 3* – Depth of Sorrow — 283
4. *Part 4* – Reign of Terror — 395

Part I
Life is a River

Here the hills do not roll gently into each other across the horizon; rather, they collide into each other and tower into the blue sky piercing the fluffy white clouds. Then they fall steeply into the gorge far below carved by the snake-like river's relentless southward flow. The slopes of these hills are covered by forests, grass and man-made terraces, and crisscrossed by countless streams and rivulets and the ubiquitous ribbon-like foot trails carved by the feet of hundreds of generations of human inhabitants. Despite their sturdy appearance, these hills are not as tough and resilient as they look. In fact, being of relatively new make in the geological clock, they are rather fragile and prone to natural disasters. Their uneven and soft surfaces are routinely ravaged by the relentless forces of nature – rain, wind, hailstorm, flash-flood, mudslide, landslide and earthquake, not to forget the corrosive effect of human action. These are the mid-hills of Nepal. They run across the length of the brick-shaped country east to west forming a chain of hills known to geographers and laymen alike as the Mahabharata Range. To the north and running parallel to the hills lie the majestic Himalaya Mountains, perennially snow-capped, aloof and foreboding, and famed all over the world as the highest peaks in the world. For the average Nepali steeped in a religion that preaches inaction and lays heavy emphasis on the hand of God, these peaks are not there for to climb but to worship as the abode their myriad gods and goddesses. Beyond the snow-capped peaks lies Tibet, once a free and peaceful (and powerful, in the days of antiquity) land, now under the vice-like grip of Red China. To the south, running parallel to the Mahabharata Range, lie the lower hills known as the Chure Hills. To the south of the Chure Hills lies the vast plain formed by the fertile alluvial soil of the great River Ganga basin and known affectionately to the Nepalese as the Terai.

The rest of the world knows this impoverished, landlocked country as the land of Mount Everest (which the Nepalese like to call 'Sagarmatha' for skyscraper), the highest peak in the world. Some also know it as the birthplace of Buddha - the apostle of peace, the Light of Asia - and yet some others know it as the home of the Gurkhas, sturdy little warriors famed all over the world for their bravery, honesty and loyalty. Although Nepal occupies a miniscule space on the world map, it is by no means a small country. If its total surface area made of mountains, slopes, precipices, valleys, ravines and gorges were to be accounted for, then one would be astonished to find that it's actually a vast country, possibly as large as some of the mid-sized countries of the world.

Only half a century ago these hills were almost entirely covered by thick temperate forests populated by a wide variety flora and fauna. But those days are long gone. These days they are largely denuded and bare, and if one were to take a bird's eye view through the window of an aeroplane, they look dishearteningly scarred, some would say as a direct result of population explosion, though there are others who disagree claiming that that is only one of the several factors. Firewood is the primary source of energy here and is arguably the cause of much of the deforestation. Large tracts of the middle and lower slopes of the hills are habitable and cultivable and covered with spectacularly eye-catching terraced fields that descend like a hundred feet tall giant's staircase down to the river bed far below. Depending upon their altitude, the slopes have different climates. The lower slopes are hot and humid in summer; the higher slopes are cool throughout the year. As the year progresses through the six seasons that the Nepalese have in their school textbooks (though there are only four in reality), the terraces magically transform from light green when the crops are in their infancy, to dark green when they reach maturity, to a sweet aroma-filled yellowish when it is time to harvest the crops, to light brown and denuded when they are being prepared yet again for the next round of crops. These terraces are the source of life for the tough and hardy people who inhabit these hills; this is where they eke out their meager living growing rice, wheat, maize, millet, barley, potatoes, soyabeans, vegetables and whatever they can grow depending upon the seasonal variation. It is said that all human activities seem futile and insignificant against the backdrop of the mighty Himalayas. The sleepy little villages perched on the slopes of the hills amidst the terraces provide ample proof of that. Here, life moves at its own slow and tranquil pace, following its own age old pattern, quietly and peacefully, far from the hustle and bustle of the modern world, as if nothing of significance ever takes place. Here houses are made of rocks, mud and wood, and occasionally of bricks and tin. They are usually two to three-storied, but no more, with low ceilings (for Nepalese as a rule are not tall), small black wooden doors and windows, and sloping thatched roof made of a thick layer of hay and occasionally of tiles or shiny sheets of tin. There may be a cowshed, a buffalo shed, a goat pen and a pigsty nearby; and half a dozen chickens and pigeons picking grains and insects, and a black or brown dog dozing off lazily nearby, with an occasional cat sneaking by on the rooftop.

To say that a Nepali loves his village would be an understatement, because to him his village is not just a collection of thatched-roofed mud-painted houses made of rocks, mud and wood. His village is the ribbon like foot trail that winds up and down the slopes of the hills, reaching every doorstep. His village is the dogs that bark at night and the rooster that wakes him up every morning before dawn with a 'kukhuri kaa' ('cock-a-doodle-doo' in Nepali). His village is the cow that moos in the cowshed when it is hungry and the goats that bleat when they get lost in the woods. His village is the hawk that swoops down from the sky to catch little chicks following mother hen and the pigeons that sing and dance their dance of courtship on the rooftop. His village is where it is bad luck when a cat crosses his path and good luck when he sees a pair of doves sitting by together. His village is the snake which supposedly carries a precious jewel on it head which only the most fortunate can see and the jackal that supposedly grows a horn momentarily every time it howls in the dark of the night. His village is the cuckoo that brings good luck to the first person who hears it sing in the Spring and the owl that hoots near one's window at night to tell him of his or someone else's impending death. Above all, his village is the farmer who prods a pair of oxen to the fields every day carrying a plough on his shoulders and whistling his favorite tune, and the womenfolk who gossip incessantly as they congregate at the village spring to fill their water jars.

And in the village people rarely refer to each other by their given names, but usually by the sequence of their birth and thus the first born male of the family is called Jetha and the first born female is called Jethi. The second born is a Maila or Maili, the third born Saila or Saili, the fourth born Kaila or Kaili and the last born Kanchha or Kanchhi, depending upon his/her sex. The same rule applies also to the wives of the men, so that the wife of the first son is Jethi daughter-in-law and the wife of the second son is Maili daughter-in-law and so on. This rule even applies to the husbands of women, so that the husband of the third daughter is Saila son-in-law. And the members of a particular family are often referred to by the location of their house, thus someone whose house is at the top end of the village becomes 'shiran-gharay', which can be roughly translated as 'the one whose house is at the top end of the village'. A particular person might be nicknamed by his mannerism or by the way he looks, such as a man who is in possession of an impressive moustache is 'Joongay', one who is overweight is 'Motay' (fatty) and one who is clever is 'Chatooray'. And in the village if one were to declare in a roadside tea shop, where men and women sit together and drink tongue-burning hot milked tea any time of the day (because it is said that any time is tea time in Nepal), that the earth is round then a myopic eyed, craggy-faced old-timer might still be found who'd give you that 'So-you-think-you-know-better-than-me-huh?' look and argue, "If it were so then how come people do not fall off lower side of the earth? And how come that field over there is flatter than the palm of my hand?" And if one were to persist and declare that the earth rotates on its axis once everyday, then the old timer would curl his lips and wag his fingers, "Now look here, grandson, I have been around for the past seventy-five or so years and I've neither seen nor heard that big rock over there move even an inch from its resting place. Now, would that be so if the earth rotated on what's-its-name? So be gone from here and don't give me that new-fangled crap anymore."

About three hundred kilometers as the crow flies to east of Kathmandu, in the far eastern hills of Nepal bordering Sikkim (formerly an independent and sovereign kingdom of the Lepcha people that became a part of India in the 1970s, thanks largely to Nepalese immigrants) and south of the majestic Mt. Kanchenjunga, the third highest peak in the world, lies a mountainous country cut almost diagonally by River Tamor and crisscrossed by its numerous tributaries, chief among them being River Kabeli. These rivers and tributaries are fed perennially by the snowcapped mountains in the north.

Unlike in the western part of the country where a village is made of houses clustered closely together, here a village is a collection of houses that are scattered far and wide. This is the domain of the Limbu (Limboo) people, an ancient and proud people of Mongoloid stock who have dwelt in these hills since prehistoric times. The Limbus call their territory Limbuan, or Land of the Limbu - a politically incorrect term in a country dominated politically, culturally and economically by the sharp-featured Bahun and Chhetri (colloquial for Brahman and Kshetriya) people of Aryan stock. Limbuan encompasses five districts of the eastern hills of Nepal – Taplejung, Panchthar, Ilam, Tehrathum and Dhanukutta. The Limbus are generally short and stocky with an olive complexion. They are a very proud race - their pride bordering on foolish arrogance at times - and fiercely protective of their language and cultural heritage.

Perched on the slope rising up from the bed of the Tawa River, a tributary of the River Kabeli, in a remote corner of Taplejung district lies the sleepy little village known to is inhabitants as Khewang. For countless generations, this little village has been home to the little known Sambiu clan, one of the more than two hundred clans that make up the Limbu tribe.

A little before sunset on a cold winter's day a young man and a woman were briskly making their way towards the village along the narrow foot-trail that winds its way precariously on the steep slope several hundred feet above the swirling waters of the river.

"I am tired. Let's take a short rest, shall we?" said the comely young woman and stopped.

"All right," the young man said and followed suit, though he didn't look tired.

"How far is it from here?" asked the woman, her voice betraying her tiredness and mounting apprehension.

"One hour for a man and two hours for a woman," he replied with a wink. This is how Nepalese still measure distance in the hills. It's always in terms of time, and never in terms of distance. "I told you it was tough," he added.

"But I didn't think it was this tough. It will be dark in no time at all. We should have started earlier," she said.

"Don't you worry! I know every nook and corner in this place like the back of my hand. Remember, I grew up here. Besides, we have a torch light." And he added, "We started at the right time, but our progress has been a bit slow."

"Then you should leave me here and go alone," she challenged him flirtatiously, with a half-tempting smile on her pink lips.

The young man eyed her with a mixture of affection and lust, and a mischievous smile drew across his handsome face. He winked his right eye and said, "Wait till we reach home, then I know what to do with you."

"What will do you?" she teased him, with an equally mischievous twinkle in her eyes. She was beautiful.

"Do you want me to show you right now, right here?" he playfully pulled her towards him. She giggled and pressed her warm and soft body against his as he caressed her taut breasts. She had a slender figure, fair complexion and a pretty face, the more so when she laughed. When she laughed a dimple formed on her right cheek which made her look lovelier still. A pair of gold earrings dangled from the soft lobes of her ears. Then abruptly she stopped laughing and pushed him away. With a somber expression on her face she said, "I am scared."

"I told you not to worry. I'll take care of everything. Don't you trust me?" he said.

"If I didn't trust you I wouldn't have followed you into this wilderness," she replied, "but still I can't help feeling scared."
A cold gust of cold wind hit them and ruffled their hair.
"It's getting colder. Let's continue walking. It'll make us warmer and take us home faster," he said taking her hand. She looked up at the darkening hills and the dark forests upon them and followed him quietly. When she turned back to take a glance at the red sun a minute later, it was already half hidden behind the dark silhouette of the western hills.

The destination of the young couple was a pair of thatched-roofed white-mud-painted houses that stood adjacent to but not facing each other on a terrace at the lower end of the village. In the kitchen of the main house, which was slightly larger of the two, seventy-two years old Narmaya, the wrinkle-faced matriarch of the family, was reminiscing the good old days as usual, while three generations of her family sat listening to her, warming themselves around the hearth. Granddaughters Amrita and Gorimaya and grandson Ratna sat by her side. Daughter-in-law Kamala, the mother of the children, sat a little further away. And granddaughter-in-law Laxmi sat near her mother-in-law. The past always looks better in retrospect, especially the older one gets. It looks safe, cozy and romantic, probably for the simple reason that one managed to survive it safely and also because it will never come back. Life-threatening situations become anecdotes to laugh about; hardship and misadventures endured become feats to brag about. Thus, it is only natural that people tend to look back at the past through a romantic haze created by the expanse of time - the good old days that never were.

"When I was young, things were quite different," the old woman said. "These days, you children are not afraid of your father. In our time we were so scared of ours that we didn't even dare look directly at his face. I was married at the age of nineteen and people said that was late. Some even said that I was in danger of becoming a lifelong spinster. But then your grandfather arrived out of the blue. At first my father was reluctant to give me to him saying that he was from a very remote village and I would have a very hard life there. But your grandfather, he set up camp with his elders and waited for a week until my father relented."

She fell silent for a moment and took a long sip of tongba with a pencil-thin bamboo pipette. Tongba is an alcoholic drink prepared by pouring hot water on fermented millet in a cylindrical wooden jar about a foot tall and half a foot wide. It is the favoured alcoholic drink among the Limbus. She added hot water to her tongba from a black kettle at regular intervals. A kerosene lamp, blackened by soot, stood on a low wooden stool nearby, its flickering yellowish flames illuminating the room dimly and casting long wavering shadows on the walls. Cups, plates and an assortment of kitchen utensils filled the blackened wooden racks along the wall; and four fully-filled water jars - one made of baked mud, two of bronze and another of aluminium - stood together on a raised platform in one corner. Directly above the mud-stove, hanging on four strings that stretched parallel to each other across the length of the floor, were several strands of buffalo meat. These would later be stored in a bamboo-cane basket after they became as dry as wood to be consumed at a later date or to be sent to relatives as gift. But the smell of the drying meat was overwhelmed by the sweet aroma of fresh cow-dung which Laxmi had applied to the floor and walls earlier in the afternoon. Cow-dung is considered clean by the

Nepalese as it is believed to kill germs and is used liberally to clean the house. It is also clean from the religious point of view. In the world's only Hindu kingdom the cow is a sacred animal. So sacred, in fact, that anyone caught slaughtering a cow gets a life sentence.

"How did you feel, grandma? Did you like him?" Amrita giggled, teasing the old woman.
"I don't know. I can't remember. It was such a long time ago." The old woman replied wistfully.
After a pause the old woman continued, "After getting married your grandfather and I didn't speak to each other properly for the next five years, I think."
"Why? Didn't you two like each other?" asked Amrita, although she had heard the story umpteen times.
"It's not that," said her grandmother, "I was just too shy to speak him."
Amrita, the flirtatious adolescent that she was, laughed mischievously and said, "You mean to say that you and grandfather had children without speaking to each other? That sounds very funny."
Narmaya replied, "You shameless youngsters of today do not understand such things. When we were young we were not as forthcoming with men as you girls are these days."
Amrita said, "But many women did fall in love and ran away with their lovers even in the old days, didn't they, grandma?"
Narmaya replied, "Yes, they did. I admit that it was quite a common occurrence, as it is now. But I was a bit too shy, I guess."
"But didn't you do the paddy-dance with the men, grandma?" asked the young girl.

Limbu men and women dance the paddy-dance throughout the year, but especially during the harvest, festivals and weddings. In this dance, which is in fact not a dance at all in the true sense of the word, men and women hold each other's hands alternately, forming a human chain, and sing duets for several hours at a stretch, making up impromptu verses as they take turns to sing. It's a kind of singing duel that can last the whole night and half the following day. It provides a great opportunity for men and women to interact with each other and fall in love, sometimes leading to sexual intercourse, pregnancy and elopement, in that order. Much of the young generation has given up this practice, however, because of its downside. In the old days many Limbu men and women wasted their lives doing nothing but paddy-dance throughout the year.

"Yes, I did, but that was only during the festivals. Some of the more frivolous girls flirted with the men openly. They even got pregnant and eloped. But I was not that type." The old woman replied.
"Did you dance the paddy-dance with grandfather before you got married?" Amrita asked.
"No, we had never met," she replied.

The reddish light emanating from the mud-stove reflected off Narmaya's craggy old face, revealing a creased and wrinkled bag of skin. She knew that she was about seventy-two, but she didn't know her exact birth date and she didn't care; hardly surprising in a country where registration of birth and death has begun only recently. Like most women in this part of the world, her life had been one of blissful ignorance. It had also been a life interspersed by physical and mental pain inflicted upon her by a husband who turned abusive when drunk. She had often fought back, quite viciously at times, but as he was bigger and stronger than her, he always got the upper hand. In spite of this, she never left him. This was partly because she had accepted it as a woman's lot to suffer at the hand of her husband, and partly because of her love for her half a dozen children.

When she was miserable she took solace in the fact that her lot was much better than that of the neighbouring Bahun and Chhetri women, whose young daughter-in-law is virtually treated like a slave even to this day. Every day the unfortunate young woman has to get up well in advance of the rest of the family and start the day by first performing the self-humiliating ritual of touching her husband's feet with her forehead as a form of worship, because to her he is God. After that she has to touch the feet of her mother-in-law, and even the feet of her older sisters-in-law in some extreme cases. Then she has to keep herself busy in household chores all day all without a break. She is always the last to eat, and sometimes gets to eat only the scraps because after everybody's finished that's the only thing left. She doesn't get to wear anything except a thin red sari and a red blouse day and night. When her husband is home late at night she has to stay awake until he arrives - without eating and sleeping. If she fails to do so then his lordship accuses her of being lazy and disrespectful, and even unfaithful. After a meager supper, she has to massage her mother-in-law's arms, legs and torso with ghee or mustard oil. Then before going to bed she has to repeat the same on her husband. Things are changing for the better in the cities, but such is the lot of the Bahun and Chhetri women in the villages. It is not for nothing that they lament that a woman's birth is a loser's karma.

"The fire has diminished, daughter-in-law," she said to Kamala, her eldest daughter-in-law. Kamala was a petite, slender woman in her early forties with long black hair that fell down to her thin waistline. Every morning she diligently braided it into a neat plait and tied it with a red lace. But before she had time to get up, Laxmi, her young daughter-in-law, got up hastily saying, "Let me bring it, mother." The young woman went out into the dark and came back shortly carrying a handful of dry firewood. She inserted a few pieces carefully into the oven and blew several times into it with a foot long bamboo-pipe crafted just for that purpose. A gust of ash-filled smoke abruptly rose out of the oven forcing her to retreat a few steps, coughing and covering her mouth. But eventually the wood caught fire, and the flames leapt out happily.

"When is eldest son coming back?" Narmaya asked Kamala, referring to Dil Bahadur, her eldest son.
"He should be back by now," Kamala replied. He was her husband.
"He must be having tongba with the men there," Narmaya said.

There meaning Jit Bahadur's house ten minutes' walk uphill. Jit Bahadur was Narmaya's brother-in-law, her dead husband's youngest brother. His young son who had gone to college in Kathmandu had returned the previous day on vacation and Dil Bahadur had gone there to collect the parcel that his younger brother's wife had sent from Kathmandu.

"He should be back by now, it's getting late. It is biting cold out there and I am worried that he might catch a bad cold," Narmaya said to no one in particular. She had been waiting for him for the past one hour on account of the stuff she was hoping her second daughter-in-law had sent from Kathmandu.

Narmaya's life, like every woman's life in these hills, had been one of waiting. Waiting for things to happen, waiting for life to take a better turn. This, of course, is true of everyone everywhere. But she wasn't in possession of a philosophically inclined mind to look at life from that perspective. When she was an adolescent she had patiently waited to become an adult. When she had turned sixteen, an age when girls are considered adult, she had waited for a suitor with a view to get married. When that had happened three years later at the age of nineteen (considered quite late at that time, though Limbus do not practice child marriage as some other communities still do), she had waited for two years to give birth. After one still birth and one miscarriage she had waited to give birth to a healthy, living child. After giving birth to two healthy girls she had desperately waited for a son. After giving birth to two sons, two more daughters and then one more son, she had waited for them to grow up and help in the house and farm. And all that time she had patiently waited for her abusive drunkard of a husband to mend his ways. As his abuse had increased she had secretly, not without an occasional pang of guilt, waited for him to die so that she could live the rest of her life in peace.

"I had four brothers and five sisters," she continued, without any encouragement from the youngsters, who she knew would be glad to listen to her story anyway, even though they had heard it many times over. "All except one are dead. My eldest brother, who was many years older than me, died eighteen years ago. My second brother, who was also older than me, became a *lahooray* and went to someplace called Burma, I have no idea where it is, to fight for the British in the Great War. He never came back. Ten years later a villager who had also gone with him returned and told us that he had died in the war. My parents, who had not entirely lost hope of his coming back, finally came to terms with what they had long suspected and performed his funeral rites. Since he was unmarried and had no children, he lives only vaguely in my memory. I can't even remember what he looked like. My eldest sister was married off to a Wanem from the village of Tembe. She died seven years ago. My second sister, also older than me, died when she was buried alive in the great earthquake of the year 1990. I was a very small girl then, but even so I remember crying for several days because she was my best friend. I am the third. My fourth sister, younger than me, married a Bhegha from Chengthapu, and the poor girl died during her fifth childbirth. My youngest sister married a Maden from Taplejung. He was a lahooray and they settled in the city of Dharan down south in the plain after he retired. I never met her after she got married. I heard that she also died of some ailment two years ago. My third brother, who was younger than me, died at the age of forty when cutting firewood from the branch of a tree which broke and fell with him. Now the only one left alive, except me, is my youngest brother. The last time I met him was two years ago when he came to see me." After this extended monologue the old woman took a long breath and stared at the fire, apparently trying to recollect the events of the past dimmed by the relentless march of time, as the red flames leaping out of the stove danced blithely before her myopic eyes.

"Tell us about the great earthquake of 1990, grandma," prodded her little grandson Ratna, referring to the great earthquake of 1934 AD. Nepali calendar is fifty-seven years ahead of the Roman calendar. In her mind Narmaya still recalled the terrible day as if it was yesterday, although there had been many other earthquakes since then. It had taken away her second sister and her youngest aunt. Both girls had been her best friends and she used to follow them everywhere. She went with them to collect grass for the animals and firewood for the kitchen. She went with them to fetch drinking water from the village spring and to wash clothes. She had grown so attached to them that their sudden and tragic death had left a deep vacuum in her tender heart.

"I can still vividly recall that day as if it was yesterday," she began as always in a melancholy voice, as if it still had the power to hurt, "I was helping my mother weed the vegetable garden when I suddenly felt the earth tremble under my feet, and as I watched with a mixture of surprise and horror, our house jumped up and down and swayed to the left and right. It was just unbelievable. It was as if they were dancing. At first I couldn't understand what was happening. Then I remember being terrified and falling flat on my face. My mother scooped me up in her arms and ran to a nearby tree and latched onto it tightly until the tremor died. I also remember my father running out of the house shouting "Earthquake! Earthquake! Everybody out!" He was followed closely by my grandfather dragging grandmother by the arm. Then just as they were clear off the house, the roof lurched sideways and the upper storey, it was a two-storey house like this, came crashing down - rocks and pieces of wood flying in every direction. The tremor didn't last long, but by the time it was over we didn't have a house; it had turned into a heap of debris. Then my father started counting heads and came up two short. My second sister and youngest aunt were missing. My ashen-faced mother dropped me and ran towards the debris and I followed her. We started shifting through the heap frantically. Then my uncles and brother and sisters, who were either out in the fields or collecting firewood or cutting grass arrived, running and panting. They too joined in the search. After about half an hour, we dug both girls out – covered in blood and dead. They had been crushed by the beams. It was the biggest tragedy of my childhood. Both my youngest aunt and second sister were still in their adolescence and they were my best friends. They took me everywhere they went – to the water spring, to the fields, to the woods and even to the bazaars. I remember crying my heart out for many days."

Then the old woman fell silent for a long moment, recalling in her mind the tragedy of her childhood with murky eyes through the thick mist of time. She took a long sip of the tongba and continued, "Later it transpired that some other houses in the village had also suffered the same fate. That day six people died in our village. Then a few days later news arrived from my mother's parent's village that one of my maternal uncles had also been killed. He had been hit squarely on the head by a flying rock as he had tried to run out of the house."

She stopped to take another sip of the tongba and to reflect upon the bitter-sweet memories of her youth. Those days were long gone and didn't matter anymore. Time is a great healer. It repairs and heals the deepest of wounds; and it has a way of covering one wound with yet another fresh wound, relegating the old would into the deep recess of memory where it ceases to hurt anymore.

After taking yet another sip of the tongba she continued, "The house was quickly rebuilt, but the emptiness left by the loss of my young sister and aunt remained in my heart for a long time. Five years after the earthquake my grandfather died of old age. My grandmother lived for another ten years, but she degenerated into a childlike state towards the end. She couldn't remember anything, nor could she recognize any one of us. People said that she had been possessed by the spirits. I don't know. Maybe she was, I don't know. We had to be constantly on guard to prevent her from harming herself. One day she got lost. We all searched for her frantically until my brother found her an hour later scrambling up a steep rock on all four. When he asked her where she was going, she said, "Can't you see your grandfather waving his hands from the top of the hill?" He looked up and saw no one there. Sometimes I worry that I'll be like her in a few years. They say these things run in the family."

Presently the dog outside broke into a howl and a man's voice said, "Kalay, be quiet."
Kalay the black dog stopped barking. It was Dil Bahadur, the old woman's son. Dil Bahadur walked in holding a smoking khosela - homemade cigarette made by wrapping finely shredded tobacco leaves in a neatly cut rectangular dry maize leaf - and made straight for the fire.

"It's damn cold out there," he said stretching his shivering hands towards the leaping flames.
"What held you up?" inquired Narmaya. She was anxious to see what her daughter-in-law had sent her.
"There were some other people as well and we were served tonga," replied her son.
"So what's the news?" Narmaya asked expectantly.
"Not much. Sister-in-law has sent some stuff in this packet," he said, handing a neatly wrapped packet to his wife. Kamala took the packet and proceeded to open it.
"Has she sent a letter?"
"I don't know. If she has then it should be inside the packet."
"How are she and the children?"
"Deepak says they are fine." Deepak was Jit Bahadur's twenty year old son.
"What about Milan? When is he coming home?" Kamala, who had remained quiet until now, asked.
"Deepak said that he couldn't meet Milan because the boy was not at home at the time. Sister-in-law told him that he had

gone out the day before and had not returned home. That was a week ago."

"Where could he have gone?" Kamala wondered in a worried voice. Milan was her second son and lived at his second uncle's house in Kathmandu.

"Nothing to worry about. He must have gone and stayed at a friends' place." Dil Bahadur said dismissively. By this time Kamala had finished opening the packet and was carefully examining the presents.

"Oh, look, she has sent a woolen sweater, two blouses, lipsticks, nail polish, hair clips and glass bangles. How very nice of her," she said happily as she held up the clothes for all to see. Amrita and Gorimaya leapt to their mother's side to examine the things.

"The sweater is for grandma, the blouses are for mother and sister-in-law, and the lipsticks, nail polish, hair clips and bangles for me and sister-in-law. It's written there," she cooed happily.

Kamala handed the sweater to her mother-in-law, a blouse to her daughter-in-law and kept one for herself. Amrita grabbed the rest of the stuff. "Sister-in-law, we'll share these," she said to Laxmi.

"Oh, how very pretty ...."

"Oh, what a fine choice of colour ...."

"Oh, what a perfect fit ....."

The women chattered effusively commenting on the thoughtfulness of the sender as Dil Bahadur listened quietly as while warming himself in the fire. He was fifty-two years old and the hard life of a hill farmer had already taken its toll on him. He had lost two front teeth and the remaining were stained a deep dark-brown by years of smoking. His forehead was creased by several lines that ran parallel to each other from temple to temple. When he frowned or laughed these accentuated to make him look older than his years. When he laughed his cheeks were segmented by a number of diagonal lines that ran across them. Of the four sons of Narmaya, he was the oldest and the only one who had remained in the village, the others having migrated to the Terai and the cities.

"By the way," he said, interrupting the women, "Chitray was also there. He is just back from his in-laws' house in Hampang. He said that our Kanchhi's husband is going to someplace called Korea next month. She is pregnant and is due in five months." Kanchhi was his youngest sister.
"Really?" Narmaya's eyes lit up, "Is she coming to live with us?"
"No, she is not, mother," he replied.
"She didn't come last Dashain. I was hoping that she would come this year," she said sadly.
"Where did he get the money?" Kamala asked. She knew that Kanchhi's financial situation was not that good.
"He pawned his land," Dil Bahadur replied.

Twelve years earlier, Kanchhi had fallen in love with a man from the Angbuhang clan from the village of Hampang, a day's walk to the south-west, and eloped with him because she had been too timid to tell her parents. Afterwards, when it had turned out that her parents wouldn't have objected to the match anyway, she had come back with her husband to seek their blessings. Now she was the mother of two teenaged daughters and a son and was on the way to having her fourth child. Her father-in-law and mother-in-law had both passed away and her two brothers-in-law had separated after getting married. They had had just about enough to eat before the breakup; the division of property had worsened the hand-to-mouth situation and her husband had been trying to go abroad to find employment.

"I hope she will come someday," Kamala added sympathetically.
"Of course, she will," replied Dil Bahadur Bahadur.
"I wish she could come soon. I'll be so happy to see her and her children. I haven't seen them for a long time," Narmaya said wistfully.

Dil Bahadur threw a glance at the Japanese wrist watch given to him by his younger brother. Although he couldn't read the numbers on them, he could tell the time accurately by the position of the hour and minute hands. It was half past ten, quite late to be up in a cold winter night. The little boy Ratna had fallen asleep by the fireside, crouched in a foetal position, with his hands between his thighs. Dil Bahadur gently patted his son on the head to wake him up. The boy awoke rubbing his eyes and Dil Bahadur told him to go to bed. Ratna got up without uttering a word and, still rubbing his eyes, went out and climbed up the wooden steps to his bedroom which he shared with his two sisters.

Dil Bahadur asked his wife, "Where is Purna?"
He was referring to his twenty-five years old eldest son.
"He went to bed hours ago. He said he was very tired," replied his wife.
"The poor boy works so hard. Doesn't remain idle for even a moment," Narmaya added affectionately. She was fond of her grandson.

Just then the dog broke into a frenzy of barking, and fell silent abruptly. Sensing that someone familiar had arrived, Kamala asked herself, "Who can it be?"

They waited for the visitor to knock on the door, but he didn't. So after some time Kamala lit another kerosene lamp and went outside. She let out a cry of surprise, for standing before her in the courtyard in the dark was her second son Milan. What was he doing here at this hour of the night? He was supposed to be in Kathmandu, where he was attending college. He hadn't even sent a message. She couldn't understand. She recollected what Deepak had told Dil Bahadur and tried to come up with an answer. The dog was jumping up and down happily, licking Milan's hands and legs while all time wagging its tail.

"Milan, is it you? We didn't know you were coming. Why didn't you inform us?"
"I had to come abruptly, mother," he replied.
She sensed uneasiness in his voice - a hint of nervousness. Her instinct told her that something was not quite right. The guilty are afraid; his demeanour gave a clear impression of that.
"Well, why do you just stand there? Why don't you come in? It's dark out here." She said to her son.
The young man scratched the back of his head self-conciously and stammered, "There's someone with me, mother."
"Who? A friend? Where's he?"
"It's not a he, mother. It's a she. Lalita, step forward."

Out of the darkness a slender young woman stepped towards her uncertainly. She was clad in kurta-suruwal, the ubiquitous baggy Indian female-wear that young Nepalese women have adopted with gusto in the towns and cities, and a woolen sweater on top of that. A foot-wide shawl of a flimsy material covered her hair and face partially and her head was bowed down self-consciously. Kamala was so taken aback by this unexpected turn of even that all she could do was to stand staring at the young woman dumbfounded. Even in the flickering yellow light of the kerosene lamp, she couldn't help noticing that the young woman was very pretty with a fair complexion. *She is beautiful*, she thought, *and about the same age as my son, too. Perhaps a year or two younger*. That was the only thing that ran through her mind.

"Who is she?" She whispered, finally regaining her voice.
"This is Lalita, mother, your daughter-in-law." Milan replied.
"My daughter-in-law? You got married?" She asked uncertainly.
"No, mother, we are not married. Not yet."

Before Kamala could think of another question to ask, Milan turned to the young woman and said, "Lalita, pay your respect to my mother." And before Kamala could react, Lalita had bent down and touched her feet with her hands.

Hearing the muffled voices in the dark the other members of the family trooped outside one after another. When Dil Bahadur saw his second son with a strange young woman at that hour of the night, he was as taken aback as his wife. He stared incredulously at the two, and said, "Milan, is that you? What is the meaning……"

But before he could finish the sentence Milan said, "Lalita, these are my father and grandmother."

With a graceful movement that comes only with youthfulness, Lalita bent down to touch Dil Bahadur's feet before he had time to react. She did the same to Narmaya, who was still trying to figure out what was going on in the dark with her aged and myopic eyes. Recovering a moment later from the shock, Dil Bahadur asked his son, "Who is she?"

"This is Lalita, your daughter-in-law, father," stammered the son, in an almost apologetic voice, mustering all his courage.

Looking at his father's face now he was uncertain of himself. Dil Bahadur's eyes shifted from Milan to Lalita and then came to rest on her face. She squirmed in discomfiture and looked at the ground. He turned to his son and said, "I thought you were in Kathmandu."
"Yes, I was, father."
"Then what is this?"
Milan made no attempt to reply. Instead, he turned to his mother with imploring eyes.

Dil Bahadur turned to Laxmi and said, "Eldest daughter-in-law, bring your husband here."
"He's sleeping, father," said Laxmi meekly.
"I know he is. Wake him up," said Dil Bahadur.
"Yes father," Laxmi hurried into the next house where her husband was sleeping.

This little incident was taking place in the courtyard of the main house, which contained the kitchen, which consisted of a single large room on the ground floor that also served as the dining and living room, and four small rooms on the first floor accessible by a rickety wooden staircase outside the kitchen door. Narmaya, Dil Bahadur and Kamala, and Amrita and her younger sister Gorimaya and younger brother Ratna slept in those rooms. In the other house, also two-storied but smaller with fewer rooms, Purna and Laxmi occupied one room on the first floor and Milan slept alone in an adjacent room whenever he was home. It was left unused at other times. The rooms on the ground floor were used as store and occasionally for guests.

A few minutes later, a bleary eyed Purna followed his wife rubbing his eyes and shivering in the cold, holding a torch light in his hand, "Why on earth do you have to wake me up at this hour of the night? Can't an honest man even ....."

When he saw his whole family gathered in the courtyard, he stopped abruptly. He stared at them uncertainly and uttered, "What's happening?"
"Well, it seems that your younger brother has got himself a wife," said Dil Bahadur.
Purna looked at his father and then at the young couple, and uttered involuntarily, "Eh!"
"Eh? Is that all you have to say?" asked his father.
"Well," said Purna clearing his throat, obviously trying to find the right words to say, "What's there to say?"
"Well, what do you think? Say something."
After a long pause Purna replied, "I guess it's all right."
"Is it?"
"I guess so," Purna replied.
Dil Bahadur turned to Milan to say something, but Narmaya overtook him and said, "It's getting late. We can talk tomorrow. They must be hungry."
"We are not hungry, grandma. We have already had food on the way," Milan replied, thankful for the old woman's timely intervention. He was finding it difficult to face his usually reticent father.

"Is she a Limbu?" Dil Bahadur asked throwing a suspicious glance at the downcast young woman. He was still examining her with his eyes.
"Yes, she is," replied Milan.
"Of what clan?"
"Jabegu."

Without saying a word Dil Bahadur headed for the staircase. When he had reached the top he turned back and said to

Narmaya, "Mother, you are the matriarch of the family. Say something to them." He climbed up the staircase and went into his room.

Narmaya peered closely at Lalita. "Show me your face, child," she said. Lalita lifted her head, removed the shawl and looked straight into the old woman's eyes.

"You are very pretty. What's your name again?"

"Lalita," said the young woman softly.

"How old are you, child?" asked old woman.

"Twenty," said the girl.

"That's two years younger than my grandson. And what village are you from?" asked the old woman.

"My parents are from Yangnam," she replied, "it's in Panchthar district."

"I know that. I've been there a long time ago when I was young. Did you say that you are a Jabegu?" Narmaya asked.

"Yes," replied the girl.

"So have you come straight from there now?" asked the old woman.

"No, we've come from Kathmandu."

"Really? Were you in Kathmandu as well?"

"Yes, grandma."

Kamala, who had been listening to the two, interrupted interrupted, "Mother, it's getting late. You will catch cold if you stay outside all night."

Then turning to Milan, she whispered, "Take her to your room. You'll find everything as you left it on your last visit."

Narmaya said to Lalita, "Go to sleep now. We'll talk again tomorrow." She followed her daughter-in-law up the stairs. When their long shadows had vanished into the darkness, Milan turned to Lalita and indicating towards Purna and Laxmi said, "These are my elder brother and sister-in-law."

Lalita again bent down to touch Purna's feet but Purna stopped her midway, muttering self-consciously, "No need to do that. No need, really. Welcome to the family."

Lalita then greeted Laxmi with a Namaste. Laxmi returned the greeting in the same manner and said, "Don't worry, sister, everything will be alright." Lalita thanked her and followed Milan.

As the couple reached the door Purna called after his younger brother, "Milan, just a moment."

Milan walked back to his brother while Lalita waited at the door.

"So? Is it her? Is she the one you told me about?" Purna whispered, putting emphasis on the word 'her'.

"Yes, it's her," replied Milan.

"How do you think you are going to do the explaining to father and mother?" asked Purna.

"I don't know. I just hope things will work out by themselves like they always do, you know," said Milan. *For better or worse things always work out by themselves*. That's the way he looked at life.

"They will in the end. But I am afraid of what will happen when father finds out," said Purna, "he will certainly not be happy, you know."

"I know. So what do you suggest?" asked Milan.

"I don't know. I am not good at such things. You are the one who is smart and clever," replied Purna.

"We'll find a way out, elder brother," he said and walked away.

Purna and Laxmi watched the couple vanish through the dark door. Laxmi gave her husband a questioning look.

"What was that all about?" she asked, her curiosity greatly aroused.
"I'll tell you later," said Purna, "You go to bed."
"Tell me now," she said.
"Go to bed. I'll tell you later," he replied.
"Aren't you coming, too?" asked Laxmi.
Purna shook his head and said, "No, you go alone. I'll come later."
Laxmi said, "Do what you like, but don't blame me if you catch cold." She locked the kitchen door and went to her bed room.

Purna stood alone under the dark starry sky, gazing at the big dipper, the group of stars that forms a question mark in the sky on a clear night. Erudite Hindus have a name for them - Saptarshi or the seven sages, but he didn't know that. He gently stroked Kalay the dog who snuggled between his legs, wagging its tail. The cold breeze blowing up from the Tawa River, whose distant roar formed a constant background to a dark and breezy winter night, struck the exposed skin of his hands and face making him shiver. His inserted his shivering hand inside the pocket of his shirt, took out a khosela and lit it with a match stick. He stood broodingly as he inhaled and exhaled the nicotine-filled smoke, which floated invisibly in circles out of his lips, giving him an illusion of warmth. This was a new situation - an entirely unexpected situation - and he was completely at a loss as to what to make of it.

Milan led Lalita up the creaky wooden steps, with a torch in his hand, to his small and sparsely furnished room on the first floor of the smaller house. Once inside, he produced a gas lighter from his pocket and lit the kerosene lamp that was on the small and bare table by the bedpost. He didn't smoke but always took care to carry a lighter when embarking upon long journeys. He noted that the room was exactly as he had left it three months ago. After throwing his shoes and socks to a corner by the door, he threw himself on the narrow bed, barely wide enough for two people to squeeze into, and pulled Lalita, who had also undressed by this time, towards him. She came easily and willingly on top of him. As they gazed into each other's eyes in the dim yellow light, with their shadows wavering gigantically against the grayish wall, Milan broke into a slow smile. So did Lalita. They had expected things to be rough and stormy, with a bit of firework between the father and son. "It might well have come to that if grandmother hadn't intervened," Milan said. He was genuinely thankful for that. "After all, what are grandmas for?" he chuckled as he wrapped his arms tightly around her warm and soft body. "Don't you worry, my love, everything will be all right and as it should be," he reassured her gazing into her dark eyes smouldering with passion.

"Mother and grandma are no problem, I can easily handle them," he said, "it's the old man who might be difficult. He is not bad, really. He is very quiet, honest and righteous. And that's the problem." Milan, though not a very conventional type of son, was nevertheless afraid of his father and respectful of him.
"I know they won't accept me when they discover who I am," said Lalita.
"Shh, stop talking like that. Trust me, everything will be all right." He reassured her.
"But I am scared," she whispered into his ear, "I can't help being scared."
"We'll face it together, you and I, the two of us," Milan said.
"You must tell them the truth," she said.

"Yes," he replied. "I guess I'll have to."
"When?"
"I don't know."
"Do it tomorrow."
"Tomorrow? Why tomorrow?"
"Because the sooner the better."
"I will."
"What will you do if they turn me out?"
"They will do no such thing. My folks aren't like that, and even if they do you'll not go alone because I'll be by you side."
"I know you will, but still …." she whispered leaving the sentence incomplete and circled her arms tightly around his neck, pulling his mouth toward her open mouth. Their lips touched and locked into each other's. They kissed passionately. Then in a quick motion Milan expertly rolled her over and climbed on top of her. She reflexively spread her thighs apart and chuckled softly, "Be careful, you might hurt the kid inside."

In the adjoining room, Laxmi waited for Purna to come to bed. Although she closed her eyes and tried, she couldn't bring herself to fall asleep. She was too excited by the night's turn of events. On top of that she was anxious to unravel the secret between the brothers. "Her," Purna had said, as if he knew the woman. *I thought my husband told me everything. Apparently he doesn't. How naïve I am. Of course, men do not tell us everything. They keep secrets from us women, same as we women keep secrets from them.*

The night's events brought back memories of her own wedding. She had come to this house as Purna's wife three years ago. It had been an arranged marriage; she had never laid eyes on him before. Her first impression of him was not much. He was a shy young man who spoke very little. *He is still like that*, she thought, *not like his younger brother at all.*

During the wedding ceremony he had sat silent and stiff beside her, without even bothering to give her a glance, though she had stolen a few glances at him out of sheer curiosity. Afterwards, to her disappointment (and relief at the same time because she was still a virgin and afraid), he hadn't made love to her on their nuptial night. He had just lied down by her side quietly, consumed by self-consciousness. Apparently, he had never touched a woman before. She had felt a bit let down, wondering whether he might not be incapable of having sex. But the next night, with subtle encouragement from her, he had lost his inhibition and done it, and that had expelled all doubts from her mind. The following morning the two had been too shy to speak to each other, or even to look into each other's eyes. But gradually, as the days had changed into weeks and weeks into months, they had overcome their shyness. In these three years she had grown to love him for what he was - a quiet, gentle and considerate man who she knew loved her and cared for her deeply, though he had never expressed his love verbally. Never! Not even once. It was not in his nature to express his feelings verbally, and she had understood and accepted that. Now looking back in a new light she wondered what it would have felt like to fall in love, and whether she would have given him a second look had they met before their marriage. *I wouldn't have*, she concluded. *He is not the sort that catches a young girl's imagination.*

An hour later she heard Purna tiptoe into the room. She turned to face him and moaned softly to indicate that she was still awake. "Aren't you asleep yet?" he asked as he snuggled into the warm bed beside her. "I couldn't fall asleep," she replied.
"Sleep," he said and turned to the other side.
"I have been wondering….." she started.
"About what?" he asked.

"The secret between the two of you," she said.

"It's no secret. She is a married woman," he broke the secret bluntly. Just like that, without any fanfare and dramatics.

"What?" she exclaimed, tugging him to face her, "She's already married? To another man?"

"Yes! When Milan was home last time he confided to me that he had got himself entangled with a married woman. She is the wife of an ex-lahooray."

"And you never told me?" she mocked a hurt tone.

"You would have talked; you women can never keep a secret," he replied.

"Have I ever talked?"

"Not that I know of, but still …. Besides, I didn't think the affair would last."

"Now I shudder to think what father will do when he finds out the truth."

"I guess he'll blow his top for a while, and then he'll accept her. What else can he do?" replied Purna and let out a long yawn. "Now let me sleep," he said and turned to the other side. He was exhausted by the day's work.

"And what's become of her husband? Poor man! He must be heartbroken. What kind of woman leaves her husband for another man?" she wondered aloud.

"You are a woman; you should know," Purna replied, "She is pretty though, isn't she?"

"And about the same age as me, too," added Laxmi.

When Laxmi next turned to say something to him, he was already asleep. *He is like that*, thought Laxmi, *works hard all day, has a tongba after supper and once he goes to bed takes no time at all to fall asleep, and then sleeps like a log.*

But she was unable to fall asleep because she, the faithful and loving wife that she was, could not even begin to understand what drove a woman to leave her husband for another man. *I will never leave my husband,* she vowed as she ran her fingers across Purna's back lovingly, *not even if he gets drunk and kicks me everyday.* She had no doubt about that.

In the room that she shared with her little brother and sister in the main house, seventeen year old Amrita couldn't force herself to enter the realm of dreams either. While her little brother and sister slept blissfully on their beds on the floor, wrapped snuggly inside their woolen blankets, she lay awake staring at the faintly visible silhouette of the wooden beams that ran parallel to each other across the dark ceiling. In the adjoining room she heard her father and mother talking in low muffled voices. Mother was doing most of the talking. She couldn't catch the words, but she knew what was being said. Her mother was defending her son's action, like all mothers do. It's the same everywhere – north, south, east and west. Mothers always defend their sons. That's why when their sons get spoilt the husband blames his wife, "You woman, you have spoilt your son with your love."

Amrita's window faced her second brother's window and she thought she heard soft moans and creaking of the bed. She listened intently but she couldn't be certain. *It's only my overworked imagination,* she chided herself, *the couple must be too tired to be at it.* Then after some time she thought she heard it again, but again she could not be sure. This brought a flood of memories into her mind, overwhelming her senses. Memories of a young man who was far, far away. His handsome face danced before her eyes and she felt a strong urge to be held tightly in his robust arms and to be kissed on her tender lips, as he used to do to her in the woods. Sharan, her boyfriend of four years, had become a lahooray and was now far away across the seven seas in England, the land of the *gora* (white people). He wrote to her every month telling her of his life in the army and of the exotic lands in the West where everything was different. In beautiful words he proclaimed his undying love for her, telling her how his lonely heart ached constantly for her in a land so far away from home, and how he missed her, pined for her and kissed her photograph every day. And in each letter he promised to her that as soon as he returned home on vacation, he'd waste not a single day to come her house to ask for her hand in marriage. She trusted him completely and believed every word he wrote. *One day he'll come back to marry me, and he will take me away to the far off land across the seven seas.* When you are young and in love and separated by a great distance from your sweetheart, time moves at a snail's pace. True love is like a sweet pain that throbs constantly in a deep, inaccessible corner of your heart. "There's still a year to go," she let out a melancholy sigh, "a year of waiting and a year filled with nagging doubt. A year so long that it seems like a decade, no a century." She feared that he'd fall for the charm of foreign girls and never come back to her. This feeling of insecurity gnawed at her subconscious mind constantly. Suddenly, without any apparent reason, her eyes filled with tears that trickled down her temples to the soft down-stuffed pillow. "Sharan, come back quickly. I am waiting for you," she whispered softly in the darkness, "I love you, and I will always love you." She didn't know when she fell asleep.

In the room next to Amrita's, her parents talked late into the night. Dil Bahadur was both shocked and upset. And he was confused. "The boy's always been a bit wayward," he declared. "I can understand that youngsters these days want to choose their own life partners and I have no problem with that," he said, "but he should have either become a lahooray or finished his studies first. Now, what's he going to do? After he has lived so long in the city he cannot become a farmer. And the girl? Who is she? Where's she from? Whose daughter is she? We have absolutely no idea. She might be another man's wife or the mother of four children or even a prostitute for all that matters," he said.

Kamala listened quietly and said, "We'll find that out tomorrow morning. But at least we know that she is not related to us. No one from either your or my side is of the Jabegu clan."
"That's true," Dil Bahadur replied.

Now Limbus have this peculiar thing about blood relation. It can be said that they are obsessed with it, literally. It runs far and deep in the community, so much so that among them it is considered incestuous to marry anyone who is even remotely related. While in many communities around the world it is the accepted custom to marry one's first cousin, in the eyes of the Limbu this is an act of incest. Everyone from one's father's clan (which is one's own clan) is related, so is everyone from the mother's clan. Everyone from one's paternal grandmother's clan is related, so is everyone from the maternal grandmother's clan. It goes much further than that - as far back as seven generations. Thus, everyone from the great-grandparents' clans (of both sides) is also related. To an outsider, this practice may seem strange and a bit weird, but with over two hundred different clans to choose from, it is actually not so difficult to find a life partner.

Now behind every tradition, there is a myth to justify it. Some believe that myth gives rise to tradition. In fact, the opposite seems to be more logical. First there was the event, and then later myth was invented to justify or explain the continuation of that event. Limbus have myths to explain and regulate every aspect of their lives. The collection of these myths is called the *Mundhum*, which is to the Limbus what the Bible is to Christians, the Quran is to Muslims and the Geeta is to the Hindus.

Now for the myth, which is but one of many. Way back in the days of innocence following creation, the earliest woman gave birth to a healthy boy. He grew up to become a brave and skilled warrior-hunter and became known as the Tall Hunter. He traveled all over the hills in pursuit of wild animals with his bow and arrows. One day while pursuing a deer in the high hills, he came across a beautiful maiden weaving cloth with her handloom. They fell in love and began to live together. This resulted in the birth of a boy. Now the Tall Hunter by no means was a faithful husband for when his wife was pregnant he made love to her maid on the sly. The maid also became pregnant and gave birth to a boy.

After some time, the Tall Hunter went hunting to the low hills and there he met a beautiful woman and fell in love with her and settled with her. She gave birth to a girl. But again the promiscuous Tall Hunter made love to his second wife's maid, who also gave birth to a boy. When the second wife found out about the Tall Hunter's infidelity, she became jealous and angry and refused to give him food. He then went to his first wife, but here again the first wife, who had also found about his liaison with her maid, refused to give him food.

Thus discarded by his wives, the distraught Tall Hunter then went into the forest in search of quarry, but he was unable to kill anything for many days and died of starvation. The children of the first wife and her maid grew up without knowing anything about the children of the second wife and her maid. One day while hunting in the forest, the sons of the two maids accidentally ran into each other. They found out about each other and complained to each other about the unfair treatment meted out to them and their maid mothers by their step mothers. There and then they hatched a plan to take revenge. Accordingly, the first wife's maid's son crafted a beautiful bamboo comb and the second wife's maid's son knitted a bag out of some creeping plants. The first wife's maid's son then took the bag home and presented it to his step-brother telling him that it was a gift to him from a beautiful maiden. Meanwhile, the second wife's maid's son took the comb home and presented it to his step-sister telling her that it was a gift to her from a handsome young man. Thus having greatly aroused their curiosity, the two conspirators arranged for their step-brother and step-sister to meet in private. Not knowing that they were brother and sister, being offspring of the same father, the two fell in love at first sight and started to live together. Over several years of conjugal life, they gave birth to several children.

One day the woman lost her temper with her dog and beat it severely. Now this bitch, for it was a female dog, knew of their incestuous relationship. She went to the gods to complain, who sent their emissaries to investigate. When they found out the truth, the gods banished the husband to the highlands in the north along with nineteen of his sons as punishment. The wife had to remain in the lower hills in the south with her remaining eight sons, who later became famous as the Eight Wise Ones greatly revered by the Limbus as their common forefathers.

So to this day when hitherto unacquainted Limbus meet, the first thing they do is to tell one another after their ancestry to ascertain whether or not they are related. This is in fact quite easy. If a person tells another person his father's, mother's and grandmother's (both paternal and maternal) clan-names, and if the other person's either father or mother or grandmother (both paternal and maternal) share the clan-name, then the two are related. Limbus usually know their father's (which is one's own surname), mother's and grandmother's clan-names.

Early the following morning, when the worried young couple had woken up and resumed discussing strategies, because one always needs strategies to survive in these modern times, there was a polite knock on the door. Lalita opened it. It was Amrita. The girl greeted her politely flashing a shy yet curious smile and asked if she had slept well. Lalita replied that she had and asked her to come in. But the girl declined politely and said, "Father and mother will see you in an hour."
"Where's he now?" Milan asked.
"He's gone out, but he's said he'll be back by then." Amrita replied and went away.

An hour later Dil Bahadur, Kamala and Purna sat on a leather-topped bamboo stool in the courtyard of the main house waiting for Milan and Lalita. Near them, warming themselves in the thin rays of the morning sun, sat Narmaya, Laxmi and Amrita on a straw mat. As usual there was a smoking *khosela* between the fingers in Dil Bahadur's right hand, its white smoke curling lazily upward. Another unlit khosela was neatly tucked above his left ear. The welcome morning sun, in all its pristine purity, pierced through the morning mist, warming the cold, crisp air. But the terraces were still covered in frost and the riverbed down below was buried under a blanket of white mist that was just beginning to dissipate.

In his room, as he prepared to face his parents, Milan was thinking up strategies - devising a plan, rejecting it in favour of another and then going back to old one and rejecting it again in favour of yet another plan. *If my father says this, I will say that.* Lalita, on her part, was preoccupied with her own thoughts. She had one simple yet dreadful question in her mind: "Will they accept me when they find out the truth?"

Milan and Lalita were the last to arrive at the scene. Without uttering a single word Lalita bowed down and touched the feet of each of the senior members of the family with her hands as a mark of respect, starting from the grandmother and ending with Purna.
Kamala smiled amiably and said to Lalita, "Did you sleep well, daughter-in-law?"
"Yes, mother," Lalita replied in a subdued voice with downcast eyes. Her countenance was was serene but beneath the calm surface a storm was brewing, and under her breast her heart was pounding furiously.

Dil Bahadur, who had been appraising Lalita with his eyes, made an act of clearing his throat and began his monologue, which he had rehearsed all night and morning:

"Now my sons and daughters, you know that I am not an educated man. I cannot read and write, because I never got the chance to go to school. There was no school in this village when I was small. And even if there had been one I doubt that my father would have allowed me to. But as uneducated as I am, even I know that the world is changing fast and we have to at least try to move along with it. Like Amrita's teacher told me one day, we may try to hold back progress but that will be to our own detriment."

He stopped to take a sip from his khosela, and then continued. "Even without the recent changes, we Limbus have traditionally been in favour of allowing adult men and women to choose their own life partners, in contrast to that of some other communities. While your mother and I went thorough an arranged marriage, some of your uncles, aunts, grand-uncles and grand-aunts fell in love and married of their own free will." He stopped to take another sip, and watched the smoke float upward in wisps that thinned and disappeared.

"There was also a tradition in the old days, which lasted well until my father's time, that if a man really liked an unmarried woman, then he could forcibly carry her off to his house and hold her captive without causing her any physical harm, of course, until she consented to marry him. As you might be well aware of, my own third uncle married his now-deceased wife that way. In today's context it's a barbaric thing to do, but they lived happily together." He took another sip of the smoke and blew it out. "Anyway, what I am trying to say is that in our culture there is no objection to a person to choose his or her own life partner, provided, of course, that he or she is of our own race, is not related by blood, has a good family background and upbringing, and is not already married."

The young couple squirmed uneasily, but except for Purna and Laxmi nobody noticed their discomfort. Dil Bahadur took a sip from his khosela, blew out the smoke, cleared his throat again and continued, "Now, our second son Milan here has chosen his own life partner, of his own free will, and your mother and I have thought deeply about it and arrived at the conclusion that his action is not entirely objectionable to us. The only thing we are not happy about is the timing – he was still in college. It is our feeling that he should have waited a bit longer. That's my view, of course. But since it's already happened, there's nothing we can do except to accept it in good faith. So let us all welcome our new daughter-in-law into the family."

This was the longest speech he had given in his life. All the time he was talking, Milan was struggling with himself with his mind in a state of turmoil and indecision. He tried but failed. He just couldn't muster the guts to tell the truth. The words froze at the tip of his tongue; they just wouldn't come out.

Sensing his discomfort, Dil Bahadur asked, "Is there anything you have to tell me?"

This is the moment. Seize it. He said to himself in his mind. Lalita glanced at him with a mixture of expectation and foreboding. Like him she was also torn between two minds. She was frightened but she also wanted to find the answer to her question. Sooner the better. Tell them now. Let's be done with it.
"No, father." Milan managed a meek reply and felt disappointed with himself.
"If there is anything, you can tell us without inhibition," Kamala chipped in.
"There's nothing, mother," he replied, cursing himself in his mind for his cowardice.

But I'll have to tell mother, he thought. Later. I'll tell her later ... when she is alone. She will understand. She always does. This thought gave him some comfort. Then he thanked his father and mother for accepting Lalita into the family. Purna and Laxmi looked relieved.

But Dil Bahadur was not finished. "Now that we," Dil Bahadur emphasized the word 'we', "We have brought this fine young woman into our family without the knowledge and consent of her family, it is only natural that they must be greatly concerned for her whereabouts and well-being. They could even be wondering whether their daughter may not have been kidnapped. The times are bad and there is no dearth of bad-intentioned people about. Therefore, we must now waste no time in informing her family and get their consent for the wedding."

Greatly alarmed by this suggestion, Milan cut in hastily, "No, not now, father. I think we should wait a few days before we do that."
"Why? Is there anything wrong?" asked Dil Bahadur.
"There's nothing wrong, father. We were just thinking to let things cool down a bit before approaching her family."

Dil Bahadur nodded affirmatively to indicate that he had understood. Turning to his wife he said, "Purna's mother, take daughter-in-law into the house and show her around."

Later that day Milan and Purna went out for a stroll. The terraces along the way lay dry and bare, devoid of greenery after the harvest, except for the yellow strands of sweet-smelling hay scattered here and there randomly. Purna was planning to plough his fields in a few days to sow maize and mustard seeds.

When he was certain that they were sufficiently far for anyone to hear, he asked his younger brother why the latter had chosen this particular time to do what he had done.

"She is pregnant, that's why," Milan stated bluntly, without any dramatics. He seldom lied to his elder brother whom he trusted completely. If Purna was surprised, he didn't show it.
"It doesn't show. How long has it been?" He asked after half a minute of contemplation.
"Two months."
"Are you sure it's yours?"
"What kind of question is that, elder brother? Of course, it's mine. Her husband has been away for the past six months," Milan replied.
"Does she have any children by her husband?" Milan asked.
"No, this is the first time she's conceived," Milan replied, "but her husband has four children from his previous marriage, all above twelve."
"Really?" Now he looked surprised. *What was a young girl like her doing with a man with four grown-up children?* But he didn't ask.
"Yes, he's about forty-four and when his former wife died of some illness, her parents forced her to marry him. You see, the deceased woman was her aunt - her father's younger sister - and you know it's quite common for a widower to marry his dead wife's niece," Milan provided the answer to his unasked question.

Then both men walked in silence. Along the way they came across men and women at work. Some of them gave Milan a curiosity-filled look and asked him after his well-being. He knew that they knew. Somehow they always know. One woman even asked him about his new bride. He replied that she was fine. News travels fast in the village.

The knowledge that Lalita was carrying a child cast a shadow in Purna's mind. Not because he was envious or anything like that, but because it reminded him of his own failure. It exacerbated his inability to father a child even after three years of marriage. He didn't know whether the fault lay with him or her, but he knew that the male-dominated society lay the blame squarely on the woman and he himself hardly knew any better. It's always the woman who gets the blame. If she gets pregnant out of wedlock, it's her fault. If she is unable to conceive a child, it's her fault. If her husband kicks and beats her, it's her fault. If he throws her out of the house, it's her fault. If he deserts her for another woman, it's her fault. If he dies a premature death, it's her fault. Why, even if she is raped and murdered, then that's her fault. The list is inexhaustible. Some things never change. In this male-dominated society, it's always the woman's fault. And in this part of the world there is no dearth of male chauvinist pigs with a holier-than-thou attitude who never fail to remark caustically: "Being a woman she should have been more careful …." or "Being a woman she should not behave in such and such way… " or "Being a woman she should dress up properly…" while he himself leers at her shamelessly and makes her the target of sexual harassment at the first opportunity available.

Purna knew that this biased social attitude hurt Laxmi terribly, and he tried his best to shield her from the pain. Laxmi was an ideal wife for him in every respect and he loved her as much as any man could love his wife. But try as he may he had never been able to express his love verbally. Sometimes he wanted to tell her how much he loved her, but he felt too inhibited to do so. The words got stuck in his throat and he ended up saying nothing or muttering something else. It was just not in his nature. But while love had blossomed between the two their inability to conceive a child cast a dark shadow in their happiness.

He was aware that pressure was slowly and subtly building on them from all quarters to produce a child.
"When are you going to have a child?" the elders would ask him every time they cornered him.
"Isn't it time you two had a child? I have been longing to hold my great-grandson in my arms before I die," his grandmother would say to Laxmi every time she got the opportunity.

"I, too, am anxious to hold my grandson in my hand. When are you going to fulfill my wish?" his mother would add. She didn't mean to hurt the younger woman, but Laxmi invariably always felt hurt, though she was always careful not to show it. With practice, she had become adept at hiding the pain in her heart.

The above was pretty tame compared to what some of the more insensitive and spiteful relatives had to say.
"When is your wife going to have a child? Is she at all capable of motherhood? I think you should start thinking of a second marriage," some of the nastier relatives would throw snide remarks at him, taking advantage of his good nature. He would try a self-conscious smile and walk away, feeling terribly wounded but powerless to do anything.

The tongue is sharper than the knife, especially when it is wielded by those with malicious intent. Lately it was beginning to get on his nerves and he was losing patience with the careless tongues whose single purpose, it seemed, was to spite him and Laxmi. He didn't tell her what he had heard because he knew that she would be deeply hurt. She was a sensitive woman who kept her feelings to herself. But he knew how she felt deep inside. He knew her fear; he knew her pain. He knew that she was afraid that sooner or later he would be forced to take another wife if she continued to remain childless. Therefore, her biggest ambition, her only ambition in life, in fact, was to have children. She did not only want a child - that would be an understatement - she pined for it every waking hour of her life and prayed silently for it before falling asleep every night.

That night as they prepared to go to bed, Laxmi said, "Lalita told me that she is two months pregnant."
"I know. Milan told me." He said.
She fell silent with a brooding expression on her face, and he instinctively knew what was in her mind.
"God has forsaken us," she lamented sadly, "otherwise, why wouldn't he give us a child?"
"Be patient," he consoled her, "The gods will take pity on us one day."
"When? When will they take pity on us?" she let out a long, wistful sigh and closed her eyes.

An hour later Purna inadvertently moved his hand across Laxmi's face. Her eyes and cheeks were moist with tears. She had been crying silently. He pulled her closer to him and wrapped an arm around her and held her until she fell asleep.

"Give us a child, all of you gods and goddesses up above and down below, one child, that's all I want from you," he prayed before falling asleep, "Not for me, but for my loving wife who is as sweet as the cool and gentle breeze that flows up from the riverbed."

Like his father Purna was a simple, honest and quiet man. One could safely say that he was a chip off the old block without making an overstatement, though he was even more taciturn than his old man. He didn't have any grandiose ambition in life, nor did he want much from life. He was a man of few needs and simple pleasures. Unlike his younger brother who had lived in the city and gone to college and thought of himself as a city boy, Purna had dropped out of school at the age of fourteen claiming that he was not cut out to read books. It had been as well because he could hardly read a written sentence without stuttering, and his father who was in need of a full time help in the farm had not objected. All he hoped for in life was to inherit a third of his ancestral land (by his reckoning the other two thirds would go to his two younger brothers), have a few children and live a quiet and contented life. He wanted to live his life quietly, in the footsteps of his forefathers, eking out his living from the farm, taking whatever it had to offer and desiring nothing more. Since his marriage to Laxmi, he had taken over much of the farm work from his father, who was happy to lend him a hand every now and then, preferring to milk the buffalo and feed the animals.

Come Spring, he would plough his fields with a pair of well-fed and robust oxen in anticipation of the monsoon rains that would shortly arrive. If the rain came too early or in too great a torrent, he'd pray for a milder rain. If the rains arrived late, as it happened some years, he would again pray to the gods and goddesses to send rain in time. In a land which is almost entirely dependent upon the mercy of Mother Nature, both the lack of and over-abundance of rain means a meager harvest. In the old days bad harvest meant starvation and death.

The 15th day of the Nepali month of Ashar, which normally falls in the last week of June, is known as '*Ropain*' in Nepal. Literally translated, it simply means 'Plantation'. Nepalese believe this day to be the start of the height of the monsoon.

On this day the entire family - men and women, old and young – help to transfer the young rice saplings to the rainwater-filled terraces, working from one terrace to the next the whole day and getting completely soaked and muddied in the process, and breaking out into impromptu songs every now and then to drive away the boredom.

The seemingly incessant downpour of the monsoon is such that it makes everything pregnant with rain water – hills, valleys, crevices, rivers, ponds, terraces, woods, houses, cattle and humans. Mud holes turn into little ponds, streams turn into rivers and rivers swell and roar angrily. Nobody and nothing escapes. The ground floors of the houses become sickeningly damp and muddy; it becomes a virtual pond if the thatched roof leaks. But all of this is amply compensated by the greenery that covers the hills and terraces. Planted earlier at the end of winter, maize is now ready to be eaten smoked or boiled, with ground green chilli and hot tea or alcohol.

Then as the rainy season fades and autumn approaches, the paddy fields assume a golden hue and a sweet aroma fills the air that goes up one's nostrils and makes one feel truly lucky to be alive. As the season progresses, the plants became top-heavy with ornaments of golden grains and bow down humbly with the weight. It is then time for the entire family to go to the fields with a sickle in hand and a bamboo basket on the back to harvest the rice. The days following the harvest are a time of great rejoicing. Limbu men and women drink jand, raksi and tongba and dance the paddy-dance, holding each other's hands, making up verses about life and love in a deliberately slow and melancholy tune, each taking his/her turn, trying to out-verse each other the whole day and night through. The men get drunken silly claiming that "it is our birthright to drink and be merry." This is also the time when amorous men and women flirt with each other in gay abandon and fall in love and fornicate on the sly, sometimes resulting in unwanted pregnancy and then elopement.

Then as winter approaches, it is time to plough and dig the fields again to plant the winter crop: potatoes, wheat, millet and barley. Those who have ploughed the terraces know that no matter how many rocks and pebbles one upturns in a year, an equal number of the same comes up the following year. Winter is cold, harsh and mostly dry. There is little rain in winter, which is merciful because rain makes the cold air colder. Winter is the time to sit in the courtyard or verandah and absorb the heat of the sun. On a sunny day people sit outside in the sun for hours, soaking up the heat. On an overcast day they sit huddled around the fire with outstretched arms and eat fried maize (pop corn) and smoked or boiled potatoes with ground chilli. Rakshi and tongba is also consumed in liberal quantities, but usually at night. Winter is the time when Mother Nature takes a break. Trees lose their old dead leaves and look denuded, twisted and ugly. The ground beneath becomes covered with dead and dying leaves. The hills look bare and bereft of greenery. The streams dry up and the rivers turns into streams.

Then in the beginning of March spring arrives and the hills become resplendent in nature's full glory, for spring is the fairest of all seasons. The once ugly trees regain their leaves, colour and beauty, in that order, and the light-green young leaves fluttering merrily with the cool and soothing breeze gives the distinct impression that nature is in resurgence. Red rhodendrons flowers, the national flower of the Nepal, in full bloom sprinkles the hills with red. There are flowers, flowers and flowers everywhere – bougainvillea, roses, jasmine, violet, primrose and poinsettia, to name a few. And the terraces are carpeted by yellow mustard flowers, millions and millions of them, where bees and butterflies dance merrily as they collect the sweet nectar.

The Limbus have a name for the beginning of spring. They call it *Oobhouli*, which means 'upward bound' or resurgence, and it is marked by the blooming of peach. They celebrate this occasion with an annual ritual worship, which is a communal affair. All the inhabitants of the village gather at the top of a hill, usually, from where all the fields can be seen and worship the goddess Yuma, the grandmother. They pray for rain, favourable weather and a bumper crop in the coming year. This is also the time when the fishes swim upriver, splashing and struggling against the mercilessly cold current in their relentless drive to reach the spawning ground near the source of the river where the water is shallow and always cold and crystal clear. Sometimes they fly out of the water, literally, flicking their silver tail, to overcome obstacles such as waterfalls, and sometimes they painstakingly wriggle up the moist and slippery surfaces of rocks covered with dark-green spirogyra. Life is tough for every living being, large or small. There is beauty in cruelty and cruelty in beauty, much of it mercifully hidden from human eyes.

At this time of the year Purna would go down to the bank of Tawa River with like-minded friends to lay handcrafted bamboo-cane traps along the fish's path. They'd then spend the night around a campfire by the river bank, each trying his best to scare the others out of their wits with stories of ghosts and malicious spirits that are said to abound in the hills, valleys, rivers, forests and desolate gorges. They'd also utilise this opportunity to catch up on the latest village gossip and boast of their sexual prowess, some imagined and some real, while waiting for the unsuspecting fish to slip into the traps in their desperate struggle against the current. They would rise up before sunrise the next morning to collect the catch. They would sometimes remain at the river bank for a stretch of three or four days, eating smoked fish and laying more traps. In a good year, the catch would be so bountiful that it would be enough to feed the entire village. The remaining fish would be dried in the sun with their entrails intact and then later packed in small handbag-sized bamboo-cane containers. This dried fish (black in colour) is known as 'bitter fish' because its intact innards give it a bitter flavour and is relished as a delicacy by the Limbus.

That was Purna's world. The only one he knew and the only one he cared for. He was as happy in it as anybody could be. He craved for nothing more and wanted nothing less.

The next day when Dil Bahadur had left home early to help a neighbour to slaughter his pig, Milan found an opportune moment to talk to his mother, alone. Lalita was adamant that the truth be told that very day. The sooner the better, she had insisted. "Let's be done with it and face the consequences," she had said. So he had made up his mind to do the same.
"Mother, I have something to tell you."
"What is it, son?"
"Well, it's a bit complicated."
"Tell me."
"It's about Lalita, mother."
"What about her?"
"Well, I ..... you see.... she is ....it is quite complicated."
"What's so complicated? Tell me." Her curiosity was now greatly aroused. Naturally, she suspected that something was very wrong.
"Well, she is ...... with a child."

"With a child? Is that why you eloped with her? I knew there was something. I had suspected something but I was not sure what."
"Yes, but that's not all. There is more ....." he continued hesitantly.
"What else is there?"
"She .... well .... she left her husband to come with me."
"What?" Kamala said sharply and looked at her son almost reproachfully. "She's got a husband?"
"Yes, mother."
"Are all the world's virgins dead that you had to fall for a married woman? Couldn't you find an unmarried girl to fall in love with?"
"Mother, love is something that is not done, it's something that happens. One cannot plan it nor can one foresee it. I can't explain it to you."
"I don't know. All I can say is that your father will be mighty upset when he hears of this."
"You will tell him, won't you, mother?"
"Yes, I will. I have to."
"And you will take care of him, won't you mother?"
She didn't reply.
"Won't you mother?"
"Why is it that every time you do something wrong you expect me to take care of it?"
"Because you are my mother and I am your son and I love you. Now, mother, won't you take care of father?"
"I don't know. I don't know if he'll listen to me."
"He will, mother. I know he always does."

Late in the afternoon that same day, Dil Bahadur came back with a bag of meat and a jar of blood, dark-red and clotted. He handed the same to Laxmi, instructing her to cook it for dinner with dry lichen. Limbus greatly relish pork curry mixed with dry lichen and blood. Lichen is found aplenty on the barks of trees in the forest. It is collected, washed and dried in the sun before it can be consumed.

After that Dil Bahadur washed his hands and legs, taking his time to do so, and climbed up the stairs to his room to rest. Kamala followed him quietly.
"Who speared the pig?" she asked sitting on the bed beside him.
"Dhan Bahadur did," he replied.
"Was it the big one that we saw last week?"
"Yes, it weighed about forty-five kilos after we killed it. It was full of fat."
"Who else was there?"
"Krishna Bir and the priest beside the two of us."
The above, of course, was just a preliminary to what she was going to say to him - preparing the 'background' for the real thing, as the Nepalese like to say. In the meantime, she was thinking of a way to break the news to him. After Milan had told her, she had decided that he must be told as soon as he arrived home and not at bed time when she usually confided to him. She knew that he was going to be upset because it was a matter of disgrace, but he had to be told the truth.

"Purna's father," she started hesitantly, "There is something that I have to tell you."
"What?" He asked laconically, without paying much attention to her. He was tired and wanted to take a nap.
"Well, it's about our new daughter-in-law."
"What about her?"
"There's something about her."
"Don't beat about the bushes. Get straight to the point. Just tell me what you know."
"Milan says that she is married."

"What?" He was stunned. For a moment he couldn't speak. "Married? To whom? What are you telling me?"
"Milan says that ..."
"That he's stolen another man's wife?" he cut her short, abruptly sitting up on the bed, "Oh, my god, what am I hearing? Have all the virgins in this world died that my son had to steal another man's wife? What will the neighbours say when they get to know of this? We'll be the laughing stock of the village."

To make a long story short, Dil Bahadur was upset. He was very upset. He was upset because his son had brought disgrace upon the family. It's one thing to elope with a virgin; it's an entirely different thing to run away with another man's wife. And he was upset because his son had lied to him. Well, not actually lied, but hidden the truth from him. More importantly, he was upset because this meant that trouble lay ahead. By his reckoning, and this was important, the jilted husband was sure to come looking for his runaway wife and he'd have to be paid monetary compensation. "Where are we going to get the money?" He lamented.

Milan stole back home at sunset, an hour of the day Nepali poets romantically call 'cattle-dust evening' because of the cloud of dust that the hooves of cattle raise on their return home from grazing just as the transverse rays of the sun sinking behind the horizon paint the clouds in the darkening sky in breathtaking shades of red and orange. He was relieved to find everything calm and quiet. *Has mother told father? He wondered. Or may be the old man has not come back. She'll probably tell him at bed time.*

Upon seeing him sneak into his room Kamala hurriedly came and said, "Listen, I have told your father and he is upset, but

he'll get over it. Avoid him for a few days. Do not say or do anything that will further upset him. Everything will be all right in a few days."
Turning to Lalita she said, "Daughter-in-law, you keep a low profile as well." Lalita nodded her head silently.

After Kamala left, Lalita turned to Milan, "Where have you been all day?"
"I was at a friend's place," he replied, "He is a teacher at the high school. What happened? Did father say anything to you?"
"He didn't say anything to me. But I know he was pretty upset. I heard him shout."
"Did he shout at you?"
"Not directly, but I heard him say things."
"I am very sorry. You must have felt pretty bad," he said.
"Don't worry about me. I am used to it. My father shouts and screams whenever he is upset, and that is quite often, and he utters a lot of obscene words regardless of who is present."
"The old man will cool down and everything will be back to normal. He is not bad, my father, you know." He reassured her, but he himself was not so convinced.

In the subsequent days Milan prudently heeded his mother's advice. He loved her, he really did. He knew that she would always be there for him, no matter what.

Unlike his introvert elder brother, Milan had always been a free spirit. He was bold and adventurous, and had big dreams in his young head. The village of Khewang was not a part of his dream. He wanted to see and experience the wider world outside, and aspired to live a life of modern comfort in the city.

Now let's rewind back to Milan's past because past is the foundation for the present and the future. At the tender age of twelve he was taken to Kathmandu by his third uncle, who was a soldier serving in the British army. There he was enrolled in one of the several English medium schools that had begun to sprout like mushrooms at that time. That was in the year 1983 AD. He had happily followed his uncle with dreams that only a teenage boy can dream. Just the thought of living in the city had filled his young heart with a mixture of nervousness and excitement. Once there, living at his uncle's house with his aunt and cousins (who were much younger than him) he had quickly adapted to city life and in no time at all metamorphosed into a proper city boy.

At first coming to Kathmandu had been a culture shock to him. The hustle and bustle of city life had overwhelmed his senses. It was a totally different world from the one he had grown up in. The ways of the Newars, Kathmandu's indigenous and majority inhabitants, are in sharp contrast to everyone else's. Unlike most other Nepalese, the Newars have lived in urban societies for over a millennium and they naturally look down upon the other races, though outwardly they profess not to do so. This is not entirely their fault. Anybody would do the same if he/she knew that he/she had a history as long as and a culture as rich as that of the Newars. These remarkable people of mixed Aryan-Mongoloid ancestry have produced some of the finest artists and sculptors of the medieval age in Asia. They proudly claim, and not without basis, that the pagoda-style architecture was exported to imperial China from Nepal. Before they were subjugated and their kingdoms annexed by a predecessor of the present monarch in the later half of the 18th century AD, they had transformed the three cities of Kathmandu valley into the fabled cities of folklore – paved streets, golden temples and magnificent palaces. In the old days the hill people literally believed that the streets of the three cities were paved with gold.

But until a few decades ago, Kathmandu was also a city unwelcoming to outsiders, amply illustrated by the following incident, which may or may not have been true but provides a peek into the typical mindset of the city's inhabitants. Once there was a knock on the main door of a Newar household and the father sent his son to see who the visitor was. After some time, the father called from his first floor room, "Who is it?" to which his son replied, "It's no one, father; it's only an Indian."

To the inhabitants of Kathmandu, all hill people of Mongoloid origin were ignorant, uncivilized and unclean brutes. They were disparagingly referred to as 'Bhotay' – a derogatory Nepali term for Tibetans. Similarly, all dark-skinned people of Aryan origin were despised as Indians. This bias is so deep-rooted that it still persists among the denizens of Kathmandu. But then in the old days, much of the civilized world was xenophobic and racist to varying degrees. Even today racism is endemic in the Indian subcontinent. It cannot be separated from popular consciousness because it is an integral part of the local culture. They just have a different name for it or pretend that it doesn't exist.

By the time he was out of high school, Milan had learnt to squeeze himself happily into the overcrowded buses that plied the pot-hole filled streets of Kathmandu, discharging a plume of black cloud of toxic fume every half a minute. He had become an authority on hot *mamacha* (Nepali style dumplings) at roadside restaurants. He had become adept at crossing the crowded streets anywhere that suited him at anytime without bothering to look left or right as the oncoming vehicles honked incessantly. And he had become deft at negotiating his way through the dark and dank narrow alleyways of the old city.

After graduating from high school he made up his mind to pursue his childhood dream. He had an enduring dream since his childhood days, and that dream was to become a *lahooray*. Even as a little boy he had enviously watched *lahoorays* on leave flaunting their wealth as the girls fawned all over them trying to catch their roving eyes. The *lahooray*'s ostentatious lifestyle had fired up his imagination like nothing else and life at his uncle's house had reinforced that dream. By the age of sixteen the lure of the foreign money that could buy him a house in the city and farmland in the fertile plain, not to mention fancy Japanese wrist watches, cameras, television, and music and video systems and television that the lahoorays exhibited so flamboyantly had become too irresistible to ignore. *One day I am going to have all of that and more*, he had promised himself.

He had enrolled in a commerce college but his mind was hardly there, naturally, with the dream that he carried in his head. He was going to become a lahooray and travel the world and make a fortune. He would buy or build a beautiful house in the city and fill it with all the modern amenities. He would not go back to village where there was nothing for him. He would live a life of comfort in the city. That was what preoccupied his mind.

But the competition was tough - as tough as it could get. With hundreds of boys vying for a limited number of seats it was extremely difficult, if not impossible, to get through. Not at all like in his uncle's time when one just had to line up and one was in, provided that one didn't have any major ailment or pronounced physical disabilities. Much before his uncle's time, there was a time when weary recruiters scoured the countryside trying to woo unwilling men. But those days were long since gone. Driven by the dream, he had jogged every morning, did skips, push-ups, pull-ups and other forms of physical exercises to tone up his body. When he was confident that he would get through he had boarded a night bus, with the blessing of his aunt, to the city of Pokhara, a picturesque tourist destination in mid-western Nepal. With scenic lakes and breathtaking view of Mount Machhapuchhre (Fishtail Mountain, so named because its twin peaks resemble the tail of a fish) Pokhara is Nepal's very own queen of the hills. This is where the British Gurkhas recruitment centre is presently situated. There he had met several young men who had, like him, trekked to the city to try their luck, as they put it. The recruiting officer, a stern-faced, slitty-eyed retired major of about fifty years of age, had taken a quick look at him and said: "So you want to serve Her Majesty the Queen, do you?" The man sounded as if he was proud just to pronounce the Queen's name.

"The Queen?" he had retorted, scratching his head, unable for a moment to get who the military man was alluding to.

"Her Majesty Queen Elizabeth the Second, Queen of the United Kingdom, you fool," the major had retorted, "That's who you will pledge your loyalty to when you join the British army."

"Oh, yes, sahib" he had replied, blinking his eyes. Of course, why didn't I think of it before? My uncle has a beautifully framed portrait of the Queen and her consort Prince Philip in the living room. There is another of Prince Charles and the beautiful Princess Diana beside it. He chided himself for this lapse of memory.

"Did you say you are a college student? I hope you are not involved in any sort of political activities. A Gurkha soldier must not be involved in politics. Do you understand?"

"Yes, sahib," he had replied.

"These days, as you know, the competition is very tough. It's not at all like the old days when one just lined up and got through. We are looking for no more than seventy boys this time, but since you are educated we'll put you in the clerical group," the major had said. Milan knew what that meant.

Now for a little bit of history. The recruitment of the Gurkhas, an anglicized version of the Nepali word Gorkha, by the British had started immediately after the Anglo-Nepalese war of early 19th century. By the early 19th century, the newly unified Nepali nation on its expansionary spree had come into conflict with the fledgling East India Company which was at the time attempting to bring the various princely states of the Indian subcontinent under its dominion. The war, which lasted two years from 1814 to 1816, was fought on several fronts, with very encouraging results for the Nepalese in the initial stages. But against a numerically and technologically superior force, Nepal ultimately lost the war and as a result had to cede half of its territory to the Company government.

Although the Nepalese, who called themselves Gorkhali at the time (after Gorkha), lost the war their British foes were highly impressed by their gallantry, loyalty and military discipline. They had noticed that unlike the unreliable Indian sepoy, the Gorkhali soldier never ran away from battle, never defected to the enemy and was absolutely loyal to his commander. So when the war came to an end, the British began recruiting the Gurkhas for their various campaigns of conquest, most notably the Punjab and Afghan campaigns. It was during the Afghan campaign that Balbhadra, one of the most famous Gorkhali commanders of the Anglo-Nepal war, died fighting for his former foes. However, it was not until much later during the time of the hereditary Rana prime ministers that Gurkha recruitment was formally recognized by the Nepalese government. Apparently, the first recruitment and training center was based in the city of Lahore, now in Pakistan, and for this simple reason Nepali men who entered the service of the East India Company as soldiers began to be known by the term '*Lahooray*' (He of Lahore), and as it became a tradition for the hill men to enlist in the British army the name stuck for good. Presently, there are more than fifty thousand lahoorays serving in the Indian army and a little over three thousand serving in the British army.

Since then the Gurkhas have served their British masters with steadfast loyalty in every theatre of war. In the course of a little less than two centuries, the small, hardy, loyal and fearless men from the remote hills of Nepal have fought and died in the battlefields of Afghanistan, Burma, Malaysia, France, Italy, Turkey, Palestine, Mesopotamia and Egypt in their hundreds of thousands, and won the hearts and minds of the British officers who have led them. It's a pity that they failed to win the hearts of the stiff-upper-lipped members of the British bureaucracy who, it seems, still look down upon them with those conceited colonial eyes. In the First World War Nepal supplied over a hundred thousand Gurkhas to the British war effort. Then again in the Second World War as many as two hundred thousand Gurkhas fought in the battlefields of Europe, Middle East, North Africa and South East Asia. Many never returned home, having lost their lives in distant lands whose names they had never heard before and could not even hope to properly pronounce. For their effort, nineteen of them won the Victoria Cross, British Army's highest medal for bravery, and many more won the Military Cross.

Sometimes the Gurkhas may not like some of their British officers, but they speak with universal respect of the Queen who (though she only reigns and doesn't rule) commands their universal respect and absolute loyalty. But in recent days they have begun to grumble against discrimination by the British government in terms of pay and pension, which is paltry compared to what a British soldier of the same rank gets for the same effort. They also lament that the British government has given them (they who have fought and died so selflessly for the Empire) a raw deal as far as permanent residence status and citizenship is concerned while generously doling out the same to hordes of other Asians and Africans whose contribution to the Empire is questionable. Perhaps today's Britain wants to have nothing do with its past.

Milan had presented himself to the concerned authorities at the recruitment centre at the given time. To his dismay there were more that two hundred boys who had lined up along side him wearing vest and shorts. The boys were subjected to grueling physical tests - sprint, a hundred and some push-ups, long-distance jogging and running with a heavy sack of sand on their back. He had done his best and given it all, but it had come to naught. The other boys had been tougher and faster than him, and perhaps, he suspected, had better family connections – being sons and nephews of serving and retired officers, the sort. Nepotism works its black magic everywhere, even in the least expected places. Far from being exempt from it the Gurkhas are born and bred in a culture of nepotism, and for them it's a way of life. Even having passed high school and then having joined college didn't help; there were tens of college-going boys like him, many of them graduates.

So in the middle of the year 1990 he had returned to Kathmandu feeling dejected. That was just after the political change in the country. But he had vowed to get through the following year. In the meantime because of his preoccupation with becoming a lahooray, he had completely neglected his studies. As a result he failed and had to repeat the year.

Now back at college he had found himself spending more time outside the classrooms than inside, attending the 'cultural programs' of various students unions aligned to one or the other political parties (outlawed by the government at the time). Strikes, Chakka Jam ("Jam the Wheels") and Nepal Bandh ("Close Nepal") organized by the various political parties and their student wings was the order of the day and closed the classroom for almost half the days in a year. Milan befriended both leftwing students (aligned to the various communist parties) and the 'democratic' students (aligned with the Nepali Congress Party). But upon the advice and veiled threat of his third uncle, his benefactor, he kept a discreet distance from direct involvement in student politics. This was not an easy thing to do when every student was automatically labeled by the associations he made. There were communists, democrats and supporters of the then government – all of different colours and hues. Student unions received direct orders and funding from the political parties they were affiliated to. Not only friendship, but also romance, love and marriages were made and broken along political lines. And while fighting the government, the students fought amongst themselves viciously, sometimes with fatal consequences.

Although Milan was in no way responsible for it, and played a very miniscule and negligible role in it, the year he enrolled in college was a momentous year in the country's modern history. After three decades of political repression and economic stagnation under the King's rule, the political situation in the country had reached a boiling point. The streets were heating up with daily strikes and protest marches that turned violent at a moment's notice. That was the year 1990 AD (corresponding to Nepali year 2046 Bikram Sambat). Thirty years of economic mismanagement and corruption under the guise of the so-called 'party-less democracy' had ravaged the country's economy, and the oppressed, disillusioned and impoverished masses were no longer satisfied with the status quo. Although they were willing to keep the King (as a titular head of state, Westminster style) because he was still respected as the 'father' of the people and venerated as the reincarnation of the Hindu god Vishnu, the preserver of life, they were no longer willing to accept his autocratic rule through his sycophants. The wind of change had finally begun to blow in the Himalayas and it was going to have far-reaching consequences.

The trade embargo imposed by the Indian government the previous year (which still held and made life extremely difficult for the Nepalese) heralded the doom of the party-less Panchayat system. Initially the people sided with the government, naturally, in a nationalistic fervor whipped up by the government, but as the economic crisis deepened (land-locked Nepal is surrounded by India on three sides) they became less and less willing to support a government they began to see as the root cause of their woes. Suddenly 'democracy' was the favoured word on everyone's lips.

When the agitation, dubbed 'People's Movement for the Restoration of Democracy' by the agitating parties, finally started, Milan found himself in a dilemma. His aunt had strictly forbidden involvement. "Politics is not our cup of tea. It's only for the cunning long-nosed Bahuns and Chhetris. They only use us to further their own selfish ends," she had warned. Although she was born in a village in the eastern hills (like him) and had grown up there, she had that much sense. But as the movement gathered momentum, he couldn't remain aloof. Many of his friends were actively involved and he felt guilty sitting at home following the news on television. Also, there was a personal reason he hated the policemen who were at the forefront of the government's effort to subdue the agitation. So he did what his heart told him to do. He joined the protesters on the sly. He helped to burn tyres in the narrow and dusty streets of Kathmandu. He helped to desecrate the symbols of the government and to throw rocks and bricks at the police and run away. Luckily for him he was never caught. Neither did he get the painful taste of a policeman's baton on his head.

He was there at the conclusion of the movement when a hundred thousand people had marched through downtown Kathmandu chanting 'We want democracy' (both in Nepali and English) and he still remembered vividly how he had run through the narrow alleys along with other frightened protestors when the firing had started as the crowd had veered towards the royal palace and started demolishing the statue of King Mahendra, the King's father, along the way. That night the shaken King had granted audience to the leaders of the agitating parties and announced the restoration of parliamentary democracy.

After that Milan had no intention of further involvement in student politics. *That's for the political-minded boys and I am not one. I have got things to do, places to go, a life to live and a dream to pursue.* Next year he'd go to Pokhara to try his luck again.

Now rewind to an earlier time. His decision to take part in the Movement was prompted by the bitter experience he had had with the police a year before the political upheaval. That year he had been unfortunate enough to witness police brutality first hand and the experience had badly shaken him.

In 1989, he was returning to his village of Khewang on vacation. On the way he met a friend, a childhood friend, who dragged him to a fair near the village of Hangpang, a day's walk from his village. Now Hari - that's what his name was - was a few years older than him and a bit on the wild side. Though of a young age, he had a weakness for two things: hard drinks and the fairer sex. He guzzled the former like water and of the latter he was constantly on the lookout for an opportunity to get into their frocks (or saris for that matter).

The temporary bazaars (that usually last a day) that take place at designated places at regular intervals provide a good opportunity for people far and wide to congregate to buy and sell their wares and also to socialize and generally have a good time. While the older men come to drink and gamble, the young at heart arrive solely for the purpose of meeting the opposite sex. They eat, drink, sing, quarrel, fight, dance the paddy-dance and fall in love. For those who live in remote and isolated hamlets, a visit to such a bazaar is the only opportunity to come into contact with other people. So, while the older men drink, gamble and quarrel, and the women shop and gossip; the younger men and women flirt, sing, dance, fall in love and fornicate on the sly.

Upon reaching the fair, an annual affair of sizeable proportion on account of it being held on the occasion of Nepali New Year which usually falls in the month of April, the two young men started taking a little sip here and a little sip there, and by midday they were slightly inebriated. Milan was seventeen and Hari was nineteen. Then at one food and liquor shop (a sort of pub) they came across a comely young woman and Hari began to flirt with her out of habit. The coquettish girl willingly reciprocated to his advances and flirted with him openly, much to Milan's amusement. This, however, apparently did not go down well with another young man, a stranger, who had been jealously hovering nearby. When Hari began to touch the young girl, on her hands, back, buttock and breasts a little at a time, the stranger could stand it no longer.

"Hey, you! Take your hands off her," the stranger growled crossly. Hari was taken aback for a moment; he hadn't been aware of his rival's presence. But he quickly grasped the situation and retaliated. "Why? Why must I take my hands off her? What business is it of yours?" Hari retorted sharply, glaring at the intruder.

"I said take your hands off her," the young man said in a louder and angrier voice.

"Why?" Hari asked crossly. He had now lost his temper.

"Because the girl is mine," the other man shouted furiously, scattering droplets of saliva from his mouth.

"Is she? Do you have your name inscribed on her? Where is it? I don't see it anywhere." Hari ridiculed his rival.

"So you think you are smart, huh? Common, let's settle it with a fight if you are your father's son," his enraged rival challenged him, rolling up his shirt-sleeves and unbuttoning his shirt to reveal his chest, as Nepalese men habitually do when preparing for a fist fight.

Before Hari had time to do the same, the young man suddenly pushed him forcefully sending him staggering backward. Quickly recovering his balance, for he was a strong man, he rolled up his shirt sleeves and lunged at his rival, punching the man squarely in the face. The stranger staggered backward, ran his fingers over his lips and spat out a blob of saliva mixed with blood. Then suddenly throwing the vilest verbal obscenities, he lunged at Hari and showered him with punches. Hari retaliated in the same manner. By this time a small crowd of spectators had gathered around the two men. Deciding to intervene, some of the spectators took hold of the two combatants and separated them. The two struggled to free themselves from their captors but in vain as they were pushed away in opposite directions.

"It's not over yet, you mother-fucking son-of-a-whore," Hari's adversary screamed over the heads of his captors, "I'll be back, and I swear I'll make you curse the day you were born."

"Try now if you have drunk your mother's milk," Hari screamed back, "I'll show you motherfucker how to fight like a father's son."

That night Milan and Hari stayed in a lodge in the bazaar. Milan had urged his friend to head for home, but the latter had refused. It turned out be a foolish decision, as they found out later. At about ten thirty they were woken up by a burst of loud and frenzied bangs on the tin door of the ground floor room where they were sleeping. When an irritated Milan opened the door to inquire, he was dismayed and frightened to find a group of belligerent-looking men holding torch lights and lanterns. Before he could utter a word, a strong hand grabbed him by the chest and jerked him violently, sending him crashing to the hard earth. When he looked up in pain, fear and astonishment, at first he could only saw the glaring light of the torchlight they were shining on his face. Only when the light was removed did he realized that he was looking into the angry faces of several policemen bearing down upon him, getting ready to shower him with kicks and punches. Then he recognized Hari's rival standing among the policemen and it all began to make sense. But before he could react, a policeman kicked him in the stomach and he groaned in pain.

"Is this the son-of-a-whore who picked up a fight with you?" The policeman growled flashing his torchlight at Milan's eyes again.
"No, sir, it's not him. It's the other one," Hari's rival replied.
"Are you sure?"
"Yes, sir."

The policemen left him after warning him not to run away and went for Hari. They dragged the frightened boy by the hair showering a volley of kicks and punches on him. One of them landed a solid kick from behind and sent him flying to the earth.

Milan dragged himself to the door and remained there to watch the spectacle unfold. He now noticed that the man who had kicked him was wearing the badge of an assistant sub-inspector, ASI in short, a step higher in rank than a sergeant and a step lower than an inspector. He was the seniormost policeman in the group. He pulled the fallen boy up by the hair and screamed into his face.

"You son of a bitch, you motherfucker, you sister-fucker, you mother-fucking son of a whore who's been fucked by a hundred mother-fucking sons-of-whores, I'll teach you to pick up a fight with my man," the ASI roared with the policeman's usual gusto for vulgarity, "Do you know who you picked up a fight with? Do you? I'll tell you. It was one of my boys. Nobody touches my boys and gets away with it, do you understand?"

Hari was in too much pain and shock to answer. The ASI pulled him up by the hair and screamed, "Did you understand what I just said, you son-of-a-whore? Do you know the consequence of picking up a fight with a man who wears the king's uniform?"

When Hari failed to reply, he slapped the poor boy on both cheeks with both hands and added a kick in the stomach with such force that the poor man went crashing down to the earth again. The ASI added another kick on the fallen man.

The policeman pulled him up by the hair again and said triumphantly, "Don't think I am finished with you because I am not. I know what needs to be done with you, you motherfucker. Turn to the other side and sit up on your knees," He barked at the injured man. Hari obeyed without a squeak; the boy was too dazed and terrified not to.

By this time a crowd of curious onlookers had gathered at the scene. The enraged ASI screamed at them, "Why are you here at this time of night? Don't you have anything better to do? Be off this instant or I'll have you all flogged." The frightened spectators quickly and quietly melted into the darkness. In the old days the policeman was the king of the countryside, and his word was the law.

"All right, boys, I want all of you to line up over there," the ASI bawled, pointing to a spot about fifteen feet away from the shaking boy, "and when I blow my whistle, I want each of you to take turn to run to that son-of-a-whore and kick his ass. But make sure you don't kill him." His subordinates did as he commanded. When they were ready, he blew the whistle and the first policeman in the line began to run, but the ASI barked, "Stop! Wait! I think the first turn should be mine."

The ASI walked to the beginning of the line, blew the whistle himself and ran. He kicked the quivering boy squarely on the back with a force that send the young man went flying to the earth, face down, whimpering in pain and terror.
"Pick him up," the ASI barked and two of his subordinates ran to Hari and propped him up in position. Then at the next whistle the policeman with whom Hari had a fight in the afternoon took his turn and sent him sprawling on the earth again. After that each of the seven policemen took his turn until their bloodied victim became unconscious.

Then the ASI turned his attention to Milan. "This son of a whore was also there, wasn't he?" he growled. He had tasted blood and was looking for some more. Milan was too frightened to refute and only managed to shake his head in denial.

"He was there, sir, but he didn't do anything," Hari's rival said.
At least the man had the decency to speak the truth and Milan was thankful for that.

The ASI glared at him and barked: "Get back inside your room this instant." Milan quickly slipped into his room and shut the door, quietly, taking care not to make even the slightest squeak. He had never been so scared in his young life.

The next morning he found out where the police were camped and went to see his friend. There he was told that his friend had been put under arrest. The boy's clothes were wet and smeared with clotted blood. His cheeks, arms, thighs, legs and back were sore and swollen black and blue. Luckily for him, no bones were broken. His tormentors had splashed voluminous amount of cold water on him to revive him after he had fallen unconscious. The poor fellow couldn't see properly; his badly bruised face had swollen like a pumpkin burying his eyes. Even in such a condition he was handcuffed and secured to a wooden post. When Milan asked a sergeant what they were going to do with his friend, the policeman replied airily, "We are going to take him to the district headquarters and charge him with disturbing public security." Now that was a very serious charge, enough to land the poor boy in jail for several months.

That afternoon the policemen took Hari to the police headquarters in Taplejung Bazaar in handcuff, but fortunately for him their superiors had a change of heart and set him free two days later. It took Hari two months to fully recover from the severe beating.

That had been a year before 'democracy'. Things had changed for the better since then. The police force had made a conscious effort to change its image from 'oppressors' to 'friends' of the people. In the old days the presence of policemen struck fear into the hearts of people not only in the villages, but in the towns as well. They were viewed as enemies rather than protectors, and Milan had exacted his revenge on them by throwing rocks and bricks at them, most of which had missed their target. But he was satisfied. He was happy that the old system that had failed the country so miserably had finally fallen.

Now once every year Milan used to make the arduous journey back home to visit his parents. The aforementioned visit was only his second after coming to Kathmandu. The journey started with a fully-packed night bus that reeked of diesel from Kathmandu an hour or so before sunset. The Indian-built contraption roared and belched out plumes of toxic black fume as it made its slow journey along the perilously narrow and winding highway carved out of the steep slopes rising above the riverbed a thousand feet below. Every year during the monsoon rains one or two packed buses slide down to the swirling, murky water of the river taking the screaming passengers to their doom. But once the hills end and the plain begin, it is a monotonous ride all the way to the far east of the country known as the 'wild east' in the old days. Then the sleepy passengers have nothing to do except to sleep all the way through. Sometimes Milan spent a few days at his second uncle's house in a small village near the rapidly burgeoning city of Birtamod, a haven for electronics and textile smugglers not far from the Indian border town of Siliguri. From Birtamod he caught another dusty and crowded bus that made its way northward into the hills where a distance that would not take more than three hours in the plain took almost an entire day. The bus came to a stop at the red-earthed town of Phidim in the late afternoon where he spent the night in a creaky wooden lodge ('Hutel and Resturent', as they advertise on the badly done billboard). Then early the next morning he caught another bus northward to a place called Suketar which had a fair-weather airport. From there he made the rest of the journey on foot. It took him two days to reach home. In those days of the early 1990s the road was still under construction and it was largely untarred. By the late 90s the road would arrive within a day's walk from his village.

There was heavy rain in the eastern hills of the country in the year 1991 AD. Landslides carried away many houses, and several casualties were reported on the national radio and television. Fortunately, Khewang was left untouched. Two weeks later news arrived that a distant aunt of his from his grandmother's side in the village of Surumkhim - on the opposite slope of Tawa River from Khewang - had been buried alive. A large chunk of the hill above her house had slid down and buried her house. Since he had only heard of the woman and never actually met her, he didn't see any reason to feel sad on account of her.

Two things happened that year that was to have a profound impact on his life. First, he again failed in his bid to enlist in the British army. It was the same story as before and feeling his dignity slighted, he vowed never to go into the army, neither British nor Indian nor Nepalese. He would find the calling of his life through other routes. Second, the retired lahooray next door (ex-servicemen tend to live close to each other) brought his young wife to live with his children. She was two years younger than him, fair-skinned and beautiful, and whenever he saw her he felt his heart skip a bit or two. Unconsciously, he made it a habit to spy on her from his window. At first she ignored him purposely and acted as if she didn't notice him. But a few months later when their eyes met accidentally, she gave him a shy and sweet smile, a smile so alluring that it gave his young and amorous heart an electric jolt from which he never recovered. From that day he was so smitten by her that his eyes searched for her everywhere and her face danced before his eyes all the time. He had never felt that way before. "She is married, stupid. Don't you know that it's immoral to look at another man's wife?" he admonished himself countless times. But his head was unable to rule over his heart. She was constantly on his mind; there was simply no escape. He was in love. That's what love does to you when you are young and full of dreams. The name of the young woman who had set his young heart on fire was Lalita.

For the next three days Dil Bahadur did not speak to his son Milan. He did not admonish him either. He just ignored the latter much to the relief of the young man who was only too happy to keep a safe distance from his father.

Now a look at Dil Bahadur's history for even the most ordinary of men has a history behind him. One's life is not shaped only by one's actions; it is also shaped by the actions of those before him. Dil Bahadur was a simple and honest man by all accounts. There was no unnaturalness about him; no artificiality in his manner. He didn't know how to conceal his feelings – his happiness, his sadness, his want, his anger, his pain and his sorrow were there for everyone to see. Whatever there was in his heart came out truthfully and naturally, not in torrents of superfluous words but in small bits and parts, or didn't come out at all. He never lied because he saw no profit in that. In short, he was a man without intrigue.

He was the eldest son of his father Bom Bahadur and mother Narmaya. In those days Bom Bahadur, his father, was the hereditary chief of the village, a minor chieftain, in name only because whatever power that came with the title had waned a long time ago. But he was a chief all the same and that meant a lot to him. Unfortunately for him, he had fallen victim to the evil of drinking at a very young age. His father Jagat Bahadur had a reputation for reckless bravado in those days. The man had died at the age of thirty-five of a bear-attack when hunting alone in the forest. Bears, leopards and other predatory animals were found in abundance in the vicinity of the village in those days. When two hunters who had been tracking the same bear with loaded muskets had chanced upon the mortally wounded man hearing his mortal whines, they had come across a grisly sight. The wounded man had his eyes gauged out, his nose eaten up and his lips torn asunder revealing his teeth and gum all in their ghastliness. There were deep bite marks and gashes all over his badly mangled body. He was lying in a pool of blood that was already beginning to clot. His musket was lying twenty paces from him and it was still loaded. They had carried him home and he had lasted nine more agonizing days before succumbing to death despite everyone's prayers for him to die quickly. A few years after that, his wife had left home to live with a cousin-brother of her dead husband. Bom Bahadur was sixteen then. Angry and frustrated by his mother's betrayal (the way he saw it), but unable to do anything about it, he had taken to drinking. To stop his downward slide his kinsfolk had found him a young bride, Narmaya. But the damage had already been done. Wedded life did nothing to halt his downward slide because he had gone too far into the vice of drinking. So instead of mending his ways, as the elders had hoped, he had begun to vent his anger and frustration on his poor wife Narmaya.

A soft-spoken and kind man when not drunk, Bom Bahadur turned into the devil reincarnate when fully inebriated. Then he went berserk and shouted the vilest expletives, letting loose his slurring tongue in unbridled abandon, looking for all sorts of ways to pick up a fight with his long suffering wife and frightened children, and with neighbors and even passersby, who were careful to avoid the 'drunkard'. He would in his drunken spree beat his wife and children for no apparent reason. Narmaya used to fight back, she did. But he was stronger and reckless. On a few occasions he had even chased her away to her maiden home, only to coax her back with sweet words and promises a few days later. She came back with him every time, for reasons of her own – but mostly for the sake of the children. Other women in her circumstance would work their charm on other men and elope with them, but the thought never occurred to her. Some nights he chased her into the nearby woods, where she claimed to have encountered hideous-looking supernatural beings that harried her through the woods until her children arrived with torches and shouts to rescue her.

Those were difficult times for the whole family. Finally, after suffering for so long, at the age of sixteen Dil Bahadur had decided that enough was enough and that something had to be done. Bad people win, and keep winning, if good people are not prepared stand in their path. So, aided by his second brother Harka Bahadur who was fourteen, he had confronted his father and threatened the old man with dire consequences if his drunken rampages continued. Realizing that the angry brothers were prepared to use physical violence, the old man had backed down.

"It is said that parents are as respectable as the gods themselves," he had told his father, "but if children are expected to respect their parents, then parents should also be worthy of that respect. A man who does not fulfill his duties and responsibilities towards his wife and children is not fit to be a husband and a father." The old man had apologized to his sons, more out of fear than remorse, and his sons had let him go. Dil Bahadur had felt very badly afterwards. But he had done something that had to be done.

Four years after that Dil Bahadur had got married to Kamala. Perhaps because of his aversion to the willful and irresponsible ways of his drunkard father, he had refrained from raising his hands against his wife. He sometimes had verbal spats with her over family matters, which is only natural, but he never raised his hand against her in anger. Neither did she against him. To him she was an equal partner in all respects and he made it a point to consult her in every matter.

Although the old man's drunken rampages had stopped after that day, he had not completely given up drinking. Unknown to his wife and sons, in his quest to quench his thirst for liquor, he had written off a sizeable chunk of his large ancestral land to the crafty local Bahuns, who were only too happy to make a grab for his fertile land at a minimal price – sometimes for as little as a pair of goats. Had the old fool been allowed to continue his drunken spree, he would have sold off everything he owned within the next decade or so, leaving his wife and children destitute and at the mercy of the elements. Fortunately for Dil Bahadur and his brothers, they had come of age at the right time and stopped the old man from recklessly leading the family to ruination.

Ten years later the old man had met a rather agonizing death. Apparently, his liver and lungs had collapsed. As he had lain in coma with only a whirring sound coming from his throat, the local witch-doctor had beaten his goatskin drum all night, shaking violently and going into trance, calling upon all the gods, goddesses and spirits of long dead ancestors to help the dying man, but to no avail. When he had finally succumbed after five days, parts of his body were already in the process of decomposition, encompassing the whole neighbourhood with a horribly sickly ordour – the ordour of death. Like birth, death for some is a messy affair. As a result of this Dil Bahadur had become wary of drinking. Although he did have a tongba every day, he never had more than his limit.

Shortly after his father's death a shrewd and wily Bahun by the name Durganath Adhikari had filed a lawsuit against him at the district court claiming that the dead man had sold him two ropanis (one ropani is about a seventh of an acre) of paddy field. The field that the cunning Bahun had claimed was fed by a natural spring which spouted water throughout the year, and thus the most fertile. Durganath claimed that the old man was planning to transfer the land to his name at the time of death. He had produced a written statement with the dead man's thumb-print to substantiate his claim. There was no way to either prove or disprove the authenticity of the thumb-print because Bom Bahadur had never taken out his citizenship certificate, the only document that would have carried his authentic thumb-print. Apparently, the illiterate drunkard, who didn't know a black letter from a black ant, had taken loan - a little at a time but the final total amounting to a few thousand rupees - to finance his drinking, and had jabbed his thumb-print on the paper thrust his way without bothering to find out what was written on it. This is how Bahuns have usurped the lands of the naïve Limbus in Limbuan – as much as seventy percent by some reckoning.

The crafty Bahuns and Chhetris are experts at flattery and the proud and naïve matwali (drinker of alcohol, a general term used for all ethnic people of Mongoloid stock) are by nature susceptible to the same. Of course, they are suspicious and distrustful of the Bahun at first. But when a wily Bahun starts flattering a *matwali*, waxing his inborn eloquence with the sweetest of words, the matwali's chest swells with pride and he quickly changes his mind. This has been the cause of their ruin.

To their credit, not all Bahuns are cunning, nor are they all apathetic to the plight of the *matwalis*. And in the same vein, not all *matwalis* are simple and naïve. Some of them are as crafty as the Bahuns and have usurped the lands and properties of their brethrens in the same manner. But in spite of centuries of exploitation by the Bahuns and Chettris, the *matwalis* have no desire for war against their Aryan brothers. Neither do they wish to declare their own separate homeland and secede, fully aware that if they do so India will quickly find a pretext to gobble up the country like it did Sikkim. They want to go on living in peace, harmony and brotherhood, but on an equal footing – not as exploiters and exploited, not as rulers and ruled, and certainly not as of higher and lower castes.

With the lawsuit had begun the most miserable phase of his life and it had lasted a full decade. Although Dil Bahadur had the papers, and the history, to prove conclusively that the land belonged to him, Durganath had managed to register the case in the court. There were no other options but to fight tooth and nail. Durganath, whose family had already amassed a fortune in this manner, had bribed the corrupt and greedy court officials with money and kind. After deliberating on the case for six years which had incurred considerable expenses on both sides, the court had given its verdict in Durganath's favour.

Fortunately for Dil Bahadur, his two younger brothers had become lahoorays by this time, and this saved the day for him. The two sent money to fight the case, and with help from his uncles, Dil Bahadur had immediately set off on the five-day trek to Dhankutta, a scenic hilltop town about a hundred kilometers southwest as the crow flies, to appeal to the regional court. Dhakutta is a beautiful little town perched on a hill high above the roaring, murky waters of River Tamor. Since the old days it has been the administrative center for the whole of the eastern region, but these days it has the look and feel of a provincial town on the wane, partly because the British-built highway into the hinterland has bypassed it instead of going through it. There the lawsuit had lasted another four years. Dil Bahadur had traveled to the town so many times, always taking the foot-trail that follows the southwesterly flow of the River Tamor because there was no road at that time, sometimes accompanied by his bother and sometimes by his wife and sometimes by his uncle, that he had forgotten count of them. After spending a considerable sum of money and energy, he had finally won the case. After that Durganath hadn't had the nerve to pursue the case, finally realizing that Dil Bahadur now had the financial muscle to fight and win the case wherever he took it, even to the Supreme Court in Kathmandu.

Shortly after the restoration of democracy, bowing to threats by the local leftists, Durganath had sold off his large three-storey house along with all the land which his family had stolen from the Limbus, and migrated to the Terai, where it was rumoured that his craftier sons swindled some more unsuspecting victims and amassed an even larger fortune.

While the lawsuit was still in progress, Dil Bahadur's second brother Harka Bahadur had got married. After the lawsuit had ended the latter had asked for his share of the land and property, which he had promptly sold off and migrated to the Terai, where though he had not managed to make a fortune as he had dreamt, he had acquired enough land to support his wife and six children.

The reason for Harka Bahadur's migration had been the lure of fertile land in the plain. The exodus of the hill people to the formerly malaria-infested Terai, in fact, had begun in earnest about two decades before that. After the eradication of the dreaded disease of malaria with American aid, the economically hard-pressed hill people had begun to descend to the plain to clear the dense rainforest and grab a piece of fertile land for themselves, while at the same time destitute Indians were migrating from across the border for the same reason. This trend continues to this day, though at a somewhat reduced scale.

This mass migration had catastrophic consequences for the indigenous tribes of the Terai who were quickly displaced and dispossessed. It proved even more catastrophic for the indigenous wildlife. With the wanton destruction of their natural habitat, many species of animals simply vanished. Human need and greed are the driving forces behind the destruction of nature. The 'have-nots' are driven by their need and the 'haves' are driven by their greed. Although it is easy to justify the former and villify the latter, both are equally destructive. Thus, the government's slogan of those days, 'Green Forests are the wealth of Nepal', was reduced to nothing more than a joke owing, in large part, to the selfish designs of the shortsighted rulers and corrupt government officials in Kathmandu, and the insatiable greed of the big landowners and timber smugglers, and the ever increasing need of the poor settlers. Today, the once dense and tall rainforests where such majestic animals as the Asiatic elephants roamed and the Royal Bengal tigers prowled, and where once the blue-blooded hunted for trophy is no more but a forest in name only.

Shortly after Harka Bahadur had migrated to the plain the other two younger brothers who had become lahoorays had magnanimously written to inform Dil Bahadur of their decision to forfeit their share of ancestral land on account of their being able to buy land and house in the city. This had immensely relieved him because he knew well that one day he'd have to split the dwindling land among his three sons.

The next big crisis in his life had been the earthquake of 1988 (Nepali year 2045 Bikram Sambat) which had hit the eastern hills and plain, killing over a thousand people, among them his eldest daughter who was three years older than Amrita. The earthquake had hit in the dead of the night when everybody was asleep. When the house had started rocking everybody had run out except the unfortunate girl who had been crushed on her bed by a wooden beam that had fallen on top of her from the ceiling, though the rest of the house had remained intact. To bury one's child is the most painful experience any parent can have and so it was with Dil Bahadur and Kamala. "Had she not died she'd be twenty now, and probably married with a child or two," Kamala sometimes said sadly with wet eyes, and he would agree with a melancholy nod. The memories of the lost child were still painful for him.

But in retrospect he concluded that in spite of all he had gone through, life had been generally kind to him. His family had never suffered from acute want; there had always been enough to eat, and the family had always been together.

A few days later Dil Bahadur forgave his son. "What's written in one's forehead cannot be altered or erased," he said philosophically, reiterating the Nepali belief that the God of providence writes a person's destiny on his/her forehead at the time of birth and what's written is unavoidable. "It was written for you two to be together and so you are together. Nothing can separate the two of you." Thus saying he rested the matter. He didn't talk of a wedding though, as it was evident that there still remained some other matters to settle first, like what to do when the jilted husband came looking for his wife, as he was certain to do. Limbu men do not let their wives go that easily, especially if the wife is young and pretty. In the old days, if a married woman eloped with another man the jilted husband could go after his rival and cut off the latter's head, but within a stipulated time frame. It was legal and socially acceptable and a few angry husbands chose to do just that. For this reason the runaway couple often ran far away - either to the plain or to north-east India from where they never returned.

Lalita quickly assumed the role of the new daughter-in-law, helping Laxmi in the kitchen and elsewhere. She took to the routine housework with gusto. She was strong and enthusiastic, and above all she wanted to please her in-laws and win their acceptance. Every day she and Laxmi got up early in the morning to start the day's work. The two women swept the floors, cleaned the two houses, cooked the food, filled the water jars, washed and dried clothes, ground maize on the hand-operated stone grinder, and beat rice on the foot-operated see-saw type rice-beater. Sometimes she helped her mother-in-law in the vegetable garden and sometimes she helped to brew rakshi from fermented millet. She was always careful to cover part of her hair with a scarf in front of her father-in-law and elder brother-in-law as she knew that it was a sign of respect to do so, though nobody ever told her to do so because such a show of respect is not compulsory.

Having to leave Kathmandu had saddened her somewhat. She was getting used to the city and its rhythm of life. She would have preferred to remain there with Milan. Here, there were no roads, no cars, no buses, no motorcycles, no electricity, no television, no cinemas, no supermarkets, no fancy shops and no restaurants. Except for an occasional radio or cassette player, the place was almost completely devoid of modern machinery. Like Milan, she liked the modern way of life and missed it. But she had grown up in a village not unlike this and had decided that the sacrifice was worth making. Besides, Milan had promised her that this was only a temporary arrangement and that they would eventually return to the city. She had complete faith in him. She loved him deeply and unconditionally. She was carrying his child in her womb and she was happy. Nothing else mattered.

Kamala, though somewhat apprehensive at first, quickly warmed up to her second daughter-in-law. She was delighted with the work Lalita put in. As far as she was concerned women had two purposes in life: to produce children and to serve her husband and his family. She couldn't be blamed for harboring such views because that's the only way she knew. She herself had gone through the same chores in life. As a new daughter-in-law her mother-in-law Narmaya too had driven her hard. But she held no grudge against the older woman, unlike so many women who did and then took revenge in the latter's old age, or if the old woman was not around, then on their daughters-in-law instead. Narmaya herself didn't have any feeling of guilt either. As far as both women were concerned each was merely playing the role that she was born to play.

Now for Lalita's story, for it's inconceivable that she didn't have a story. People do not take drastic steps without a good reason. There is a reason behind everything, and everything is there for a reason.

Lalita was born and bred in the village of Yangnam, the domain of the Thamsuhang and Jabegu clans in Panchthar district, way south of Khewang two days' journey on foot and by bus. When she was just out of school she had big dreams for herself in her pert and pretty head. She wanted to go to the city to become a nurse and tend to the sick in a hospital wearing a clean white robe. Maybe fall in love with and, with luck, marry a handsome doctor. If one dares to dream then that dream is bound to take one to places. That was her philosophy on life.

But she hadn't reckoned with the bullheadedness of her stubborn and arrogant father. So at the tender age of seventeen, and against her will, her father had given her off to a forty-two years old widower, an ex-lahooray with four children from his deceased wife. The man was her late aunt's husband. Her father had taken pity on his heartbroken brother-in-law who looked sad and forlorn and, in his eyes, pined for his dead wife. Lalita's father, in all good faith, had wanted to compensate for the loss of his sister by presenting him with his own daughter, quite a common practice among the Nepalese.

Now this uncle, she called him uncle then because he was her aunt's husband, had kept alive the relationship even after his wife's untimely death. As it happens with men, once they get over their grief they start looking for a new wife, most for sexual reason. And by that time Lalita had blossomed into a sexually desirable young woman and his roving eyes had not missed the development in her body. Lalita, on her part, had not failed to notice his interest in her. She was a smart girl with observant eyes. Whenever an opportunity presented itself, he teased her and tried to flirt with her and she did her best to avoid him. But when he caught her alone (she suspected that he stalked her) he stared at her longingly - his gaze shifting from her face to her taut breasts – to her extreme discomfort. Sometimes when their eyes met by accidentally a slow and deliberate smile spread across his slitty-eyed mustachioed face. It was not difficult for her to imagine what he wanted. Two years of bachelorhood had made him sex-starved and the very sight of this beautiful young thing aroused his senses. As his visits had become more frequent, she had found it increasingly difficult to avoid him. She felt his eyes follow her everywhere. When she was turned towards him, his eyes were glued to her face and breasts. When she was turned away from him she knew that they were glued to her waist and buttocks. She found his attention infuriating. She detested the man. She hated him from the core of her heart. She was angry that an old man like him should lust after a young girl like her.

Then one day the uncle talked to Lalita's father about his loneliness and desire for a second marriage. Her father promptly offered him his daughter without bothering to consult either Lalita or her mother first. The uncle was elated, to say the least. He had been planning to propose himself but hadn't found the courage. She was constantly on his mind. He was tormented by his growing lust for her young body. Just the thought of her filled him with sexual desire and gave him an erection. On a few occasions he had sought refuge in the arms of prostitutes in Kathmandu and other towns along the way, but they had been unable to quench his thirst for her.

Lalita was devastated, to say the least. In her nightmare he had become the demon who tried to whisk her away to his lair against her will. She abhorred the very idea of having to sleep on the same bed with a man who, at forty-two, was only seven years younger than her father. She protested, she threw tantrum, she cried, she howled and screamed; she threatened to run away from home, she threatened to throw herself off the cliff; she threatened to drown herself in the river; and she locked herself in her room, but all in vain. Her father was adamant. His decision was final and there was no going back. He couldn't go back on his word for fear of losing face. He told her that it was for her own good. He told her that if there was anyone who could give her a good life then it was the uncle. Her mother was no help. She did put a word or two on her distraught daughter's behalf, but that was all. Then she meekly went along with her husband.

Thus, her father had prevailed upon her, and at the tender age of seventeen and three years after her aunt's death, the heart-broken girl had miserably made the journey to the village of Dumrise, for that was her husband's ancestral village, the domain of the Samsohang clan, by the Phawa River, a tributary of the Kabeli River, as the lawfully wedded wife of a middle-aged man who was formerly her aunt's husband.

Two weeks after the wedding Bhim Prasad, her husband, had taken her to Kathmandu for that was where he lived with his four children. Her cousins, one of them older than her by a few months, were waiting for her apprehensively.

Bhim Prasad had wasted no time in spreading his eager hands and weight all over her young body. But his performance in bed, like everything about him, was lackluster. From day one sex with him had become a daily chore, something that she anticipated with dread. He could neither arouse her, nor excite her nor satisfy her and her prejudice against him didn't help. She didn't like him touching her and kissing her, especially in the mouth. Nevertheless, every night she quietly let him have his way, lying inert under his loathsome weight as he huffed and puffed, and prematurely spilled the fluid of his lust into her. Afterwards, as he turned to the other side and fell asleep, she went to the bathroom and thoroughly washed the repugnant fluid off her flesh. Luckily for her, she didn't become pregnant, and whatever the reason may have been, she was thankful for that.

She spoke to him as little as possible, and spent the better part of the day conjuring up a pretext to avoid submitting herself to his lust - mostly by claiming that she had a headache or a stomach-ache. He was nice, and kind and loving to her. Who wouldn't if at the age of forty-two he had a lovely seventeen year old girl for a wife? It is said that the older men grow the more they crave for the soft and delicate flesh of young girls. But Lalita could never love him. Although she could tolerate him, she could not love him and that was her final decision, as far as she was concerned. She may have been forced to marry an older man, but she couldn't be forced to love him for love is something different. It must come from the heart, not from the head.

As one miserable day passed after another, she felt utterly alone, misplaced and homesick. Unlike in the village where everybody knows everybody, one hardly interacts with the next door neighbour in the city. Everyone is busy with one's own life. Lalita found herself alone in the middle of the crowd. The older children didn't know how to react to a 'mother' who was about the same age as themselves, and the younger ones were suspicious of her. She herself did little to remedy the situation. She cooked for them and fed them, but that was all she did. She had never wanted to become a mother to grown up children at such a young age. She thought of joining a girls' college and made some inquiries, but found out that the year's session was already a third of the way through and she had to wait till the following year. Then six months after marriage, Bhim Prasad went abroad for employment, to her utter relief.

It was at such a dark phase of her life that she had thought of the young man next door as a spark of hope. She knew that he liked her, and she felt attracted to him as well. Whenever she stole a glance at her next door neighbour's house, she found him either at his window or on the attic stealing glances at her. But she deliberately ignored him at first, or tried to. *Boys are no different from older men. All they want to do is get into your skirts, and once they get what they want they do the disappearing act.* But one morning she woke up from a pleasant dream. In her dream she and the young man were locked into each other's arms, making passionate, wild love. She found it a strangely fulfilling dream. Perhaps it was a harbinger of things to come, she thought. That very day she decided that she would lock eyes with him, just once, and see what happens. And that was the day when their eyes had first met and she had given him a shy and sweet smile which had captured his heart. The moment had been electric for both of them.

As the days passed the two continued to exchange stolen glances and smiles, and afterwards advanced to communicating with gestures and hand-signals. One day, after pondering for many days, she came to the conclusion that she was in love with him and if there was anyone who could rescue her from her dreary existence, it was him. By the time they started meeting in private, both had long understood implicitly the intensity of the fire smouldering within each other's heart. This was real love. This was love at its most pristine form – love that comes straight from the heart, not arranged by or imposed by a third party.

Suddenly life took an exciting turn, filling her with renewed hopes, dreams and possibilities. She felt as if her life had been completely rejuvenated. In the heady days that followed they made their rendezvous at different locations all over the city. They went to the cinema and sat in the dark holding hands and touching each other profusely. They went to the temples to seek the blessings of the gods and goddesses (at Lalita's insistence, Milan didn't care much for the gods and goddesses), and exchanged vows of everlasting love and companionship. They went to quiet secluded places and restaurants where they sat many hours cuddling each other. And they shared their dreams and planned their future. In about a year he'd go abroad to seek his fortune (that's what young people were doing since there was hardly any fortune to be made in the country) and she'd wait for him for three years. In the mean time she'd avoid getting pregnant and study to become a nurse. When he returned, they'd elope and get married. They'd build a house in Kathmandu, have two children – a boy and a girl - and live happily ever after. This was being unfaithful to her husband and she knew that. *But why must I be faithful in a marriage that I never wanted? Why must I remain faithful to a husband I do not love?* She argued with herself.

They conducted their affair so clandestinely that nobody suspected anything in the beginning. But emboldened by their success (in eluding prying eyes) they became careless. Six months into the affair Milan took her to a friend's rented room in a quiet corner of the city. His friend had magnanimously lent him the key for the day. As soon as they entered the room, by tacit understanding they fell all over each other hungrily, with all the fury of pent-up desire. It was as if a dam had suddenly collapsed and thousands of tons of water had gushed out sweeping away everything in its path. In no time at all the two had undressed each other; hurriedly, eagerly, with urgency. Their clothes lay scattered all over the floor as they locked into each other on the bed, both stark naked. They made love passionately, with all the eagerness and forcefulness of youth - she lying on her back with her thighs tightly bound around his legs as he mounted her thrusting vigorously. She kept whispering into his ears between her ecstatic moans, "I love you. I love you. I love you with all my life and heart. Don't ever leave me." It was the first time she had enjoyed sex and she craved for more. They made love three more times that day. From that day on, their sexual escapades ran unrestrained, like a brand new racing car in the hands of a wonder-eyed juvenile.

In any neighbourhood nothing escapes people's eyes forever and in the course of time the neighbours got wind of the affair. It was inevitable. People are good at putting bits and pieces together and coming up with a picture. Lalita quickly became the topic of gossip in the neighbourhood. Milan's aunt admonished him for being involved with a married woman. She warned him that if things got out of hand he'd have only himself to blame.

Now one truth about life that everyone knows is that things do not always go according to plan. And sooner or later one must pay the price for carelessness. One morning, three months after their first sexual intercourse, Lalita discovered that she was pregnant. At first she was scared, naturally. She didn't want to become pregnant, that was not part of the plan, and she panicked. She was eaten by anxieties. What will happen when people find out that I am pregnant? They will vilify me and make my life hell. And what will Milan do? Although she trusted him completely, deep inside her heart she had a nagging fear that he might get cold feet and desert her, as so many young men do leaving the jilted girl with no other way but to commit suicide to escape social disgrace. This prospect frightened her. If that happened to her, what was she going to do? She didn't have an answer. She didn't even want to think about it.

For many days and nights she was tormented by anxiety. *How will Milan take it? Will he be man enough to accept his responsibility and do the needful? Or will he shirk responsibility and abscond? Where will he take me? He has no house and employment here? Will he take me to Khewang? If we go to his village then what will happen to our plan for the future?* She asked herself these questions over and over again. Finally, she decided that she could not be certain until she told him.

Two weeks after she discovered that she was pregnant, she broke the news to him. They had just finished making love, and he was still on top of her.
"Milan, there's something I have to tell you," she said looking into his eyes.
"Go on," he said, "I am listening."
She paused for a long moment and he waited.
"I am pregnant," she said.
"You are what?" He sat up with an expression of shock and disbelief on his face.
"I said I am pregnant. With your child. What are you going to do about it?"
"You are .... pregnant?" He said slowly. It was more a statement of shock than a question and he looked as if he had been hit by an electric rod.
"Yes, I am pregnant." She repeated. "I have your child in my womb."
"Are you sure?"

"Absolutely."
"But where's the bulge? I can't see it."
"It's too early for that."
He got off her and sat staring at her belly, trying to grasp the significance of her words. She could see beads of sweat on his face, and his lips had lost their colour.
She persisted, "What are you going to do about it?"
"Let me think," he replied.
"There's no time to think. You men get away with it so lightly, as if it's just a child's play, while we women are left to suffer the consequences of your actions."
"Oh…." he groaned in pained confusion, "What am I going to do now? What are we going to do now?"
"Oh, you men, you are so mercurial and untrustworthy," she lamented, "You use us, abuse us, suck us dry of our youth and then discard us like dirty rags when you get tired of us."
"My aunt and uncle will be mad at me."
"And this heartless society will make my life hell. Have you thought of that? I had sex with you because I love you. I have given you my love, my body, my soul and everything I have. All because I love you," she said.
"That's why I love you so much. And that's why I will never let you down ever," he replied.
"Then what will you do?"
"Let me think. We'll find a way out." He pondered for a long time as she waited for his answer. Both were stark naked. Then finally he said, "How about an abortion? Do you want an abortion?"
"No, I don't want an abortion," she objected.
"I've got friends who might be able to arrange it in a nursing home."
"I said no. I don't want an abortion. Don't even mention it."
Then he again became quiet and thought for a long time and said, "Will you come away with me?"

"Where?"
"To my home."
"Khewang?"
"Yes, Khewang."
"I am a married woman. Will your parents accept me?"
"They will have to."
"If they do not allow me to set foot in their house ……"
"They will not do such a thing. Trust me."
"But if they do …."
"Then I'll take you away from there."
"Where?"
"I don't know. I guess to a place ……. where love never dies."
"And where is that place?"
"I don't know. But there's got to be a place somewhere where love never dies."

She gave him a long, tender and loving look and said with a smile, "Milan, you are an idealist. Your head is full of dreams. That's what makes me love you so much. I'll come with you. I don't care where you will take me, but I'll gladly follow you. Come rain or shine, I'll be with you - not because I am carrying your child, but because I love you, truly, deeply, from the bottom of my heart."
"I know that. And I also want you to know this. I'd have taken you away with me sooner or later, pregnant or not pregnant. It hardly matters. Do you want to know why?"
"Yes."
"Because I love you. I love you so much that I cannot think of a life without you."

Two days later she packed her clothes and jewelry (excluding the ones given by her husband) and boarded a night bus out of Kathmandu with Milan. She left a note for the older children. "I am going away for good. I won't be back. Please don't look for me. I hope you will be able to take care of your siblings." She didn't tell them where she was going. Neither did she bother to leave a message for her husband. "That will be for him to find out," she said to Milan, and added silently to herself, "And my arrogant father, too. It's my little revenge on him."

Sure enough, a distraught Bhim Prasad, Lalita's ex-husband, and his kins came looking for her exactly a month after they had eloped. When they arrived late one morning, Amrita was in the buffalo-shed stroking the beasts gently and talking to them tenderly. This was a daily ritual for her. She talked to them as if they understood her. She was fond of the animals. They were mute and innocent, without any malice in their hearts, and that's what she liked about them. There were a couple of buffaloes in the shed – a large female and a young male. Not far from the shed was another shed where a pair of oxen was kept. Her father had already fed the animals hay and salted water, and the two oxen had been taken by her brothers to the fields. Upon seeing her, four black pigs grunted in their smelly and muddy pigsty a short distance away in anticipation of food, though they had already been fed. But then pigs are always on the lookout for food. As always when she was alone she sang softly to herself and day-dreamed about the one person who mattered the most to her. Sharan had been gone for the past two years and she could not remember a single day when he hadn't been in her thoughts. Before leaving he had presented her a colour picture of himself – he gazed at her with a quizzical smile - and she had given him hers – she gazed at him with a serene expression on her face. She had hidden the picture in an old book deep inside a metal box under the bed, where her parents were unlikely to find it. However, she knew that her mother had somehow got wind of the affair and had even asked her about him casually one day. But she had given evasive answers, telling her that it was nothing more than useless gossip by jealous people. Her mother, though skeptical, had let the matter rest. But she was certain that mother knew the truth and was thankful that she had not told her father.

Every time she got the opportunity she would take out that photograph and gaze into it lovingly, with dreamy eyes. Then she would hold it close to her heart and plant several kisses on it, wondering each time if he did the same. His letters had kept coming and in every one of them he expressed his undying love for her, telling her how much he loved her and how much his heart ached to be with her. The lahoorays get a six months' home leave at the end of every three years, and Sharan had only one year before his first leave. That's when most lahoorays get married. *One more year and he'll be here. He'll come straight to our house with his father. Only one year. Father will readily accept the proposal because he is a lahooray. I will be so happy that I just can't imagine how happy I'll be. They say that a bride must shed tears during her wedding, but I will not. I'll be too happy to cry on that day. After our wedding we'll leave this place for good. We'll settle in either Dharan or Kathmandu because our children – there'll be two of them, a boy and a girl - will need a good school for education and hospital when they are sick.* She smiled contentedly, secure in the knowledge that the day she had been waiting for was coming nearer each day.

As she gave the doleful-eyed buffalo a last pat on the head uttering words of endearment, she heard some male voices at a distance. She looked up and saw a group of strangers coming along the footpath leading to the house. There were five of them, all male. Two of them were older than the other three.

She heard one of them say, "This must be the house." She peered at them carefully wondering who they were. They were certainly not from this area, because she had never seen them before. The oldest man among them was wearing the traditional Nepali costume - *daura-suruwal* and a black coat complete with a *dhaka* topi (a colourful hand-woven Nepali headgear straight out of a village woman's spindle-wheel). The others were wearing modern clothes – trousers and shirts, one in jeans and T-shirt.

Instinctively, she decided that they had come looking for her younger sister-in-law. It had to be them. Without wasting any more time, she picked herself up, tore across the courtyard and straight into the kitchen where her elder sister-in-law Laxmi was busy dung-painting the floor.
"Elder sister-in-law, where's younger sister-in-law?" she asked breathlessly.
"At the back of the house," Laxmi replied without looking at her. "What's the matter?"
"I think it's her folks. They are here." Amrita said and ran out to the back of the house.
"Quick, sister-in-law, I think they have come looking for you," she almost shouted.

"Who?" Lalita's dropped the bronze cauldron she was ash-painting to brew *rakshi* by distilling fermented millet. Ash protects the cauldron from turning black with the smoke.
"A group of men," Amrita replied.
"Are you sure they are looking for me?" Lalita asked, trying to conceal her anxiety, but her voice betrayed her anxiety.
"Yes, it's got to be them. I have never seen them before. They are coming straight to our house," Amrita said.
"How many are there?" Lalita asked nervously, her heart pounding furiously.

"Five. If you don't believe, go have a look."
"No," replied Lalita.
"What will you do now, sister-in-law?"
"I don't know."
"You stay where you are, I'll run to inform father and mother," said Amrita as she dashed away. She immediately returned to ask, "Where's he?"
"Upstairs with mother. They are peeling dry maize-seeds," replied Lalita.
"And where's second brother?"
"He must be in the fields with elder brother."

Amrita hurriedly climbed up the wooden stairs, making loud stamping noises with her feet. She found her father with her mother, younger brother (Ratna) and younger sister (Gorimaya) peeling dry maize seeds.
"Father, mother," she said breathlessly, "There are five men outside the house."
"Five men? Who are they?" Dil Bahadur asked.
"I don't know. They are strangers. I think they are looking for second sister-in-law."

Dil Bahadur got up and walked to the window and peered out. The men had already reached the courtyard and were looking up at the doors and windows. He quickly came back and said, "I think you are right. I think they are looking for her."
"We must call uncle," Kamala said, meaning Jit Bahadur.

He thought for a moment and said to Amrita, "Run as fast as you can to your youngest grandfather's house. Tell him to collect some men and come as quickly as he can. Tell him it's an emergency. Now run!" Then he turned to his little son Ratna and said, "Run as fast as you can to the fields and tell your brothers to leave everything and come home immediately."

When Laxmi and little Ratna ran down the stairs, the men called out to them.
"Where are your parents, children?" the oldest of the group said.
"Upstairs," Amrita answered with a quick glance and the two continued on their way. A moment later Dil Bahadur came out followed by Kamala carrying her little daughter Gorimaya.

The oldest of the group, a craggy faced man of about sixty-five, said "Sewaro!". That's 'greetings' in Limbu language. Though he uttered the word with a smile, there was little warmth in his voice. In fact, Dil Bahadur sensed an undercurrent of hostility there.
"Sewaro!" Dil Bahadur replied, somewhat hesitantly, in the Limbu language.
"Is this the house of one Milan Limbu?" the stranger asked gruffly.
"You are right. I am his father." Dil Bahadur replied.
"Then we have come to the right place and met the right person," said the stranger. His younger companions grunted in agreement.
"Gentlemen, who are you and what can I do for you?" asked Dil Bahadur trying to be as amiable as possible, reverting to Nepali.

The old man turned to the middle-aged man standing beside him. As if on cue the middle-age man said: "I am Bhim Prasad Samsohang. I have just arrived from Kathmandu. This is my uncle and these are my brothers from Dumrise."

"Yes, that's right," added the craggy faced man, "My nephew here has lost his wife and we have come a-looking for her. He was abroad and came back as soon as he heard the bad news. We have reasons to believe that your son knows her whereabouts."

Dil Bahadur examined the middle-aged man with his eyes. *So this is Lalita's husband*, he thought. The man was unimpressive. He was of average build with a prominent bulge above his waistline. With a pair of slitty eyes, a short nose and receding hairline, he was not handsome by any standard. The thin line of mustache above his upper lip made him look comical rather than formidable as he had obviously intended. No wonder she left him for my son. Then he threw cursory glances at the three young men – they were all about his sons' age. He noticed that they stood awkwardly, feeling quite unsure of themselves, being of young age.

While Dil Bahadur was still searching his mind for the appropriate words to say, Bhim Prasad said, "I have come here to take my wife back home." Surprisingly, there was no hint of anger in his voice. He sounded calm and composed, very sure of himself. He wanted his lawfully wedded young wife back and there was nothing wrong with that. She was, technically speaking, still his wife.
"If you agree to send our daughter-in-law back with my nephew, who is her rightful husband, then we'll consider this matter solved amicably," the craggy faced old man added.

"I am sorry, gentlemen," said Dil Bahadur politely, "But I am afraid that's not up to me. You see, my son did not kidnap her. He did not use force or threat. He did not blackmail her. She came with him of her own free will. If she is willing to go back with you, then we cannot stop her, she is free to go. But I cannot allow you to take her against her will. Since she has already come with my son, she is my daughter-in-law now, and I consider it my duty to protect her."

"It's my wife you are talking about. Your son stole her from me when I was away. I have come to take her back." Lalita's husband said.

"Calm down, Bhim," said the craggy faced man to his nephew, touching his arm lightly, "Let us try to solve this problem peacefully."

"Yes," said Dil Bahadur. "Why don't we all sit down so that we can talk in an amiable manner?" he added, pointing at the skin-topped bamboo stools nearby. But the men made no move to take the stools.

"Where is she? I want to see her," said Bhim Prasad.

Just then some voices were heard and half a dozen men arrived. Two of them came and stood by Dil Bahadur's side and the rest mingled with the men from Dumrise.

"What's going on here?" asked Jit Bahadur in a cheerful voice. He was a silver haired man of about sixty-five, slight of build but hardy of appearance, with a well-trimmed mustache below his sharp nose that added to his persona. He assumed a natural air of authority because he was a sort of patriarch of the family and, more importantly, because he was a local politician. In the previous local election he had stood as an independent candidate and lost. But that hadn't dampened his spirit. He was planning to stand in the next election again.

"Well, these honourable men have come from Dumrise looking for my son and daughter-in-law," Dil Bahadur told his uncle.

"My name is Jit Bahadur Sambiu and I am the boy's granduncle," Jit Bahadur introduced himself, "Let us all sit down and talk. After all, we are all brothers. And at the moment you are our guests. Our culture says that guests are like gods and they should be treated as such."

"Yes, let us by all means," said the old man from Dumrise, with a wide smile breaking on his craggy face for the first time, making his slitty eyes even narrower, and motioned his men to take the stools moving to pull one for himself. Then the old man introduced each of his men. "I am Nar Bahadur Samsohang. This is my nephew Bhim Prasad, my elder brother's son. That one over there is my youngest son, and those two are my grandsons from my eldest son." Then he told them his father's, mother's and grandmother's clan-names, and then his nephew's mother's and maternal grandmother's clan-names.

After he had finished narrating his side of the family tree, Jit Bahadur proceeded to do the same on his side. He told them of his father's, mother's and wife's clan-names and then his nephew's wife's and mother-in-law's clan-names. It turned out that there were a few people who were known to both parties and they exchanged information about them. It made the talk easier and smoother, and feelings of hostility that existed between the two parties subsided.

Just then Purna and Milan arrived. Milan looked reluctant at first to approach the group, but on Jit Bahadur's beckoning he walked to his father's side and took a stool. The arrival of Milan made the situation tense again. Bhim Prasad glared at him crossly and Milan looked away. He wasn't afraid of the man; he had his folks all around him. He was just embarrassed.

"As you may have guessed, this is my grandson Milan," said Jit Bahadur with a smile as the men from Dumrise sat stiffly, glancing at Milan from time to time. It was evident from the expression in their eyes what they were thinking. *So this is the motherfucker who's stolen our woman*.

"In the old days," Jit Bahadur continued with an amiable smile, "our forefathers had the tendency to settle their disputes by violent means. It is said that they were prone to brandishing their khukuri at the slightest provocation and not one village fair or bazaar ended without a fight induced by a liberal dose of alcohol. They used to boast that 'to cut three inches deep is child's play'. But after 'slashing each other three inches deep just in jest' they would readily make peace over a bottle of rakshi and become friends the very next day. Thankfully, we have come a long way from those days. In these modern times, there is no disagreement that can't be solved peacefully."
"Yes, that's right," Nar Bahadur agreed, "And we mean to do just that – solve this problem amicably, in a civilized manner."
While the two old-timers talked, the younger men sat still, listening quietly.

"Good," said Jit Bahadur, "Now that we have all agreed to settle this matter in a peaceful and amicable manner, let us all try to put forth our views and understand what it is that each side wants so that we can come to a mutual understanding beneficial to both sides. Now could you please kindly explain to us what it is exactly that you want?"
Nar Bahadur cleared his throat and said, "I think we have already made it very clear. What we want, or rather what my nephew here wants, is very simple and straight forward. He has been profoundly wronged by your grandson. You all know as well as we do that it's immoral to steal another man's wife."
"Yes, we understand that," replied Jit Bahadur.
"As my nephew here still loves his young wife deeply and cares very much for her, who lawfully belongs to him, he would be

happy to go away peacefully if you agree to send her back with him," Nar Bahadur said and waited for the answer.

"We will not stand in the way if the woman in question agrees to go back to her former husband. What do you say?" Jit Bahadur turned to Dil Bahadur, his nephew, with a questioning look.
"No, we won't," replied Dil Bahadur, who in turn looked at Milan, who nodded his head silently. Milan was confident that Lalita would never leave him.
"But as we all know very well, the times have changed," continued Jit Bahadur, the local politician, with his well-practised oratory skill, "In the old days some of our forefathers treated their women like their personal property. I don't want to be disrespectful to our august ancestors, but that is the truth. For us to continue to do so is very wrong in today's context. Of course, there are still people in the world who shut up their women and treat them like slaves in the name of religion, culture and tradition, but they are not in step with the time and it would be unwise for us to emulate them. You might have heard how well the white men from across the seven seas treat their women. Of course, we cannot be as advanced as them either. But still I believe that we must at least try to keep up with the changing times. And in these modern times a woman is considered a man's equal in all respects. She has a mind of her own and she must be allowed to make her own decision concerning her life. In any case, our women have always been freer than other women in this country. What do you say?"

"Agreed," replied his counterpart on the other side, "We are not against our daughters and sisters making their own choices in life. They have as much right as we have."
The men around him silently nodded their agreement.

"Therefore, we must let the girl speak up for herself and find out what she has in mind and accept what she says as the truth" said Jit Bahadur, "Are you in agreement with me?"

"Yes," said Nar Bahadur and looked at his nephew, who nodded his head quietly.

"Good. I am glad that all of us are in agreement. Then let's summon the young woman and hear what she has to say," said the old man.

Dil Bahadur turned to his wife and said, "Purna's mother," that's how a Nepali man usually addresses his wife, as the mother of his first-born son or daughter, "Bring daughter-in-law here."

At a signal from Kamala, Laxmi quickly disappeared through the door into the kitchen. After some time she returned with Lalita by her side.

"Daughter-in-law, please step forward," said Dil Bahadur to the young woman. She did as she was asked, nervously. Her eyes quickly singled out Milan in the crowd and locked with his for a flitting moment. Milan gave her a reassuring look and a nod. She didn't look at her Bhim Prasad, her former husband, who was staring at her intently. Not even once.

"Now, daughter-in-law," said Jit Bahadur, "I am going to ask you some questions and I want you to answer them as truthfully as you can for the benefit of all of us here. Will you do that?"

"Yes," replied Lalita, looking at the floor.

"Did my grandson Milan make you run away with him by threat or force or any other unlawful means?"

"No!" she replied.

"So you eloped with him of your own free will."

"Yes!" She replied.

"Daughter-in-law, your ex-husband is here to take you back. Are you willing to go back to him?"

"No!"

"Is that your final answer?"
"Yes."
"You will not reconsider your decision?"
"Never."
Turning to the men, Jit Bahadur said, "Did you hear that, gentlemen? She came here of her own free will. She was not threatened or forced in anyway, and she doesn't want to go back."

Bhim Prasad stood up abruptly and demanded, "Lalita, I want to have a talk with you in private."
"No," Lalita protested hastily and firmly.
"Give me just a minute," the man pleaded, changing this tone.
"No," Lalita was adamant, "I don't want to talk to him in private. There's nothing he can say that will make me change my mind. I am not going back to him." She didn't directly address him, but spoke of him in the third person.
"Please listen to what I have to say. Just once! Then I won't bother you again." Bhim Bahadur pleaded in an imploring voice.
"No," said Lalita, "It's over between you and me. There is no going back." This time she addressed him directly. An expression of profound hurt mixed with disbelief spread across Bhim Prasad's face. He had come with the certainty that he would be able to persuade his wife to come back to him.

"I gave you everything you ever needed. I would have given you my own life if you had only asked. But apparently that was not enough for you. Now for the last time, tell me one thing. Why did you leave me?" he asked her.

Looking at Bhim Prasad's stricken face now, Lalita almost felt sorry for him. This man, who was still technically her husband, had never treated her badly. In fact, he had always taken care to treat her with the utmost love and affection. And in spite of her betrayal he still wanted her back, because he loved her. She saw it plainly in his sad eyes. But she knew that though she pitied him, love was a different matter altogether. She could never love him. Love needs a common platform where two hearts can meet, as they say. There was no such thing between them. He was not only too old for her; he was also incompatible to her in every other way. Then she glanced at Milan and in him she saw the man she had always dreamed of – young, virile, exciting and adventurous, and with big dreams in his head. True that he didn't have money, but there was long road ahead for them together and there was plenty of time for that. This was the man she loved. This was the man she would readily follow anywhere.

"Because you are too old for me," she replied bluntly. She uttered these harsh words boldly and clearly, loud enough for everyone to hear. She felt no remorse afterwards. The truth must be told at some point, even if it hurts. Bhim Prasad was devastated by these stinging words and looked crestfallen.
"But you knew that when you agreed to marry me, didn't you?" he asked in a quivering voice.
"I never consented to marry you. My father forced me against my will," she replied.

Slowly he sank down on the stool and didn't look at her again. Seeing the pain in his eyes, Nar Bahadur whispered something into his ears and he nodded. Then the old man said to his hosts, "Allow us to discuss the matter among ourselves for a minute."
"By all means, go ahead" said Jit Bahadur, "Take all the time you need." Then he turned to Lalita and said, "Daughter-in-law, you can go now." With a look of tremendous relief, Lalita

quickly disappeared through the door. She didn't bother to look back.

The five men got up and walked to the end of the courtyard and discussed amongst themselves while Dil Bahadur and the others waited. They couldn't hear what was being said, but Nar Bahadur was doing most of the talking and the others were nodding their heads in agreement. The discussion dragged on for ten minutes, and then twenty minutes and then half an hour. Finally, the group walked back.

"All right," said Nar Bahadur, "Here is what we have decided. Since she has made it clear that she will not come back to my nephew, we can't take her against her will."
"You have made a very sensible decision," said Dil Bahadur, "Because we wouldn't have allowed you to either."

Ignoring Dil Bahadur's remark, the old man continued: "Now my nephew here has spent a fortune on his wedding. He has provided his wife with expensive clothes and jewelry. Therefore, according to our tradition, we'd like monetary compensation."
"She hasn't brought any jewelry with her save the earrings and bracelet given to her by her parents," said Milan.
"Is that true?" asked Nar Bahadur to his nephew.
"Yes," replied Bhim Prasad truthfully.
"Then that's settled. Now let's talk about the compensation." Jit Bahadur said looking at Dil Bahadur.
"How much is it that you want?" asked Dil Bahadur. He knew it would eventually come to that. He had known it all along and even calculated the amount in his head.
"Fifty thousand rupees! That's all we want. Actually, twice more than that was spent on the wedding. You know how

costly marriages are these days. But we don't want to look mean," Nar Bahadur replied, carefully weighing his words.
Dil Bahadur said, "Fifty thousand? That's too steep for us. We don't have that kind of money."

Then the negotiation began in earnest. Nar Bahadur insisted on the stated amount, while Jit Bahadur insisted on lowering the same. Finally, after a negotiation of a little over an hour, they reached an agreement. Twenty-five thousand rupees in cash. With that, Bhim Prasad agreed, reluctantly, to forfeit his claim over his wife forever.

That very day the money was raised from various sources - partly from Kamala's safe box and partly borrowed from relatives and neighbors. With the money paid in full, the men from Dumrise departed in an agreeable mood, except for Bhim Prasad who looked absolutely heart-broken. But it all ended peacefully. No voice was raised in disagreement, no fist was raised in anger, and no grudge was held.

After the men left, Kamala said, "Now the way is clear for the wedding." Dil Bahadur didn't reply, he only shook his head. He was thinking of the money he had just paid out. Children can be a liability. You bring them into this world, feed them, clothe them, send them to school and then as if that wasn't enough you have to buy them a wife or a husband depending upon their sex and then pay for their wedding as well. It's not easy being a parent, he was thinking.

"When are we going to have the wedding, Purna's father?" Kamala asked. Dil Bahadur didn't reply. He was still engrossed in his thoughts.

Milan and Lalita's wedding was held with a simple ceremony two months later. With the colour and sound of life in every nook and corner of the hills, spring was already in full swing. Dil Bahadur invited all his relatives and neighbours to his son's wedding and slaughtered a large pig and some chickens for the feast. As is the custom, the guests came with money and kind as contribution towards the wedding cost. Amrita, at the behest of her mother, carefully jotted down in a notebook what (or how much) each guest had brought. This would be referenced later when deciding how much to give to a particular family in case of a wedding in that family.

While the guests ate and drank (for no Limbu feast is complete without alcohol), the bride and groom sat cross-legged on a woolen mat to receive the well-wishers. The younger ones (by relation and not by age) paid their respect while the older ones (again by relation and not by age) gave their blessings. "May the two of you remain together forever," some said, while the others said "May you have many, many children to cover all the hills and lands," to which Milan replied in jest, "Who wants many children these days? The days of twelve sons and thirteen grandsons are over. Give us a more modern blessing." Lalita spent a better part of the day getting up and bowing down to touch the feet of the elders or simply greeting them with joined palms – Milan's granduncles and grandaunts, uncles and aunts, brothers and sisters-in-law, sisters and brothers-in-law; most of them once, twice or thrice removed. There were so many of them that she just couldn't keep count.

Then the older men danced the drum dance. Half a dozen men carrying large double-sided cylindrical drums (called *chyabrung*) with leather straps slung across their shoulders danced in a circle to the synchronized beat of the drums. The drums went dang, dang ... dang, dang .... dang, dang, dang,

dang .. dang, dang .... while the men moved in a circle in a fluid and rhythmic motion - left leg swing to the right, right leg swing to the left, three quick steps forward and then two quick steps backward. Every now and then they cried "Hurrr........." which was picked up by the spectators who excitedly crowded around them. The drum dance is not accompanied by any song. The spectators stand around the dancers and watch, making comments when a dancer unwittingly makes a wrong move or does something funny to attract the attention of the spectators. Every now and then a tired man was replaced by one of the bystanders. In this way, the dance went on for more than an hour.

After the feast all the relatives and neighbours stayed behind to attend the wedding ceremony which takes place at night. It was a long and protracted ceremony conducted by the priest, but Lalita enjoyed every minute of it. The first time had been a nightmare and she had shed voluminous amounts of tear under the cover of her wedding veil. But this time it was different. She looked stunningly beautiful in resplendent red and Milan gaped at her awestruck. "You shine like the full moon in a dark sky," he said and she blue him a kiss. It was the happiest day of her life. If one could measure happiness in terms of physical quantities such as kilometers, then she was a million kilometers happy. She looked radiant with a wide, if a bit shy, smile on her face all day. She was happy, and that's what mattered the most to her.

But while it is true that every dark cloud has a silver lining, it is also true that every clear blue sky has a patch of cloud in it. For her the cloud was the non-response of her parents. She had written to them explaining why she had done what she had done. She had profusely begged for their forgiveness and blessing. She had been hoping for a reply, but there had been none. Their complete silence had hurt her deeply. She took it as proof that they were still mad at her for leaving the husband of their choice. *But I am their blood. I will have to make peace with them one day. And they will have to forgive me in the end. That day will surely come, for time comes for everything.*

Milan was happy, too. He was happy that he had got to marry the woman he loved, something that not every man is lucky enough to do. At the same time he was also aware of the responsibility that had fallen upon his young shoulders. With a wife to take care of and children (not yet born, but he was sure there were going to be a few) to bring up, he sensed that his life had already taken a different turn. He also realized with a tinge of sadness that his student life was over and along with that his carefree days. He couldn't possibly go back to his uncle's house and live there as if nothing had happened. For his father to pay for his education in the city would be too big a burden for the family. But in spite of this he hadn't abandoned his urban dream. *There's nothing for me and Lalita in this village. One day we will go back to the city, because that's where my heart really belongs.*

Dil Bahadur also had reasons to be happy. Both of his grown up sons were now married, and both daughters-in-law were good natured, respectful and hardworking, though very different in every other way. Now he had Amrita to think of. He had not failed to appreciate the physical changes in her over the past couple of years. From a fun-loving sprightly teenager, she had blossomed into a sexually mature young woman. Many a young man's wandering eyes were bound to fall upon her pretty face. Sometimes he worried that she might fall for the wrong sort of boy and run away, or worse get pregnant and give birth to a fatherless child. This is a worry that every father of a grownup daughter has. Having been boys once they know what boys want of naïve young girls, and every father thinks that his daughter is naïve and innocent. Unlike in the Chhetri and Bahun communities where parents start looking for eligible young men by sending out feelers once they decide that their daughter has reached marriageable age, the Limbus cannot do that. Limbu parents must wait patiently for suitors to arrive for their daughter. If neighbours find out that they have been actively looking for a son-in-law, then they will lose face. Many a girl prefers to find her beau of her own, which is a good thing because as long as the boy possesses a good moral character and is not a pauper then the parents do not object.

Kamala, too, was happy. In fact, she was happier than her anybody else except the bride and groom themselves. Not only both grownup sons were married, but one of them was actually going to make her a grandmother. And pretty soon, too. That was what was important to her, becoming a grandmother and holding a plump little grandson on her lap. But when her eyes caught Laxmi, she felt a sense of pity for the young woman. She had talked to the couple several times urging them to produce a child. She had been to village astrologers and roadside fortune-tellers. She had summoned the priests and shamans many times over to perform elaborate and expensive rituals to 'drive away evil spirits' that she thought were plaguing her daughter-in-law. Every one of them had predicted the birth of a child "by next year". But still Purna and Laxmi were childless. How long was she prepared to wait when it had become the personal business of every bitchy neighbour and relative? If a woman fails to conceive, then suddenly it becomes everyone's business. "Why is she still childless? Isn't she capable of giving birth? Perhaps she is infertile." The same is true for an eligible young woman who fails to attract a suitor. Thus Laxmi's problem had become her problem. *Perhaps people are right,* she thought, *perhaps she is really barren.* And lately she had even begun to view their advice in a more favourable light: *Perhaps Purna should take a second wife. But will he agree to be the husband of two wives? He probably will if he is forced into it.* This thought troubled and saddened her because she liked Laxmi. In her eyes the young woman had all the qualities of an ideal daughter-in-law – soft-spoken, hardworking, obedient and respectful.

Kamala had no way of knowing, but this was exactly what occupied Laxmi's mind that day. She had been carried away by the celebration around her and happily scurried to and fro tending to the needs of the guests until her eyes accidentally caught the bulge above Lalita's waistline. She had nothing against Lalita, who was polite, courteous and nice to her at all times. The two got along quite well, Lalita and she, though they were very different in nature and could never become the best of friends. Now looking at Lalita she couldn't help feeling envious. She tried to fight the feeling but it persisted and cast a dark shadow in her mind.

Lalita caught her eyes and gave her a radiant smile. She smiled back at her. *Look how happy she looks. In less than a year she is going to become the mother of a cute little baby sucking greedily at her luscious nipples, and I will still be barren. She will be the toast of the family, and everyone will fuss over her and her child while I, poor wretched me, will be completely ignored.* This thought filled her with melancholy and nearly brought tears into her eyes. *I mustn't cry today. I must not. It is a day to be happy. My younger brother-in-law is getting married. I must be happy.* She wiped her eyes, put a brave smile on her face and went back to work.

Jealousy is the most complex of human emotions. It rises from deep inside the subconscious mind. It drives men and women to do things that they wouldn't even think of doing in a normal frame of mind. It is the reason for some of the most heinous hate crimes that people commit. But jealousy is not limited to individuals. It extends to groups of people, communities and races. When one community becomes more successful than others, then the other (less successful) communities become jealous. It does not end there either. It also exists between nations. When one country becomes more successful than others, the other (less successful) countries become jealous. This leads to misunderstanding, conflict, terrorism and war. But jealousy is also one emotion that people never admit that they have. When confronted they find one or another pretext to conceal this most shameful of emotions, for even the most jealous person is ashamed of it. But while the truly 'bad' make jealousy the guiding principal of their life, the 'good' recognize it as a dark and evil force and fight against it.

Being of a good and tolerant nature, Laxmi's jealousy was only flitting. Her good sense quickly prevailed and she blamed only herself, or rather her own fate, for her misfortune. *It's not Lalita's fault that I am childless.*

At the conclusion of the ceremony an hour before midnight, most of the guests (except those who were staying the night) returned to their respective homes. The newly wedded couple went back to their nuptial bed. Although she was tired by the day's work, Laxmi couldn't sleep. She stayed awake by her bedroom window as some men and women danced the 'paddy-dance' in the courtyard. A man sang in his melodious voice:

"The streams are full of crabs, younger sister, they make me dizzy,
If you fail to reciprocate my love, younger sister, I will go crazy."

A woman immediately replied in her mellifluous voice:

"Life is very short; it's only for a few days, older brother,
How can I trust someone who loves me today only to ditch me tomorrow?"

An hour after midnight she went to lie beside Purna who was fast asleep and snuggled up to him, but he didn't respond. The last lines she heard before she descended into the kingdom of dreams was:
"We don't know if we'll be dead or alive tomorrow,
But we'll dance the paddy-dance to our heart's fill tonight."

A month and a half after the wedding, when everything had settled down and fallen into their respective places, Lalita made up her mind to visit her parents to ask for their forgiveness. This was very important to her because ever since she had eloped with Milan, she had been tormented by the thought that she had hurt their feelings badly. In spite of what her parents had done to her, she still loved them and had tender feeling for them. They were, after all, her parents.

After the wedding she had written to her parents again, and this time her father had written back a harsh reply telling her that he wanted to have nothing to do with her because she had hurt his feelings badly by putting the family name to shame. In spite of this scathing letter she was determined to make peace with them and receive their blessings. She planned to go to Yangnam before the arrival of the rainy season.

But like the oft-quoted Nepali proverb goes: 'I aim at the log and the axe aims at my knee', the early arrival of the monsoon rains forced her to put her plan on hold. Black clouds pregnant with water rushed inland from the Bay of Bengal and swiftly swept over the eastern hills. They collided with the perennially cold Himalaya mountains, precipitating torrents of rain accompanied by deafening thunderstorms and blinding flashes of lightning that threatened to tear the hills apart. It rained interminably for four days and four nights – sometimes in a torrential downpour and sometimes 'drip, drip, drip' the whole day and night. There is something very romantic about the monsoon rains. It makes everything wet. It cools the air and washes away the dust and dirt. It makes the trails muddy and slippery. It's a time for the family to huddle around the hearth munching boiled potato and fried maize seeds with ground chilly and washing the same down the throat with tea, water or alcohol. But the one thing truly disagreeable about monsoon is the sticky mud that clings to every surface, from the sole of one's shoes up to the knees. It sticks thick and fast to the hooves of cattle and even on their itchy horns. It's everywhere. It follows one into the house and even into the bed if one is not careful. And then wherever there is greenery, there are the hateful, slippery leeches, constantly on the lookout for animal flesh to latch onto. They stretch out of the nostrils of the hapless cows and buffaloes to quench their thirst when the animals drink from springs and ponds. And mysteriously frogs appear as if out of nowhere, thousands of them, and croak incessantly calling out to their mates. After a few days these amphibians fill the ponds with millions of slimy, slippery tube-like things that contain their eggs which hatch into slippery tadpoles.

With four days and four nights of incessant rain, the foot trails turned into impromptu rivulets. The potholes filled to the brim with muddy water and turned into miniature ponds. Then when these were trampled by the hooves of cattle, the road became muddy and slippery. The terraces filled with water and turned into ponds – the upper one feeding the one immediately below it and so on until the bottommost terrace fed the river. The swollen Tawa River roared with such vehemence that the usually subdued roar could now be heard from miles above, prompting people to express fear of an impending landslide somewhere. And a minor landslide did occur. A few kilometers to the west from the village a stretch of foot trail was swept away into the river. At that particular corner there remained nothing of the trail, just a large and ugly impassable scar forming a steep cliff precariously hanging over the roaring river several hundred feet below. The village became inaccessible to outsiders.

After the rain dwindled to a drizzle and then took a respite, the men went with spades and shovels to cut a bypass near the damaged section. But a few days later another spate of heavy rain brought on by a new of wave of elephant-trunk clouds, so called because they look ominously like the dark spiral-shaped trunks of the pachyderms, swept away another large chunk and made it impassable again. Lalita was forced to shelve her plan until Dashain, the biggest of all Nepali festivals. There's nothing a woman, or a man for that matter, can do when nature itself conspires against her. For all human's technological progress, he still hasn't acquired the ability to accurately predict or tame the forces of nature. There's nothing he/she can do to prevent earthquakes, hurricanes, typhoons, flooding, landslides and avalanches.

Milan, who had been uneasy about Lalita's plan from the beginning, because he didn't relish the idea of facing his in-laws so soon, was relieved and secretly thanked the rains. "Festival season would be a more appropriate time to meet your parents. People are generally in a more agreeable and forgiving mood then," he had argued with Lalita. But she had persisted until he had been forced to acquiesce out of his desire to see her happy. Now he was secretly happy that the rains had come to his aid.

The months of June and July are perhaps the most important in a Nepali farmer's life, for the hard work put in these two month yields the harvest to feed the whole family in the coming year. For the first time in his life, Milan helped his father and brother to plough and till the fields for the upcoming paddy plantation. During this time young men show off their dexterity with the oxen and the heavy wooden plough with an iron blade, challenging each other to a competition. Then on the day of plantation the whole village becomes busy in transferring young rice saplings to water-filled terraces. Everybody chips in to help; even the children do what they can. As always there was great competition among the planters and from time to time the men and women broke out into impromptu songs in their melodious voices. The village untouchables – the damai (tailors/weavers), the kami (ironsmiths/goldsmiths) and sarki (shoe smiths), some of them so destitute that they only had dirty, tattered rags for clothes on their backs – came to help with their whole families for the price of two square meals a day and the liquor that flowed freely during and after work.

Fifty years ago when Dil Bahadur's grandfather was a hereditary village chief, called 'Subba', the whole village irrespective of caste and social standing used to come to help in the fields. He owned a large swath of land which his drunkard son later squandered. He was treated with deference, and he referred to the villagers as his subjects like a king. His one duty to the government of the time was to collect the land taxes from his subjects and surrender the sum to the land revenue office in the district headquarters. A handful of Limbu chiefs were shrewd enough to enrich themselves with their collection, but the majority of them, being simple and honest to the core, didn't profit a single *paisa* from that endeavour. Instead, they unwittingly helped to fill the private coffers of the corrupt district officials of various ranks – starting from the lowest to the highest level, who grew fat on the peasants' earning.

The clout of the hereditary village chiefs began to wane after the fall in 1951 of the hundred and four year old absolute rule of the hereditary Rana prime ministers. The executive powers of the state once again reverted back to the hitherto titular Shah king who in turn, after a few years' of experiment with parliamentary politics, seized control in a bloodless military coup in 1960 and ruled the country with absolute authority under the guise of the so-called party-less democracy called the Panchayat (Council) System. The Land Reform Act which King Mahendra, the founder of the party-less Panchayat (Council) System, implemented in 1966 abruptly ended whatever power and privilege the hereditary Limbu chiefs still had until then. But their loss was nothing compared to the catastrophe suffered by the Limbu community as a whole. As a result of this act almost seventy percent of their communal lands went into the hands of non-Limbus. Thus reduced to near-penury they saw no other alternative but to leave their ancestral land and migrate to the Terai in search of livelihood. The wave of migration started at that time continues to this day, though at a reduced scale. The lopsided Act was highly successful in redistributing the lands belonging to ethnic minorities, but it largely left untouched the vast amounts of lands belonging to the really wealthy and powerful absentee landowners (akin to feudal lords) based in Kathmandu and in other urban areas. When formulating and implementing this obviously well-meaning but badly implemented Act, the King did not care to consult the ethnic minorities, who combined form half the country's population. At the time they were inconsequential. They still are today. Centuries of cultural repression and political marginalization has rendered them powerless and voiceless. As a result they are unable to speak up for themselves and they have no one to speak up for them. That's why they watched mutely when a prominent member of the ruling community flew to Paris to represent them in an international conference of the world's ethnic minorities. That's also why they watched mutely when a handful of Hindu fanatics forced the makers of the country's constitution to declare their country a Hindu state.

'In the months of June and July
When the rain soaks everything,
How can I console this
Solitary heart of mine?'
Laments my sweetheart,
With teardrops in her eyes
'Across the seven seas
The land where he's gone lies.'

Amrita hummed along with the melancholy song playing on the radio – a perennial favourite of all lahoorays. She was washing clothes with elder sister-in-law Laxmi in the backyard. Her younger sister-in-law Lalita was in the kitchen preparing morning meal as a plume of black-gray smoke streamed out of the two small square holes that served as ventilators. This sorrowful song dwelt on the pain of a soldier in a distant land as he remembers his home and sweetheart. It had a mournful sweetness that emanated directly out of the heartache and homesickness of a lonely man. Ever since Sharan's departure, the song had become one of her favourites, too. Every time she listened to it she felt its sweet melody permeate through her heart to touch her very soul, and a lump came up her throat and stuck there for a long time. At such times she couldn't help but miss him terribly. She closed her eyes and pictured his smiling face. *I love him. I love him with every beat of my heart. I love him so much that if I could tear apart my breast, I'd show him how it beats for him and only him. If only he were here with me.* Being young and naïve, she had a very romantic notion of love. Love that is boundless, pristine, indestructible and everlasting. Love that has the power to conquer all.

But today, as hard as she tried to concentrate, she could not recollect with clarity the face that she loved with such intensity. It came only as a vague and blurred image and she wondered why. "Maybe he doesn't love me anymore. Maybe he's found a frivolous white girl to give him company," she murmured softly. This thought filled her with melancholy. She had heard that many young soldiers had tall and pretty foreign girlfriends.

"Excuse me! Did you just say something?" Laxmi's question startled her.
"No, I didn't." She said, blushing profusely.
"I thought I heard you say something."
"I didn't say anything."

"Yes, you did. You said something but I couldn't catch the words clearly."
"Did I really? I must have been wondering aloud."
"About what?"
"Nothing," she replied.
"I know what," Laxmi teased her with a smile. "You were thinking of him, weren't you?"
"No." She contradicted, blushing deeply.
"Yes, you were," Laxmi persisted; "This song reminds you of him, doesn't' it?"

She didn't answer. Maybe at this very moment he's embraced in the arms of a pretty white girl, caressing her golden locks and kissing her pink lips. She quickly reprimanded herself for being so suspicious and fickle-minded. The only white girls she had seen were American Peace Corp volunteers, and they certainly did not go out with the local boys. *The reason I am not able to recollect his face clearly is because he's been gone for so long.* And she liked this explanation better than the previous ones. *I must look at his picture more often.* With this thought she got up and ran up to her room. Laxmi wondered what she was up to. *Perhaps this is what love does to you. It makes you laugh; it makes you cry; it makes you babble; it makes you brood; and it makes you act strangely.* She thought with a smile. *How unfortunate that I never had that experience.*

Once inside her room, Amrita locked the door. Then she pulled out the metal box from under her bed and took out a photograph. She gazed at the smiling face for a long time and pressed it against her breasts. After some time she planted several firm kisses on it. Then she gazed at it longingly again, wondering whether he did the same. After about five minutes, she put the photograph back into the box, which she locked

and pushed under the bed. Then she went back to where Laxmi was washing the clothes. Laxmi gave her a puzzled look and said "What happened?"
Amrita blushed and said, "I remembered something."
"And what was that?"
"Math homework," she replied.
"Really?" Laxmi gave her a knowing smile, "Did you manage to do it in five minutes?"
"There were just a couple of sums," she replied with a blush.
School started only at ten in the morning and she still had an hour left. Luckily for her, it was only ten minutes walk away, some of her classmates had to walk for an hour each way every school day. After they finished washing the clothes, she helped Laxmi to hang them out at various places, some on ropes and some on the branches of shrubs. She asked Laxmi to collect them if it rained. It usually rained in the afternoon, but one never knew when the sky would suddenly turn dark and open up in a torrent. Then she went to her room to prepare herself and her siblings for school. At seventeen she was still in the ninth grade. She should have completed the tenth grade and left school by now, but she had started a year late and then had failed once along the way.

She called out to Ratna and Gorimaya to get ready and when they were ready, she shepherded them to the smoke-filled kitchen to gobble up the morning meal Lalita had prepared for them. There was rice, *gundruk* (dried spinach soup) and potato curry with a few pieces of fresh red chilly. They hurriedly washed down the food with cold water and then started for school. Amrita couldn't wait to finish school that day because she was going to Manju's house in the afternoon. Manju's soldier brother had just returned from England on leave - he had arrived the previous day - and she was hoping that there was a letter for her. Sharan was Manju's aunt's son. He and

Manju's brother Kiran were close friends and the two had joined the army together. It was through Kiran that they had met and fallen in love. *What if Kiran hasn't got a letter for me? What if Sharan has fallen in love with a pretty English girl and forgotten me? You never know with men.* Such thoughts nagged her persistently because feeling of insecurity is a part of being in love. But she needn't have worried. The moment she ran into Manju, the girl pulled her aside with a wink and said, "If I give you something, what will you give me in return?"

Her heart beat faster and she blushed. "What could you possibly have for me?" She feigned ignorance.
"All right then. I have nothing for you." Manju giggled and pretended to go away. But Amrita caught her arm hastily and said, blushing profusely, "Ok, I'll give you anything you ask for. Just hand it over to me."

"Is that a promise?" Manju teased her.
"Yes, it's a promise. Now give it to me." Amrita pleaded.

With a secretive and knowing smile, Manju produced a folded envelope from her bag and handed it to Amrita, who hastily read the writing on the envelope. There was only her first name on the scented envelope and nothing else. She quickly pushed it inside a book in her bag and thanked her friend, who flashed a mischievous smile at her. She dared not open the letter at school. If a teacher found out about it he would confiscate it and either report her to the Headmaster or worse vilify her in front of all her classmates.

Throughout the school hours that day Manju kept giving her that special smile and an occasional nudge with her elbow as the two sat beside each other. Amrita liked Manju, she really did. She was her best friend. She was also her cousin. And her confidante. The two knew everything about each other and shared the deepest of secrets, including Manju's crush on a young Bahun teacher. When Amrita's romance with Sharan was at the budding stage, it was Manju who had acted as the go-between, carrying messages and letters and setting up rendezvous.

Sharan's mother was Manju's father's younger sister. She had married into the Yonghang clan from the village of Medibung, a day's walk to the south. The young man often visited his maternal uncle's house in Khewang. There the two had exchanged coy glances and shy smiles, and afterwards wondered about each other. And with subtle encouragement and help from the brother and sister, the two had fallen in love.

She recalled in her mind that their 'love' had really taken off with the first letter that Sharan had sent her. When Manju had handed her the letter one day, she had been thrilled, nervous and terrified all at the same time. At that time she was an adolescent girl of thirteen. Her periods had just started that year and the nipples on her her newly-developed fist-sized breasts were just beginning to push the shirt up. Every part of her body was beginning to exhibit signs of the sensual woman she was growing into. At her age the world was a fun-place to be in and she laughed, smiled and giggled at everything. And everytime she saw Sharan she blushed profusely. She couldn't help liking him; there was something irresistible about the boy.

After seeing him a few times she had realized that she had a crush on the boy – he was seventeen, fair-complexioned and good looking with dark, searching eyes and an infectious smile. His smiling face danced in her eyes constantly. At first she had been frightened by this new feeling inside her and was unable to understand it fully. She had also been terrified that her parents and elder brother would find out. "They will kill me if they find out," she had said to Manju and refused to send a reply.

But Manju had insisted that she write a reply, telling her that he would be heartbroken if she rejected him and that he would never come back to Khewang. It was an emotional blackmail and it worked. Not being able to see him again was a prospect she didn't want to think about, and she had written back to him. That was the beginning of their romance, which had blossomed into love by the time he had left to join the British army.

Before leaving he had come one last time to Khewang to say farewell. "Wait for me for three years," he had said as they had stood holding hands in an abandoned cowshed, "and I'll come back to marry you."
"I will," she had replied through tears, "If you promise that you will come back."
"I promise," he had said, "that I'll come back to you. Do you trust me?"
"With all my heart," she had replied, "I will be right here waiting for you, no matter what. I will think of you and pray for you every day. Will you do the same for me and write to me every week?"
"I will," he had said, "I'll think of you and write to you every day."

With that the two tearful lovers had embraced tightly and kissed each other in the mouth. Then they had parted unwillingly, with tearful eyes. That had been the sweetest and saddest day of her young life. She had cried herself to sleep that night. Two years had passed since then. After his departure Amrita had ticked off every month of the calendar counting the days he'd be back. Three years is a long wait. Almost an eternity when you are young and in love. *How difficult it must be for the young wives of lahoorays to wait for their husbands, who come at the end of three years and then leave again after a six-month stay?* She thought sadly.

When the last bell of the day rang at four o'clock in the afternoon, Amrita hurriedly shepherded her little bother and sister home. Since she had already got what she had hoped for, there was no reason to go to Amrita's house.

"Give your brother my thanks," she said to Manju, "And tell him that I'll come to see him in a few days."
"Come to visit him someday." Manju had said.
"I will," she had replied.

As soon as she reached home, she locked herself inside her room and carefully opened the letter. It was written on a beautifully watermarked (a bridge with a clock tower near it) scented paper. She read the content hurriedly.

Dearest Amrita,

A thousand kisses to the queen of my heart! No, a million kisses. Amrita, you are the essence of my being. Without you I am nothing; my life has no meaning. I love you from the bottom of my heart. I love you with every breath of my life. And I pray every day to all the gods and goddesses up above and down below to always take good care of you and keep you from harm's way.

I spend my days here in this foreign land thinking of you all the time. It aches deep inside my heart to be so far away from you. Not a day goes by when you are not in my thoughts. I carry your photograph in my wallet and everyday I take it out and shower it with kisses. Sometimes I go to bed holding your picture near my heart and then I dream of you. In my dream I am always running towards you and you towards me with outstretched arms, but somehow I never reach you. Just at the moment when I am about to reach you, I wake up. What does it mean? My mother used to interpret dreams and you used to do the same. Some people say that dream is a premonition of things to happen. But I have my doubts. Dream, a better educated friend of mine here says, is a product of our subconscious mind. He says that our hidden desires and fears manifest themselves in our dreams and release us from tension. He read that when he was in college. And I believe that to be true because I always fear that I might lose you to someone luckier than me. That's why I have these dreams.

I wish I could be with you always – holding your tender hands and looking into your beautiful eyes. But a soldier's life is a life of hardship and loneliness brought by long periods of separation from family and loved ones. These two years have been like a decade to me. The first nine months of training were the most difficult and I almost felt like giving up. After that things eased up a bit. In the end it has been worth it in a way. I have had the opportunity to travel far and wide, to such wonderful places as I had never heard of or imagined. I have seen beautiful girls of every race and colour – white, black and brown - that one can only dream of. But you, my love, are prettier than them all. And in all the fabulous places I have been to, the only thing I have wished for is for you to be by my side, holding my hand. It sometimes occurs to me that if our country were not so impoverished then I wouldn't have to serve in a foreign army and be away from you for such a long period of time. We would be together, you and I, everyday of our lives. But what can we do? We are all slaves to circumstances and prisoners of our own desire to escape poverty. Only after coming here have I realized how utterly impoverished we are. We may be rich in culture and tradition, but they cannot be worn and eaten. One cannot sing and dance on empty stomachs and bare backs. What people really need is material progress. Do you know why our country never seems to make any progress? Because people say that it is a land cursed by a heartbroken sati whose patriot husband was treacherously put to death by jealous courtiers, and I am inclined to agree with that.

On the surface we are happy, but deep inside every one of us is lonely. Sometimes we show each other the pictures of our sweethearts. My colleagues never fail to remark how beautiful you are. At such times my chest swells with pride. Some of my friends have English girlfriends. But believe me when I say this: I have always been true to you and I always will be. Otherwise, I wouldn't have told you this.

My darling Amrita, I have a sweet little dream and in that dream there are the two of us, there is a beautiful two-storey house in Kathmandu built of our own sweat, and a couple of children running about merrily. You do not know how anxious I am to share this dream with you, and turn it into reality. Be patient, my love. There is only one year to go. Come next July, I'll be at your doorsteps with my father, asking your father for your hand. That day is not very far. Wait for me. You said that you'd be there waiting for me, no matter what, and I have faith you. And write back to me as soon as you can.

Yours and only yours forever,

Sharan

She kissed the letter several times and then read it all over again, this time slowly, without haste, crunching and digesting every word. She had innumerable letters from him in her box. It wasn't the first and she knew that it wasn't going to be the last. She loved the way he wrote and she loved the way he proclaimed his undying love for her. She smiled smugly. Her dreams were taking shape.

"Amrita, Amrita! Where are you?" She heard her mother's voice outside.
"I am in my room mother. I am changing. Why?" She yelled back.
"Does it take so long to change? Come down here and help me to weed out the grass from the vegetables."

But she went to see her grandmother first who was recuperating in her room. The old woman had caught a bad cold and was coughing. After inquiring after her health and giving her assurance that she would recover soon, she climbed down the stairs and went into the kitchen. Her two little siblings were having fried maize seeds. Laxmi offered her a plate of the same with a cup of tea. She thanked her sister-in-law and stuffed that down her throat. Then she went out to the vegetable garden to help her mother.

While weeding the vegetables her mother said casually, "There's something I have to talk to you about."

"About what, mother?"
"About a proposal...."
"A proposal? What proposal?"
"We have indirectly received a proposal for you through a relative. There's a young man who wants to marry you."
"Mother, I don't want to get married."
"He is a young lahooray of about 24 years of age. He is of the Angbuhang clan from the village of Hampang."
"I don't care and I don't want to know. I am not going to marry. Maybe some day in the future, but not now!"
"They say he is a good looker."
"I don't care."
"They say he is of a good character and will take care of you well."
"Mother, I told you I don't care."
"If you agree to marry, then he will come with his folks to take a look at you next week. You can at least agree to see him."
"No, I don't want to see him, or anyone else for that matter. Please tell them not to come."
"Why don't you want to marry?"
"Because I am still at school."
"School is not that important. You can leave it any time you like. You are all of seventeen now and it's about time you got married, you know."
"Don't do that to me mother. I told you I am not interested."
"Your father thinks you should marry."
"I don't care what he thinks. It's my life, not his."
"How can you say that? If he hears of this he will give you a good thrashing."
"I still won't. And how can he give his grownup daughter a thrashing?"
"He will, if you are not too careful how you talk of him."

"He can't. Don't you know that it's a sin to beat grownup daughters?"

"He will if you are disrespectful to him. Now tell me the truth. What's the real reason?"

"I told you ……….."

"No, it's not that." Kamala paused for a moment and then lowering her voice to a whisper said, "It's because of that Yonghang boy from Medibung, isn't it?"

For a moment, Amrita was too stunned to say anything in reply.

"You think I don't know?" continued Kamala, "I have known about your 'friendship' with Manju's cousin all along."

"Who told you, mother?"

"I heard it from some people."

"Who?"

"I won't tell you."

"Does father know, mother?" She was scared of her father, though he never did more than rebuke her.

"No. I haven't told him. Now tell me the truth. It's because of him, isn't it?"

"Yes, mother. He has asked me to wait for him."

"For how long?"

"He's coming back next year."

"Are you sure he's going to marry you?"

"He has given me his word."

"Words do not mean much these days. What if he breaks his promise? What will you do then?"

"Trust me, mother. A promise is a promise and he is going to keep it. He'll come."

"You may have faith in him, but I have doubts. Young men are fickle and untrustworthy. They carry their heart at the tip of their finger. When they see all those pretty and coquettish girls in the city, they lose their hearts there. They never come back, not for a naive village girl like you. I know a few women who

have wasted their life waiting for unfaithful lovers who never turned up."
"Mine is different, mother. Believe me. He is not like others. He'll come back for me."
"I hope he does." Kamala said, "But if he doesn't you'll have only yourself to blame."

That night when Kamala told Dil Bahadur, he listened quietly and said at the end, "My daughter has a boyfriend? Unbelievable." He was surprised. Fathers are the last to know about their daughters. But then it occurred to him that Amrita was no longer a child; she had grown into a woman. He didn't lose his temper and didn't think badly of it. He accepted the news quietly and matter-of-factly. Many Limbu girls have boyfriends; they've always had boyfriends. *If Amrita wants to marry the boy of her choice then so be it*, he thought. *If a man can choose his wife, so can a woman. But the boy better be good.*
But he said to Kamala, "I don't know. We've got a very good match here."
"Yes, that's the point," replied Kamala.
"It is unlikely that we'll get another proposal as good as this one," he said pensively.
"That boy of Amrita's also a *lahooray*."
"What's he like? Is he worth waiting for?"
"I think he is. I have met him a few times. He used to frequent Manju's house before going away to become a *lahooray*. That's where Amrita met him."
"So you think we should reject this proposal and wait for that boy?"
"I don't know. He may not come, you know."
"Exactly! That's what I am afraid of. If he fails to turn up, we'll be the laughing stock of the whole village."

"You are right. But Amrita is adamant. You know how she is. If she doesn't have a mind to do something then no amount of persuasion can make her do it."

"She is very obstinate, isn't she? But we all are. That's our family trait, I guess," Dil Bahadur said with a smile.

"Perhaps that's a common characteristic of all Limbus," added Kamala with a chuckle.

"I guess all humans are basically the same. So shall we decline this proposal? You know, your cousin and his wife won't be happy." Kamala said.

"They certainly won't. They will feel slighted by the rejection because the boy they are proposing is the woman's sister's son."

"Then what shall we do?"

"I'll talk to Amrita tomorrow to see if I can make her change her mind."

"And if she still refuses?"

"Well, in these times we mustn't force our children against their wish. Why, even our forefathers never stopped their sisters and daughters from marrying the men of their choice. So I guess we'll have to wait for that boy of hers, and hope for the best."

The next day Dil Bahadur summoned his daughter to his presence and broached the topic, knowing fully well what her answer would be. As expected, Amrita refused, flatly and with finality. Dil Bahadur was prepared for her answer and accepted her refusal quietly and sympathetically. He knew that his cousin who had brought the proposal would be upset. *My cousin will complain that they (he and his wife) were in danger of losing face in the boy's village because of this. He will also warn me that I couldn't possibly hope to make a better match than this for my daughter. But I will courteously apologize to him and tell him firmly that my decision is final and unalterable. My daughter is not going to marry. Not now anyway.*

Lalita had long given up trying to tame her rapidly bloating abdomen. Looking at her bloated belly, the women made speculations as to what would come out of that. Some said that since her abdomen was big and round it would definitely be a girl, while others claimed since it was conical-shaped it would be a boy. Different people see the same thing differently. "Mark my words," said the aged Chandra Maya, wife of the nearest neighbour Khem Bahadur, "it's going to be a girl." Kamala and Narmaya were hoping for a boy, naturally, and they argued that it would be a boy. "You must have a boy," they said to Lalita, as if she had a say in the sex of the baby. If anyone dared to declare to their face that it would indeed be a girl, they immediately suspected jealousy and dismissed the person curtly. As for Lalita, since it was her first child, she didn't care much for the sex of the baby. All she wanted was to give birth to a healthy child.

Now for a bit of mythology once again. The daughter of the all-powerful creator goddess Tagera Nimaphungma was the earliest woman in the world. Since she had no siblings she grew up alone and entered womanhood without any knowledge of the opposite sex. One day in the forest she chanced upon a naked young man who entered a state of great sexual excitement upon seeing the beautiful naked woman. He touched, caressed and prodded her breasts and vagina with his eager hands and erect penis. To her astonishment and delight, this greatly aroused her and there and then they had sexual intercourse. The enjoyed it so much that they repeated the act many times over and began to live together. As a result she became pregnant. In the first month of pregnancy her complexion turned blue. In the second month her body began to itch. It itched even more in the third month. It itched so terribly in the fourth month that she became irritated even by mild rain and gentle breeze. In the fifth month she became confused and disorientated. In the sixth and seventh months, the foetus began to move inside her womb and she longed for hot, sweet and sour tastes. In the eighth month her appetite increased so much that she felt like eating everything, including snails. In the ninth month she felt irritated and angry. In the tenth month she made up her mind to face the consequence of her action (i.e., sexual intercourse) and readied herself for delivery. Then within that month she gave birth to a baby boy. This child later became famous as the Tall Hunter.

Now, because a pregnant woman has to go through several precarious stages, the Limbus believe that she should impose certain restrictions upon herself. She must not cross a river, she must not step over a rope tied to cattle, she must not eat unripe fruit, she must not slaughter or witness the slaughter of animals, she must not see the melting of gold and silver, and she must not quarrel or fight. And before delivery, her parents are required to perform a special womb-worship ritual to propitiate the goddess Yuma, the grandmother, who is the earthly reincarnation of the supreme goddess Tagera Nimaphungma and is the chief deity of the Limbus, to protect the child in the womb and to ensure safe delivery. As she was estranged from her parents, this was not to be for Lalita. In any case, economic and other circumstances do not permit all Limbus to go through this three-day ritual.

The wet monsoon, which gets onto one's nerves after a while, neared its end in the beginning of August. The Limbus have a special name for this time of year. They call it *Oodhouli*, or downward bound, as opposed to *Oobhouli* (upward bound) which falls in March. They celebrate this occasion by a communal ritual worship. This is the time when rivers and streams begin to lose their volume, and the mostly deciduous trees that cover the hills prepare to shed their leaves. This is also the time when the fish lings that have hatched in the crystal clear cold water near the source of the rivers flow downriver with the current which carries them the deep blue sea on their journey of life.

One sunny morning Lalita complained of pain in her abdomen and went into labor immediately, two days earlier than her mother-in-law had predicted. Kamala, however, was ready to deal with the situation. Realizing that delivery was imminent, she sent Amrita to fetch the village midwife (by experience and not by training) and helped the whining young woman to her bed with the help of Laxmi and gently laid her down. The midwife arrived within a quarter of an hour.

Milan anxiously waited outside the house with his father and brothers while the women helped Lalita to push the baby out. After two hours and several heart-rending whines of agony, she finally gave birth. As soon as the baby came out emitting a sharp cry of pain as it sucked in the cold, fresh air for the first time, the midwife cut the placental chord neatly with a rupee coin, wrapped the thing with a piece of old cloth and handed it to Kamala dispose it. Kamala in turn sent Amrita to bury it. After that she cleaned the baby and then placed it on the bed beside its mother. "It's a girl," she said to Lalita who managed a feeble smile.

A short time later Kamala came out and said to her anxious son, "You have become a father. It's a girl."

Milan smiled shyly and said, "I can't believe I am a father." Milan didn't care for the baby's sex. He was happy that Lalita had given birth safely, without any complication.
"How are the mother and child?" he asked.
"Go inside and see for yourself!" replied his mother.

Milan hurriedly made his way inside, followed by his little brother Ratna. Lalita was lying on the bed with a little bundle by her side. She looked pale and worn out; labour pain had drained away all her energy, but there was a tranquil look on her face. When their eyes met, she smiled weakly and motioned at the baby with her eyes. Laxmi, who was standing by the bed next to the village midwife, a fussy and talkative woman who was quiet for once, picked up the baby and handed it to him. "Congratulations, brother-in-law! You've become a father," she said with a smile.

He smiled back at her and slowly stretched out his arms to take the baby, and then hesitated and stopped midway. He was overcome with shyness. *Take the baby, it's your daughter*, he urged himself in his mind.

But something held him back. It was inhibition borne out of his youthfulness. He stood motionless while Laxmi eyed him with mounting curiosity. She seemed to sense what was going on in his mind; it was plainly evident on his reddening face.
"Why are you so shy, brother-in-law? Take the baby. She's your daughter." Laxmi teased him.
"I am not shy," Milan lied and his cheeks turned redder, which enhanced his good looks, thought Laxmi.
"Yes, you are." Laxmi insisted.
"Take the baby," Lalita said feebly, gesturing with her eyes.

Milan gave one look at his wife and reached for the baby. He took it into his arms and held it up awkwardly. The expression on his face betrayed his embarrassment. He was clearly uncomfortable with the idea of fatherhood. In the old days it was quite common for men his age to become fathers of two or more children, but things had become quite different since then. None of his friends had become fathers; most hadn't even married. And here he was, holding the baby, literally, his own pink little baby, and completely at a loss as to what to do with it.

All of a sudden the baby let out a shrill cry and he almost dropped it. Then composing himself, he fixed his eyes on the infant's pink little face. It was a cute little thing, so soft and delicate and yet so full of life, with bluish veins running under its translucent skin, and a few strands of soft black hair on its head. He smelled the infant. There was a milky 'freshness' about it that only a newborn baby can have. He gently ran his fingers across the soft and delicate spot above the baby's forehead. Why do babies have that? He wondered. It makes them so vulnerable. And suddenly all his inhibitions faded away. He felt at ease with himself. He held his little daughter firmly and kissed on her cheeks.

"The baby will be cold. You can put her back now," the midwife said to him. He handed the baby back to Laxmi who laid it carefully by its mother's side. Lalita looked lovingly at her newborn daughter. Then she looked up at him and their eyes locked. He saw profound love in her dark eyes and his happiness was boundless. Life is a river, he thought. It flows constantly, overcoming all obstacles until it reaches its end in the ocean.

Limbus believe that the birth of a child makes the house unclean. Therefore, a purification right has to be performed to make the house clean again. This is done together with the name giving ceremony which takes place on the fourth day for a girl and on the third day for a boy. After performing a lengthy ritual in which he sought the protection of the supreme creator goddess Tagera Nimaphungma for the newest member of the family, the priest gave her the Limbu name Tanchona, meaning 'morning star'. This name would be used for all religious rites. Afterwards Lalita gave her the modern Nepali name Kalpana, meaning 'imagination'. This name would be used for all other purposes.

It was the year 1994 AD (Nepali year 2052 Bikram Sambat). At about the same time in Kathmandu the first democratically elected prime minister after the restoration of democracy dissolved the parliament and called for mid-term polls, all because he was unable to tame the three dozen dissenters in his own party. Thus, with one single stroke of whim he sowed the seed of political instability that was to wrack the country for years to come and adversely affect the lives of all Nepalese. Things would never be the same again. The mid-term elections held the following year produced a hung parliament, and the country had to suffer one corrupt and ineffective coalition government after another, frustrating the people's aspirations and paving the way for the bloody Maoist rebellion that was to ravage the whole countryside.

Part II
Acts of Destiny

The monsoon rains petered out and stopped completely by the beginning of September; and with that the weather became more agreeable to the mind and body. The end of the monsoon is followed by autumn - three months of pleasant weather before the onset of the harsh winter. During this period summer heat is gradually replaced by the winter cold. Each day becomes colder than the one preceding it. Paddy fields loose their green cover and turn yellow, and a sweet aroma fills the air and goes up one's nostrils and makes one truly happy to be alive. This is the season for boys to fly their home-made kites and vigorously engage in impromptu dogfights in the sky. Then in the beginning of October when the yellow and orange marigold flowers are in full bloom in every courtyard, the ten-day festival of *Dashain*, the greatest of all Nepali festivals, arrives in all its myriad colours.

To the Nepali Hindus *Dashain* signifies the triumph of good over evil. It is a time for the family to get together. It's a time to eat, drink, laugh and be merry. It is a time to construct swings and swing high up into the sky. It's a time to visits one's parents, grandparents, uncles and aunties, grand-uncles and grand-aunties and all other elders to receive red *tika* (wet raw rice grain mixed with red vermillion powder or the blood of the sacrificial animal) on the forehead from their hands along with their blessings and monetary gifts. Dashain, however, is also of time of great difficulty for the poor and the destitute. This is a time when they are forced to borrow money and kind they cannot possibly hope to pay back from crooked moneylenders who seldom fail to add one or two zeros to the amount the illiterate wretch has taken. Thus a principal of five hundred mysteriously becomes five thousand and the poor man unwittingly embarks upon his quick road to destitution.

At least that used to be case with the Limbu and their brethren the Rai, Dewan and Sunwar as well until a decade ago. After the restoration of democracy, it suddenly became possible for the politically and culturally suppressed ethnic communities to speak up and organize. That was when the educated among them decided that rather than signifying the triumph of good over evil, Dashain in fact signifies the victory of the migrant Aryan race over the indigenous Mongolian race in the days of antiquity. From a historical point of view, this theory seems more plausible than the one offered by the Hindus.

Limbus and Rais have their own indigenous religion they call *Kirat Dharma*, or Kirat Religion, which is as ancient as time and is animistic in nature. They worship numerous gods, goddesses, divinities, semi-divinities and spirits that are supposed to reside in the hills, mountains, forests, rivers and valleys. The language they speak belongs to the Tibeto-Burman family of languages, and uniquely among Nepal's indigenous people Limbus have their own script called the Sirijunga script. And most importantly they have the *Mundhum*, which is a collection of myths that includes the story of creation. The *Mundhum* governs every aspect of a Limbu's life from birth to death.

Now the question arises, who are the Limbus? Along with the Rais and two other smaller ethnic minorities, namely Dewan and Sunwar, who inhabit the eastern hills of Nepal, Limbus trace their ancestry back to the ancient *Kirat* people who were among the first to arrive in the Himalayan foothills in prehistoric times to clear and cultivate the harsh land. When the great Roman Empire was at the zenith of its power in Europe, North Africa and the Middle East two thousand years ago, the Kirats were ruling over a large swath of mountainous lands in the foothills of the Himalayas from their capital in the fertile Kathmandu valley. A fierce-looking bow-and-arrow-carrying warrior-hunter named Yalamber is credited with establishing a royal dynasty that lasted for over five hundred years until the 29th king was defeated by the invading Aryan princes from India.

After their rout from Kathmandu valley, the Kirats moved to the eastern hills. Not much is known what happened after that, except that in the subsequent centuries they established several petty kingdoms that warred against each other. Thus weakened by internecine warfare, many of these petty kings became vassals to the more powerful Hindu kingdoms in the south that rose and fell at different times. At least once there appears to have been an attempt at unification but without success. Then in the course of time, no one seems to be certain when, they subdivided into different ethnic groups of today – Limbu, Rai, Dewan and Sunuwar, each with its own language and culture. The Kirats inhabiting the hills east of River Arun became Limbu. Those living in the hills west of the river became Rai, and those occupying the area further west became Sunwar. Those living between Limbus and Rais became Dewan. Rai are the most numerous of the Kirats.

In the middle of the eighteenth century, Limbuan, like the rest of Nepal, was made of several small principalities ruled by petty chieftains who called themselves king anyway. Then in the middle of the 18th century Prithvi Narayan Shah, the shrewd and ambitious young king of a small hill principality called Gorkha (not much of a town even today) in mid-western Nepal, decided to conquer all the other hill principalities. Now he was a singularly unique figure in the history of Nepal. He ascended the throne of his little hilltop kingdom in 1742 AD at the age of twenty and immediately embarked upon a mission of conquest. His quarter-century campaign turned out to be a resounding success, owing to his brilliant military strategy, astute diplomacy, relentless attacks and counter-attacks and ruthless battlefield tactics aided by the modern weaponry he had clandestinely smuggled in from north India, at that time under the jurisdiction of the fledgling British East India Company. He declared himself the King of unified Nepal after the conquest of the three affluent kingdoms of Kathmandu valley in 1769 AD, describing his newly conquered kingdom as a yam between two great boulders for obvious reasons. His campaign of conquest did not end with his death six years later. His descendents carried on his work and within the next quarter of a century managed to push the boundaries of the country as far as River Sutlej in the west (now in Pakistan) and the Kingdom of Sikkim in the east (now a state of India).

The conquest of Kirat land, however, was not as easy as Nepali history textbooks make it out to be in a single sentence - *"Then the Kirat territories were conquered"*. It took several bloody attempts to subjugate the Rai chieftains of Near and Middle Kirat. After finally conquering them the Gorkhali army proceeded to conquer the Limbu chieftains of Far Kirat. In the old days the Kirat land west of the River Arun were known as Near and Middle Kirat and the area east of the river was known as the Far Kirat. Upon failing to do so after several attempts, a fact rarely mentioned in Nepal's history books because they are all written by Aryan historians, the King succeeded in persuading the Limbu chieftains into signing an agreement according to which they would get full autonomy while the overall sovereignty would lie with himself. Wary of the expansion of British rule by the East India Company in neighboring India, and falling prey to the Hindu propaganda that the British rulers would forcibly convert all to Christianity, the Limbu chieftains reluctantly agreed.

After the agreement King Prithvi Narayan Shah made the following royal decree and handed it to the Limbu chieftains with his royal seal:

To the Limbus of Far Kirat:

We have received your reply to our previous letter. We desire peace and harmony in our kingdom. Our intention is good. We had afforded you refuge previously also. We have conquered your land by dint of our valour. You were defeated and your country now belongs to us. But you belong to us and we undertake the protection of your kinsmen. We hereby pardon all your crimes and confirm the customs and traditions, rights and privileges of your country. Therefore, join our courtiers and render them assistance. Take care of the land as you have done when you were ruled by your own chieftains. Enjoy the land from generation to generation as long as it remains in existence. You are different from the other people we have conquered; their kings and chieftains are to be replaced, but not you. We fully understand your intent. But since truth remained in your heart, there was conflict between Sikkim and us. We have sent our officials there and you will understand everything from them. As we have said above, remain under your own chieftains and enjoy your traditional rights and privileges and your lands. If we confiscate your land, may our ancestral gods destroy our kingdom. We hereby inscribe this pledge on a copper plate and also issue this royal decree and hand it over to you our Limbu brethren.

The above is mentioned here because it is important to the Limbus. Thus, the subjugated Limbus were given full autonomy by the magnanimous King in Kathmandu and their land was declared communal land and outsiders were forbidden to buy or occupy it under any circumstance. Over time, however, the authority of the local chieftains waned and disappeared completely due largely to the active drive of the Hindu nationalist agenda of the successive rulers in Kathmandu, aided by the ignorance and naivety of the Limbu chiefs themselves, not to forget their love for alcohol and disdain for education. Then in the course of time the economically hard-pressed Limbus began to sell their communal lands to the immigrant Hindus.

Even after the conquest of their lands some Rai and Limbu chiefs fought back sporadically for many years, but they were all captured and killed, and over a period of time their rebellion died out. One rebel who particularly stands out is the Rai king Buddhikarna Rai, who was captured and killed in the most brutal manner. But that's another story. After that pressure from the Hindu migrants, chiefly the priestly caste Bahuns, increased and the staunchly animist descendents of the Kirats were gradually forced to adopt the customs of the immigrants, and before they knew it they were counted among the Hindus. The priestly Bahuns did not come to the hills with a missionary zeal, they had none. They came in search of livelihood and saw economic profit in converting the indigenous people to their creed. This was also compatible with the interest of the rulers in Kathmandu who saw political advantage in obliterating the language, religion and culture of the indigenous people by integrating them into the so-called national mainstream, dominated by the Aryan Hindu culture, so as to render them incapable of ever rising up again.

Because of this, educated Limbus and Rais actively campaigned to give up the Hindu practices their forefathers had adopted in ignorance. At the same time, a similar movement was going on in the mid-west where the ethnic Gurung community, one of the largest indigenous ethnic groups, decided to convert back to Buddhism, quite unsuccessfully because they were too far entrenched in Hindu practices.

Hinduism is not all that bad. In fact, it is decidedly the most tolerant and inclusive of all the world's major religions. Here, God can be worshipped in any form and in any way one chooses to. Although Hindus believe that there are altogether three hundred and thirty million gods and goddesses (of which only a small number are actually known and worshipped), the more erudite among them also readily admit that all of them are manifestations of one supreme God. Although they worship rigid idols made of rocks and metal, some of them bizarrely-shaped, they also admit that God is invisible, colourless and formless. Buddhists insist that Buddha was a rebel against Hinduism, but Hindus insist that he is the tenth reincarnation of their God Vishnu. Christians would be mighty surprised to learn there are actually Hindus who believe that Christ is just another name for Krishna who has hundreds of names. If both Christ and Muhammad were born in India, they would probably have been worshipped as reincarnations of Vishnu.

But this same tolerant creed has brought catastrophe to the indigenous people of Nepal - not so much because of religious philosophy, but because of ethnic politics. King Prithvi Narayan Shah insisted that 'Nepal is the only true Hindu state' (India had been overrun by Muslim invaders time and again) and this became one of the guiding principals of his successors. It still is to Hindu fanatics. After the unification of the country, they set about forcibly converting the non-Hindu tribes to Hinduism, with disastrous long-term consequences for the indigenous communities. Before adopting Hinduism, the Limbus were engaged in reading and writing in their own language and script. After the conquest and conversion to

Hinduism (without their being aware of it; many of them were too drunk to remember anyway), they were actively discouraged to do so. Like the rest of the *matwalis* they were placed near the bottom of the Hindu caste hierarchy and taught that according to ancient scriptures it is sinful for non-Bahuns to read and write. The Hindus even chased out of the country one Sirijunga Thebe who tried to teach his people to read and write. He was murdered in exile in Sikkim and is today revered as a martyr.

Thus, slowly and surely, as intended by the rulers in Kathmandu, all indigenous people of Nepal turned into illiterate ignoramuses and their communities sank into the depth of darkness. Not very long ago the older men of the village would severely admonish (and even threaten to beat up) any person who wished to read and write ignorantly repeating the line that the wily Bahuns had planted in their brain: "Don't you know that it's a sin for non-Bahuns to read and write?"

The uneducated minds of simple rural folks like Dil Bahadur, however, were not sophisticated enough to understand the intricacies of emerging ethnic politics, and they found it difficult to give up this almost two-centuries old tradition immediately. Therefore, they tacitly made a compromise. They would do everything as usual (two hundred years is a pretty long time), but with some minor exceptions. In Dashain they would visit their relatives, eat, drink and be merry, but they would not perform ritual worship and they would not put *tika* on their forehead which signifies the victory of the Aryans over the indigenous people. This suited everybody fine. The children were happy because they could get to wear new clothes, eat to their fill and get a few rupees as gift. The men were happy because they could get together and drink *rakshi* and *tongba*. The women were happy because they could visit their parents. The weary Bahuns took comfort from the fact that despite objection to Hinduism the Limbus still followed their tradition.

That's more or less what really happened. But Limbu priests and shamans (there are several different types) have their own mythical story of migration which they recite during the various ritual worship ceremonies. Just as the study of ancient Egypt, Greece and Rome cannot be complete without their mythologies and pantheon of gods and goddesses, the Limbus' identity cannot be complete without theirs. The following is a mythical story of their migration:

Human beings were created by the gods according to the instructions given by the supreme creator goddess *Tagera Nimaphungma* in the 'Land of Human Creation' shortly after the creation of the world. In time they became efficient hunter-gatherers, and lived innocent, peaceful, happy and plentiful lives. But when they became numerous, lack of food forced them to disperse into different directions. The names of the places mentioned by the priests are difficult to pronounce and in any case no longer exist, but they give a general idea. One branch moved south towards a great plateau (probably Tibet) and settled there. Another branch headed further south to a great lake surrounded by high hills and settled in the hills around the lake (probably Kathmandu valley). Yet another branch moved further south towards a great plain (the Gangetic plain) and settled there. After several generations the descendents of those who had settled in the plain moved northward in search of the promised land and settled on either side of the River Arun. Much later, descendants of those who had settled in the great plateau came into conflict with the followers of a new religion called Buddhism. They were defeated by the Buddhists and trekked southward across the mountains to join their kinsmen already there. Thus, Limbus believe that they are of two different ancestries: descendents of those who migrated from the plain (Kashi) and the descendents of those who migrated from Tibet (Lhasa). Each clan picks up its own particular story of migration from this point onward.

Now when her human children fell into disarray and into vice and sinful living, as it inevitably happens, a greatly concerned Tagera Nimaphungma appeared in human form to protect them and to lead them on the true path. This earthly reincarnation of the supreme creator goddess is known as Yuma, the grandmother, and all Limbu clans worship her as their chief deity (among the several lesser deities that they have, including Theba, the grandfather, who is not Yuma's husband and is of a lesser status than her). After landing on earth, Yuma retraced the migration of her children. First she went to *the* plateau in the north with her retinue of followers and worshippers. From there she went south to *the* big lake surrounded by high hills. There she cut a gorge with her sword and drained the water out of the lake, making it habitable for humans. Then she headed south into *the* great plain until she came to the confluence of three rivers where she took a holy bath. After that she went to several places, most notably the confluence of all rivers, which suggests that she reached the River Ganga delta in the Bay of Bengal.

Finally, she went to Limbuan. There she took possession of a sage of the Mabohang clan and through his mouth she taught her children about god and religion, and gave them laws to govern their lives. The laws laid down by her are pretty much the same as the teachings of Buddha, Christ and Muhammad.

'Be compassionate towards all living beings. Love your fellow human beings. Show gratitude to your protectors. Do not be jealous of others. Revere the gods and goddesses as your father and mother. Always act with a clear conscience. Do not steal or plunder. Do not quarrel, fight or murder. Do not lie, slander or backbite. Do not be conceited and arrogant. Do not covet another person's wealth. Do not be corrupt. Look after the poor and the orphans. Be kind and just towards widows. Do not commit incest and other sinful acts.'

Now back to more earthly matters, for that's what's more important. Until a few years ago Kamala used to make it a point to visit her parents during Dashain, but since they had both died of old age, she had stopped. With their death, the purpose had simply ceased to exist. She, however, made it a point to send her daughters-in-law to their respective maiden homes. It was a matter of prestige to her, because if the young women were not sent at such an important time of the year, their parents would suspect ill-treatment of their daughters, naturally.

Until a decade earlier Dil Bahadur used to slaughter a young buffalo with a swift and powerful blow of an axe on the unsuspecting animal's forehead on the day of *Maar* (slaughter). This year he slaughtered a pig and a goat. Purna severed the goat's head with a single blow of his Khukuri and Dil Bahadur impaled the squealing pig with a spear through the heart, a single stroke again. No Limbu can slaughter a pig without a ritual worship to propitiate the goddess Yuma, so a priest was at hand from early in the morning, happily swilling tongba at every break. Half of the pig was intended for Lalita's planned first visit to her parents' home.

The day of slaughter is followed by the day of *Tika*, the last and the most important of the ten days' festival. On this day, at the most auspicious hour chosen by the royal priests in Kathmandu and announced solemnly on Radio Nepal, the state radio, Hindus all over the country perform 'pooja' (ritual worship) and senior members of every house confer tika on the forehead of juniors members and give them their blessings along with token monetary gift. Now, since the Limbus had given up 'tika', they only exchanged visits with relatives and neighbours.

That day Laxmi's otherwise happy mood was clouded by the blessings she received from the elders: "May you give birth to a child this year!" She knew that they were asking for the near impossible and it hurt her deeply. In spite of this, she put on a sweet smile and presented a brave face, thanked them for their kindness and expressed hope that their blessing would bear fruit. When all else fails, hope remains and she had plenty of that. Hope is what gives purpose and direction to life. She doggedly held on to the hope that this year the elder's blessings and her prayers would be answered and she would conceive. This was her most fervent wish. She prayed for it every day and every night.

Early the next day Laxmi, accompanied by Purna, started for her parent's village of *Tharpu*, of the Yonghang and Mabo clans, two and a half days walk away. She was a daughter of the Mabo clan. Between the two of them, they carried pork curry cooked with dry lichen and blood, mutton curry, a jar of fermented millet, dried buffalo meat and dried fish among other things. Along the way they had to pass through or near a number of villages belonging to different clans and cross a number of streams and rivers, chief among them River Tawa and River Iwa further south, by precariously hanging suspension bridges that swung like cradles above slippery rocks and swiftly flowing river currents.

As always, Laxmi's parents were delighted to see their daughter and son-in-law. It was not often that Laxmi came for a visit and they treasured every moment she spent with them. The women gossiped late into the night, sharing their joys and sorrows, catching up on the news of relatives long separated by marriage, migration, death and other reasons. Many of Laxmi's childhood girlfriends had married, though a few unfortunate ones still remained virgin. The married women visited their parents at about the same time resulting in an unplanned happy reunion. They brought along their children who tottered about the house, urinated and defecated anywhere at their convenience, and cried in pain or squealed in delight depending upon their childish whim while their young mothers fussed incessantly over them. Laxmi watched them wistfully, with a heavy heart. Meena had a two years old son, Phulmaya had a year and a half old daughter, and Sita had a four years old daughter and a two years old son. The unmarried girls, on the other hand, were embarrassed that no suitor had arrived to take them away and sad that time was running out for them. They tried to put on a brave façade, quite unsuccessfully. Laxmi felt luckier than these girls who had the prospect of lifelong spinsterhood staring at their wrinkling faces, and secretly sympathized with them, though to do so openly would be an insult to them. The annual visit to her parents' house was the happiest time of the year for her. It was a trip down the memory lane and she cherished every moment.

As usual Purna and Laxmi slept in separate rooms – Laxmi slept with her two young sisters and Purna slept in his young brother-in-law's room. The boy graciously gave him his bed while he prepared another bed for himself on the floor. Purna had no problem with sleep apart from Laxmi, one didn't sleep in the same bed with his wife in his in-laws' house. The annual visit to his in-laws' provided him with ample opportunity for relaxation and reflection. Having nothing to do, he got up late in the morning. He was served a jar of warm *tongba* first thing in the morning, then another in the afternoon and finally one more at night before bed. Thus he spent the days blissfully in a state of mild inebriation, free of all cares in the world. In the afternoon he strolled about the village, smiling amiably to all and sundry and stopping to give brief answer to anyone who cared to inquire after his well-being. And in the evening before going to bed he sat with his father-in-law sipping tongba. His father-in-law, a wiry and alert-eyed man of fifty-four years and not more than five feet tall, was excited about the road that had arrived at a neighbouring village and talked effusively about it, "You know, son-in-law, now the road has come up to Gopetar which is, as you know, only a few hours walk from here, it is only a matter of a couple of years before it reaches our village. With road other things will follow, such as electricity and telephone. Then just you watch, son-in-law. This place will grow into a town, and the price of my land will increase by tenfolds." Purna nodded his head complacently in agreement. That, of course, would make no difference to him as he would still have to walk from his village.

While Purna was thus spending halcyon days, his mother-in-law was worried about Laxmi's lack of fecundity. A day after their arrival, she broached the subject with her daughter, as she always did.

"It makes me very sad that you are still without a child," she said to Laxmi. "I constantly worry about you."
"I know that you are greatly concerned for me, mother. I worry a lot too. I hope the gods will be kind to me some day."
"If this goes on too long I am afraid that your husband will be forced to marry a second wife."
"He won't do that mother."
"How do you know?"
"I just know that he won't. He is a very good, honest and loving man. He won't do anything to hurt my feelings."
"But you must know as well as I do that it's not up to him. His parents may force him, you know."
"My father-in-law and mother-in-law are very nice. They treat me like their own daughter."
"I am happy to hear that. But they still want grandchildren from their eldest son, don't they?"
"Yes, they do."
"Of course, they do. It's only natural."
"I can understand that, mother."
"And for your sake we too want grandchildren from you. It is every parent's wish that their sons and daughters have a good, stable and secure married life. That cannot happen unless there are children in it."

Her mother's candid remark stung Laxmi. She said despairingly, "Mother, tell me. What is there that I can do?"
"Do whatever you can to have a child, daughter," her mother replied.
"I know that, mother. Everybody wants to me have a child. I desperately want to have one. My mother-in-law has done every ritual there is to propitiate the gods and goddesses. What else can I do? Do you think I should go to the hospital in the city?"

"I doubt they can help you. And besides, they say that it costs a lot of money which I suppose you don't have. Maybe you should go to the temple of Pathibhara Devi instead? People say that she is the most potent wish-fulfilling goddess in eastern Nepal, and if properly placated, she will grant any wish that one makes. Why don't you give her a try?"

"I have heard of her mother," Laxmi replied. Suddenly she saw of spark of hope. "Why hadn't I thought of that before?"

"It's a long and arduous journey to her temple up north, at the foot of the high mountains, but I think you should make the trip."

"Yes, I will mother. I'll do anything that will help me to conceive a child."

"But be careful before you make any promises, because it is said that once you make a vow to visit her, you cannot break the vow otherwise a great misfortune will befall you. Are you aware of that?"

"I am mother," Laxmi replied.

"Good, then make a vow now. Promise to the goddess that you will visit her temple within a year and that you will sacrifice a goat in her honour."

Laxmi took a deep breath, closed her eyes and said in the most solemn voice, "Oh, mother goddess Pathibhara Devi, I solemnly promise that I will visit your temple within a year, and I will sacrifice a goat in your honour. In return, I beg that you endow me with a child. That is all I want, and nothing more. If I break my vow then give me any punishment you see fit, even death."

Laxmi felt her spirit rise after making the vow. She didn't doubt for a moment the ability of the goddess to fulfill her wish. With her blessing she hoped to hold a plump little baby in her arms by this time in two years. But first she would have to talk to her husband and mother-in-law. She knew they would be only too happy to accompany her.

A day after Purna and Laxmi's departure, Milan and Lalita started down the same trail for the village of Yangnam. There had been no communication between Lalita and her parents after her father's scathing reply to her letter sometime after the wedding. This had hurt her deeply and made her very unhappy. In spite of this, or rather because of this, Lalita was determined to make peace with her parents, and make them see things her way, if possible. The sooner the better, she had said, and so they had embarked upon this journey. Beside other gifts, there was a special gift of one half of the pork (vertically split from head to tail, complete with the trotters) slaughtered on the day of *Maar*. Every newly married Limbu daughter is expected to take this gift to her parents on her first visit home with her husband. The pig carcass was shaved and cleaned, and a paste of turmeric powder (in mustard oil) was rubbed to the skin until it acquired a deep yellow hue. It was then decorated with marigold flowers and carried by a hired porter in a conical bamboo-cane basket. Like Purna and Laxmi the couple first went to Sinam to visit their maternal uncles where many curious folks came to take a look at Lalita, of whom they had heard through the grapevine, and her child. The women gossiped about the mother and fussed over the infant. Some cooed that the baby looked just like her mother while others claimed that she had definitely taken after her father. They also made the inevitable remarks about Lalita behind her back.
"She is pretty, isn't she?"
"Yes, she is. But don't you think she is too skinny?"
"Well, it's fashionable to be slim these days."

"I think her elder sister-in-law who was here yesterday is prettier."
"No. This one is definitely prettier."
"But the other one is better endowed with womanly qualities, such as modesty. This one looks rather modern."
"I've heard that she was married to a *lahooray* before she eloped with Milan."
"They say that he was heart-broken. Did he mistreat her?"
"No, I've heard that she left him because he was too old for her."
"No, the real reason is that she became pregnant. But the child might not even be Milan's, you know. You never know with young girls these days and the city is full of young men like Milan."

Milan and Lalita reached the village of Yangnam late in the afternoon on the third day of their journey. Yangnam is a village perched on a slope high above the Phemay River; about six hours walk from Phidim Bazaar, the domain of the well-known Nembang clan and the administrative center of Panchthar district. The sun was about to sink behind the darkening hills in the west when they reached their destination. Lalita's father was sitting alone in the verandah leisurely sipping *tongba*. He was a big man, much taller than the average Limbu, with a thick mustache above his upper lip. He was in his mid-fifties. In his youth he might have been as strong as a bull, but now age had diminished his strength and mellowed his mettle. When his eyes fell upon the approaching couple, he looked incredulous at first. "What on earth am I seeing today? How the fuck .... could this happen?" he muttered in disbelief and ran his eyes over the contiguous vicinity to make sure that he wasn't imagining things under the influence of *tongba*. When he was sure that what he was seeing was flesh and blood and not apparitions, his cheeks turned red as anger surged in in his mind. He stood up abruptly and bellowed angrily, "Why have you come to my house? Go back immediately. There is no place for sluts here. I don't want a woman who whores herself to step into my house. And who is that tramp with you? Take him and go back to wherever you've come from this instant."

Milan stopped in his tracks and became rooted to the spot he was standing on. He couldn't decide whether to turn back or take a step forward. At the moment all he wanted to do was to vanish into thin air. He wished he were invisible. He wished he were not there. This was a nightmare he had imagined, and played and replayed in his mind, and dreaded while Amrita had dragged him along. She had told him repeatedly that though her father was a big man with a quick temper and a foul mouth, he was not all that bad. Looking at the bellowing man he wasn't so sure now. He looked at Lalita for cue. But she herself looked confused. She hesitated a moment, looked at him with a red face and whispered, "That's my father." Milan heard her but didn't reply. *Yes I can see that's your father, but what now?*

Then Lalita gathered her composure and said in a conciliatory tone, "Father, I have come to ask you for your forgiveness."
"If you think I'll forgive you, then you are gravely mistaken, because I will not. You have whored yourself and brought disgrace upon me. Because of your thoughtless and willful action I am unable to face the villagers with a straight face. You have let me down. You have betrayed me. You have hurt me and I can never forgive you. Never!" The old man shouted furiously, words flying out of his mouth in a torrent. If she had been a man, she was certain that he would have already landed a few kicks and punches on her.
"Father, please ..." Lalita implored.

"No! Never!" the old man cut her off. "Go back this instant. I won't let you enter my house."

"Father, please listen to me just once..... Forgive your daughter. I have come from so far away and I am your flesh and blood."

"I won't listen to you anymore. Go back to where you came from this instant. And what is it that you have brought? A pig? I won't touch it. I won't eat anything you have brought. Take them all back."

"Father, I have done nothing wrong ...."

"Oh, you haven't, have you? Say that again! Say that again! You have the guts to say that after what you have done? Shame on you!" He spit on the floor. "Shame on you! And after we did so much for you ...."

Seeing her father's intransigence, Lalita suddenly felt anger rising inside her. The anger inside her built up and turned into uncontrollable fury. She was, after all, her father's daughter. She yelled back: "You didn't do it for me, father. You did it for yourself."

"What? What is it that you just said? You talked back to me, did you? You insolent girl, I will ...." The man yelled and thrashed his hand in anger.

"You cannot strike me, father. Not anymore. I am not your little girl anymore, you know. I am a grownup married woman with a child."

"You are an ungrateful daughter. You never thought of us. You didn't care how your thoughtless action might humiliate us; make us the laughing stock of the whole village. You thought of only yourself. You young people of today are selfish and ungrateful, you care only for yourself and naught for your parents," shouted the old man angrily.

Lalita trembled in fury at this baseless accusation. It was he who had nearly wrecked her life. And now it was he who was accusing her of betrayal. This was a grave injustice and she was not going to go away without a fight. She yelled back at the top of her voice, "What about yourself, father? Don't you think you are selfish, too? Did you ever think of my likes and dislikes, father? Did you consider of my feelings when you married me off to a man more than twice my age? Did you ask for my opinion? Did you?"

"You are my daughter. I don't have to ask you. I did what was best for you."

"No, you didn't. You did what was best for you, not for me. You took pity on your dead sister's husband. You wanted to continue your relationship with him, that's why you married me off to him. Did you ask me when you gave me away to that old man? Did you, father?"

"He was rich. He had a house in Kathmandu and he had the means to keep you in comfort all your life. What more could a girl want?"

"What about my happiness? Did you ever think of that? I too had a dream of my own. I had just completed high school. I wanted to become a staff nurse in a hospital just like my cousin Devika. I wanted to do so many things. There was so much I was looking forward to in life. And you wrecked it all. You destroyed all my hopes and dreams. You destroyed my life."

"What dream? Being a daughter, you should learn to be happy with whatever you are given," shouted the old man.

"Being a father, you should learn to give your daughter what is best for her. And did you say that a daughter should learn to be happy with whatever she's given, father? Where did you get that outdated idea? Learn to be happy with a man who is almost as old as my own father? Never!"

"You should be ashamed to talk back to your father like that, you insolent girl," the old man hollered.

"And you should be ashamed to call your own daughter shameful names like that," Lalita yelled back.

By this time, Lalita's mother and sisters had come running out of the house hearing the angry exchange outside the house. When they saw her they wanted to run to her and embrace her. But since the father and daughter were in the middle of a heated altercation, they couldn't. They looked at the two in utter bewilderment.
"Husband, that's enough. Leave her alone." Lalita's mother, who was in her mid-forties, implored breaking her silence.
"What? What did you say?" The old man turned angrily at his wife.
"Stop this madness. She's our daughter, no matter what. And she's come to see us after a long time. We should be happy, not angry." The woman said to him boldly and calmly. In spite of his size, she was apparently not intimidated by him.

The old man glared at his wife, then at his daughter, and then back at his wife again. Finally, his eyes came to rest on Milan and he scowled contemptuously. Milan winced thinking that he was going to become the next target of the fuming man's ire. The old man turned to Lalita and speaking of Milan in the third person remarked sarcastically, "Is this the ruffian you have chosen for a husband? He looks like a thug to me. What does he do for a living?"

"Husband, stop!" Lalita's mother interrupted sternly. "That's enough. Now let me handle the situation." He glared at his wife, but she stood her ground. He opened his mouth to say something but changed his mind in midcourse. After a moment's silence he said, "All right, do what you like. But I won't have anything to do with her or that tramp of a husband of hers." He stormed off and vanished behind the banana

grove. He didn't come back. After he disappeared, the mother and daughter turned to each other. Lalita's sisters came running to her and hugged her happily. "Elder sister, we thought we'd never see you again."
"Here I am," she said. "How are you, girls?"
"We are so happy to see you. What a beautiful baby." They took the infant in their arms.

"Mother," Lalita said looking at her mother, relieved that the worst was over.
"My daughter," her mother said. Both mother and daughter looked flushed.
"Come, my daughter," Lalita's mother said, "Come! Forget what your father said. You know what he is like."
Lalita urged a reluctant Milan towards her mother and said, "Mother, this is your son-in-law."
Milan bent down to touch the older woman's feet, but Lalita stopped him.
"Aren't you forgetting something? Do it the proper way," Lalita said to Milan who looked askance. "With a rupee coin," she added.
"Oh," Milan uttered and hastily taking out a rupee coin from his purse put it at his mother-in-law's feet and bent down to touch them.
"May you become fortunate, son-in-law," his mother-in-law said.
Then Lalita pointed to her baby in her little sister's arms and said, "And this is your granddaughter." The older woman took the infant into her arms and cooed, "Ooh, how pretty! She looks just like you." She was smiling.
"Some say she looks just like her father," Lalita replied with a smile.

"They are wrong, all of them. She looks just like you, very pretty." Her mother replied lifting the baby up in the air. "What have you named her?" She asked happily.
"Kalpana," Lalita replied.
"What a beautiful name! As beautiful as she is."

Asking Milan to wait on a wooden chair in the verandah, Lalita climbed up the stairs and disappeared into the upper floor of the two storey house with her mother and excited sisters. Milan waited uneasily, wearily glancing left and right, fearful that the terrible old man might reappear and pick up a fight with him. After what he had seen, it seemed highly probable. Thankfully his fear didn't materialize. But the feeling of humiliation at the unbecoming reception he had received persisted. It made him hurt and angry. He wanted to return home straight away, and were it not for his love for Lalita he would have done just that. But he reigned in his anger and prepared to suffer further humiliation for the sake of his wife. "Oh, what indignity a man has to suffer for love," he muttered.

Lalita came down the stairs and ushered him to a small room on the ground floor containing a bed, an old table and a chair. "This is your room. I'll sleep upstairs with my sisters," she said.
"You didn't tell me your father was a tiger," said Milan.
"No. He is not a tiger, he is an ogre. If I had told you that you wouldn't have agreed to come," she replied. "But I did tell you that he is a big man with a quick temper, didn't I?" She added.
"What does your mother say?"
"She said that she was angry at first, but then she forgave me."
"And what does she have to say about me?"
"She says you are young and good looking, much better than she had expected," she replied with a smile.

"How long are we going to stay here?" He asked. He didn't relish the idea of staying too long, as he knew that would inevitably bring him face to face with the ogre.

"A few days, maybe. What do you say?" She asked him.

"No. We'll go back tomorrow. That ogre of yours scares me to death," he said.

After some deliberation the two agreed to return home early in the morning on the fourth day. Milan wanted to go back as soon as possible, but Lalita wanted to spend some time with her mother and sisters. He wondered how he was going to spend the remaining three days, anticipating with dread the moment he would have to face the wrath of his father-in-law again. *That crazy, foul-mouthed old man doesn't look at all the forgiving type,* he thought.

A quarter of an hour later, Lalita's younger sisters arrived shyly with a jar of *tongba* and a plate of fried meat and potato curry. They remained to chat with him and he was glad to have their company. Munu and Shanta, the giggling teenaged girls, were both slim and pretty like their elder sister, though one was a bit darker. They were self-conscious at first, but after a few minutes of talk they opened up to him and chatted away happily, and later even flirted with him.

After dinner Lalita brought her mother and sisters to Milan's room to talk to him. While sipping *tongba* he told them funny stories and anecdotes which made them laugh heartily. Then suddenly Lalita's father walked in and everybody became quiet. Milan had been dreading this moment the whole afternoon. He knew the meeting was inevitable and had rehearsed it several times in his mind, each time with a different scenario. Without ceremony, the old man took a stool and began to inquire Milan about him and his family gruffly. Milan replied to the old man's sarcastic questions as politely as he could, taking the utmost care not to look at the old man in the eyes.

When Milan told his clan name, the old man said contemptuously, "What's that? Is there such a clan in Limbuan? I have never heard of a Sambiu."
Milan replied, "No, I don't think you have. There are over two hundred clans in Limbuan and not all are well-known. We are a small and little known clan confined to that particular area."
"That's too bad, because every one knows and respects our clan. Ask any man in Limbuan and he knows what and who a Jabegu is," the old man said sarcastically. Milan was tempted to reply that there were other clans that were far better known, but he checked himself. It was useless arguing over such trivial matters.

"Our Jabegu men have become ministers in His Majesty's Government. Have any of your kinsmen ever been anywhere near a government minister?" The old man added insult to injury.
"No, they haven't," Milan replied calmly.

Then the old man proceeded to ask him about his village. When Milan told him, the old man remarked insultingly, "Yes, I have been as far as to Tellok, Surumkhim and Mehele in my younger days, but I have never set foot in your village. From what I have heard Khewang is so remote, isolated and wild that only monkeys and bears live there."
"The trail leading to the village is certainly difficult and the village is isolated, but it is not wild. It is as large as this village, if not larger. There used to be bears, leopards, wolves and jackals in the forest near the village in the old days during my

grandfather's time. But not any more," Milan replied politely but with a hint of defiance in his voice.

"That may be so, but your village is still in a very remote corner of the hills." The old man insisted. Milan agreed and did not say anything lest he aggravate the matter.

"Where do you shop? You need to buy things like salt, cooking oil, kerosene, etc., don't you?" The old man continued his insult.

"We have a few shops in the village. And we can always go to *Tellok Bazaar* which is at a distance of only a few hours walk, or the bigger *Panchami Bazaar* which is about half a day's walk," Milan replied.

"Where do the children go to school? I don't believe you have a school there."

"There are two, actually, and one of them is a high school."

"I can't believe it. Anyway, will your village ever see the face of road and electricity? I don't think so. Not even in the next one hundred years." The old man added another insult, caressing his moustache triumphantly.

At this point Lalita's mother intervened. "That's enough, husband. You've gone far enough. Now, please leave us alone."

Apparently, the old man had run out of words to harass his young son-in-law, so he mumbled something about being late for bed and went out. There is only so much you can say when the other party refuses to hit back. Milan was immensely relieved, and yet angry at the same time. In a period of less than twelve hours he had taken more insult than in the rest of his young life. His mother-in-law was right, the old man had pushed him far enough. If it had been any other man he would have punched him and knocked out a front tooth or two.

After the initial confrontation, both Lalita and her father took pains to avoid each other for the next two days. But the old man watched his daughter from afar. He watched her and said nothing. On the third day she decided that he must be confronted again. Her mother had forgiven her. Now it was his turn to do the same. That's what she had come here for. So in the evening when the old man was sitting with his usual jar of *tongba* in the verandah, caressing his mustache and brooding, she stood submissively before him and said, "Father, please forgive this daughter of yours."

The old man didn't look at her directly, but said, "You have made me angry."

"Yes, I have, father. That's why I have come to apologize to you. Please forgive me."

The old man said, "You have hurt my feelings. You have brought shame upon me."

"Yes, father, and I am truly sorry for that. Please forgive me."

"That I will never do," said the old man dismissively.

"Father, I beg you to forgive me." A lump rose and stuck on her throat. "I am your daughter, father, a product of your own flesh blood, not a stranger, not your enemy," she said with tears in her eyes.

"I admit that you are my daughter, my own flesh and blood, and because of that I will not stop you from coming and going as you please. But I won't welcome you with open arms either. I don't care what your mother does. She is a woman and like all women she has a tender heart. But as long as I live I will not forgive you."

That was his final answer. Knowing her father very well, Lalita didn't see any benefit in pursuing the matter further. "All right, father," she said, "But I hope you will be able to forgive me someday."

"I don't think so. Life is like a river that flows but only in one direction. Once a wrong turn is taken, nothing can make things the same as before," the old man said philosophically and dismissed his daughter with a gesture of his hand.

The old man was unrelenting, blinded by his misguided sense of pride and self-importance, as many men of his age and generation are. Half blinded by tears she ran to her room and threw herself face down on the bed.

Early in the morning of the fourth day, Lalita and Milan departed for home. Every member of the family was there to see them off. Even Lalita's father was there on his favourite chair in the verandah. Her mother and sisters gave Lalita a tearful farewell, asking her to visit again, and asked Milan to take good care of her and love her always. On the way back, Lalita told Milan of her conversation with her unyielding father. After listening to her in silence Milan said, "I can't stop you from visiting your parents. They are your parents, after all. And I hope that in the years to come I will be able to forgive your father for subjecting me to such humiliation. But as long as he doesn't forgive you and accept me as his rightful son-in-law, I will not accompany you to his house again."

Dashain is immediately followed by another great Hindu festival, Deepawali or the Festival of Lights as it is known in India, and Tihar as it is known in Nepal. The Limbus celebrate this festival with gusto but for a very different reason. For the men it's a time for gambling and drinking; for the women it's a time to receive gifts in money and kind from their brothers; and for the youngsters it's a time to play 'deusi' and 'bhailo' by reciting verses and singing and dancing at every doorstep for money. Then after the annual harvest in the month of November, another harsh winter set in and then gave way to the joyful spring. Spring is the queen of all seasons. Although school children in Nepal learn (in their textbook) that there are six seasons in a year, there are actually only four climactic seasons. It is *winter* from December to February, *spring* from March to May, *summer* (or Monsoon) from June to August and *autumn* from September to November. In winter the trees shed their leaves and look bare and bereft, and the hills and the forests acquire a derelict and forlorn look. But with the arrival of spring, they regain their leaves once again. Then the hills are once again covered by greenery. The light green coloured young leaves flutter and sing happily with the cool breeze that sweeps across the hills, valleys and forests. Flowers of myriad colours bloom everywhere and fill the air with a sweet aroma and the hills become alive with the sound of life. Spring is the season favoured by all – man and animals alike – when Mother Nature is at her best.

"Cuckoo .. Cuckoo…" the cuckoo sang high above on the branch of a tree. Amrita stopped singing and looked up joyously but was unable to locate the bird. Only the young leaves of the trees were fluttering in the cool, gentle breeze. It was a quiet, lazy afternoon and she was cutting the succulent green grass for the animals, singing her favourite tune softly to herself when she heard the sweet song of the cuckoo, which added to her happiness. It is said that if one make a wish the first time one hears the cuckoo sing in spring, then that wish will surely be fulfilled.

"Cuckoo …. Cuckoo.." The bird sang again and Amrita's heart raced and danced with joy. *The bird is asking me to make a wish and I must make a wish*, she muttered to herself breaking out into a smile.

Only a few days earlier, she had received a letter from Sharan. He was coming back in July and there were only three months to go. After her father had given her his permission to wait for him, Amrita had written to him conveying the good news. In his reply he had written that come July he would be at her doorsteps, come rain or shine. Nothing would be able to stop him. Since that day, she had gone about with such gaiety that people never failed wonder aloud what it was that made her so happy. She smiled sweetly and went her own way, making people remark whether she had not gone off her head. But it's hard to keep a secret when you are that happy. So she confided to her closest friends, who in turn confided to their close friends. So the reason behind her happiness quickly became a common knowledge.

"Lucky girl! She is very pretty, well mannered and hardworking, too," some people remarked.
Some were inevitably envious of her and remarked caustically, "She shouldn't count her chickens before they are hatched."
Some jealous girls and their mothers were downright nasty, "What did that *soldier* see in her? I don't think she is pretty. Our so-and-so is prettier than her." But they always said it behind her back.

"Cuckoo .... Cuckoo ...." The bird sang again. She looked up squinting her eyes and this time she saw it. It was perched high up on the branch of a tree to her right, flicking its tail merrily as it cooed.
"Sweet little bird, this is the first time I have heard your beautiful song this spring," she said to the bird, "and I would like to make a wish because it is said that if I make one now it will surely come true. Now what do I wish for?" She touched her forehead with the palm of her right hand and said, "I wish .... for Sharan to come back soon." Then she said, "Wait a

minute, he's coming back anyway, so I need a better wish. ....I wish to be married to him as soon as he comes back." She was satisfied with the new wish. "Yes, I wish to be married to him as soon as he comes back." The enamoured bird didn't pay any attention to her; he was too busy calling out to his own mate.

Half an hour later, she happily made her way back home with a bundle of grass on her back fastened securely with a flat belt-like rope slung across her forehead. She sang softly to herself as she walked with light and brisk steps. As soon as she reached home, she flung the bundle near the buffalo shed and threw some at the expectant beasts who began to munch away. Then she ran into the house to confide to Laxmi.

"Sister-in-law," she said excitedly, "Do you know what happened today? I was up by the woods cutting grass and I heard the cuckoo sing."
Laxmi smiled at her and said, "And did you make a wish? You must make a wish when you hear the cuckoo sing the first time in spring."
"Yes, I did," Amrita replied.
"And what wish did you make? No, don't tell me. Let me guess," Laxmi teased her.
"Yes, guess what wish I made." Amrita challenged her with a giggle.
"You wished for ...... a young man," Laxmi said with a playful smile. Amrita laughed joyously throwing back her straight black hair.
"And you wished for him to ...... marry you ..... and take you away .... and let me guess. You wished for him to cuddle you in his arms and ...." Laxmi teased her with a wink of an eye.

"No," Amrita said, "I didn't make that wish," and slapped her sister-in-law playfully on her back.

"Sister-in-law, did you make such a wish when you married my brother?" she asked.

"No," Laxmi replied, "I wasn't in love with your brother. I hadn't met him."

"Where is younger sister-in-law?" Amrita asked changing the topic.

"She is in her room, breast-feeding the baby, I think."

Then again, abruptly changing the topic Amrita asked, "When are you going to the temple of Goddess Pathibhara?"

"Mother said we'll go before the monsoon starts."

"Is mother going, too?"

"Yes, she, your brother and myself - the three of us."

"Take me with you, dear sister-in-law." Amrita implored with big, round eyes fixed upon her.

"I would love to. But it's not up to me. Ask mother." Laxmi replied sympathetically.

"She might not agree to take me. I've got school and there'll be no one to help younger sister-in-law at home, and on top of that she will be busy with her own child."

"It's just a few days' journey. I think she'll let you go if you ask her to."

"Ok. I'll talk to her. But will you speak to her as well on my behalf?"

"I'll do what I can. Have you also made a vow?"

"Well, no. Because if I make a vow and if mother refuses to take me along then the goddess will be angry at me for breaking the vow and send me misfortune."

"Yes, that's true. She might even stop your soldier from coming here." Laxmi teased Amrita.

"Oh, please don't say that, sister-in-law. It will break my heart." Amrita said in alarm.

"And mine, too, to see you heart-broken. You are like my younger sister."
"I am your younger sister, aren't I?"
"Yes, you are. That's why I love you so much."

Amrita was touched by her sister-in-law's admission of sisterly love. She was thankful that her relationship with both of her sisters-in-law was cordial, unlike many of her friends who constantly bitched about their sisters-in-law, who in turn did likewise.
"Sister-in-law, I hope that goddess Pathibhara will grant you your wish, and you will have a cute little fair-complexioned child next year."
"I hope so too, Amrita. I pray for it every day and night." She had no doubt that the goddess would make her wish come true.

While Amrita was anxiously waiting for Sharan, and Laxmi was eagerly looking forward to make the trip to Pathibhara, and Lalita was busy taking care of the child who was now big enough to crawl energetically across the floor, Milan was busy planning his future. He had a persisting dream. A beautiful two-storey house in Kathmandu with all the modern amenities like television, music player, computer, refrigerator, microwave oven and the stuff. A shiny Japanese motorcycle to tear across the streets of Kathmandu. These were the things that he dreamt of. Perhaps not at all a big deal in the affluent countries of the world, but almost an unattainable dream for the average man in an impoverished land where more than half the population languishes under the line of poverty. Nevertheless, he dared to dream - a dream that dies a premature death everyday in the pitiless grind-wheel of Nepali life. Let the old folks worry about preserving culture and tradition, the young ones want material progress. Just as it is every person's birthright to be free, it is every person's birthright to have an opportunity to enjoy the fruit of human progress. So even after failing twice in his bid to become a *lahooray* (which would have given him all that he dreamt of), he had kept his dream alive. Now after living quietly for a year in the village, he had become restless. Kathmandu beckoned him constantly - all his waking hours and even in his dreams. He missed the bright lights and television, the constant honk of motor vehicles and the crowds of people in the streets.

But in a land where employment opportunities for *unconnected* young men like Milan are just above nil and those that are available pay so meagerly that it won't even buy a black-and-white television in six months, there is only one option available to the young and ambitious. Go abroad. Just get the hell out of the country. It doesn't matter where. Put up your house and land as collateral to pay a hefty sum to sharks who go by the name foreign employment agents and grab any job they can find for you. Cook, driver, waiter, construction worker, porter, butcher, house servant, security guard. It doesn't matter what. Just go. Get the hell out. Thousands of Nepali young men and women had been streaming out of the country - to India, Japan, South Korea, Taiwan, Malaysia, Hong Kong, Saudi Arabia, Kuwait, Qatar, Bahrain and UAE. Some of the richer and more educated ones were heading for Europe, North America and Australia. Rich or poor, literate or illiterate, male or female, all were driven by one common goal. They were all going out in search of a dream impossibly out of reach in their own beautiful but impoverished land.

But getting out is not as easy as it sounds. There are horrible stories of hope turning into tragedy, dream turning into nightmare. Many of the so-called 'manpower agents' prowling the streets of Kathmandu are nothing more than viciously greedy sharks who unscrupulously rob naïve young men and women of their life's savings leaving them totally destitute. Most of the young people aspiring to go abroad raise the requisite amount (running into several hundred thousand rupees) either by taking loan at exorbitantly high interest rates by putting their house (and land) as collateral or by selling them. After handing over the money to the agent they have to wait many months for work permit and visa. The process is long and grueling and sometimes takes more than a year. Some unscrupulous agents collect the money from a number of aspirants and then disappear. Even after the visa is obtained one cannot be absolutely certain of reaching one's destination because some unscrupulous agents are known to leave their clients stranded along the way in New Delhi, Bangkok and such places as these. It is for this reason that many innocent Nepalese have been languishing in foreign prisons, most notably in Thailand, where they are subjected to the most inhuman treatment by the prison wardens. But it's a risk that young men and women are willing to take. The question of livelihood takes precedence over everything, even death.

Already largely dependent upon foreign aid, the country had now become heavily reliant on remittance economy. How did this once largely self-sufficient country come to this? Thirty years of the King's authoritarian rule was largely successful in maintaining peace and order in the country. But it was a disaster in every other way. While the well-meaning monarch surrounded himself with his army of sycophants and crooks, the country's economy went to the dogs. And while the government constantly paid lip service to the slogan of the time, 'Let us bring a flood of development' and many other ridiculous slogans such as that, the long-suffering people never saw their economic standard rise. While the rest of the world marched on, Nepal stagnated. Thus, from the land of peace, the country turned into the land of broken dreams.

Even a brief period of parliamentary democracy in the 1960s and the restoration of the same in 1990 did nothing to alleviate the plight of the people. The leaders of the major political parties squandered valuable time, money, opportunity and people's goodwill by squabbling constantly over trivial matters and trying to unseat each other. Thus the growing frustration of the people found vent in the bloody rebellion by a ragtag army of ruthless Maoist guerillas hell bent on overthrowing the democratic system and installing their own extremist brand of communism.

When Milan was planning his future, the Maoist insurgency was in its infancy, limited to a few dirt-poor hill districts in the mid-west. In fact, the outfit hadn't even formally declared war. And although Milan was aware of the ominous rumblings in the mid-west, he paid no interest to it because like the majority of the Nepalese he had no inkling that the insurgency was going to have a profound impact on his life. But that was for the future, and nobody can see into the future – not even the wisest of sages who claim to see everything.

Every night, lying in bed beside Lalita's warm and soft body, he talked to her about his dream. She was as enthusiastic as him. One night he said, "Lalita, I think it's getting on time for me to translate my plan into action."
"Yes, I know," she replied.
"I've grown restless sitting here doing nothing. I practically grew up in the city and a farmer's life is not for me. The time has now arrived for me to go away. What do you say?" He asked.

"Whatever you decide to do, I am with you. Where will you go?" Lalita asked.
"I don't know, but I'll decide after I have talked to the agents in Kathmandu," he replied pensively.
"Do what you think is best. You'll always have my full support," she said as the baby greedily sucked at the dark nipples of her bare breast.
"Will you wait for me here until I return?" he asked.
"I will. I have always wanted to go to college and become a nurse, but that's out of the question now," she replied.
"When I make enough money, with luck, I'll come back and take you away. We'll buy or build a modest house in Kathmandu and live there for rest of our lives."
"And our children will go to a private English medium school, like your uncle's children," Lalita added dreamily.
"And there will be a television and a VCR in the living room, a refrigerator and a gas oven in the kitchen, a washing machine in the bathroom, and …." added Milan wistfully, "and I'll have a big, shiny motorcycle to zip through the streets of Kathmandu. With you riding behind my back, of course."
Lalita was suddenly hit by a waft of memories. She had owned all of these in Kathmandu. But she quickly pushed the memories away because they also reminded her of her former husband.
"But how will we raise the money? The 'agents' charge a fortune, don't they?"
"I guess I'll have to ask my uncles for a loan. They are rich."
"What if they refuse?"
"They won't refuse. The last time I met my youngest uncle, that was about two years ago, he told me that he was ready to help me in whatever way he can. I'll write to him tomorrow."

The next day, Milan talked to his father and mother about his plan. Dil Bahadur, who was aware of his son's aspirations, was apprehensive at first, but Kamala was supportive of her son's desire to go abroad to seek his fortune.

"Why would you want to go to work for foreigners?" Dil Bahadur asked. "We have enough land to survive," he added.
"But not enough to live a decent life, father. Besides, you know that I cannot live in this village. There's nothing for me here. If I am able to make a lot of money, I can even take you there to live with us."
"Oh, no! Not for me the city life. I am very happy where I am. This is where I belong and this is where I intend to breathe my last. I don't want to live in a congested place where you don't even know your next door neighbour."
Kamala chipped in, "I support Milan's plan. Everybody is going abroad these days. Why not my son? It would bring us prestige. Neighbours will look up to us."
Dil Bahadur didn't counter his wife. He said to his son, "All right, do what you think is best for you. After all, it's your life. Everyone must seek his own fortune. But first write to you uncle. If he says that he's willing to help you, then go ahead with your plan."
"I'll do that, father," Milan said happily.

After thinking for some time Dil Bahadur added, "You will go only if your uncle agrees to send you money. Your sister Amrita might be getting married shortly. I've heard that her soldier is coming back on leave. We'll need some money for the wedding, too."

Milan thanked his father for his support. But even if the old man hadn't given his consent, he'd have gone ahead with his plan anyway. The next day he wrote a long letter to his uncle in England asking for a loan. His youngest uncle had not yet built a house in Kathmandu, though he owned a small piece of land in a quiet suburb.

A month later, in the windy and dusty, but altogether pleasant month of April when roses and bougainvillea flowers were once again in full bloom in the courtyard of every house, childless Laxmi accompanied by her husband Purna, mother-in-law Kamala and sister-in-law Amrita made the arduous journey to the hilltop temple of Goddess Pathibhara, considered the most potent wish-fulfilling goddess in the eastern hills of Nepal, with an unwilling black sacrificial goat in tow.

The temple of Pathibhara is a two and a quarter days walk (one and a half days for men, as they say) in a north-westerly direction from Khewang, past several villages inhabited by various Limbu clans. On a hill about twenty-five kilometers as the crow flies to the southwest of Pathibhara temple lies Fungling Bazaar (also known as Taplejung Bazaar), the administrative centre of Taplejung district. This hilltop town, with two long streets running parallel to each other, is mostly inhabited by *Newars*, the trading community originally from Kathmandu, and the surrounding rural area is the domain of the well-known *Maaden* clan, among others. Members of a sub-clan of the *Maaden* clan do not eat buff (buffalo's meat) because they consider the animal their 'grandmother'. Clan folklore has it that in the days of yore one of their ancestors had saved himself by latching onto the tail of a buffalo when crossing a flooded river. Since then they have stopped eating buffalo meat out of gratitude. But the *Maadens* are not unique among the Limbus in tabooing the flesh of a particular animal. Members of the Yonghang clan do not eat mutton (goat's meat) because they consider the animal their grandmother.

Similarly, members of a sub-clan of the Nembang clan of Panchthar district also do not partake of mutton because according to clan folklore one of their sex-starved ancestors was caught red-handed in the act of fornicating with his she-goat in the dim past. It is said that the goat became their grandmother from that day. The Yonghangs might have a similar story.

Anyone who has heard of the Limbus find it hard to believe that there are those among them who do not eat pork (pig's meat). They need pork for everything – festivals, birth rite, death rite, wedding ceremony and all other rituals. But there are actually Limbus who do not partake of pork meat. Members of a sub-clan of the Angbuhang clan do not eat pork. Myth has it that in the dim past an Angbuhang woman called from the bottom of a hill to her son at the top of the hill to kill a pig and bring its head for dinner. The son misheard her and asked her to repeat what she had said. He again heard exactly what he had heard the first time. Greatly perplexed and distressed, but not wanting to look disobedient, he cut off his younger brother's head and took it home for dinner. Since that day, it is said, the clan has tabooed the eating of pork in sheer disgust.

The temple of Pathibhara Devi sits at the top a 3,794 meters high hill. As pilgrims from all over the eastern hills throng to the temple all year round, there is no shortage of company along the precarious trail. The scenery from the peak is breathtaking. Mt. Kanchenjunga, the third highest peak in the world, looms in the north-east as if it is only a stone's throw away, flanked by a sea of lesser hills that collide into each other. At the hilltop temple the Hindu priest sprinkles cold water on the unwilling goat's head before slitting its throat. It's a practice among the Nepalese to sprinkle water on the sacrificial animal's head. If the animal shakes its head (to remove the water, obviously) they say that the goat is willing to be sacrificed. If it doesn't (which happens sometimes), then they say it is unwilling and sprinkle water on it again and again until it becomes willing. After severing the goat's head, the priest sprays the blood oozing out of the still trembling torso on the altar. As in other temples where animals are sacrificed, here also the head of the animal belongs to the temple, and for that reason the priest (or his helper) severs the head from the base near the shoulder (to get more meat) and not at the middle as is generally done. The bare-feet pilgrims ring the bells and circle the temple clockwise. As the priest applies the blood-soaked tika on their forehead, each asks the goddess for the boon he/she has come for. Then the pilgrims head back home the same day as there is no hotel or lodge there. Because it's said to bring ill fortune to anyone who takes the animal's carcass back home, they stop at a place at the bottom of the hill and clean, cook and eat the meat.

The tired and worn out, but elated, group arrived home on the fourth day. Laxmi came back with renewed hope, vigor and enthusiasm. She truly believed that the deity would fulfill her most cherished dream that very year. Life for her once again became full of promises, and she carried herself with an expectant air. The long-lost exuberance was back in her eyes. She had complete faith in the goddess.

The Nepalese are children of fatalism. They believe that 'whatever is bound to happen will happen, no matter what'. Talk to anyone and it's at the tip of his/her tongue. They are poor because it's written for them to be poor. They suffer in this life because they had done something bad in their previous lives. But history stands testimony to the fact that gods and goddesses have nothing to do with either the happiness or the sufferings of mankind. Man's destiny lies in his hands alone and it is only he who can shape it by his thoughts and actions. He alone has the power and the will to do so. If things were to be left in the hands of the apathetic gods alone, then there would be no justice in the world for the simple reason that justice per se doesn't exist in nature; it is purely a human concept. Take for example, the holocaust in Europe during the Second World War, the Killing Fields of Cambodia in the late 1970s, the mass starvation in north-eastern Africa in the 1990s, or the genocide in the African nation of Rwanda in 1995. These are but only a few examples of many such tragedies of diabolic proportion. In the end it was not divine intervention but pure human compassion and determined action of a few that brought hope to million of doomed lives. God may have got the credit, but it was the humans who did the immense act of kindness.

The truth as espoused by Charles Darwin, the eminent English evolutionist, is this: in nature the fittest survives and the weakest perishes. He called it natural selection. It may sound cruel but it's the way nature works. All life on earth has evolved through this process. In the natural world there is no system of punishment for the strong and protection for the weak. But man, though himself a product of nature, is different because he has the power to reason. As he left his home in the trees and caves and built civilizations to escape the vicious predator-vs.-prey cycle, he realized that his greatest enemy – his nemesis – was not another predatory animal. It was much closer home. It was another man. So as human civilizations grew, he created the concept of justice – a powerful tool to bring order in a world of chaos. When that was not enough, he created the concept of an unseen, omnipresent, omniscient and omnipotent force to strike fear into the hearts of offenders. That imaginary force is called God. But God (or the belief in an all-powerful supernatural being) is not the panacea to earthly ills. It has never been. If it were, then why is there so much injustice and suffering in the world? Why do the 'bad' prosper and the 'good' suffer everywhere? Why are governments across the world filled with corrupt politicians and bureaucrats while honest people die of disease and starvation everyday? Why do criminals and terrorists who use God's name to justify their crimes go unpunished? Why are they hailed as heroes by half the world instead? And why do lovers of peace march in their thousands to protect ruthless dictators who brutalize and murder thousands of their own countrymen? The fact that justice is not a natural phenomenon has a lot of say about human nature. Deep inside their heart, most people do not really care much for rule of justice, though they may pay unending lip service to it. What they really do care about is where their allegiance lies. It's natural selection at work once again. It happens instinctively. So there are leftists and rightists, conservatives and liberals, East and West, North and South, Jews and Muslims, Muslims and Christians, Christians and Hindus, Hindus and Muslims, Muslims and Buddhists, Buddhists and Hindus, all at each other's throats at one time or another, regardless of where truth and justice stand.

Talking of justice and power - somehow these two seem to go together - take a man named Junga Bahadur Kunwar in Nepal's case, for instance. Junga Bahadur Kunwar was another truly remarkable figure in the history of Nepal. Some would say that this small, dark-complexioned soldier with a cruel streak was destined to change the course of the country's history. That's real power - the power to change not only one's own destiny, but the destiny of a nation. Compared to this, the supposed power of a goddess to grant an individual's small wish is nothing. Seven decades after the death of King Prithvi Narayan Shah, the royal court had fallen into a sorry state. Selfish and sycophantic courtiers with allegiance to different clans (and queens) constantly conspired against each other, openly, and against the crown, secretly. The situation was made worse by a succession of weak kings who inherited the throne in their infancy and who as adults preferred to hand over the executive powers of the state to their unscrupulous and incapable queens, who constantly conspired to install their own sons on the throne rather than to tame the recalcitrant courtiers. The time had become ripe for a drastic change and Junga Bahadur seized the opportunity by a stroke of fate.

Junga Bahadur was the son of an impoverished nobleman who had served the palace loyally until he had lost everything in a political purge. By his twenties he had become a well known gambler and adventurer. By his thirtieth birthday he had earned fame (but not fortune) as the most fearless man in the kingdom by his legendary exploits. He had caught and sold wild elephants in the malaria-infested plains, and performed feats of astounding bravery. At the order of the mentally unstable crown prince, he had jumped down a bridge into a swirling river on the back of his horse and survived. Then again at the order of the same prince he had jumped bare-feet into a deep well and come out alive. When an angry elephant had gone berserk and gone on the rampage killing a number of people, he had caught the elephant single-handedly. When a man-eating tiger had struck terror in the outskirts of Kathmandu, he had gone alone and killed the tiger. At an age of chivalry and heroism, he was the people's undisputed hero. But he was also a controversial figure, and a man of many contradictions. He was as cunning as he was daring, as kind as he was ruthless, as magnanimous as he was mean, and as ambitious as he was down-to-earth.

One dark August night in the year 1846 (Nepali year 1903 Bikram Sambat) the queen's favourite courtier (her illicit lover by some accounts) was assassinated while performing *pooja* (prayer) at his residence. The enraged queen summoned Junga Bahadur, who had by then become a powerful general at a young age, and ordered him to immediately find and punish the murderer. Some historians claim that the assassin was Junga Bahadur himself; two years earlier he had assassinated his own maternal uncle, the then prime minister, at the king's order and thus had been promoted to the rank of general. Seizing this opportunity, he summoned all the courtiers at the royal court that very night, and with the help of his brothers massacred all of them including the then prime minister under the pretext of finding the assassin. But history is unclear as to whether he actually planned the massacre or whether he was just an instrument (and the surprise victor) of circumstances not of his own making.

This dark new moon night is known in the country's history as the infamous Kot Massacre. Was Junga Bahadur punished for this and other subsequent crimes that he committed? No, sir, he wasn't. The terrified queen, who held the reign of power because the weakling of a king had handed it over to her, promptly made him prime minister surrendering all her royal prerogatives. By the fateful stroke of swords, he became more powerful than the king and queen. Later when the queen plotted against him, unsuccessfully, he exiled her to India. After consolidating his power, he claimed royal pedigree by proving (most historians agree falsely) that he was a descendent of the famed Rajput maharajahs of western India, and changed his family name to Rana. Then he forced the now titular king to declare him the maharajah of two districts in western Nepal and decree that the post of the prime minister and all the executive powers and privileges that came with it would pass on to his brothers and then to his sons after his death. And that was exactly what happened. The hereditary Rana prime ministers ruled the country with an iron fist for over a century as their personal fiefdom, much like the shoguns of Imperial Japan. They closed to country to the outside world. They imprisoned and killed all their detractors. They collected tax from the impoverished people to live a life of opulence and decadence while doing absolutely nothing for the development of the country. The civil code enacted by Junga Bahadur Rana further entrenched the discriminatory caste system in the Nepalese society and contributed to the economic and political marginalization of the indigenous minorities. But to give credit to him, he probably saved Nepal from becoming a part of British India by extending a hand of lasting friendship to Nepal's former foes the British.

Junga Bahadur Rana himself became the first Hindu prince to cross the 'dark waters' (considered a sin for a Hindu at that time) to go on an official visit to England where he was feted by Queen Victoria and conferred knighthood. After coming back from England he was said to have made the following observation in the presence of one of his courtiers: 'In England even little children can speak English fluently.' This may or may not have been true, but the truth is that neither he nor any of his successors did anything to improve the lot of the people. In fact, after inaugurating a college, the first of its kind in the country, one of his particularly ruthless (and long-serving) successors was recorded to have remarked to his equally ambitious sons, "Today I have driven a nail into my heart with my own hands .... Until now I have been fortunate enough to rule over a land populated by animals. In your time you will have to rule over a country populated by human beings."

⤶

A month later, Milan received a reply from his uncle. The soldier had written back expressing his willingness to provide monetary assistance. He would send the money to his elder brother's house in Kathmandu, and Milan was to collect it from his aunt in about two weeks. Milan was elated. The very next day he left for Fungling Bazaar, the administrative centre of Taplejung district, with a testimonial from the chairman of his ward (a village is made of several wards), to apply for the dark-green coloured Nepali passport. A week after he got his passport he left for Kathmandu.

Approximately three hundred kilometers to the west as the crow flies from the sleepy little village of Khewang, but by a tortuous route that's three times as long, lies the ancient city of Kathmandu. The city sprawls over every nook and corner of the cup-shaped valley made fertile by the rivers Baghmati and Bishnumati, both considered holy by the Hindus but both filled with rancid squalor. Once famous as the city of temples where a pedestrian was bound to encounter a temple or a shrine around every corner of the narrow streets and alleys, Kathmandu is now an overcrowded, dusty, and polluted city perennially covered by a thin layer of haze. It is a city irreversibly damaged and scarred by decades of haphazard development, with unsightly brick and concrete structures of bizarre shapes and sizes rising abruptly out of every conceivable space, along side, and in many cases dwarfing, the almost dilapidated medieval structures and neo-classical Rana palaces. Many old and historic temples and structures have lost their shine, and some are crumbling, with grass and trees growing on their roofs and walls, which adds to the city's antique ambience. The city's pot-hole filled narrow streets are clogged with all sorts of old and new motor vehicles - four-wheelers, three-wheelers and two-wheelers of myriad shapes and sizes - spewing toxic black smoke and honking incessantly at the crowd of pedestrians who hardly ever bother to take a second look before crossing the street at any place of their choosing. If someone is hit and injured or killed it's always the driver's fault, and the bystanders waste no time in falling upon the hapless fellow like a gang of thugs if he is not lucky enough to make an extra-quick getaway.

Despite this, Kathmandu still retains its old world glory and charm, and proudly proclaims it to those who are enamoured by it beauty, for the city is indeed beautiful. Its slope-roofed temples, dome-shaped stupas, towering pagodas and magnificent palaces never fail to catch one's eyes in their grandeur, and make one wonder when and who built these wonderful structures. It's also a city where the past meets the presents, where the modern mingles with the medieval, and the two reside uneasily side by side.

Kathmandu means different things to different people. To some it's a city of astounding beauty and exquisite taste, and to others it's a city of rancid squalor. To the angry young generation who desperately want to move ahead into the new age, it's a city struggling unsuccessfully to escape the iron grip of its medieval past. To the conservative older generation (and they are also angry) who want to return back to the supposed good old days (the past always looks better in retrospect), it's a city that is blindly embracing the supposedly decadent ways of the West. But one thing is certain. It's a city struggling between the ambivalent mindset of its modern-living yet traditional-thinking guardians.

And this was the city with which Milan had fallen in love and where he aspired to live the rest of his life. Three days after leaving home, he arrived in the city one early morning by a dusty night bus that spewed black smoke from its blackened exhaust pipe at its rear end into the nostrils of the pedestrians who didn't seem to mind. They had grown used to such indignity and took it in their strides. To Milan, Kathmandu was a city of many different faces. When he had first arrived here, he saw it as a city of splendor. When he went to college he saw it as city dominated by politics. When he fell in love, he suddenly saw it as a city of love and romance. Now he saw it purely as a springboard. The place was filled with young men and women from every part of the country – all trying desperately to go abroad for employment.

Milan had lived six wonderful years here. Those were his formative years and his character had been deeply influenced and shaped by it, so much so that he considered himself a city boy rather than a village boy. He made hi way straight for his uncle's house in Maharajgunj where his aunt welcomed him back happily and served him a breakfast of tea and fried egg, while his cousins – two teenage boys and a girl – hurriedly ran out on their way to school after a few customary words of greeting. His aunt, a woman in her late thirties, had grown up in the village but had now comfortably adapted to the modern lifestyle of the city. She didn't miss the village; if she did she never mentioned it. She wasn't angry with him for running away with her neighbour's wife. In fact, she teased him about it and asked after Lalita's well-being. He was immensely relieved to learn that Lalita's ex-husband was not in the country. His aunt also told him that four months earlier the man had married a spinster in her late thirties who was in good terms with her and visited her quite often.

He handed over the stuff his mother had sent – a jar of homemade butter, several strands of dried buffalo meat, and half a kilogram of 'bitter fish' and some *goondrook* (smelly dark-brown dried spinach) – all items that the Nepalese crave for anywhere in the world.

After making himself comfortable on the soft and cozy sofa in front of the television and exchanging the news of relatives with his aunt, he inquired if she had heard from her younger brother-in-law. She replied that a soldier was shortly coming on leave with his money. She added that he was welcome to stay as long as he liked and showed him to his old bedroom which was now occupied by his cousin-brother. As he entered the room, he was filled with a wave of nostalgia as his past life came flooding back to him. It was from this room that he had first seen Lalita and spied on her. It was from this room that he had plotted his romance with her. He peeped through a slit in the window curtain at Lalita's ex-husband's house. He saw a dark-complexioned woman of mid-thirties hanging clothes. She looked happy and contented. For some reason, this scene made him happy and he smiled.

The following day he met up with an old friend at his favourite restaurant and had hot Newari *mamacha* (dumpling) which he had missed so sorely in the village. The Newars of Kathmandu valley have an exquisite taste for food and revel in preparing and eating a variety of dishes that are delightful to the tongue and light on the stomach. When it comes to cuisine the rest of the Nepalese are practically barbarians compared to them. Then in the following days, he caught up with other old friends and sought their help in finding a reliable manpower agent. Over the past decade, manpower agencies and freelance agents claiming to send people abroad had sprung up like mushrooms all over the country. Most of them were nothing more than frauds and thieves involved in daylight robbery of naïve and desperate young men and women. They were known to collect large sums from their trusting victims and then vanish into thin air. There were others who accompanied their clients up to New Delhi, Bangkok or Hong Kong and then disappeared, leaving their unfortunate victims stranded without cash or hope. Thus many naïve rural Nepalese young men with big dreams have become destitute. Worse still, many have landed up in the torturous and inhuman foreign prisons where they are routinely insulted with the vilest expletives and brutalized by the cruel strokes of rattan.

Two weeks later his money arrived. After spending half a month checking out several of manpower agents, he finally decided to try his luck with a company owned by an uncle of a friend, a former classmate of his. The large billboard above its glass-panelled front door proudly proclaimed its name: Pacific Sunrise Manpower Pvt. Ltd., whatever that was supposed to mean. As he entered the ground floor office, a smartly-dressed friendly-looking man in his mid-thirties finished his conversation on the phone and wheeled around on his revolving chair to face him and welcomed him with a warm smile. The nameplate on the table read Managing Director in white on a black background. After the initial introductions he said, "I am not a swindler like the others who so callously rob honest young men like you. I have been in this business for the past five years and sent over two hundred men abroad. Honesty is the best policy, as they say in English, and I have made it my motto. You cannot survive in this business if you are not honest. Or else how do you think that I could own that car out there?" The man pointed proudly to a shiny red Toyota Corolla standing outside his door. "It's the result of honesty and hard work. And the goodwill of satisfied clients," he added as Milan wistfully looked at the expensive vehicle with undisguised admiration and envy. *Will I ever be able to own such a beautiful car?*

"I have received no complaints from any of my clients so far. If I cannot get you where you want to go, then I will return your money. And believe me, this company is perfectly legal," he pointed at a framed certificate on the wall, "I always strive to give my clients their money's worth. I send people to all places – Korea, Taiwan, Japan, Malaysia, Saudi Arabia, UAE, Qatar, Kuwait and so on. You name it and I'll send you there. But, of course, it all depends on how much money you have. Where is it that you'd like to go?"

Milan replied that he was prepared to go wherever there was good money to be made.

"Have you done any professional training such as electrician, plumber, brick-laying, security guard, etc.?"

"No!" Milan replied truthfully.

"That's the problem with us Nepalese. Most of our workers are unskilled. That's why all the skilled jobs go to the Indians and Bangladeshis, even in our own country."

"But I have some college education," Milan added.

"Your college certificate is useless out there," the man replied without sarcasm. "What they require are labourers, factory workers, construction workers, security guards, waiters, butchers, porters, loaders, drivers and the lot. They have plenty of educated men in their own country."

"I am prepared to learn and do whatever is necessary," Milan replied.

"Can you drive?" the managing director asked.

"Drive what?" Milan asked.

"Car, jeep, bus, truck, anything with four wheels."

"No."

"Then I suggest you learn to drive. Starting today. I think a driver's job would be more suitable for someone like you."

Then the managing director, who was hardly more educated than Milan but was adept at interspersing half of every sentence with English words, which gave him an air of an educated man, went on to list the going rate for each country. After a few visits to ascertain the reliability of the agent, Milan made a deal with Pacific Sunrise Manpower Pvt. Ltd. He handed over his passport and the stated amount with the understanding that the company would arrange a work permit and visa for him as soon as possible. The process would take anything from two months to more than a year, the managing director told him. In the mean time he was to learn to drive and then wait and check with the office from time to time. *And hope that the man will not swindle me*, Milan added thoughtfully to himself. A few days later Milan joined a driving school. The learning part was easy, but the part when he had to get the license was not so easy. Anyway, two months later he applied for and got a license. He was ready to go. He returned home a happy man. His dream was finally taking shape. By this time, the monsoon rains were in full swing.

When Milan was running after manpower agents in Kathmandu, Amrita was anxiously waiting for Sharan. As it happens with young people in love, her mood shifted daily. She was joyous, excited and nervous on different days and sometimes all at the same time, and her heart constantly fluttered like a butterfly in anticipation. *He is coming! He is coming! He'll be at our doorsteps soon.* Every day she stretched her eyes towards the trails until they hurt, although she knew that his arrival was still days away, and every morning she counted the remaining days on the knuckles of her fingers.

But she was unaware that some other people were also waiting for him in the city of Dharan about a hundred kilometers as the crow flies down south-west in the plain. Dharan is a relatively new city settled by retired *lahoorays* who saw no profit in going back to their old life of hardship in the hills and merchants of Indian-descent who saw money to be made at their expense. The city that had a humble beginning about a century ago lies on the gentle slope where the Chure Hills (the lower hills) meet the Terai (the plain). Despite its rapidly burgeoning size and population, it still has the look and feel of a provincial town (which it is) – relatively quiet and less polluted, semi-urban, cozy, friendly and familiar. The hills become successively higher as one travels northwards; and to the south lies the rainforest, once dense and impenetrable but now a forest in name only. Until the eighties this hot and humid city was famous for the British Gurkha Transit Camp, a recruitment center for the whole of eastern Nepal, which was so clean and well-maintained that people called it a piece of Great Britain in Nepal. The city also had a reputation for its fashionable girls who never missed a Hindi film and who were said to carry their hearts at their fingertips, and gangs of belligerent looking youths who broke into vicious street fights at the slightest provocation, mostly over the girls. In those days the town was made of mostly wooden houses that stood on a storey-tall wooden stilts, their ground floor lying open and vacant for protection from snakes, chiefly the deadly cobra, and poisonous insects such as the centipede. Now it's a well-planned city with wide streets and modern brick-and-cement houses. The snakes and centipedes disappeared with the increase in human population. The British Camp closed down in the late eighties and was replaced by a hospital that serves the whole of the eastern region of the country. When the British Camp closed there was palpable fear that the stagnant city's economy would completely crumble and the city would die out. But fortunately for its denizens that didn't happen. In fact, with the establishment of a regional hospital, aptly named after the country's foremost freedom fighter BP Koirala, the city survived and thrived. The boys, all diehard fans of the Kung-fu superstar Bruce Lee, who fought each other so viciously, in many cases fatally, either got married and settled down to quiet lives or left the place in search of livelihood. The wildest of Nepali towns thus mellowed down and its mantle passed to smaller and newer towns further east.

As the day for Sharan's arrival came nearer, Amrita's twenty-one year old college-going cousin-brother Suraj found himself in an increasingly difficult situation from which he found it hard to extricate himself. He had received a letter from his friend Sharan two weeks earlier. Sharan had written that he would be staying at his elder sister's house in Dharan for a few days before going to his house in the hills and then from there to Amrita's house with his father. Three years earlier, Suraj had tried along with Sharan and failed to enlist in the British army. Now he was a student of commerce in a local college in Dharan and stayed at his aunt's house in a quiet street that faintly reeked of fermented millet. Every night the retired *lahoorays* sat down to a jar of *tongba* and a dose of reminiscence before going to bed. The residue became was the staple diet of the fat white pigs that grunted contentedly and slept happily all day in a mildly drunken state in their wooden enclosure. Suraj had become so accustomed to the smell that he had stopped noticing it a long time ago. His mother and aunt were Dil Bahadur's sisters. The aunt's husband was a retired *lahooray* of about forty-eight, who spent his days doing nothing in particular. He had served for over fifteen years in the British army and retired in the rank of sergeant. With the money he had been able to save he had bought a farm in the Terai which he leased to tenants on a fifty-fifty basis. This meant that half of whatever grew on it came to him and the other half went to the tenant. The couple had two teenage sons and two pretty teenage daughters, one of whom had become ripe for marriage, in their reckoning. And this was the reason for their interest in the young soldier coming back on leave.

Now one mistake Suraj had made unwittingly, as he looked back in regret, was to tell his aunt and uncle about the imminent arrival of his soldier friend. When they heard that the young man would be passing through town, they became very excited and began to have ideas in their heads. From that day they began to pester him constantly, asking him everything about Sharan and telling him how he must bring his friend to their house. He knew what they were after. The couple wanted the boy for their own daughter, and this put him in a big predicament. This was in direct contradiction to Limbu tradition, but these were competitive times. He didn't know how the girl in question, his cousin Anita, felt because she remained tight-lipped, but he suspected that she too was also secretly excited about the prospect of marrying a *lahooray*.

On the day of Sharan's arrival from Kathmandu, Suraj's aunt looked animated from early in the morning.

"Isn't your friend arriving today?" She asked him as he prepared to take the twenty minutes' walk to his college.

"According to his letter, yes." He replied.

"When did he arrive in Kathmandu?"

"Three days ago, I think. His plane is landing at Biratnagar airport at about three in the afternoon, and then he'll hire a taxi to Dharan."

"Where did you say he is going to stay?" She asked again. This was not the first time she had asked this particular question.

"At his sister's house," he replied. He was getting fed up with these questions, and began to move off saying, "I've got to be on my way now. It's getting late."
"Aren't you going to pay him a visit?" she persisted.
"Of course, I am, aunt. He is my friend." He replied.
"You must bring him to meet us then," she said. That he was not willing to do knowing their intentions very well. But he also knew that he had no choice. These people were his benefactors. They had provided him with free board and food, and he was indebted to them. Provoking their wrath would mean that he would have to find another place to live and he could think of none. He certainly could not afford to rent a place of his own.
"I will," he said reluctantly.
"When?" she asked impatiently.
"Let me meet him first, and then I'll fix a date." He said and climbed down the wooden staircase noisily.
"Suraj," she called after him, "Don't forget."
"I won't," he yelled back.

He met Anita examining some plants near the main gate. She gave him a warm smile and waved her hand. He smiled and waved back at her. He wondered whether she was in it with her parents. He never mentioned Sharan to her, but every time he was with her, he had a vague feeling that she wanted to hear of him. She was an attractive girl of seventeen and just out of high school. As far as he knew, this quiet and soft-spoken girl didn't have a boyfriend, though there were boys who telephoned her and wrote to her from time to time. She didn't mix with or care for the local boys who passed by her house hoping to see her and maybe strike up a conversation with her every evening as she watered the plants. Sometimes he heard whistles and catcalls directed at her from the road, but noticed that she didn't respond.

All that day he thought of his poor cousin Amrita back in Khewang. He liked her immensely. She was sweet and fun-loving. He hadn't told his aunt and uncle about her. *She is waiting for Sharan right at this moment. The two have been in love for the past four years. What will she do when she finds out?* He felt very sorry for her. Fate had conspired to make him an instrument of betrayal, he thought sadly. *I cannot betray Amrita; I cannot stab her in the back. I must tell them about her and Sharan.*

When he returned home that afternoon, his aunt said, "Well, what's the news? Have you met him?"
"No," said Suraj, "I didn't have the time to go to his sister's place."
"You could go now, couldn't you? You must go now." She was pushing him to make haste and he knew why. They were afraid that Sharan's sister might fix him up with some other girl. There was no dearth of eligible young girls with their parents on the lookout for the increasingly rare *lahooray* in the city.
"I'll go in the evening," he said, "It's too hot to walk outside now." During the summer Dharan can be exceedingly hot and steamy from which torrential rain provides the only respite.

But he didn't have the courage to tell her about Amrita. *I'll tell her when the right time comes*, he kept promising himself. The more he thought about it, the more he hated the predicament that he was in. He knew that once he brought Sharan home, they would scheme and plot and create such a situation from which the unsuspecting young soldier would not be able to escape. And the worst part of it was that he was going to be the main instrument of their plot. So he stalled making several excuses.

Three days later, after much nagging from his aunt, Suraj reluctantly brought his friend Sharan to his aunt's house. The cropped-haired, alert-looking, smartly-dressed young soldier was received with remarkable deference by Suraj's calculating aunt and uncle in the living room which had been revamped and given a new face for that purpose. The sofa sets had a new set of cover, the windows new curtains and the floor a new carpet. The table was adorned with authentic looking plastic flowers and fruits. Sharan, the naïve young soldier that he was, didn't suspect a thing. Until he laid his eyes on Anita, he didn't even know that his friend had a pretty cousin-sister. After the initial introduction, Suraj's aunt asked Sharan what he'd like to have.

"I'll have nothing. Thanks," Sharan replied.
"You must have something. Anything you like. It's against our culture to send a guest away with nothing." The aunt said.
"In that case, I'll have tea," replied Sharan with a self-conscious smile.
"With or without milk?" she asked with an ingratiating smile.
"With milk," he added. Somehow he began to feel at home. It was the ambience, perhaps.
"And you, Suraj?" Aunt turned her attention to Suraj. It was rare that she treated him like a guest. In fact, this was the first time as far as he could remember. Usually he was the errand boy of the house. *Suraj, come here. Suraj, go there. Suraj, do this. Suraj, do that.* There were always orders for him that he obeyed without complaint. But then this wasn't any ordinary occasion.
"I'll have the same," replied Suraj.
His aunt then called to her daughter. "Daughter Anita, could you please kindly bring four cups of milk tea?"

The two girls had, of course, been peeping at Sharan from behind the door of their bedroom. Anita went into the kitchen without a sound, and because the tea was already made and waiting, she returned promptly carrying four shiny porcelain cups on porcelain saucers on a silver tea-tray. She walked lightly and self-consciously, in a very feminine and graceful way. Her head was bowed down modestly and she didn't look at Sharan. She didn't even glance at him. The girl's father said as a way of introduction, "This is our daughter Anita. She's just completed high school. She is now thinking of joining college."

"Namaste!" Sharan greeted her awkwardly. He was struck by her frail, feminine beauty.

"Namaste!" She replied timidly in an almost inaudible voice. Her voice was soft and quiet, and she was fair-skinned and pretty with dark, watery eyes and a dimpled chin which added to her good looks. There was a flitting look of approval in Sharan's eyes which lasted long enough for the others to perceive. They were watching his every move intently. After the introduction, the girl quickly retreated back into her bedroom.

Sharan stayed for half an hour and in that short period the scheming couple interviewed their prospective son-in-law with much gusto and managed to extract from him all the information they needed. After Suraj accompanied the young *lahooray* to his sister's house and returned, his aunt declared to him, "We like the boy. He is tall, fair complexioned, good looking and well mannered. He'll make a good match for our beautiful daughter. We would like you to ......"

Suraj didn't let her finish. He couldn't. He had decided to seize this moment to tell them about Amrita.

"I don't think so, aunt and uncle," he said quickly, his heart pounding.

"Why?" Aunt cut him short harshly, "What's wrong with Anita. Isn't she your sister?"

"There's nothing wrong with Anita, aunt. The problem is with Sharan. You see, he is Amrita's boyfriend and he is going to marry her." He blurted out in a single breath.

"Amrita? Amrita who?" she said sharply.

"Your niece Amrita in Khewang. Uncle Dil Bahadur's daughter. Amrita and Sharan have been in love for the past four years, since a year before he joined the army. He's is going to marry her."

Suraj's aunt and uncle were dumbfounded. They didn't speak for a long moment, thinking that such a good catch was slipping out of their hands. In Dharan it was every marriageable girl's (and her parents') dream to catch a *lahooray*. But since the British army had drastically cut down the number of Gurkhas in the mid-eighties, from more than ten thousand to just over three thousand, young and eligible *lahoorays* had become as scarce as stars in a cloudy night. They searched each other's eyes, waiting for the other to speak first. Finally, aunt cleared her throat and asked, "Are they engaged?" she asked.

"No, they aren't. But he's given her his word," Suraj replied.

"Mere words mean nothing." She said triumphantly.

"A promise is a promise, aunt," he said.

"In these days? These days a promise means nothing. Really." She shot back.

"But she is your niece, aunty, your own niece. She has done you no harm. How can you even think of doing this to her?" He blurted out exasperatedly.

"Amrita can find plenty of men who can make her happy in the hills. We want this young soldier for our daughter. Besides, she is just a simple village girl; she doesn't know the ways of the city. A smart and good looking boy like Sharan needs a smart city girl like our daughter who can speak English and dress up fashionably," she lectured him.

Suraj didn't respond. He had no words in his vocabulary to reply to such callous selfishness. Dejectedly, he started to go to his room, but his aunt stopped him, "Suraj, we count upon you to help us."
"Yes, aunty," he said unenthusiastically.
Sensing his reluctance, aunty said, "Don't forget what we have done for you. We have provided you food and shelter these past three years. Without our help you wouldn't have been able to go to college."
"Yes, aunty, and I am grateful for everything you have done for me."
"We know you are. You are such a good-hearted boy. Now will you help us get this boy for our Anita?"
"Yes, aunty, I'll do what I can."
"Thank you. That's all I wanted to know. You can now go to your room." His aunty dismissed him.

Two days later, as planned, Suraj persuaded Sharan to accompany him to the cinema to see a Hindi film. Outside the theatre, they suddenly ran into Anita, her younger sister Ranjana and a young but married aunt of theirs. The meeting was arranged, of course, but Sharan didn't know that.
Anju, the girls' young aunt, looked very surprised and exclaimed, "Suraj, what're you doing here? And who is this nice young man with you?"

"This is my friend Sharan. He is in the British army and has just come back on leave. We have come to see the film. Are you also here for the same reason?"

"Of course, we are. Why else would we come to the cinema hall? If we had known you were coming, we could have come together."

The two girls, Anita and Ranjana, looked shy and didn't utter a word. They didn't look at Sharan either, who in turn looked awkward in their presence. He didn't know how to react to his friend's pretty young cousins. He tried to think of something to say to them, but couldn't think of anything. When his eyes accidentally met Anita's, she blushed profusely and to his surprise he found his heart miss a beat. *God, she is pretty*, he thought. *She looks so delicate.*

"Have you got your tickets?" Suraj asked Anju.

"No, we have just arrived. Have you got yours?" Anju asked him in return.

"Same here," replied Suraj, "but not to worry, let me get the tickets for all of us."

"Oh, will you do that for us? Thank you. Here, take the money." She opened her purse as Suraj stretched his arm to take the money, but Sharan stopped him and said magnanimously, "Let me pay for all of us this time."

Anju mumbled an objection, but Suraj told her that it was all right.

Suraj fought his way into the crowd and bought five tickets. When they entered the dark hall, they successfully contrived to sit Sharan and Anita together, beside each other. Both of them sat stiffly, talking very little to each other but acutely aware of each other's presence in the dark. On a few occasions Sharan inadvertently touched Anita's arms. It felt soft and smooth and warm, and he felt an electric sensation pass from his hand to his head. It had been a long time since he had come into contact with female body. While in England he did not go out with girls and unlike many of his friends was not in the habit of visiting brothels.

The film, starring a pair of Bollywood matinee idols, was a run-of-the-mill dance-around-the-tree love story, unabashedly sentimental and with half a dozen groovy song and dance sequences thrown in. These films usually have a long poetic name, such as 'The Groom Takes Away the Bride' or 'This Heart of Mine Belongs to You'. The boy meets the girl. The boy is from a rich family and the girl is from a poor or disgraced family or vice versa. The richer family objects vehemently to the union and plots to separate the lovers. The poorer family does the same feeling their pride slighted. In the end an accident takes place conveniently and the lovers get the chance to do something to change the mind of their detractors. In this way love wins the day. In Bollywood films the doctor always leaves the life of his patient in the hand of the God, and the protagonist is invariably always seen praying in front of a garlanded photograph of his (or her) dead parent repeating the same monologue heard in every other film. Sharan, though his eyes were glued to the screen, was able to follow little of the story; his mind was preoccupied with the owner of the soft, smooth and warm flesh sitting next to him.

Afterwards, the unsuspecting young soldier magnanimously proposed they go to a restaurant. Suraj and Anju agreed readily. That was exactly what they had in mind. At the restaurant Sharan and Anita sat opposite each other, and exchanged shy glances. Sharan asked her a few questions about her school; she answered shyly. Every time their eyes met, her cheeks turned crimson and he found that very attractive. The two, however, did not talk much. Most of the talking was done by Suraj and Anju, and they mostly talked about the film they had just seen. Then as dusk approached the two boys walked the girls home. Dusk is when it is relatively cool and people come out to water their garden or just to exchange gossip with their next door neighbours. The incident did not go unnoticed and inevitably tongues began wagging. That was also a part of the plan, of course.

"How did you find Anita?" Suraj asked Sharan afterwards, as he accompanied his friend back to his sister's home where he was staying.
"I must say that she is fair and pretty," Sharan replied. "And very shy," he added.
"Would you marry her if she were willing?" Suraj probed him.
"I don't think so," he replied.
"You don't like her?"
"It's not that. But because I love Amrita and I am going to marry her. I cannot betray her." Sharan replied with conviction.

That night during supper, aunt said conspiratorially to Suraj, "Now the boy and the girl have been to the cinema and restaurant together, and all the neighbours know of this and have seen them walking together, it's become very difficult for us to manage the situation. You know how our neighbours are. They always add two and two and make five. Now if your friend doesn't propose to Anita, we'll lose face in the community. Everybody will laugh at us. So, I think it is high time you talked to your friend about it."
"Yes, aunty." Suraj answered dutifully as he swallowed a handful of rice. He felt anger rising up inside him, but did his best to subdue it.
"We leave it up to you to do whatever it is necessary to win him over," ordered the aunty.

"Yes, aunty." He replied.

After dinner he went to his room and sat on the bed for a long time, thinking. *I must be frank and honest with Sharan. I must tell him the truth.* He firmly decided. He had a troubled sleep that night.

The next day, he went to see Sharan to explain his predicament. He told Sharan flatly, without mincing words or beating about the bush, what Anita's parents expected of him.

"Anita is very pretty and attractive, I admit," Sharan said, "And if I were not attached, I'd probably marry her. But I love Amrita and she's the only girl I'll ever marry."
"I know that and I too don't want you to marry anyone else," replied Suraj.
"Then why are you telling me this?"
"Because I have no choice, that's why," Suraj replied, "They have been pestering me ever since they heard about you. I admit that it's my fault but I am not in a position to disobey them."

Sharan didn't reply; he only let out a low whistle accompanied by a smile. He rather liked having a beautiful girl thrown at him. All he had to say was yes and she was his for the taking. But he loved Amrita.

Suraj continued, "Aunt says everybody knows that you dated her and took her to the cinema. Now they expect you to ...."
"Wait a minute," interrupted Sharan, "I didn't date her. You know as well as I do that our meeting them was merely a coincidence, and it was only out of sheer politeness that I offered to buy everyone a ticket."

"Yes, but people don't know that. They think you asked her out for a date."
"Wait a minute. It was fixed, wasn't it?" Sharan said suddenly, "Wasn't it?" The truth of the matter had finally dawned upon him.
Suraj didn't reply immediately. He sat silently gazing out of the window. Sharan continued, "Now I am beginning to understand. That meeting was no coincidence. It was no accident. You people fixed it up. Didn't you?"

But in spite of this Suraj saw that Sharan wasn't angry. He was more amused than angry. It was a big boost to his male ego and he loved it. Like every young man he relished the idea of pretty girls running after him or being pushed his way. *And this girl is certainly very pretty. I wouldn't mind asking her out for a date. Really.* He thought smugly. Then he quickly reprimanded himself. *I mustn't be thinking like this. I love Amrita, I must remain faithful to her.*

"Yes, it was fixed," replied Suraj, "I am sorry but that's the way it is. And to tell you the truth I am here again today to fix another meeting."
"Well, friend, you know I can't ..." But the young soldier found his conviction wavering. The faces of the two girls danced before his eyes – Amrita and Anita. A part of him told him that he shouldn't allow himself to be manipulated like this. *I love Amrita. She is the only one I'll ever marry.* Another part urged him to listen to his male ego which craved for female attention. A delicately beautiful girl was being pushed his way and all he had to do was take her. As easy as that. *I can take a look, can't I? What's the harm in that? After all, it won't affect my final decision.*

"You don't have to say yes," said Suraj, "Pretend to have a look at her, talk to her and then tell her parents politely that you can't marry her because you've already got a girlfriend. This will take the heat off me. You can do this much for an old friend, can't you? They are after me all the time and I have lost much sleep since your arrival."

"You are a dear old friend. We grew up together running up and down the hills, and this is the least that I can do for you. But I beg you not to force me to go any further than that. Just a look and a chat, that's all. Ok?" Of course, he knew that he didn't really mean it. The thought of seeing Anita again filled his heart with anticipation, in spite of Amrita.

"Thanks," Suraj expressed his gratitude, "You have done me a great favour. I now feel as if a great weight has been lifted off my chest. By the way, is your sister looking for a bride for you as well?"
"No," replied Sharan, "She knows about me and Amrita."

Afterwards they talked to Sharan's chirpy sister Mankumari, a young wife of a soldier serving in the British army and a mother of two, one of which clung to her succulent breasts greedily. Her husband was away in England and she lived alone with her two children (a son and a daughter) in her two-storey house with marbled floor and a well-tended flower garden inside a large walled compound. But much of the year she hardly got any respite from her husband's and her own relatives who descended from the hills for one reason or another and stayed at her place for months at a stretch, enjoying the free board and food she provided so generously. When she heard what the two boys had to say, she was greatly amused. She laughed heartily and said, "You don't know how hard I am finding it to fend off the people who want to give him their daughters. It's not like Limbus at all. It seems the whole of Dharan is after him. Young *lahoorays* are hard to come by these days." After a thought she added, "I don't see any harm in it though. You can see her, talk to her and then at the end tell them 'no'. They can't force you. After that you can go to Khewang or wherever it is and marry your Amrita." Both Sharan and Suraj were immensely relieved to hear this.

The next day, as planned, Sharan came to see Anita late in the afternoon. Anita's father was conveniently unavailable. He was happily sipping *tongba* at one of his relative's house boasting that his daughter was so pretty that all the young *lahoorays* were flocking to his house to court her. Suraj slunk away mumbling something about having to go to the shop to buy something. He slipped into his room on the ground floor on tip-toe, threw himself on the bed, picked up a novel and began to read it quietly. Nepali pop novels are usually cheap tear-jerkers. The boy and the girl fall madly in love with each other, but the whole world stands in the the path of their love and the story usually ends in tragedy. Anita's little brothers had gone to play football with their friends. They wouldn't be back until late in the evening. Only Anita, Ranjana and their mother remained in the house.

Anita's mother graciously welcomed her intended son-in-law into the beautifully decorated living room. The glass windows were covered by maroon-coloured curtains, and a dim 40 watt bulb illuminated the room from the ceiling. As soon as he entered the room, Sharan sensed a seductive aura about it. He was served hot milk tea. As per her mother's instruction Anita sat timidly on a sofa opposite him, avoiding direct eye contact with him. She was wearing jeans trousers and a plain red T-shirt, through which her tight cream-coloured bra could be vaguely discerned. Sharan's eyes wandered to her twin peaks and he quickly looked away. He found himself wondering what it would feel like to take them in his hands. But the expression on her face gave away nothing. She didn't even give the slighted hint that she knew what was going on. After asking after each other's health aunt said, "We can't force you young people of these days to do what you don't want to do. That's an archaic custom of the past. Therefore, we'll leave the two of you to talk to each other, feel each other's hearts and minds, and find out if you like each other. We'll be downstairs. If there's anything call us. We'll be back in ten minutes."

She got up to leave and as if on cue her younger daughter Ranjana followed her out of the room and out of the house. She didn't forget to close the door softly behind her. She made straight for the next door neighbour's house and whispered to them, "The young soldier has come to propose to Anita. He is in my house with my daughter now. Come quickly." Her younger daughter Ranjana did the same in another neighbour's house. In no time at all, a dozen curious women and young girls had gathered in the courtyard, whispering conspiratorially and speculating what was going on inside.

In the living room Sharan and Anita sat awkwardly for some time in utter silence, thinking of something to say to each other. It was utterly quiet. The only sound that could be heard was the sound of their nervous breathing. Then Sharan looked at her and she at him. When their eyes locked into each other's, Sharan found himself thrown off balance. *God, she is so beautiful*, he kept thinking. *So delicate that I could take her in my hands and break her.* As he gazed into her moist eyes, finding himself unable to look away, her cheeks turned a deep rose-colour and then crimson, and when she suddenly blinked her eyes, Sharan felt his heart miss a beat. He was swimming. Swimming out of control in those mesmerizing eyes. At that instant, he forgot Amrita. He forgot his love and his promise to her. She seemed so far away and remote that she didn't matter any more. This girl in front of him was the girl of his dreams.

Regaining his composure, he began to ask Anita about herself, her school, her friends and her likes and dislikes. She replied hesitantly at first. But after some time, she became more confident and eloquent. As the conversation progressed, she turned out to be a lot smarter than he had thought and carried the conversation very well. After half an hour, the two were still chatting amiably, and even laughing at each other's jokes and anecdotes. Then suddenly there was a knock on the door and the women waiting outside entered one by one, quietly and curiously. Sharan didn't realize that the trap had closed upon him.

"Have you two decided?" Anita's mother asked looking at her daughter first and then at Sharan.
Anita sat quietly. She didn't reply. After half a minute she threw a quick questioning glance at Sharan, got up and went into her room.
"Well?" aunt turned to Sharan.
"No, we haven't decided ..." said Sharan, ".... to do anything."
"But it's high time you decided," an elderly woman chimed in, "Your affair with our Anita is the talk of the neighbourhood, and today you remained behind closed doors with her doing god-knows-what. The whole neighbourhood knows."
"Yes, it has become common knowledge," added another woman, "if you do not propose now, it will give her family a bad reputation. In fact, it will give the whole neighbourhood a bad reputation. Our daughters are not others people's playthings, you know."

Now Sharan panicked. He thought of Amrita and his promise to her and it troubled him. "I'll have to talk to my sister first," he said as a way of escape, "Only then can I give you my answer."
"All right then, talk to your sister first. But whatever you and your sister decide, remember not to sully our good name in the neighbourhood," Suraj's aunt said to him.

On his way out he ran into Suraj who looked at him intriguingly. "Let me accompany you," the latter offered his nervous-looking friend.
"No, thanks," replied Sharan, "I can find my way alone." He briskly walked away, without waiting for Suraj who ran after him anyway.
"I am sorry, friend," Suraj murmured. Sharan ignored him. He was thinking of Amrita and Anita, and comparing the two cousins. *Which one will it have to be? Which one?*

Next day in the evening, an old couple paid a visit to Mankumari's house at the behest of Anita's mother (Suraj's aunt). The old woman was Suraj's aunt's aunt in relation. The old man was Mankumari's husband's grand-uncle in relation. But they were more closely related to Anita's family. After Mankumari had generously served her guests a jar of *tongba* each, the old man briefed her on the situation and went on to elaborate the customs and culture of the Limbus, interspersing his long monosyllabic monologue with "…. you young people of today may not know ……", a phrase as old as time itself oft repeated by the older generation and much resented by the younger generation. The brother and sister listened to the old man intently without interrupting him.

At the end the old man said to Mankumari, "Our culture says that after what has happened it will be wise for your brother to marry Anita."

"But grandfather," Mankumari retorted, "My brother has done nothing to her, so he cannot be forced to marry her against his wish."

"All the women in the neighbourhood insist that he remained behind closed with her for almost an hour." The old woman quipped in.

"But that means nothing," Mankumari said, "They didn't ….."

"It may mean nothing to you. But it means a lot to the girl's family. If nothing comes out of this, they will lose face. They will become the laughing stock of the neighbourhood. It's a very serious matter."

The old man and his wife stayed late into the night, and Mankumari was forced to serve them dinner. Initially, Sharan pretended to put up a feeble objection, but gradually he gave in. He was in a state of indecision. He was strangely excited by the prospect of marrying Anita, taking her in his arms and making love to her. At the same time he felt guilty and chided himself for feeling that way. But he couldn't help it. In the end the old couple managed to extract a promise out of him to marry Anita. When they left, both slightly inebriated, Mankumari scolded Sharan, "You should have been more careful."

"I have been, elder sister," he replied, "but there was nothing I could do. Maybe this is how one's fate works."

"And what about Amrita then? Are you going to throw away four years of love just like that? Don't you feel any guilt in your heart?" Mankumari asked, perplexed at his brother's behaviour. Sharan didn't reply.

"I feel terribly guilty, and my mind is in such a big turmoil." Saying this he got up and went to his bedroom.

"This is why men can't be trusted." She said. "The moment they see a pretty face, they leave everything and go after her skirt." Sharan did not hear her.

That night Sharan couldn't sleep. He thought of both Amrita and Anita. The faces of the two girls danced before his eyes alternately in the dark. One a girl he had loved for four years, and the other a girl he didn't even know well. But while he could recollect Amrita's face only vaguely after a gap of three years, he could vividly recall the pretty face of her cousin Anita. Whereas on one hand he had a promise of more than four years to keep and felt burdened by a sense of guilt, on the other hand he felt an overriding sense of excitement at the prospect of making love to the fair and fragile-looking Anita. In his fantasy he kissed her tender lips, and caressed her soft and smooth cheeks with his lips. He cupped her small, taut breasts in his hands, and kissed her nipples. She parted her warm and smooth thighs for him as he stroked them gently with his hand. This thought gave him an erection he found difficult to subdue. Then suddenly Amrita's face danced before his eyes and he reprimanded himself for such thoughts. In London an English friend had once taken him to a theatre to see a play by a famous playwright called Shakespeare. It was called Hamlet and it was in old English. He would not have understood anything had his friend not explained the story to him. He now compared himself to Shakespeare's Prince of Denmark who was eaten inside out by a state of perpetual indecision.

At the end he decided that it was fate that was to blame. *It is said that one gets to marry only the person one is destined to marry, and not the one that one chooses,* he reminded himself. *Perhaps there's some truth in it. Perhaps I was not destined to marry Amrita. Perhaps we were never meant to be together.*

With this he once and for all made up his mind to forget his love of four years. But still haunted by guilt he fervently prayed for forgiveness for his betrayal. *It's not my fault, I am just a victim of a difficult circumstance,* he kept repeating to himself. But he was also generous in his prayers. *Oh, God, please give Amrita someone who'll make a better husband than me.*

Two days later Mankumari led a small delegation of relatives and neighbours with a proposal to Anita's house with two bottles of Scotch whiskey, which Sharan had brought from England, and which was happily and most graciously accepted, signifying the acceptance of the proposal. Anita's mother asked Sharan for two *tolas* (a tola is roughly 11 grams) of gold as a token of his good intention, which he produced immediately. He had it ready for Amrita. After that the wedding dates were discussed and agreed upon by both sides. At the end of the negotiations the would-be groom and bride were packed off to take a 'look around' and acquaint themselves with each other. "In these modern times the bride and groom must know each other before they get married," Anita's father said and the others agreed. Sharan tried to wipe the memory of Amrita off his mind. But as he tried to concentrate on Anita with a feeling of excitement and anticipation, he was also beset with a nagging feeling of guilt. That day as they rode on the ubiquitous three-wheeled open rickshaw sitting closely beside each other, he touched her arm voluntarily and she gave him a shy smile. And as he locked his eyes with hers savouring her alluring smile, he realized that he couldn't wait to take her into his arms and make love to her. The gap-toothed wrinkle-faced rickshaw driver glanced back at the couple and smiled knowingly. Many a young and amorous couple had taken a ride on his rickshaw in this city of romance.

That night, a greatly distraught Suraj sat down in his room under a yellow sixty watt electric bulb to write a long, mournful letter to his cousin Amrita, asking for her forgiveness for the part he had been forced to play in her heartbreak.

Two weeks later Amrita received the letter and went through it in utter disbelief. She went through it again because she couldn't believe what she had read. When finally the full meaning of the message sank in, she felt as if the ground underneath her had suddenly opened up and she was falling into a deep, deep chasm. Her hands trembled and tears filled her eyes and flowed thick and fast down her tender cheeks. Discarding the letter on the floor, she threw herself face down on the bed, sobbing uncontrollably. Half an hour later Lalita arrived looking for her. As soon as she entered Amrita's room, she sensed that something was wrong. She picked up the letter and went through it. "Oh, God, your own aunt and cousin-sister! How could they do this to you? How could they be so cruelly and utterly selfish?" she exclaimed angrily. "And how unfaithful and untrustworthy men can be? The moment they see a pretty face, they forget everything." She went on, "To play such a cruel trick on such an innocent girl. What has she done to deserve this?"

"One can't even trust one's own relatives these days," she continued angrily. "It's better to have an enemy than to have relatives such as these. At least you can always trust the former to act against you. But don't cry, Amrita. Please, stop crying! So what if a feckless boy has deserted you? You are young and pretty, and there are plenty of men out there waiting to fall in love with you."

Amrita went on sobbing without acknowledging her presence. Lalita sat by her side gently caressing her hair to give her solace. "Amrita, stop crying. This is not the end of the world. You are young and beautiful. You can have a hundred boys better than that boy if you want." But the heartbroken girl was inconsolable.

When the rest of the family got to know of Amrita's misfortune, a deep sense of gloom and anger prevailed in the family. Dil Bahadur was deeply hurt by this family betrayal. "My own sister," the bewildered man lamented, "my very own sister has stabbed me in the back. How could she do such a thing? I just can't believe it."

Kamala's rarely exhibited wrath broke through her dam of patience. "The bitch," she ranted, "That shameless whore, that slut, that witch, that daughter of a whore, that wife of a philandering sex pervert! How could she even think of doing this to her own niece? Is this how she pays us for our kindness? Look at what she had done. We have always thought of her children as our own, and instead of reciprocating our goodwill, look what she has done to us. Why didn't god strike that accursed witch and that whore of a daughter of hers dead before they had time to carry out such a callous act?"

She turned to her husband and targeted her wrath at him, "And you, Purna's father? What can you do? Nothing. Absolutely nothing. You are incapable of doing anything. Why, you are so nice and kind that you can't even hurt a fly. 'She is my sister', you say. 'My sister is so nice, my sister is so good', you say. 'My sister is not capable of doing such a thing', you say. Look how your goody-goody sister has repaid your brotherly love." There was so much pent-up anger inside her that she went on and on for a good hour.

Dil Bahadur tried to calm her. "Calm down, Purna's mother, all is not lost yet. Our daughter is still young. So what if one worthless boy has betrayed her? There will be others. Don't they say that if you have your feet intact you will find plenty of shoes?" But he knew as well as Kamala that such talk was hardly any consolation to the distraught woman. He thought of writing a long scathing letter to his sister and brother-in-law, but later decided against it. What was done was done. Nothing could change it.

At length Kamala's ire turned towards her daughter. "You are also to blame for this. You trusted that boy, and made us reject a good proposal. Now look what has happened. The whole village will know of this tomorrow and they will laugh at us. It's all your fault."

Narmaya was sad. She wasn't angry; she was just sad and it reflected in her aged lusterless eyes. She was sad at the misfortune that had befallen her favourite grand-daughter, she was sad for the love lost between brother and sister – her own children. She kept shaking her head and saying, "My daughter shouldn't have done such a thing. It was extremely mean and selfish of her."

A week later the whole village got to know of Amrita's misfortune through the grapevine. Many were sad for her and expressed their sympathy. But there was no dearth of jealous folks who were joyous at her misfortune. Amrita lost her jest for life. She stopped laughing. She spoke very little and her eyes were shadowed by a profound sadness. Sometimes she had a distant look in her eyes, as if she was taking solace in the safe and cozy world of fantasy, where everything goes according to one's plan and nothing is left to chance. She lost her appetite for food and grew thinner by the day. "Keep an eye on her all the time," Dil Bahadur instructed, "She has been profoundly hurt. She might do something rash." And fearing that she might actually do what her father suspected – it's the young people who mostly commit suicide - Laxmi kept her constant company, comforting her with words of endearment.

Amrita's tragedy is the tragedy of every human life. The one thing that one covets the most is the one that is the hardest to get. The one person you trust turns out to be one who betrays you. The one person you love becomes the one who hurt you the most. But in this lies the sweetness of life, because it makes that thing that much worth fighting for, or if you are not capable of fighting, then crying for. The sweetness of love does not only lie in the joy that it brings, but also in the pain and heartache that it causes for love is a dull pain throbbing somewhere deep inside the heart. The more it hurts, the sweeter it becomes.

When Milan returned from Kathmandu and heard of his sister's misfortune, he was angry at Sharan and his aunt. He also berated his sister for her foolishness. But there was little else he could do. There was not much joy in the family for many days. They had been expecting a wedding and instead what they got was a 'heartbreak'.

But time is a great healer. The despondency lasted only as long as the monsoon rains. As the days changed into weeks and weeks into months, Amrita stopped crying and began to smile occasionally. But it was a smile tinged with sadness; there was no laughter in her eyes. Nevertheless, Laxmi was satisfied that her sister-in-law had embarked upon the healing process. It would take a long time, but it was a start, at least.

By the beginning of October Milan had become restless again. He had not heard from his agent since his return, and feelings of doubt had began to nag his mind. "I must go back to Kathmandu to follow up," he said to Lalita. "They will not work if you don't chase after them." Two weeks later he left for Kathmandu again.

That same month Lalita discovered that she had become pregnant once again, and since she had already given birth to a girl, everyone expected it to be a boy this time. Both Narmaya and Kamala said, "Daughter-in-law, you must have a boy this time." She felt like they were not just expressing their hope; they were insisting that she have a boy.

"Yes, mother. I am certain that it's going to be a boy this time." She replied confidently. Though it was an unplanned pregnancy once again, she was happy. She felt sure that she was going to have a boy this time. Somehow she knew it. Her instinct told her. The other women scrutinized her rising abdomen and said, "This time it's going to be a boy." It delighted her to hear this. But her happiness was tampered by Milan's absence and his impending departure. *Milan won't be home to witness the birth of his son. He won't see his son grow. And when he comes back his son will recognize him.* These thoughts made her sad.

Milan didn't return for a month and a half, but wrote three letters. He didn't come home for Dashain and Tihar, and Lalita didn't visit her parents that year. He returned home in mid-November. His agents had finally confirmed (after he had chased them every day) that his papers were ready. He was to leave for Malaysia within a fortnight and he had returned to bid his family farewell. "I am going to work as a driver in a private company," he told them.

On the day of Milan's departure, Lalita decorated the main door of the house with flower-garlands and placed two copper water-jars filled to the brim with water on each side of the door for good luck. Nepalese believe that it brings them bad luck if they see empty water jars on the way out. She painted a yellow swastika on each of the jars for good luck according to Hindu custom. When Milan walked out of the door between the two water jars, his mother sprinkled water on his head and body with the stem of a herb from a brass amphora. Then his grandmother, father and mother took turns to apply the customary red tika on his forehead for good luck, and a flower garland around his neck. He touched their feet with his forehead while they gave him their advice and blessings. After that he turned to his elder brother, Purna, and elder sister-in-law, Laxmi, who also gave him their blessings. Then he said goodbye to his little brothers and sisters. Finally, he took his little daughter Kalpana in his arms and lifted her up. He kissed her on the forehead and cheeks, and blew into her palms, as instructed by his mother, to make sure that her spirit would remain behind with her and not follow him, for the Limbus believe that if a child's spirit follows a departing person, especially a loved one, then the child will fall ill and may even die.

Finally, he turned to Lalita and said in a whisper, "Look after grandmother, father and mother well. I'll write to you often," he said. "I'll always love you and think of you every day." Her eyes filled with tears.

"Come back soon," she whispered through tears.

"I'll will," he said, "I will come back as soon as I can and take you away from here."

Now fast forward. Two years had passed since the departure of Milan. In these two years, things had changed much in the country, though not all were either aware of or affected by them.

As far as Laxmi was concerned nothing had changed. She was still childless. The goddess in whom she had put so much faith had failed her. But she didn't blame the deity. Gods and goddesses never get the blame, they only get the credit. So she blamed her own wretched karma. *I must have committed an immense sin in one of my past lives,* she lamented. To forget her growing despondency, she immersed herself in house work and kept busy all the time. But she knew that time was quickly passing by, and this realization made her sadder still. She did her best to hide the pain in her heart, but the sadness in her eyes betrayed it. She was a simple village girl, not a polished actress.

Seeing his wife's despondency, Purna too felt miserable at times. But that was only the beginning of his problems. Pressure was growing on him from all quarters for him to take a second wife. Some of the more insensitive men and women, who included some of his close relatives, openly taunted him. They called Laxmi an infertile wench incapable producing children, though what business it was of theirs he was at a loss to understand. Though their remark left him hurt and angry, he was too polite and good-natured to hit back at them. But he was slowly losing his patience at the people who had made it their business to interfere in his life. People can be exceedingly cruel, especially to those whom they deem less fortunate than themselves. After becoming the recipient of one particularly tasteless remark he had vowed: "If I ever hear it again, I am going to tell them to go to hell."

But there was no way he could tell his mother and grandmother to go to hell. "If daughter-in-law is unable to give birth, then we think it will be best for you to marry again. Although we love Laxmi – she is the best daughter-in-law any one could have - being a good wife is not enough. There must be children in a marriage; otherwise the union has no purpose." She repeated at least once a month and grandmother agreed with her wholeheartedly.

One day Laxmi said to Purna, "We can't go on like this forever. We have to come to terms with the fact once and for all that I am infertile; that I can never give you children. You should go ahead and marry another woman."

"Don't ever say that," Purna chided his wife with a hurtful expression. "I can never do that." He loved Laxmi. He really did, though it was not in his nature to articulate his feeling in words.
"Yes, you can. It's not uncommon for men to have two wives. My own father had two wives and they lived quite happily with each other until my stepmother died."
"That was in the old days, it's not done these days," replied Purna, "in any case it's against the law."
"Only if the first wife objects and files a lawsuit, according to what I have heard," Laxmi said. "And I won't object. The children you have from your second wife will be like my own children."

"No," objected Purna, "I don't want to hear of it anymore." And he refused to discuss the matter with her afterwards. He was steadfast in his loyalty to her.

But that didn't solve Laxmi's problems because wherever she went, she was constantly reminded of her deficiency. It was not that people made cruel remarks to her face (though she knew that they did it behind her back); it was their physical gestures - the expression on their faces and the look of pity in their eyes. Even at her parents' home, which she visited once a year, there was no escape.

Eight months after Milan's departure Lalita had given birth to a healthy baby. No, not a boy, but another girl. Again. Kamala and Narmaya were dismayed. They said: "Next time, daughter-in-law, you must have a boy." But that had not dampened her spirit. *There is always a next time,* she said to herself. *As long as there is life, there is hope. And as long as there is hope, there is a way.* She had named the little girl Samjhana, remembrance, for obvious reasons. The little girl was now a year and a half old, and together with her older sister Kalpana, she was the light of the family, as Dil Bahadur was fond of saying. The house was once again filled with the laughter, cries, quarrel and frolics of the little girls, who kept their grand-parents busy and cheerful. Milan sent home money from time to time and wrote long lovelorn letters to Lalita expressing his undying love, telling her how much he loved her and missed her, and how lonely he felt in an alien land so far away from home and how he yearned for her company and dreamed everyday of making love to her.

And in *Dashain* she dutifully visited her parents, and although her father still refused to forgive her, he had become more accommodating towards her. This, she concluded, was on account of her two little daughters of whom he had grown immensely fond of. "The stars of my eyes," he called them. He loved them and showered them with kisses, and looked forward to seeing them.

Amrita had finally recovered from her heartbreak. No more a naïve girl of seventeen, she had become older and wiser. She no longer pined for the boy who had so heartlessly jilted her for her cousin. She rarely thought of Sharan and never uttered his name. There were, of course, a few young men who had an eye for her, but she ignored them because they were not to her liking.

She had stopped going to school after failing the tenth grade exams. She devoted all her time and energy to helping her sisters-in-law in the household chores. But as any eligible young woman, she secretly harboured the dream that one day a good looking young man would arrive from somewhere to win her heart and take her away. Until then the only thing to do was to wait patiently. The tragic end to one affair doesn't mean the end of life. Nor does it mean the end of hope. She was young and pretty, and there was still much to hope for, and much to see, and much to achieve in life. One must always move forward with life. One must leave the past where it belongs – in the past. Otherwise, there will no place for the future because that's what really matters. Humans may remember and take lessons from the past, but they live for the future. This is what makes them different from other less intelligent animals.

One day Amrita's friend (and cousin) Binita paid her a visit. Although the young woman tried to act normal, she looked flushed with happiness. There was a curious restlessness and excitement about her, as if she was anticipating something

exceedingly pleasurable. After greeting the older members of the family and exchanging the customary pleasantries, the girl dragged Amrita to the latter's room and whispered excitedly, "I've got something to tell you."
"What?" Amrita's curiosity was greatly aroused. She had already sensed the excitement in her friend.
"Promise that you won't tell anyone," Binita said, blushing profusely.
"I promise," replied Amrita.
"Last night we had some visitors from Medibung," Binita said. Amrita's heart began to beat faster; she could almost hear it pounding furiously under her breast. That was Sharan's village.
"Who?" She asked weakly, the colour draining from her cheeks. For a brief moment she almost expected to hear of Sharan.
"They came with a marriage proposal," Binita whispered eagerly.
"For you?"
"Who else?"
"And what did you say?"
"I didn't have to say anything. My parents said 'Yes'."
"Have you seen the boy? What does he look like?"
"He was there with them. He is about twenty-five and he is good looking that you have to see to believe," Binita uttered excitedly.
"You are so lucky," said Amrita, not without a tinge of envy, "When's the wedding?"
"In three weeks," Binita replied. "Oh, I am so happy that I don't have my feet on the ground," she chirped on, "but please don't tell anyone that I told you."
"No, I won't." Amrita laughed happily. She was happy at her friend's happiness.

"Amrita, my darling, will you be one of my bridesmaids and accompany me to my future husband's house for the wedding?"

"Let me think," Amrita said teasingly, "Medibung is a long walk away and ……."

"No, don't think. Just say yes. Even if you won't I'll drag you along with me."

"Of course, I'll accompany you. I am so happy for you. So happy, in fact, that I cannot tell you how happy I am."

"Tell me," Binita said blushing, "What happens on the first night?"

"Which first night?"

"The night the husband and wife ……… you know, sleep together?"

"How should I know? I am not married. But I think they have sexual intercourse."

"And when that happens what am I supposed to do?"

"I don't know. I guess you just lie down on your back and let him do whatever he's supposed to do."

"Oh, Amrita, I am so scared. It's only two weeks away. Will it hurt? Will I get pregnant?"

"I don't know. Why don't you ask your sister-in-law?"

"I can't. She might think badly of me. Besides, you know that I am not in very good terms with her."

"In that case, you can talk to my sisters-in-law. They are both nice and friendly and might be of help," Amrita suggested.

"I can't. What will they think of me?" Binita replied.

The two girls talked and laughed happily for a very long time.

When Binita left four hours later, Amrita found herself wondering about her own future. At nineteen and approaching twenty, she felt her youth silently stealing away. *Life is like the water under the bridge*, she sighed sadly, *it flows in only one direction, never to return. Once one's youth is gone, it never comes back. If only it weren't for my scheming aunt in Dharan, I'd be happily married by now with a toddler in my hand. If no suitor arrives in the next few years, I might end up an accursed spinster.* The thought frightened her. She didn't want to end up a spinster. Those unfortunate women were forever at the receiving end of derisive comments.

Three weeks later, Binita got married. Amrita and her friend Manju accompanied the young bride along with half a dozen other bridesmaids. It was a one and a half day's journey on foot. The wedding party reached the groom's village late in the afternoon the next day. As Medibung came nearer, Amrita became uneasy and nervous. The ghost of her past began to haunt her. She was afraid that she might run into Sharan, although Manju had told her that he was in England. He might have come back on leave. She didn't want to come face to face with him. She didn't know what she would do if such a situation arose and this frightened her. But at the same time a part of her wanted to see him once again, just for a brief moment, to see what he looked like and find out if he still had feelings for her. Thus by the time they entered the village, her mind had become a ball of contradiction. Her eyes kept darting towards the young men of the village – with hope and dread at the same time. One moment she was glad he wasn't there and then the next she was disappointed.

After a night's rest, the wedding ceremonies began early the next day. During the feast in the afternoon, Amrita noticed an immaculately dressed mustachioed man in his mid-thirties following her every move with his eyes. He wore a light blue shirt and a pair of finely pressed dark-green trousers. She thought he looked very modern and handsome. *He must be a lahooray on leave,* she thought. *He definitely looks like one. Probably married, with a plump wife and a few kids. But why does he keep looking at me?* As the day wore on, she felt his attention more acutely and found it impossible to escape his smiling eyes. The man made deliberate attempts to catch her attention. When her eyes met his accidentally, he smiled at her and she couldn't help but blush.

She found it difficult to drive the man out of her mind. *Who is he? What does he do? How old is he? Is he married? Is he divorced? How many children does he have?* She loved the masculine attention that he showered upon her; it made her feel like a woman. She hadn't felt this way since ..... Sharan. But on second thoughts she had misgivings about him because he was obviously much older than her. But try as she may, she couldn't help stealing glances at him which he caught every time and reciprocated with a warm smile. *Whoever he is,* she thought, *he must be a regular womaniser, with an eye for young girls. That's what he must be. There is no dearth of such men in the world, roving married lover boys who run after young girls and other men's wives to satisfy their lust. Oh, what am I thinking? How could I have such awful thoughts about a man I don't even know? I must find out about him. I must,* she said to herself.

She whispered to Manju, "Who is that man over there?"
"Which man?" Manju asked.
"The man with the mustache," she replied.
"I can see three or four men with mustache," said Manju disinterestedly, "Which one do you mean?"
"The one over there in light blue shirt and dark-green trousers," she whispered. She was afraid that someone might overhear their conversation.
"Oh, him?" said Manju, "Why, that is Uncle Rajkumar."
"Uncle who?"

"Uncle Rajkumar. He is Sharan's uncle, his father's youngest brother. Why?"
"I was just curious," she replied. She glanced at him again and he caught her eyes and smiled. She smiled back at him. Manju didn't show much interest in her curiosity in the man. She was too engrossed in looking at the younger men.

A quarter of an hour later, Amrita whispered to Manju again. "Tell me about that man," she said.
"Which man?" Manju asked.
"Your uncle Rajkumar."
"Oh, him? He is an officer in the British army, a lieutenant, I think. He lives in Dharan and Kathmandu where he has houses."
"What's he doing here then?"
"Can't you see? He is here for the wedding."
"But what about his wife and children? Are they here as well?"
"He doesn't have a wife. He is a widower. His wife died two years ago, leaving behind three children – a son and two daughters."
"A widower?"
"Yes, I've heard that he is thinking of getting married again."
"Really?"
She didn't know why, but it made her feel ..... happy and ..... hopeful. *Yes, that's the word, hopeful. His wife is dead and he's thinking of marrying again. I wonder who he will marry.*

Manju didn't question her interest in her uncle Rajkumar, and Amrita was glad for that. The knowledge that he was single made her look at him in a new light. But that whole afternoon Rajkumar made no attempt to talk to her. She wished he did. But he was taking his time. So Amrita got bolder and obliged him with a coquettish smile every time their eyes met, which was quite often. *What's the harm in flirting with a man who obviously likes you, even if he is much older than you? He is not that old, really. In fact, he is good looking and rich and looks quite young, too.*

Late in the afternoon, the older men brought out their *chyabrungs* (drums) and they and some women danced the drum-dance. When Rajkumar joined in, with obvious intent to attract her attention, Amrita followed his every move with unfeigned interest. He was good looking and danced gracefully. Unlike the other men, his belly didn't protrude out of his shirt. He had a full head of short, slick black hair, and the neat mustache above his upper lip gave him a manly air. She thought he moved with a grace that the other men were incapable of. She fixed her eyes upon him as he swung to the left, then to the right and moved forward and backward in a circle with the other men to the rhythmic beat of the drums. At every step forward, Rajkumar threw a glance at her and she met his eyes with an approving smile. When he smiled back and winked at her, her heart skipped a beat and she realized that she had a crush on him.

Later at dusk, a couple of hours before the start of the main part of the wedding ceremony which takes place at night, Amrita found Rajkumar relating an incident to some young men and women at one corner of the courtyard decorated beautifully with fresh flowers and crepe papers. Lalita shyly joined the group, and her arrival did not go unappreciated by the delighted storyteller. He was a good talker and an eloquent story-teller, and had the capacity to captivate his audience.

"I saw them hack Balbir to death. That was about twenty years ago. At that time Balbir was the terror of these hills. He was as big and as strong as a bull, and he always wore a shiny khukuri tucked neatly in its leather scabbard on his waist, like all Limbu men used to do in the old days, ready to be brandished at a moment's notice. People said that the handle of his khukuri was made of pure ivory, but unfortunately I never got to lay my eyes on it. When he and his cronies walked into any bazaar, the frightened people hurriedly made way for them. He had four or five wives, some of whom he had forcibly taken, but they were all faithful to him and bore him many children. Now every strong man has enemies and Balbir was no exception. People like him always have their nemesis. One such man was Laljung, a pugnacious little fellow of ferocious disposition. He was a known drunkard and a gambler. And a fighter, though he was of a small stature. Man to man he was no match for Balbir who could smash him to pulp with a single hand. But the little man had in abundance what an average man lacks – guts. It was said that Lal Jung was not afraid of anything. And with four or five brothers to lend him support, he was definitely not scared of Balbir."

Rajkumar stopped to give Amrita a special smile and then continued, "I forgot how their enmity began. But I think it started when Lal Jung was gambling as usual in a bazaar. Balbir joined in and when he lost a considerable amount of money he accused the little man of cheating. A quarrel ensued and the bigger man threatened to beat up little man. Unlike the other men who would have quietly slunk away hiding their tail between their legs, Lal Jung stood his ground defiantly which resulted in a fist-fight. Severely beaten up, the bloodied little man was carried away by his friends, but he did not depart without vowing vengeance. Immediately after his recovery, he collected his brothers raided the home of Balbir, but the man was not there. They kicked down the door, smashed up some furniture, and threatened his wives and children. When Balbir came to know of this he became incensed and vowed revenge. A month later when Lal Jung was at his father-in-law's house, Balbir got wind of it and he and his khukuri-wielding cronies surrounded the house yelling at the man to come out. But the quick witted little man jumped down from the attic and, before his enemies could react, made a clean getaway. After this undignified escape Lal Jung and his brothers vowed to kill Balbir anytime anywhere they encountered him. When Balbir came to know of this he laughed and boasted that he was ready to face the brothers single-handedly, anytime, anywhere. He would make mince meat of Lal Jung and his brothers. He was not afraid of anyone."

Rajkumar gave Lalita another special smile. She blushed and smiled back at him. He continued, "I was just a boy of fifteen then, on my way to the British camp in Dharan. But when we heard that there was going to be a fight between Balbir and Laljung in Sankranti Bazaar, we changed course and went there instead. We didn't want to miss the fight of a lifetime if there was going to be one. This kind of thing doesn't happen every day. I had never laid my eyes on either Balbir or Laljung and his brothers, though I had heard plenty of them. The day I reached Sankranti Bazaar with a friend there was a big fair because of a festival. We found that the place was wild with the rumour that there was going to be a fight between Balbir and Laljung. It was on everybody's lips. People were excited and nervous at the same time. We waited expectantly all morning but nothing happened. There was no sign of fight. We had almost given up when we heard in the afternoon that both parties had arrived. Upon this news the bazaar became tense. Wherever Balbir and his associates went, a hush fell and people quietly made way for them. It was the same with Laljung and his brothers. Both adversaries walked with a confident swagger, as if they owned the whole bazaar. But for some reason the two parties avoided each other. In fact, the two war parties didn't come face to face the whole afternoon. Perhaps they were afraid, despite their boasts, we suspected. We were anxious to see the fight and when there was no sign of one, we were dismayed. We attributed this to the presence of four or five policemen in the bazaar. We waited the whole afternoon shifting from one teashop to another with feelings of anticipation, excitement and dread."

Amrita couldn't help being impressed by the repertoire of words Rajkumar used. He was good at talking, he was. He continued, "When the fight failed to materialize by dusk, we had given up and declared the day a waste, when suddenly there was a commotion. People started running about in great alarm – some towards the open space at one end of the bazaar and some away from it. We ran towards the source of commotion. When we reached the place, we noticed that the main pathway was empty and there was a ghostly quietness about it. Everyone was silent; no one spoke, not even a whisper or cough was heard. Frightened men tried to make themselves inconspicuous behind pillars and walls, and terrified women peered cautiously from behind half-open doors and windows. Roadside hawkers quickly gathered their wares and took refuse at the verandah of the nearby houses and shops. Then at one end of the field I saw Balbir standing alone with a shiny *khukuri* in his hand. His muscular frame stood tall and terrible under the darkening sky. Then he began to pace left and right as he bellowed vile obscenities at his enemies challenging them to come out in the open. This put the shiver into my heart. It is said that in the old days our forefathers boasted that "to cut one's flesh three inches deep is just a jest". It is also said that when one drew out a khukuri in anger in those days one couldn't put it back without drawing blood, and from time to time there were deadly confrontations which almost always ended in fatalities."

"But why was Balbir alone? Did you not say he had friends with him?" A young man asked.

"I don't know. But I later heard that he had instructed his men not to come to his aid telling them that he alone was more than enough for the diminutive Laljung and his equally diminutive brothers. The people, superstitious to the core that they were, claimed afterwards that it was *written* for him to die that day, that's why he faced his enemies alone. Whatever the reason, there he was, standing alone and daring his enemies to fight him."

"Where did the policemen go? Didn't they intervene?" Amrita suddenly blurted out. Rajkumar smiled at her, surprised that the question had come from her and she blushed profusely.

"I didn't see any policemen there. People later said that as soon as there was a sign of fight, the policemen disappeared. Perhaps they were afraid. Perhaps they sensed that this was not going to be an ordinary fight and didn't want to get involved. Anyway, there was Balbir shouting the choicest obscenities at his as yet unseen enemies. Then suddenly there were whispers and murmurs and I saw five men swagger confidently and purposefully towards the field with naked khukuris in their hands. Someone pointed out Laljung to me in the middle of the group, just a pace or so ahead of his brothers. He was just a couple of inches more than five feet and looked puny in comparison to his arch-enemy. His brothers were not much taller either. But I noticed something about him. Though small in stature, he had a broad chest, wide shoulders and muscular arms and he walked with a confident swagger. The group stopped about a hundred feet from their enemy who had momentarily fallen silent seeing his enemies approaching. Then Balbir waved his khukuri and bellowed at them once again to come to him. Laljung shouted back that he needn't worry because they were there to kill him. That was it. They were not just going to beat him up. They were going to kill him. Then there was silence. I was under a shed about fifty paces away from the brothers. I was thinking that they were going to make a single concerted attack on their enemy from all sides. But that didn't happen. Apparently the brothers had a different strategy. Suddenly, Laljung ran towards Balbir and attacked him with his khukuri. I heard the terrible sound of metal striking metal three or four times. Then as abruptly as he had gone on the attack, he ran back. Balbir didn't follow him. Before he was halfway back, one of his brothers went on the attack in the same manner. Then when he came back another went. In this manner all the brothers took turns to attack the bigger and stronger man who stood his ground defiantly. I realized that the brothers were going to tire him out. That was their strategy. Until then nobody seemed to be hurt, but by then the sunlight was fading and I wasn't able to see properly. Then two of the brothers went on the attack together. Balbir fought off both of them. When the two ran back to their position, I noticed that one of them was limping. Then the remaining three went on the attack. They attacked Balbir from three sides, and the big man fought all of them swinging his khukuri in all directions. Then suddenly I thought I heard the dull thud of metal cutting into flesh. I am not sure whether I really heard the sound or not, but I thought I did. Then abruptly the three brothers ran back to their positions. Balbir still stood tall and erect, but I saw him sway a little. Then again three of the brothers went on the next wave of attack. Balbir fought them off same as before. There was another dull thud as metal cut through flesh. The brothers walked leisurely back this time. They didn't hurry. The reason became clear when I turned my attention back to their enemy. Balbir still stood erect, but his khukuri-wielding hand, the right hand, had been chopped off neatly from just below the elbow. Curiously, there was no howl of pain from the wounded man. He slowly bent down and picked up the khukuri with the remaining hand. Then two brothers went on the attack again. Balbir, whose name means strong and brave, fought them off valiantly with one hand for a while, but when they returned his left hand was also gone. But he still stood tall and erect. He had nothing to fight with now. But Laljung and his brothers were in no mood for mercy. Laljung strode towards his armless enemy leisurely and hacked him diagonally across his chest, and walked back. Balbir still stood but he began to sway left and right. He was strong, mighty strong. Then another brother walked lazily towards the wounded man and hacked his abdomen horizontally. Someone later said that his entrails poured out, but I didn't see it as I was too far away. Then another one hacked the wounded man's right thigh, and then another hacked the left thigh. Then the wounded man swayed and crashed to the ground like a tree. After waiting for a minute, the five men walked towards their victim and inspected him. I saw Laljung kick his fallen enemy. Then they walked back slowly and deliberately, as they had come at the beginning, and walked away. As they passed close by me, I noticed that their shirts were red and blood was dripping from the khukuris that they still held in their hands. Three of them had large gashes on their body and one limped visibly. All of them had deadly expressions on their faces. After they vanished into the night, frightened men and women slowly emerged out of their shelter and walked cautiously towards the wounded man. Somebody shouted murder and the others rushed to help the dying man. I too went to see the wounded man, but I didn't have the heart to look for long. His body had been slashed at several places. His entrails had poured out of his abdomen. His arms were scattered a few feet from where he had fallen. The fallen man was soaked in his own blood but he was still breathing. We headed for our lodge, and I later heard that Balbir lived through the night and died the following morning."

"What happened to Laljung and his brothers?" someone asked.

"I later heard that they crossed over into India and never came back," replied Rajkumar.

"And the police?"

"They came back the next morning. But we didn't stay to see what happened next. We'd seen enough."

The wedding ceremony came to an end an hour before midnight. Most of the guests went home. But some of the more amorous and energetic ones stayed behind for the paddy dance. The young men of the village coaxed the unwilling bridesmaids to dance, but since none of them had danced before they refused. Rajkumar, however, had chosen this moment to seize the opportunity to make his move. He cornered Amrita as she was trying to make her escape.

"Younger sister," he said politely, "May I know your name?"

"Amrita," she replied shyly, taking care not to look directly into his smiling eyes.

"Do you know who I am?" he asked.

"No, how could I?" she lied.

"I am your friend Manju's uncle," he replied. "Do you have any family relation with Manju besides being her friend?"

"We are cousins."

After a moment's silence Rajkumar asked again, "You are very young and pretty. If you won't mind, may I ask how old you are?"

"I don't know. Why don't you make a guess yourself?" She replied coquettishly. To her own surprise she was becoming bolder.

"Eighteen?" He asked. "You must be between 16 and 20, not more and not less."

"You may be right," she said glancing at him, "and then you may be wrong." He caught her eyes and she blushed.

"Are you related to the bride?" He asked.

"Yes, she is also a cousin but more of a friend." Amrita replied.

"I've been watching you all day." Rajkumar said.

"Have you?" She feigned surprise.

"Yes, I have."

"Why?" She was blushing profusely by now.

"Because you are very pretty," he said. She smiled but didn't reply. "You look prettier when you smile." She still didn't reply. She felt blood surge into every part of her body. She hadn't felt this way in a long time. She looked up at the yellow moon hanging in the sky and thought she saw a human face there and that face resembled Lieutenant Rajkumar's. A sudden gust of cool breeze ruffled her hair and brought her back to reality. She turned her eyes to Rajkumar and their eyes locked.

"My wife died two years ago," he said, without blinking his eyes.

"I am sorry for you," she uttered softly, "What did she die of?"

"Cancer," he replied, "I have been lonely ever since."

"But you have your children," she said.

"Yes, but they are busy with their own lives. They live their own world, I in mine."

"How old are they?" She was curious. For some reason unknown to herself, she wanted to know about his children.

"Twelve and nine! Both of them go to school."

By this time some men and women had already formed a chain happily holding each other's hands and getting ready to do the paddy dance. Rajkumar glanced at the group and said, "Will you dance with me?"

"I have never danced," she replied truthfully. She had never danced the paddy dance, but she felt like doing it now, with him.

"It's easy. Actually, it's not much of a dance. You just hold my hand and sway your body slowly left to right and back along with the others." He said.

"But I don't know the lines," she replied.

"You don't have to," he replied, "Just listen to what the others sing, and then make your own as you go along."

When she still hesitated, he caught her right hand and pulled her along. At his masculine touch she felt an electric sensation pass through her body and that made her shiver. She had felt this way only with Sharan. She felt powerless to do anything and followed him meekly

When Manju saw her join the dance, the girl couldn't believe her eyes at first, and then slowly the significance of it began to dawn on her mind as she remembered her conversation with Amrita earlier that day, and realized why her friend was so curious about the man. *There's something going on*, she whispered to herself, *something very interesting, and something worth a good gossip.* But for the moment she decided to keep the secret to herself. The dance lasted a long time. As usual the men and women sang of pain and suffering, and of life's trials and tribulations, and mostly of unrequited love. When Amrita broke away from the chain an hour after midnight saying that she was too fatigued to continue, Rajkumar did not protest. He left the dance as well and bade her goodnight promising to see her again. When Amrita fell asleep beside her friend Manju a quarter of an hour later, the others were still dancing. That night she had an erotic dream.

Rajkumar was kissing her lips and fondling her breasts and the valley between her thighs was all wet.

The next day Rajkumar came again to talk to Amrita and her friends. He regaled the young girls with several jokes and anecdotes. This was the first time Amrita had laughed so much and with such abandon after her heartbreak. All that day he was constantly on her mind. When she closed her eyes, he was there – smiling at her, and when she opened her eyes he was still there. Before falling asleep that night she decided that she was in love. Even while asleep there was a smile on her face.

The next day was the day of departure for the bridesmaid with their escorts. They got up early in the morning, had breakfast and prepared to depart. A few minutes before their departure, Rajkumar arrived and asked her to come aside. She followed him hesitatingly, glancing shyly at her curious friends with a reddening face.
"Can I talk to you?" he asked looking steadily into her eyes.
"I guess so," she replied. Suddenly she felt afraid and her legs trembled. Her instinct told her that Rajkumar was going to say something of importance.
"I've been thinking," he began nervously. She waited without uttering a word, avoiding his eyes. "I have been thinking that if you ………." He fumbled to find the right words. He was nervous, and it amused her to see an adult man become nervous in her presence. He made an act of clearing his throat and continued, "… that if you are not against the idea, I would like to ……" He stopped. She remained silent. He cleared his throat again and continued, "You can slap me if you want to but I have to tell you this. You know I like you ….I mean I have been …… smitten by you. Ever since I laid my eyes on you I cannot think of anyone but you. I know that there's a considerable age difference between you and me ……… I was

married once until my wife died …… and I have two children from that marriage ……and you are so young and pretty ……. but if you are not against it, I would like to ……….. to come to your house to ask your father for ……. for your hand in marriage. I am an officer in the British army …… and I will take you to England and take good care of you."

He was proposing to her, she realized. She didn't know how to react. She hadn't expected it so soon. They had met only two days ago. She was scared, but at the same time she liked the idea of a mature man nervously stuttering in her presence, begging for her love. It gave her a sense of power. This is how women conquer, she thought – by capturing the hearts of men. She didn't know what her parents' reaction would be. She knew that they were anxious to marry her off, but he was almost twice as old as her.

"What's your answer?" He said after waiting nervously for a minute.
"I don't know," she replied, her voice quavering, "You'll have to ask my parents."
"But do you want me to come to your house?"
"I don't know," she replied.
"I've got houses in Dharan and Kathmandu. If you marry me I will take you to England. Trust me, I can give you a good life – a happy life," he blurted out in a single breadth. "Will you be happy if I come to your house with a proposal?"
"I don't know," she said again.
"Does it mean yes or no?" he persisted.
"I don't know," she replied.
"I'll take that as yes. I'll come in a month. If you don't want me to, then say no now," he said. She did not reply. She left him standing and walked back to her intrigued friends who looked at her inquiringly. Manju smiled at her conspiratorially

and said, "What is it between you and my uncle? What did he say to you?"

"Nothing," she replied, then added a moment later, "I'll tell you later." As the party started their journey back home, Amrita stole a quick glance back at Rajkumar. He was still standing where she had left him, watching her intently, with a barely perceptible smile on his face. In his eyes there was a silent appeal. *He's in love with me..... as I am with him,* she thought, and she liked the idea immensely. She thought of the dream she had two nights ago and blushed. She thought of him all the way back home.

Lieutenant Rajkumar was true to his word. He arrived in Khewang within a month with a delegation of the senior members of his clan. Amrita had not told anybody about him except to Manju and that too only after extracting a vow of secrecy from the latter. Since returning from Medibung her mind had been in turmoil, beset by contradictory thoughts. One day she was hopelessly in love and the next day she wasn't so sure. One day she would decide that he was too old for her and the very next day she would decide that age difference didn't really matter and becoming his wife would not be such a bad idea. Whatever the thoughts, he was constantly on her mind; not a single day passed by without her thinking of him.

The relentless storm in her mind tormented her day and night. It reflected in her moods that swung to the extremes every day, and aroused the suspicion of her sisters-in-law, mother and grandmother. But she remained tight-lipped.

Rajkumar didn't come straight to Amrita's house. He sent a feeler to test the water first, as they say it. The feeler was none other than Manju's mother. She was a coarse-skinned middle aged woman with an almost masculine voice who liked to decorate her face with gold ornaments of various shapes and sizes as Limbu women like to do. Kamala served her a bowl of *jand* (soup of fermented rice or millet). The elliptical gold pendant hanging down from the cartilage between her nostrils dipped into the liquor as she drank from the bowl but she was unperturbed. As with many women of her generation, this was a usual occurrence with her, whether drinking tea, water or alcohol. After exchanging the usual small talk and village gossip, she raised the topic of Amrita's marriage.

"Amrita has grown into a beautiful woman," she said, as a way of embarking on the topic of importance.

"Yes, she has," Kamala replied, "and so has your daughter. The two are almost the same age, aren't they?"

"They are just a few months apart, I believe. Don't you think it's time to marry her off?"

"Of course, I do," Kamala replied, "but there are no good suitors at the moment."

"Well, there is one actually, if you are interested."

"Is there? Who's he?"

"He is a relative of mine. He is in my house right now. If you are interested my husband will bring him and his folks to see you."

"I'll have to talk to Purna's father," Kamala said, "But what is he like? Is he a man of good character? Is he the right age for my daughter? Does he have enough assets to support my daughter?"

"He is a man of good character and very well off. He is in the British army and has houses in Kathmandu and Dharan. But there is a small problem." Manju's mother said hesitatingly.

"And what's that?" Kamala asked, alarmed.

When they say that there's a problem with the potential groom, it usually means five things: either the man is physically disabled, or already married, or divorced or widowed or destitute. There was no way she could give her daughter to such a man.

"He is much older than Amrita. Thirty-five, in fact. He is a lieutenant in the British army and a widower."
"A forty year old widower? It's out of the question. I can't give my daughter to a forty year old widower. What will the neighbours say? Won't they laugh at us?" Kamala protested.
"Thirty-five," said Manju's mother.
"It's the same. There's not much difference between thirty-five and forty."
"He is a lieutenant in the British army and he is rich. He has a house in Dharan, another in Kathmandu and plenty of land in the plain."
"I don't care. My daughter cannot marry a thirty-five year old widower with children. I won't hear of it." Kamala said.
"I wouldn't have come to you," Manju's mother added in a calculating tone, "had he and Amrita not already met and talked about it."
Then she related to the surprised woman everything that she had heard from her daughter. Kamala listened, open-jawed. But still, she was adamant that she wouldn't give her daughter to an older man.
But Manju's mother was a persistent woman. She begged and pleaded with Kamala to consider the proposal in good faith, and at length the latter gave in. Kamala told her that she'd talk to her husband about it and let him make the decision. After the woman left, she summoned Amrita to her presence and asked her about Rajkumar. Amrita did not deny having met the man and dancing the paddy dance with him.

"You didn't like that man, did you?" Kamala asked hoping to get a negative response, but her daughter remained silent. She repeated the question again and after a long pregnant pause Amrita replied with a self-conscious smile, "I don't know, mother. Do what you think is right, but please don't ask me. I don't want to talk about it."

Kamala was mystified by this puzzling response. *What's the matter with this girl?* She wondered. *I just can't understand her these days. How can she like a man twice her age?* That night she talked to Dil Bahadur who agreed that the man was too old for his young daughter. Besides, he was a widower with two children. But as the night deepened the two also agreed that it was high time Amrita got married and at nineteen it was getting rather late. People were already beginning to talk.

"Perhaps a proposal from an army officer, even if he is much older than our daughter, is better than no proposal at all," Dil Bahadur wondered aloud. "Many women are known to lead happy lives with older men. Why, my cousin Hitman's second wife is thirty years younger than him and she seems to be quite happy with him. In fact she has even given him two healthy sons."

"Do you think we should, you know, give it a try then, I mean just for the sake of it?" Kamala asked. She was not as vehemently opposed to the idea now as she was before. The solitude of the night has a sobering effect on people.
"Let's think it over again," Dil Bahadur replied. "If we reject this proposal outright, which we can do, Manju's parents will be displeased."

Two days later Manju's father led a group of men to Dil Bahadur's house. The latter had given the green light the previous day and was waiting for them. As it is not considered proper to make a marriage proposal without a 'go-between', Manju's father acted in that capacity. Behind him walked Rajkumar's eldest brother, who was Amrita's ex-beau Sharan's father. As the oldest man, he was the leader of the group. Amrita learnt this from Manju as the two peeped down from a vertical crack in the window. Manju had sneaked into her room half an hour before the arrival of the men. *How ironic it is*, Amrita wondered, *that the man who should have led his son's delegation was instead leading his younger brother's.* After the customary exchange of greetings, Manju's father introduced the two parties to each other. Then he explained the reason for their visit which of course everyone knew and was only a formality. While Laxmi served the men *rakshi* at the behest of her mother-in-law, they inquired after each other's family branches. After that the hosts and the guests returned to the real purpose of the visit.

Rajkumar's elder brother knew that he was treading on difficult ground. Therefore, he went about it with utmost care, doing his best not to offend the girl's parents.

"Now to dwell on the matter of importance," started the silver-haired old man of about sixty, "My younger brother here is an officer, a lieutenant, in the British army." He had two upper and one lower front teeth missing and the remaining were stained a dark-brown by smoke, and like Dil Bahadur he had a *khosela* neatly tucked above his ear. "He has a house in the city of Dharan and another in the capital Kathmandu. In addition to these, he has a few acres of land in the Terai not to mention many other moveable and immoveable assets. Unfortunately, he has no one to help him look after them and share his happiness and sorrow as his former wife tragically died of cancer. Poor woman, she was such a good wife and mother. They say that God always takes away the nicest person first."

Dil Bahadur listened intently, without uttering a single word. Purna sat quietly on a stool near his father. One of his oxen had stepped in a hole and acquired a nasty gash on its hind leg and his mind was preoccupied with that. He had applied some ointment on the wounded hoof and bandaged it with a piece of cloth but more needed to be done. The poor beast limped badly. He hoped it would recover before the arrival of the monsoon rains; otherwise he would be in trouble. Next to him sat Kamala, Narmaya, and younger brother Ratna. Laxmi and Lalita remained in the kitchen, and Amrita remained in her room with her friend Manju, nervously awaiting the outcome of the meeting.

The old man continued, "My brother had the good fortune to meet your daughter when she visited our village as a bridesmaid last month during one of my nephews' wedding, and had the opportunity to talk to her."
"They may have," Dil Bahadur said. "People meet and talk all the time."
"Yes. They have met," the old man continued, "and danced the paddy dance, and talked to each other. I daresay that they have already exchanged their hearts as well. Although my brother is much older than your daughter, he liked her instantly and also discovered that a marriage proposal would not be objectionable to her in spite of the age difference. Therefore, if I may be permitted to, I'd like to ask your daughter's hand in marriage for my brother in good faith. If my proposal has offended you in any way, then please forgive me."

Dil Bahadur didn't reply immediately. He thought for some time, cleared his throat and finally spoke. "Gentlemen," he said glancing at Rajkumar but addressing the latter's brother, "I have nothing against your brother. He seems to be a fine man. The only problem is the age difference. My daughter is not even twenty; only nineteen, in fact. And I have been told that your brother is about forty. Don't you think that will cause any problem in the future?"

"I am thirty-five," Rajkumar spoke for the first time.

Dil Bahadur said to him bluntly, "That's almost twice my daughter's age."

Rajkumar did not reply and looked uncertain.

"Nevertheless, considering all things we are open to the proposal," Dil Bahadur said and the other party looked relieved. He turned to Kamala and said, "Well, what do you say?"

"Well, I think it would be best to ask our daughter again. She's the one whose future is at stake." She replied.

"And what's your view?" Dil Bahadur turned to Purna. The latter sensed everybody's eyes fixed upon him and squirmed in discomfort. He made an act of clearing his throat and said, "I think that's the thing to do." *That damn hole had to be right in the middle of the path.*

"You're right," said Dil Bahadur. He turned to the old man and said, "Allow us to talk to our daughter. Young people these days have their own ideas and we must listen to them."

After a short pause he added, "Please give us some time to think things over. We'll give you our answer tomorrow. I hope there will be no ill feelings between us even if our answer is in the negative."

"Agreed," said Rajkumar's elder brother, "We are prepared to wait as long as it takes."

After Rajkumar and his group left, Dil Bahadur called Amrita and explained the situation to her. Amrita listened calmly. She already knew everything and the expression on her face did not betray the violent storm in her mind.

"Well, what do you say?" Dil Bahadur asked her.

Amrita didn't look directly him, or to anyone else. "I don't know," she said with downcast eyes.

"My daughter, are you prepared to become the wife of a thirty-five years old widower with two children?" Dil Bahadur asked again.

"I don't know, father," she replied.

"We want the truth, daughter," Kamala interjected, "Just say yes or no."

"It's for you do decide, father. I am your daughter and I will be happy with whatever you decide for me." Amrita replied.

"Does that mean your answer is yes?" Kamala said.

Amrita didn't reply. She stood quietly, fidgeting nervously.

"All right," Dil Bahadur said, "If we decide to marry you off to him, will you be happy?"

"Yes. No. I don't know," she replied, her cheeks turning crimson.

"Will you or will you not?" Dil Bahadur persisted.

"I'll be happy with whatever you decide for me," she replied and ran up the stairs to her room.

Dil Bahadur watched his daughter disappear through the door. He made no effort to call her back. He looked at the puzzled faces of the others and sighed, "It's funny, but I have a feeling that she is more than willing."

"I think so, too," replied Kamala, "If it is her wish then let it be so."

Afterwards, Lalita asked Amrita, "Why are you doing this, sister-in-law?"

"Doing what?" said Amrita.
"Consenting to marry a man twice your age," Lalita replied.
"I have not consented," the red-faced Amrita protested feebly. She knew it was a lie.
"Yes, you have. You gave the distinct impression to all present."
She blushed and looked away.
"Look at me, Amrita," Lalita said, "I, too, was married to an older man with children. My father forced me into it against my wish. People of older generation believe that marriage is only about social obligation. They forget that it is also about love. For a man and a woman to be happy together, there must be love. There was none in my marriage. I wasn't happy. Every day was like hell. You can only imagine what I went through. That's why when your brother came along I saw a glimmer of hope and took the chance. It was a gamble, but it was better than nothing at all. I risked everything to be with your brother and I have absolutely no regrets. I am happy though he is far away now. What makes you think you will be happy? How can you love a man almost twice your age?"
"He is nice and kind ….." Amrita replied.
"How do you know that?"
"I have had opportunities to talk to him," Amrita replied.
"Yes, but not more than two or three times. That's hardly sufficient time to know a man. All men talk sweet and act kind and seem considerate at first," Lalita replied, "But they cannot be easily trusted."
"You trusted my brother."
"That's different. We are the same age, and we saw each other for half a year before we spoke to each other. And when I fell in love with him, I knew that I could trust him."
"Sister-in-law, I too know that I can trust this man. You may not believe it, but somehow I know I can."
"You do?"

"Yes. Besides, I have always wanted to live in the city." Amrita said.
"You, too? That's news to me. I didn't know that," Lalita exclaimed, "I thought it was only your brother who had that dream. Like brother like sister."
"Yes, you can say that I am my second brother's sister. But that's not the only reason. There's also another reason."
"And what's that?"
"Rajkumar is Sharan's uncle." Amrita said.
"Sharan's uncle?" asked the greatly surprised Lalita, trying to grasp the significance of this revelation.
"Yes," retorted Amrita, "His own youngest uncle, his father's youngest brother."
"Then why are you doing this?" Lalita asked, still unable to understand.
"Can't you see? When I marry Rajkumar I will be Sharan's aunt, senior in relation to him. He will come to my house and call me 'aunty' and speak to me respectfully. Every time he sees me he will be reminded of his betrayal and he will forever be tormented in my presence. This is my little revenge on him. Destiny has given me this opportunity and I'll take full advantage of it. It was all predestined. Do you know, sister-in-law, that everything in life is predestined? Your first marriage was predestined, your falling in love with my brother was predestined, your marrying him was predestined, my being jilted by Sharan was predestined, and now this marriage between me and his uncle is predestined. Why, even this conversation between you and me is predestined."
"That's very superstitious; I doubt it goes as far as that," Lalita said, "I believe that we do have control over our lives. We have the capacity to mold our lives the way we want through the choices that we make. All we need is the courage and the will to do so."

"Sister-in-law, please don't mind my asking, but why did you not resist when your father forced you to marry against your wish?"
"I did resist. I resisted as much as I could. But I was young and naïve then and my arrogant father was obstinate. He wouldn't listen to a word I said. I had only two options before me - either marry him or throw myself off the cliff. I was afraid to die so I chose the first."
"See, sister-in-law, it proves that even the choices we make are predestined."
"How is that so?"
"Because it was your destiny to marry my second brother, that's why you were predestined to make the first choice."
"I still don't agree with your point of view," Lalita replied. "I fell in love with your brother of my own free will; and I eloped with him of my own free will. Destiny's got nothing to do with it. It was purely by choice."
"No, sister-in-law, everything happens because it's destined to happen – from one's birth to death and everything in-between." Amrita was adamant. Her belief in the hand of destiny was unshakeable.

Amrita, like the majority of her superstitious compatriots, was a child of fatalism. For her everything that happened in life was an act of destiny. It was not her fault that she looked at life that way. At home, at school and everywhere, she had been fed a constant diet of fatalism. She had grown up with the belief that nothing in one's life is under one's control – not even the choices that one makes. This belief is actively propagated by the greedy gurus and self-proclaimed living gods (Bhagawan) in neighbouring India and their ascetic-looking but vain and intellectually blank devotees. This fatalistic mindset has done immense harm to the Nepalese nation. It has irreversibly corrupted the minds of the people, both old and young, and rendered the whole society incapable of pursuing a productive lifestyle commensurate with the modern world. Thus Nepal, in spite of being rich in natural resources, remains one of the poorest nations in the world.

The next day Dil Bahadur sent his answer to Rajkumar's elder brother. Shortly afterwards the immensely relieved future groom's party came back with the customary two bottles of *raksi* to confirm their intention, which was accepted in good faith by the hosts. Then the 'guests' and 'hosts', as they called each other, sat down to discuss the wedding date and other details, such as the gift the prospective groom has to give his prospective bride as a testimony of his good intention. Kamala asked her future son-in-law for four *tolas* of gold (a *tola* is about 11.66 grams) for her daughter. Rajkumar did better than that. He took out a small velvet sachet containing eight tolas of twenty-four carat hallmark gold and happily handed it his future bride. He also gave her some beautifully-patterned and brightly-coloured saris and blouses, a pair of very expensive looking white sandals and a velvet-coloured make-over kit. He had brought all of these from England. Then he went back to his village to make preparation for the wedding.

Two weeks later, Lieutenant Rajkumar arrived accompanied by his best man and a group of smartly attired young men. After a simple farewell ceremony, Dil Bahadur carried his daughter on his back out of the house and handed her over to the groom's party. Amrita wore a red bridal sari and a matching blouse, and her face and arms were adorned with gold ornaments and makeover. She looked so beautiful that Rajkumar couldn't keep his eyes off her. Thus, Amrita left for her wedding, which was to take place at the groom's house according to Limbu custom. Half a dozen bridesmaids, including her best friend Manju, accompanied her. As she turned back to take a look at the house where she was born and where she had spent all of her young life, she found herself unable to stop the tears that blocked her sight. She wiped them off with a handkerchief and covered her face with the loose end of her sari. She left with a mixed feeling of profound sadness at having to leave the home of her birth for good and in anticipation of a new life with her husband. Her parents did not accompany her, though her brother Purna did along with some other men (all cousins). Strange as it may seem to others, Limbu custom dictates that the father and mother of the bride must not witness the wedding ceremony of their daughter.

They reached their destination late in the afternoon the following day. That night the bride and her bridesmaid were treated to a sumptuous dinner with liberal amounts of rice, pork, mutton curry and vegetables on the menu. Some young bridesmaid even partook of *raksi* and *tongba* at the insistence of the hosts. Several amorous young men came to flirt with the giggling girls, some of who were only too happy to have so much male attention showered upon them.

The elaborate wedding ceremony began early the following day. After the morning meal the bride and her bridesmaids were taken to a relative's house a short distance away. This is known as 'hiding the bride'. It is a custom no doubt derived from the marriage practice of the old days when Limbu men and women married mostly by elopement and on the day of the wedding a house belonging to a relative of the groom substituted for the bride's maiden home. There the bridesmaids proceeded to decorate the bride with facial makeover and an assortment of gold ornaments – dangling earrings on both earlobes, a disc-shaped nose-ring on the left side of her nose, a beaded chain with a heart-shaped locket around her neck, bracelets and brightly coloured bangles on her wrists, a ring on her finger and a crescent-moon-shaped ornament on her forehead. She wore an expensive-looking ornamented bright red designer sari with a matching red blouse that Rajkumar had bought in an Indian shop in Kathmandu.

Just before noon the groom came to fetch his bride with a procession. He was immaculately dressed in a dark suit (which he had brought from England) and a pair of dark designer sunglasses. After living so many years abroad, it was his desire to mix the modern with the traditional. On his previous wedding he had worn the traditional Nepali attire - *daura* (a long tight-fitting shirt with two pairs of laces instead of buttons) and *suruwal* (a tight-fitting pocket-less long pant that's fastened by a lace instead of a belt) again, and a black coat. When the marriage procession arrived, Amrita came out into the courtyard surrounded by her bridesmaids. Bedecked in jewellery and makeover, she looked the embodiment of feminine beauty and Rajkumar gasped audibly. He couldn't take his eyes off her and had to be nudged out of his dream-like state by his best man. Then he applied red *tika* on her forehead with his right hand and she bowed down to touch his feet. After that she was handed a flower garland which she put around his neck.

Then she was carried in a palanquin to the groom's house. When the procession reached its destination, the people waiting there welcomed the bride and groom with a shower of curd and rice. At the main door, which was brightly decorated with fresh flowers and crepe papers, the older members of the groom's family took turns to put tika on the her forehead and welcome her with words of blessing. Instead of the usual band of *Damaais*, who traditionally take a respite from tailoring to double as the musical band during the weddings, Rajkumar had a 750 watt Japanese cassette player fitted with amplifiers that boomed continuously with the beat of modern Nepali pop songs.

Later in the day, the whole village arrived for the feast. There was plain white rice, yellow spiced rice, pork curry, mutton curry and buff curry on the menu, and *raksi*, *tongba* and *jand* flowed freely until well into the night. The guests came in their best clothes with presents for the bride and groom, and gave the couple their blessings. *May you have a successful conjugal life! May the gods never separate you two! May the gods keep you happy! May you have many beautiful children!* The usual stuff.

The most important part of the wedding ceremony began after dinner at night. A large room had been selected and prepared in advance. A wooden post was erected in the middle of the room to serve as the altar and the floor around it was covered with fresh banana leave. Two water jars, each festooned with flowers, two oil lamps on leaf-plates, a flower garland, red lead powder, and pieces of fried pork among many other things were spread on top of the leaves. The priest instructed the groom and the bride to sit cross-legged beside each other, with the groom on the right and the bride on the left. He then instructed the groom to place his right thigh on top of the bride's left thigh, and his left palm on the bride's right palm. The groom's best man was instructed to sit on the groom's left side and one of the bridesmaids to sit on the bride's right side with instructions to assist the bride and groom in the course of the ritual. Then the priest placed a long white shawl on the back of both the groom and bride. When the couple was thus seated – Rajkumar with a smiling face and Amrita bowed down with her face covered by a flimsy red shawl - the priest began the ceremony in earnest. He chanted a lengthy incantation in the Limbu language, his melodious voice rising and falling, rising and falling, from a whispery low to a pitched high and then back, sometimes intelligible and mostly unintelligible, sometime audible and sometimes inaudible. In the course of the ritual he sacrificed a pair of chickens in the couple's name (a rooster for the groom and a hen for the bride), and sprayed the blood on the altar. He carefully examined the blood and declared that the couple's conjugal life would be successful and long lasting.

Near the end the priest declared that marriage is a union of not only two bodies but also of two souls; therefore, the couple should strive to love, respect and support each other to make the union successful. He then asked the groom and bride to take a vow to remain faithful to each other, to co-operate with each other and to bring forth offsprings to continue their lineage, which they happily did. After that the priest turned to the men and women present in the room and asking them to bear witness he queried the mother of the groom (the father had died sometime back) whether she was prepared to behave properly towards her daughter-in-law and maintain a sincere, cordial and affectionate relationship with the young woman. Rajkumar's mother, a craggy-face, myopic-eyed, stooped–backed woman of eighty gave an affirmative answer with a complacent smile. She was happy that her widowed son was married again.

The priest then placed a rupee coin on the banana leaf and asked the groom and bride to press the coin with their fingers and take a vow of conjugal fidelity, which they did promptly. With this he declared them husband and wife.

"In the old days," a silver-haired, craggy-faced old man reminded the others, "this was done by beating a shiny white pebble three times with a knife to produce sparks. After declaring them husband and wife, the priest would then declare that the couple would be considered divorced if the wife hit her husband's head with the white stone if she was not treated properly by him and his family."

The priest then invoked all the gods and goddesses, the sun, the moon, the sky, the earth, fire, water and all other natural forces (for Limbus are animists in essence) to bear witness to the union, and asked the supreme goddess *Tagera Ningwaphuma* to bless the couple with a successful conjugal life and abundant children to continue their bloodline. Then at the behest of the priest Rajkumar picked up red lead powder from a leaf-plate with his fingers and sprinkled it at the parting of Amrita's hair at the middle of the forehead – a custom no doubt borrowed from the Hindus in the recent past. After that both husband and wife stood up. Amrita placed a flower garland around Rajkumar's neck and bent down to touch his feet. With this the wedding rites were over. It was almost midnight.

The newly married couple slept on separate beds that night for a Limbu couple does not share the bed on the first night of wedding. Early next morning Amrita took charge of the kitchen to prepare food for the family and the guests. This is known as the 'bride's feast'. It's a test for the new bride. It provides her with an opportunity to demonstrate her dexterity in the kitchen. Since Amrita had grown up helping in the kitchen, she passed the test easily and some of the guests praised her cooking generously. Rajkumar beamed with pride. "Would I have chosen her if she wasn't good?" he said with a happy smile.

Now back to mythology once again, because among the many stories recited by the priest as part of the wedding ceremony the following is worth a mention. During the time of the Eight Wise Ones (who were grandsons of the unfortunate Tall Hunter by his incestuous children), a lady of wealth became so impressed by the eldest of the brothers that she promised to give him her little daughter in marriage. But when the girl grew up and learnt that she was to be married to a man much older than herself, she objected to the union vehemently. She complained bitterly that he was too old and uncultured and was incompatible to her. But her mother was adamant so to spite her mother she ran away in search of a better husband. First she went north and asked the king of the northern lands to marry him. The king, who knew about her, refused on the ground that he was not powerful enough to offend the Eight Wise Ones. Then she went to the king of the southern lands, but he too declined on the same ground. Then she went to the east and west, and both kings refused on the same ground. The Eight Wise Ones were too powerful to antagonise. Finally, she returned to her own land and asked each of the Eight Wise Ones, except the eldest to whom she had been betrothed, to marry her. But they all refused. Finally, she decided that the one she had despised as old and uncultured was in fact the most suitable husband for her because he was the wisest and bravest of all. When she finally approached him, he forgave all her mistakes and accepted her as his wife. They sired many children and lived happily.

A week after the wedding Amrita returned to her maiden home with her husband. The couple was accompanied by a small retinue of porters. As is customary, she brought as gift a whole pig – slaughtered, shaved, cleaned, boiled and painted yellow with paste of turmeric powder and decorated with flowers – and bottles of *rakshi* among many other things. Every Limbu parent in the village expects this gift from his/her newly married daughter and son-in-law. Rajkumar placed a rupee coin at the feet of each senior member of the family as a token of respect, which was duly accepted with words of blessings. Amrita looked the epitome of happiness; it was as plain as day to everyone that she was deeply in love with her husband, and people did not fail to remark upon that. When her close friends teased her about her sex life, she told them that it was great without going into the details.

In the days following the wedding Rajkumar told Amrita everything about his life, which his young wife found fascinating. He was a good talker and when he began talking Amrita listened to him awestruck, with a twinkle in her eyes. She absolutely adored him. He told her about his dead wife whose colour photograph (taken somewhere in England) he still carried in his purse. *That would have to go in the future*, Amrita decided silently. She couldn't help being jealous. "Poor woman, she suffered terribly until death finally took her away from me. What didn't I do to save her? I did everything I could. She was such a lively woman when I married her, full of life and vigour, just like you. But by the time she died she had turned into a withered flower. It makes me sad to think of her." Upon hearing this Amrita couldn't help but sympathise with him, though a part of her felt jealous at the feeling that Rajkumar still seemed to harbour for his dead wife.

He told her how as a starry-eyed teenager he had journeyed to the British camp in the city of Dharan to enlist in the British army. "In those days, the road had not reached these hills. One had to walk uphill and downhill for about a week, always following the south-westerly course of the Tamor River, taking shelter at any house that one reached before sunset. In those days people were trusting and welcoming, and finding shelter was not difficult. Nobody trusts strangers these days. Now the road has come right up to my village, but I no longer live here."

He told her about his life in the army. "The best thing about joining the British army is that I got an opportunity to see the world and also to make some money. I have been to Hong Kong, the UK, America, Canada and Australia to name but a few places, which is no mean feat for a high school dropout from the hills of Nepal. Many of my colleagues could not even read and write when they enlisted. They had never seen the inside of a classroom until they joined the army. But now all of them can read and write, and speak a smattering of English."

He told her about Hong Kong where he had started his military career but which had ceased to be a British colony since 1997. "It's a very large, very modern city of high-rise buildings. Until the handover to Red China in 1997, we guarded the territories' borders. We stared at the Red Chinese soldier across the border with our fingers ready on the trigger and the enemy did the same from his position on the opposite side. But our real job was to catch the desperate refugees who tried to sneak in from all directions. Some even swam across the sea; that's a measure of how desperate they were to escape communist rule. When we caught them, and there were many, they were sent back to the mainland. We felt sorry for them, but there was nothing we could do. One mustn't mix one's duty with one's emotion. We heard that they were shot. Sometimes half-starved Vietnamese refugees would try to sneak in on their rickety boats and we detained them, too. Some of the Vietnamese girls were breathtakingly beautiful."

He told her about the exotic places he had been to. "In the rainforest of Belize, which is a small country in Central America, there are flies that lay their eggs on your skin. The locals are immune from the pest but outsiders like us aren't. The boil itches so terribly that one feels like scratching the damn thing out. When on exercise in the dense rainforest we used to cut out the writhing larva out of the boil with our knives."

He told her about the Falklands war of which she had heard from other soldiers. "The place is so cold, barren, isolated and desolate that it's a wonder why the British even cared to fight for it. I was a young soldier then. I believe you were just born then. The weeklong voyage from England on the cold sea was nauseating. Being hill men we Gurkhas are not fond of the sea. We didn't see much fighting, though. When we made an assault on a hill called Mt. Williams that the Argentines were holding, the enemy didn't even put up a decent fight which was rather disappointing. They abandoned their weapons and ammunitions and fled. But there is one incident I can never forget. In the dark of the night one can actually see bullets flying. One night we came face to face with the enemy. They were a few hundred meters away from us. One of them fired a tracer bullet in our direction and our Gurkha officer shouted, "Boys, Look, Look!" We all ducked down to hide as he had instructed, of course, in Nepali. But the tall British officer who was with us didn't know a word of Nepali and stretched to his full height to take a better look. And as we watched in utter fascination the bullet flew straight at him and went right through his body knocking him down. But luckily the man didn't die. We later heard that he fully recovered in a hospital."

He also told her about the soldiers' garrulous Philipino girlfriends (who sometimes ended up as their lawfully wedded wives) in Hong Kong and Brunei and the chirpy English girls (who didn't) in England. He told her how the soldiers showered their girlfriends with money and gifts in exchange for "well, you know, sex". He also told her of the sexual prowess of a Gurkha soldier stationed in England in the Eighties who had sex with a prostitute eleven times in a single night.

During his four-day stay Rajkumar, the new son-in-law, was treated regally. Neighbours and relatives asked the couple to dinner every night. This was nothing new to Rajkumar as he'd gone through the same before, but it thrilled Amrita infinitely to become the centre of so much attention. As the couple prepared to leave early on the fifth day, Dil Bahadur gave the age-old advice to his new son-in-law:

"Son-in-law, what can I say to you? You yourself are wiser and more knowledgeable than me. Nevertheless, I have some advice for you handed down to me from my forefathers. I hope you will take them in good spirit. Now that we have submitted our daughter, who is as dear to us as our own lives, in your care we expect you to take good care of her and keep her happy for the rest of her life. We brought her into this world and brought her up in the best possible way we could. She is a piece of our heart and it grieves us to let her go so far away from us. But we must accept the law of nature. This is how human societies operate. This is what daughters are born for. And this is what they are prepared for all their childhood because it is a daughter's destiny to leave her birthplace and make home somewhere else. If you mistreat or harm or kill her then we can take no action against you but you will become a sinner in the eyes of the God and suffer in the afterlife. If you love her and keep her in comfort and happiness, then God will be happy and your path to paradise will be clear."

Amrita was given a tearful farewell. It would be many years before she would come back for a visit, if she ever did. "Don't forget us. Write to us from time to time," a tearful Kamala said as she hugged her departing daughter.
"I'll be back," Amrita said with teary eyes, "I will come back to see you all after three years. I promise I will."
"Amrita, remember your poor sister-in-law sometimes," Laxmi said as she hugged her sister-in-law.
"You will always be in my thoughts and in my heart, sister-in-law," Amrita cried. She said the same to Lalita.

Those remaining behind watched them sadly, waving their hands until the couple and the porters turned into minute dots in the horizon. After spending two days in Medibung, they caught a bus from there to Dharan where they planned to spend a month. Then they planned to spend a month in Kathmandu before flying to the UK on a special flight chartered by the British army for vacationing servicemen and their families.

It was the year 1996 AD (Nepali year 2053 Bikram Sambat). In Kathmandu, the ineffective leftist minority government formed after the general elections had collapsed, and a more ineffective coalition government with the largest cabinet in the country's history (to appease the various interested parties) had come to power. The cabinet was aptly dubbed the 'jumbo cabinet' by the ever-critical media. Quite understandably, the Nepalese people were beginning to feel disenchanted with the democratic process which had failed to deliver the much expected fruit at the hands of inept, selfish and corrupt politicians who were unable to give the country a proper sense of direction.

Then in a little hamlet in a remote corner of mid-western Nepal, a small group of extremist communists calling themselves Maoists after China's Mao Ze Dong declared 'people's war' with the expressed intent to overthrow the monarchy along with the democratically elected government and install a communist dictatorship in its place. The outfit was led by a small group of ultra-leftist intellectuals who saw Deng Xiao Ping's economic reforms in neighbouring China as a betrayal to the communist cause. These firebrand politicians had previously participated in the electoral process and met with dismal results. Now they were determined to do through violent mean what they had failed to do by peaceful means – grab absolute power in the name of people.

This little incident was dismissed as a non-event by the incumbent coalition government. All but a handful of diehard supporters of the rebels gave it any significance. Most Nepalese were not even become aware that such an incident had taken place. And no one, not even the rebels themselves, expected it to grow into a political and military juggernaut in such a short period of time and sweep the entire rural areas in its terrifying wake.

Part I II
Depth of Sorrow

Three months after Amrita's departure, her friend Manju got herself pregnant by the young and amorous school teacher she had been infatuated with. As he was a Bahun from a distant village, she had no option but to elope with him. She knew that her fiercely proud father would never agree to an inter-racial union. Neither would her lover's family, who being Bahuns consider themselves above all other races, but apparently that was a risk the lovers had been prepared to take. The Limbus are a very proud people, sometimes to their own detriment. The conceited Bahuns think that they are above all other races according to their archaic caste hierarchy, but the equally conceited Limbus think quite differently. They think that the Bahuns are beneath them because they know that not very far back in the past their forefathers were the sole masters of these hills, and most of the Bahuns and Chhetris had arrived as destitute migrants and were magnanimously accommodated by them.

"My daughter has cut off my nose," Manju's father lamented to all who cared to listen to him. A Nepali's chest swells when he is proud and his nose gets cut off when he is in shame. As always the older generation was vehemently opposed to the union. But some expressed the view that as long as it wasn't with the 'low caste' there was not much wrong with inter-racial marriage. The younger men and women expressed the view that race and caste did not matter in these enlightened times. They were of the opinion that all human beings are born equal and the same red blood flows in their veins regardless of caste, race and creed.

A month later there was another scandal in the village. Milan's friend Hari, the one who had had the misfortune to be beaten up by policemen six years earlier, eloped with his own elder brother's wife to the plains. Apparently, he had carried out an illicit sexual relationship with his elder sister-in-law in his brother's extended absence and made her pregnant. Although this kind of incident is not uncommon, the villagers were aghast. "How could he do that to his own brother?" People wondered. "It's the adulterous bitch's fault," some declared, "She could not wait for her husband for even a year." Most of them were quick to find fault in the woman. "Men are men, they do it naturally, but women should be more careful," they said.

While the village was abuzz with these two back to back scandals, a shattered young man trudged wearily back home unannounced one evening. He looked dark, emaciated haggard and broken. His arrival did not go unnoticed because nothing goes unobserved in the village.

After uttering a few words of greeting to his bewildered parents and wife, Milan made straight for his room saying, "I am very tired now. Let me have a good sleep." He threw himself on the bed without changing and immediately fell asleep and slept like a log. Lalita followed him and sat by his side gazing at his gaunt face. It had been days since he had last shaved the hair on his face. The hard life of physical labour had made him leaner, thinner and darker. He looked more mature and worldly-wise. He seemed like a stranger - no longer the same man who had left home two years earlier. This man lying asleep on the bed was not the same carefree and vigorous young man she had fallen in love with. He was a different man - a tired and beaten man, a man who had been through the grind-wheels of life, a man who had suffered much, and a man whose hopes and dreams had shattered. But she was happy to have him back. He may have changed, but he was her man - her Milan. She gazed at his face lovingly for a long time, kissed him on his lips and went back to the kitchen.

Milan said very little the next day. When asked why he had returned so suddenly, he gave a short and laconic reply, "I was caught by the police and sent back home." His face lit up when he saw his daughters. He spent the whole day with the little girls. He held them in his arms, threw them up and down in the air, and showered them with kisses. "My lovely little daughters, I am back," he said, "I am back to be with you, and I'll never leave you again." The girls didn't recognize their father and were hesitant at first but when they realized who he was they squealed in delight and jumped on his back and shoulders.

When the couple made love that night after the little girls had fallen asleep, she felt a number of long marks on his back. When she inquired about them, he replied that he had once slipped on a wet floor and fallen on his back on top of some iron rods. She believed him and inquired no further.

A week after arriving home, Milan was ready to tell his story. "I didn't tell you the truth in my letters, because I knew that you would have taken it badly. I wasn't working as a driver like I wrote to you. The agent who took us to Malaysia had arranged a three months' tourist visa for us, and when I asked him about it he told me that we'd be given a new visa along with work permit once we landed at the airport in Kuala Lumpur, which is the capital of Malaysia. Of course, that never happened. Instead, he took us to a rundown hotel and left us there. I was in a mind to return at once, but my friends said that since we had already thrown so much money down the drain, it would be better to remain there and find work to recoup the money and also to save face. That seemed quite reasonable to me. We were lucky enough to meet a Nepali man who found us work at a plantation near Kuala Lumpur. The city is big, beautiful, very modern and very rich. I wish we could make our country like that. After working there for six months, we met another Nepali who said that there was better pay and living conditions in a textile factory in the south and with his help we moved there. The factory was in a place called Johor in the southern part of the country near Singapore. There were half a dozen of us Nepalese but most of our co-workers were Indians, Bangladeshis and Indonesians. It was a hard life of labour. Just think of it, I had never done any menial job before. Here I was my own master; there I was someone's servant. We had to work from early morning till late in the evening. On top of that many of us were illegal workers without work permit, I being among them."

He paused for a sip of *tongba*, which Lalita had prepared for him. Since returning home, she had served him the alcoholic drink twice every day – afternoon and evening. *Tongba* is bad for those with high blood pressure and good for those who want to add a little weight. "I mustn't go on like this. It keeps me drunk all day," he had complained to her earlier that day. But Lalita had replied lovingly, "You must have it everyday until you get better. You are so thin and weak. This will help you regain your health."

He continued, "We had to make ourselves inconspicuous at all times because the Malaysian police regularly conducted raids to net illegal foreigners. Our living quarters were cramped and uncomfortable; we lived eight men to a small room. Despite the hardship we were doing all right, thinking of our home and future. Almost every week we heard news of other illegal foreign workers, mostly Indonesians, being caught and sent back home, and we were scared. But by being careful we managed to elude the police."

He paused again for a sip of *tongba*. "We would have remained undetected. But then a month ago a group of Indians broke into a local man's house and stole a television and a VCD player."
"I know what a television is, but what is that other thing?" Narmaya asked.
"It's a thing to play films on television, grandma. You've never seen it. We were unaware of this incident. But the next day it made a lot of splash in the local newspapers and there was a public uproar. Then after a few days one of the accursed idiots was caught, and it seems that besides spilling the beans he also told the police that there were many illegal foreign workers. The police conducted surprise raids in every factory, plantation and workplace in that area. We were tipped off in advance and hid in the nearby forest. But it was no use. Five of us were caught. Our visa had expired a long time back and we had no work permit. They handcuffed us and took us to a police station. There we were interrogated and moved to another place where they locked us up. The sadistic jail wardens beat us up, sometimes with baton and sometimes with rattan. After holding us for a month, they marched us to the airport in handcuffs and sent us back with nothing except the clothes we were wearing."

He stopped and calmly unbuttoned his shirt. "Look at my back," he said and turned to reveal several elongated marks running randomly across the length of his back.
"My son, you have suffered so much. Why didn't you come back sooner?" Kamala said with wet eyes.
"I had a dream, mother," he said sadly. "That helped me to endure the hardship. But I have nothing left now. Nothing,

except that dream! No money to show for my hard labour. The little saving I had was confiscated by the police."

"Don't lose hope, my son," Kamala said, "You haven't lost anything. You have us – your father, mother, wife and children. We are your family. And we have our land which yields sufficient harvest to feed us. All is not lost yet."

"Yes, your mother is right." Dil Bahadur added, "We are happy that you have come back in one piece. That's the main thing."

"It's all the work of destiny," remarked Narmaya. "You were fated to suffer in a foreign land so far away from home. That's why you had to go there."

"You may be right, grandmother," Milan replied, "but it's not only my fate to suffer like that. It is the fate of thousands and thousands of young men and women born in this impoverished land. The only way for them to escape from the never-ending cycle of poverty is to go abroad, and even there they are not secure. They get beaten, tortured and insulted in the jails of Thailand and Malaysia. They lose their hands and legs in the factories of Korea and Taiwan. They get harassed, abused and murdered in the deserts of Arabia. And nobody cares for them. Their plight doesn't even get a cursory mention in the international news media. Not only the poor, but even the educated are not insulated from this fate. Why? Because while the rest of the world has moved on, we are still stuck in the medieval age. Do you know it is actually easier to endure the physical beating than the insults they throw at you? The former only hurts your body but the latter hurts your heart and your pride."

Narmaya didn't understand half of his angry outburst. The others nodded their heads silently in agreement.

"I am so happy that you have come back alive and in one piece," Narmaya repeated what Dil Bahadur had said earlier. "I am getting old and I was beginning to be afraid that I'd die without seeing you ever again. I feel death creeping up on me more acutely since the day Amrita left. I am afraid I'll never get to see her again. Poor girl! She loved me so much."

"She will come back, grandmother," Milan consoled her. "You'll get to see her again."

Narmaya said, "You will not go away again, will you?"

"No, grandma, I will not. I am through with this stupid dream of mine. In a foreign land you are nothing but a slave. You have no right and no social standing there. You have to work from dawn to dusk and put your life at the mercy of snobbish foreigners who look down upon you. Some of them treat you like vermins. Here, I may not be rich but I am my own master. There is nobody to order me around, nobody to look down upon me with disdainful eyes, nobody to insult my race and country, nobody to rebuke me for trivial mistakes, and nobody to push me around or threaten to fire me. I am a free citizen of a free country."

Milan quickly recovered from his ordeal and settled down to a quiet life, helping his father and older brother. This time he felt more comfortable doing so. For the first time in two years he found peace of mind. But he knew that the feeling of bliss was temporary; it would not last. He knew that he would become restless once again because notwithstanding the ordeal he had been through his eyes were still firmly fixed on the city. *One day I am going back to the city. I don't know how and when, but I am definitely going back.* He had seen the world or at least a part of it, and this remote little village in a corner of the hills was too small for his ambition. *There is a demon inside of me. It's in recess now, but sooner or later it will rise to the surface once again. It will not be let me remain in peace.* Most days he tried not to think. It made him happy.

When he was born there were no roads and electricity in the village. There were still no roads and electricity in the village. In fact, there was little, if any, hope of road and electricity ever arriving. The story, sadly, is the same for every part of the country. The lot of the long-suffering Nepali people never improves because the apathetic politicians and corrupt bureaucrats in Kathmandu think only of lining their own pockets while giving unending lip-service to nationalism and patriotism.

To think of it, the Nepalese people have always been at the mercy of corrupt and apathetic governments. Until the middle of the twentieth century, there was no concept of economic development. Before Junga Bahadur seized power the King used the state treasury for his own end and distributed large tracts of land to courtiers and soldiers to ensure their support. After he seized power, the country fell further into the Dark Age. One hundred and four years of autocratic Rana family rule (from 1846 until 1950) proved ruinous for the country. The hereditary Rana prime minister ruled the country as his personal fiefdom. The national treasury became his personal property, to be dispensed at his pleasure for his personal ends. He distributed vast tracts of lands to his family members and army of sycophants, thus reducing the country to virtual serfdom. The legal code introduced by Junga Bahadur further helped to institutionalize the inhuman caste system and social division, and marginalize the indigenous people and the so-called 'untouchables'. While the Ranas built magnificent neo-classical palaces for themselves, they did nothing for the benefit of the people. And while the rest of the world marched on into the modern age, Nepal remained closed to the rest of the world. It required an armed rebellion by the Nepali Congress and defection by King Tribhuvan along with the entire royal family to New Delhi to finally bring the autocrats to their knees.

But the path to freedom and democracy doesn't lie easy anywhere in the world. It is fraught with danger around every corner. Freedom has many enemies and they come in many different guises. Some come as nationalists, some as traditionalists, some as religious fundamentalists and some as communists. And paradoxically, many of them are found among those who profess to believe in freedom and human rights. One thing, however, is true. Most of those who are against freedom have vested self-interest. The well-meaning and much-loved King Tribhuvan died an exasperated man after four years of experiment with chaotic parliamentary democracy. His son King Mahendra, who was only fourteen years younger than his august father, had even less patience with the political parties that had sprouted like mushrooms since the fall of the Ranas. The Nepali Congress won the general elections held in 1958 and formed the first democratically elected government with BP Koirala, Nepal's foremost freedom fighter, as the prime minister. But in 1960, just a year and half after the formation of the government, the ambitious king seized power in a bloodless coup and imprisoned and exiled all political leaders. He banned the political parties and imposed his own brand of 'dictated democracy' called party-less Panchayat (Council) System with a unicameral parliament made entirely of his handpicked sycophants. With this he effectively set the clock back. The main mantra of the day was 'nationalism'. But a misguided sense of patriotism does more harm to the country than good. This system of governance, which was in effect a cover for the King's autocratic rule (it is no secret that the autocratic King

Mahendra loved the feel of power in his hand) with the national assembly as his rubber stamp, lasted for thirty long years until Mahendra's well-intentioned son King Birendra was forced to restore democracy in 1990.

The party-less Panchayat System turned out to be another catastrophe for the Nepali people. While it can be given the credit for being able to maintain peace and order - but what is peace without progress? If humans had only wanted peace then they'd still be living in caves - the country's economy went down the drain. Even with a flood of foreign aid the economic condition of the people failed to rise. Material poverty brings spiritual poverty, which in turn brings about general breakdown of public discipline. Corruption became rampant from the lowest to the highest level in the government. Development funds were grossly misappropriated and the culprits were never punished. Civil servants refused to lift a finger without bribe. Even the common man in the street wantonly damaged or destroyed public property without any sense of guilt. Thus when public telephone booths were placed at street corners, they were immediately vandalized and the sets and cables stolen. Public buses had their seats slit with razor blades or torn to shreds for no apparent reason. Streetlights were made the target of hand-thrown projectiles and subways were quickly turned into stinking lavatories.

The system proved even more catastrophic for the indigenous people. Under the aggressive Hindu nationalist agenda of successive Panchayat governments, the already weakened indigenous people lost much of their land, language and culture, and above all their self-respect. They were forbidden to organize, and to read and write in their own language. Any community wishing to protect its cultural identity was viewed with suspicion and hostility by the government, and such an act was branded 'anti-national activity', while Hindu culture, idea and philosophy were promoted aggressively. Thus, in the ancient land eked out by the sweat and blood of their forefathers, the indigenous people, collectively known as the *'matwalis'* (alcohol drinkers), were rendered insignificant, powerless, voiceless and connectionless - to be used, abused and manipulated at will by the Aryan rulers. They had no 'source and force' (a popular Nepali English euphemism) in the government that was indifferent to their plight. And with the conversion and integration of these people into the so called 'mainstream' Hindu culture, the victory was complete. Never would these people be able to rise again to challenge the position of the ruling Aryan Hindus.

Thus, they became victims of political marginalization, actively pursued in the past by the governments in Kathmandu. Although the so-called *Matwalis* (alcohol drinkers) constitute about half the country's total population, they have a negligible presence in the government bureaucracy and upper rungs of the major political parties. This is by no historical accident; it's the end result of deliberate political marginalization. As a result they do not have any real say in the governance of their country, nor are their voices ever heard. They are among the voiceless people of the world.

Their silent cry goes unheard because they are unable to speak up for themselves. They cannot speak up because centuries of political and cultural suppression have rendered them incapable of speaking up. The very fact that a majority of them are not even aware of this gross injustice speaks volumes. When they do speak up, as the educated among them are starting to do lately, their voices of dissent are curtly dismissed as the whines of losers. When the formulators of the democratic constitution declared Nepal a Hindu state at the instigation of right-wing Hindu fanatics in Nepal and India, the voiceless people largely remained silent. Most of them had no idea what was happening, and even if they had known, the significance of the event would have been lost on them.

Although Aryan Hindus had arrived in Kathmandu valley and established their petty kingdom as far back as two millennia ago, they arrived in significantly large numbers in the outer hills only after the twelfth century AD. Unable to repel the tide of invasion by Muslim warriors from central and western Asia (Islam was the most modern and forward-looking creed of that time), the staunchly Hindu Brahman priests and Kshetriya warriors fled to the hills of western Nepal as refugees. There these politically astute migrants overwhelmed the simple and naïve indigenous people by their sheer number and cunning. Slowly the stronger and shrewder among them carved out their own petty kingdoms and assimilated the ethnic people into their religion and culture, placing the latter much below themselves in their caste system which was alien to the hills until their arrival.

The *voiceless* people did not rebel against these new masters of the hills. At least there is no written historical record of that. On the contrary, they began to ape the new masters of the hills. The Magars of the western and mid-western hills readily adopted Hindu customs and practices with the hope of elevating their newly acquired lowly position in the Hindu caste hierarchy. The Gurungs of the mid-western hills stopped eating pork for the same reason (high-caste Hindus do not touch a pig, dead or alive, for fear of losing their *caste*). They didn't even let out a squeak when later Hindu rulers forcibly forbade them to eat beef. Thus the subjugated people adopted the customs and practices of the conquerors. But this strategy apparently hasn't been of much help to them, for in the eyes and minds of the conceited Bahuns and Chhetris they are still at the bottom of the social ladder - only a step or two higher than the so-called 'untouchables'.

The Sherpas of the higher hills are the only ethnic group untouched, as yet, by this Hindu cultural invasion. This explains why they have a more vibrant culture, and are economically more successful than the others. Unlike the high-caste Hindus whose sole aim in life, it seems, is to live off the labour of others; those untouched by Hinduism still have their work ethics intact. The attitude of the high caste Hindus towards work can be summed up as follows: *Work is shameful. It is only for servants, not for masters. It's only the stupid and the uneducated who work; clever people do not have to work.* Sadly, and this is true, the Limbus, Rais, Magars and Gurungs and others have also adopted the same attitude towards work.

Narmaya was at peace with herself. She had arrived at an age when one can be self-indulgent with impunity, secure in the knowledge that her material needs will be taken care of by her children and grand-children, and happy that her responsibilities are over and the only thing left to do is to enjoy life while awaiting death which will surely come. She had been to places few other village women of her generation had had the opportunity to. She had descended to the plain twice to live with her second son but after having lived there for about half a year each she had declared that the place was too hot for her comfort and she didn't like the mosquitoes singing to her every night. Then she had flown on a Twin Otter to Kathmandu to live with the family of her *lahooray* son. And what an experience it had been! As the small 20-seater airplane had taken off she had shut her eyes and held on tightly to the seat in front of her and prayed for dear life until, halfway to the destination, she had suddenly begun to enjoy the ride. She had returned after half a year complaining that the city was too crowded and congested for her taste. She had concluded that she couldn't live in a place where one didn't know one's next door neighbour and where one couldn't walk freely without the danger of being run over by a motor vehicle. Upon returning to the village she had firmly declared that this was where she belonged and this was where she intended to breathe her last.

Every morning she lazed in the sun, sitting on a straw mat with her grandchildren and great-grandchildren. Sometimes she helped the younger women peel dry maize seeds, beans and potatoes, to husk the rice, wheat, barley and millet, and to sort out and clean vegetables. Sometimes she helped to feed the cattle, goats and pigs. Some days she visited her neighbours and relatives to catch up on the latest village gossip, and always returned home slightly inebriated. In the evening she sat in the kitchen with a jar of *tongba* until sleep overcame her. And when she was in the mood, she told her grandchildren, in whom she always found more than willing ears, of the good old days that seemed so distant now. At such times her mind was filled with nostalgic thoughts of people long dead and their escapades, and of ghosts, witches and evil spirits that roamed the hills and made people's lives difficult and interesting at the same time.

"How can you tell a woman is a witch, grandma?" Her youngest granddaughter Gorimaya asked as they sat by the wavering light of the kerosene lamp in the kitchen one night. Gorimaya, who was eight, was listening to her grandma's tales of the old days with rapt attention, and Ratna was doing his homework under the flickering light of another kerosene lamp which cast a long shadow of his Chinese fountain pen on his book.

"You have to look at her tongue, because they say that a witch has a black spot on her tongue," she replied.

"Have you seen any woman with a black mark on her tongue, grandma?" the girl asked again.

"No," replied the grandmother, "But I have known people who have. In my maiden village a long time ago, when I was a little girl like you, there was an old widow who was said to have a black spot on her tongue. She was poor and childless. People said that she had 'eaten' her husband. Witches eat the hearts of men, mostly their husbands because that's the easiest, and they gather at a secluded place under the moonlight and dance naked around a tree. They are able to change into black cats and back into human form any time they like."

Narmaya paused for half a moment trying to recall the myths of her childhood. She believed every one of them to be true. Ratna, her youngest grandson who was by now a hotheaded adolescent of fourteen, put away his books and moved closer to her, pricking up his ears.

"What happened to the old woman, grandma?" He asked impassively.

"A short distance from our house lived our neighbours. They had been complaining of being harassed by a witch for some time. One morning we heard that they had caught a witch in a basket and we ran to see it. The whole neighbourhood had gathered there. The witch was inside a bamboo-cane basket and on closer inspection I realized that it was the same poor old woman. She was cowering in fear; her sad and frightened eyes filled with tears. Although she was a witch, I couldn't help feeling pity on her."

"How did they catch the poor old woman, grandma?" asked Ratna, "Did they simply accuse her of witchcraft and grab her or was she caught red-handed?"

"They said that a black cat had been visiting their house at night for some time, and that night they snared the cat and imprisoned it inside the basket. When they looked in the morning, there was the old woman instead of the cat."

"That couldn't have been true," interrupted Ratna skeptically. "Such things do not happen, grandma."

"Why can't it be true, older brother?" his innocent little sister chirped, "There are ghosts and witches everywhere."

"There may be, but I don't believe that the cat transformed into the old woman overnight. The truth is that they picked on her because she was poor and helpless. It was an act of grave injustice and extreme cruelty. This is how the poor and helpless are victimised in our society."

"But I saw her with my own eyes," his grandmother protested.

"But you did not see the cat transform into the old woman, did you, grandma?" he asked her.

"No, I didn't. But why would they lie?"

"There could have been many reasons, grandma; reasons you could not have understood at such a young age. People always victimize the poor, the weak and the helpless for one reason or another. It could have been to usurp her land and house. Such things happen all the time in our country. My teacher says that there is too much injustice in our society, grandma. He says that's why the poor and oppressed people are now rising up against injustice all over the country. He knows such things, he is a communist," Ratna said with a touch of anger in his voice which was, of course, not directed against his grandma.

"I don't know," sighed the old woman, "I am too old to understand such things. All I know is that she was a wicked old witch and they said that she deserved to be punished."

"Did you take a look at her tongue, grandma? Was there really a black spot on it?" Ratna asked.

"Yes, tell us grandma, was there a black spot on her tongue?" Gorimaya added out of curiosity. She wanted to know if the woman was really a witch.

"Yes, I think I did but I can't remember with clarity, but everybody said afterwards that there was a small black mark on it and that she was definitely a witch."

"What did they do to the poor old woman after that, grandma?" Ratna wanted to know.

"They beat her up, made her eat bits of faeces and marked her hand with a red hot iron rod. Then they let her go warning her never to harass anyone again. I believe she died a month after that."

"Poor woman, she was an innocent victim of a cruel and unjust society," Ratna spat out angrily, "I wonder how many helpless women have suffered her fate in this country."

Outside, the dark silhouettes of the trees and bamboo groves stood tall, shadowy and foreboding in the moonlight. Except for the intermittent chirp of crickets, everything was quiet and still. At night people try to avoid bamboo groves because they are said to be inhabited by wicked ghosts and evil spirits who take pleasure in frightening passersby out of their wits. Sometimes bamboo stems are said to make ghastly creaking noises and bend down to touch the ground of their own accord to block the path of wayfarers. But this doesn't deter the villagers from going about their business when they have to. The business of living takes precedence over the fear of the supernatural.

Presently, the unmistakable sound of the rhythmic beat of a witchdoctor's goat-skin drum came from a distance – 'dang-dang, dang-dang, dang-dang' – piercing the still of the night.

"Whose house is that drumbeat coming from? Is somebody ill?" Narmaya asked of her grandson.

"It's from Lal Bahadur's house. His young son has been taken ill since this afternoon. Something has happened to him, but they say that he was struck by the spirit of the forest when he went into the woods in the morning to collect firewood," replied Ratna.

"Sometimes when you go into the forest the spirit of the forest strikes you," said his grandmother, firm in her belief.

"But he wasn't struck by any evil spirit, grandma. There are no such things in the forest. People become sick because they are infected by invisible germs or because they have problems inside their body. Only a doctor can cure them with his medicines, grandma"

"You may be right. But when you are struck by an evil spirit then only the witchdoctor can cure you," said his grandmother. "Ghosts and spirits are everywhere. When people meet with untimely death, like in accidents, pregnancy and suicide, their unsatisfied and discontented souls turn into evil spirits and haunt the living. When I was young, there was a boy in my village. He was a strong lad with no physical problems, and then one day after coming back from the forest he suddenly complained of pain in his abdomen. The witchdoctor chanted his mantra and beat his drum all night, while the sick boy clutched his stomach and cried in pain. Finally, by morning the boy stopped whining and he was dead. All the elders of the village said that the spirit was too powerful for the witchdoctor to subdue," said Narmaya.

"Poor fellow, he died because it wasn't a disease that a witchdoctor can cure. My teacher says that this happens when one's appendix swells and bursts, but people blame the spirits in ignorance," Ratna said.

"What's an appendix?" Gorimaya asked.
"It's a part of our stomach," Ratna wasn't too sure either.
"I don't know about that. But everybody said that he was struck by the spirit of the forest. You do not believe in such things, but I have seen it happen with my own eyes," the old woman was adamant.

Ratna gave up trying to convince her. It was futile to argue with his grandmother. Her belief in superstitions and the supernatural was unshakeable, like a rock, and at the age of fourteen he was not too sure of his own beliefs either. At home and everywhere he was fed a daily diet of superstitions, while at school his teachers, the young ones among them, taught him otherwise. They taught him of the world outside that had moved hundreds of years ahead into the future while his own languished doggedly in the past. They taught him how social injustice, inequality, nepotism and corruption had pervaded every section of the society and made it hollow from inside. They taught him of the need to rise up to rid the country of these ills. They taught him of the need to bring drastic changes to the society, through violence, if the need arose. But here was his grandmother who had an unshakeable belief in superstitions. He knew that his father and mother were not much different from her.

To change the topic he said, "Tell us about the *syokpa*, grandma." Syokpa is the mythical hairy man of the mountains.

As always, the old woman was eager to relate the story that the children had heard tens of times. But they never tired of hearing it.

"*Syokpa* was the hairy man of the mountains. He walked on two legs like us humans but he was much taller and bigger and his whole body was covered with a thick layer of hair. He lived high up in the mountains and occasionally descended to the lower hills in search for food. There was once a lonely cowherd who lived alone in his cowshed with his buffaloes high up in the hills where the air is always cold and grass plentiful. Every night after dinner he made a fire and sat near it with outstretched arms to warm himself. Every night he heard the blood-curdling howl of the syokpa and became afraid. Then one day a syokpa walked into his shed without any warning. The frightened cowherd sat still with his eyes fixed on the terrifying creature. But the fearsome creature did not attack him. It came and sat by the fire opposite him and stared back at him. It sat until after midnight and then quietly got up and disappeared into the black night. From that day the syokpa made it a habit to visit the frightened cowherd and sit by the fireside. Although the beast did not appear to threaten him, the boy could not trust it with his life. He dared not fall asleep in the presence of the beast for fear that it might kill and devour him."

"As the days passed, the syokpa started to mimic the boy. Whatever the boy did, the frightful creature did the same. If the boy touched his head, the creature touched its head as well. If the boy stretched his hand, the creature did the same. This frightened the cowherd even more. One day he thought up an idea to get rid of the beast. He prepared two cups of butter, one for himself and one for the syokpa. When the animal arrived as usual, the boy began to apply the butter on his body, slowly – taking care to rub it liberally on his face, hair, arms, legs and torso. The syokpa did the same. Then when he was ready, the boy picked up a piece of flaming firewood and brought it near his face. The syokpa did the same. As the boy had intended the animal's hair caught fire and quickly spread all over its body. Letting out a series of blood-curdling howls the animal ran out into the black night. From that day it never visited the boy again."

"Are there any *syokpas* these days, grandma?" Gorimaya asked in a frightened voice. The tale of the hairy beast never failed to fascinate and frighten her.

"I don't know," the old woman replied, "I don't know. But when I was a small girl like you, we heard strange howls from the forest high up in the hills and the elders said it was a syokpa."

"There aren't any syokpas, grandma. They exist only in myths and folklores. These days people know it by its Sherpa name. They call it the *Yeti*," Ratna said.

Just then Milan arrived to take some hot water. Narmaya said to him, "I see very little of you these days."

"I am busy with the upcoming 'vote', grandma. I am helping grand-uncle in his campaign."

"When is the 'vote'?"

"Two months from now," he replied, "You are going to caste your vote, aren't you, grandma?"

"No," she replied, "I can't separate one symbol from another. In the last election, I went to vote for your grand-uncle and only after coming home did I realize my mistake." The old woman laughed aloud heartily. "He'd told me that his election symbol was the lantern, but I had mistakenly put my thumb-print on the bucket. They looked the same to my weak eyes."

With an amused chuckle Milan said, "When I was in school my teacher told us that when the first general elections were held many years ago, the villagers were confused by the English word 'vote' because it is pronounced exactly as the Nepali word for Tibet, and when the cadres of the contesting political parties went to the villages asking for their vote the

bewildered villagers retorted, "Bhot? How can we give you Bhot? It belongs to the Bhotays (Tibetans), not to us." Everybody laughed.
"What party is he in?" Narmaya asked.
"He is an independent," Milan replied.
"What's that?"
"It means he is not with any party, grandma."
"I don't understand the world these days. Life was so much simpler when I didn't have to vote. Whenever 'vote' comes I worry that there will be violence."
"But there hasn't been any violence in our village, grandma."
"No, there hasn't. But didn't someone get killed in Sinam in the last 'vote'?"
"Yes, but Sinam is different. It's a much bigger place than ours. It has a bigger population and the people there are much more politically active. It won't happen here."

The rhythmic beat of the drum continued to pierce the silence of the night. Declaring that she was feeling sleepy, Narmaya pushed the jar of tongba aside, stood up with an effort, coughing a few times in the process, and prepared to go to bed. She told her grandchildren to do the same. Presently, from outside came the 'twoo-hoot' of an owl. It was repeated three more times, and instead of barking the dog let out a long melancholy howl and the other dogs in the neighbourhood followed suit.

Narmaya said, "Did you hear that? Some one is going die. Someone always dies when the owl hoots near the house like that. And on top of that it is a bad omen when dogs howl like that. Milan, go outside and silence the dog."
"Nothing will happen, grandma. These are all superstitions. The owl is probably looking for a mate, and the dog is lonely," Milan said, but went out to silence the dog anyway.

"You youngsters of today do not believe in any thing," the old woman complained.
"I do believe, grandma. I do believe that the sick boy was struck by the spirit of the forest," Gorimaya said.
"I hope he will not die. I hope death will take me away, instead," Narmaya said with a faraway look in her eyes.
"Why you, grandma? Why not that sick boy?" asked Gorimaya.

"Because the boy is young; I am very old. It's about time I died; that's the only thing left for me. The old must make way for the young. I have lived long enough and I have seen many things. I am like the old sun sinking behind the hills and you are like the new sun rising above the hills."

As she made her way out of the kitchen to the stairs leading up to her room, she suddenly tripped on a low wooden stool near the door and stumbled, crying out in pain. Ratna quickly jumped to her side and tried to pull her up saying, "Grandma, are you hurt? You should have been more careful." He examined her arms and legs to make sure that no bones were broken. "Poor grandma, it must be very painful," Gorimaya said as she supported the fallen old woman in her arms. Narmaya tried to rise on her feet but an excruciating pain ran through her leg and she sank back whimpering in pain, "I think my leg is broken. Someone must have cursed me. Who can that accursed person be?"

Hearing sudden cries of pain and alarm, Milan, who was on his way back to his room, came back running. He saw his grandmother lying on the floor. After Ratna related to him what had happened, he gently picked her up and carried her to her room. The others followed quietly. He laid her on her bed and caressed her leg gently for some time.

"Sleep, grandma," he said, "I hope your bone has not broken. If it has then we'll know for sure tomorrow because then it will swell."

Gorimaya took over the task from him and caressed her grandmother's legs until the old woman fell asleep.

The next morning, Narmaya's skinny and wrinkled leg was swollen tight halfway between her knee and ankle, a sure sign that she had broken a bone. Purna, who came to know of the mishap in the morning, tied the broken leg with a thick layer of cloth. Kamala called the priest (witchdoctor), but Milan protested.

"Grandma's leg is broken, mother. There's nothing a witchdoctor can do about it. We'll have to take her to the hospital," he said. Purna agreed with him, though he would have preferred to give his grandmother the traditional home treatment – a thick layer of nettle paste and bamboo straps. That very day the two brothers carried their grandmother on a bamboo-cane basket to the district hospital in Taplejung Bazaar, a day's walk away.

The plaster was taken off after three months, poor old Narmaya was incapacitated for a long time and although she was able walk, she never fully recovered. For six months after the accident she had to be carried out into the sun every morning and then back into the house again as the sun shone brighter as the day got warmer. Her grandsons took turns to do that.

The sick boy for whom the witchdoctor had beaten his drum didn't die. He survived the night and fully recovered in a few days. When Narmaya got to hear of it she said triumphantly to her skeptic grandsons, "See! What did I tell you? You youngsters of today do not have faith, but the witchdoctor has cured the boy, hasn't he?"

Ratna didn't counter that claim. He knew that no matter how much he tried, he would never be able to change his grandmother's mind because her belief was so strong and deep-rooted that it could not be shaken by mere words. Besides, hadn't she declared that it was a bad omen for an owl to hoot near one's house at night, and immediately afterwards she had broken her leg? He knew that it was the little things like this that made sense to her.

In the hills of Nepal demons, ghosts and witches still rule the human psyche. They are an integral part of the local culture, and the older generation, and even a sizeable section of the new generation, is superstitious to the core. They trust the witchdoctor completely and view the medical doctor with skepticism. Even in the towns and bazaars where doctors are available, they seek the help of both the witchdoctor and the medical doctor at the same time, and when the sick person gets cured the witchdoctor is the first to get the credit. The medical doctor only gets only a grudging acknowledgement. This is just an example of the social afflictions that stubbornly refuse to let go of their stranglehold and help to keep the Nepalese people backward.

Seven months after the departure of Amrita, and a month after Narmaya had broken her leg, a young soldier on leave arrived at the doorsteps carrying a large parcel. It was from Amrita. In it were presents for the whole family – expensive looking and fragrant-smelling saris and blouses for the women, shirts and T-shirts for the men, and dresses for the children. During these seven months she had written to her parents exactly four times. This time around, along with the letter to her parents, she had written a letter to Laxmi to the unmitigated delight of the recipient.

With lines of happiness etched across her cheeks, her dark eyes twinkling and her face glowing with happiness for once, Laxmi read the letter effusively to her husband that afternoon while he sat on the bed grinning from ear to ear, seeing her so happy. He loved it when his wife smiled and laughed, and it had been quite a while since she had last done that with such vigour. He thought she looked lovely.

"Dearest elder sister-in-law, Sweet, sweet remembrance from your loving younger sister-in-law!" Laxmi read. "My husband Rajkumar and I are in good health by the blessings of the almighty gods and goddesses. I hope they are also keeping you in good health. First of all, let me apologize for not writing to you earlier. Please forgive me. I have been meaning to write to you for a long time, but I hope you understand how hectic my life has been since I left Khewang. It seems such a long time ago and I miss you so much."

She stopped to take a breath and continued, "We arrived in the UK safe and sound. This land of the *gora* (white man) is alien to a Nepali village girl like me, and I have a lot of learning to do. England is very beautiful country; the cities are big, modern and clean, and the countryside is refreshingly green. The only problem is the weather. It drizzles quite often here. They say that winter is exceedingly cold and wet, but I have yet to face it. I'll tell you more in my next letter."

Laxmi stopped and remarked, "How lucky she is! We can only dream of such wonderful places."

Purna smiled and said, "To each one's own *karma*. It was not in your *karma* to see such wonderful places; otherwise you'd have married a *lahooray* like her."
"I didn't mean it that way," Laxmi protested.
"I know," Purna replied with a smile.

She continued to read: "Now let me tell you what happened in Dharan. A week after we reached Dharan, we paid a visit to my aunty. As she had already learned that I had married an officer in the British army, she was very nice and polite to me and even deferential. When I went without my husband on subsequent visits, she herself raised the topic and apologized to me profusely laying the blame squarely on my poor cousin Suraj and his friend Sharan. She lied so blatantly that it made me squirm in shame. She said that it was Suraj who had first suggested the match and Sharan had liked her daughter so much that he had visited her house everyday to pursue her. She said that had Suraj told them about me and Sharan, they wouldn't have given him their daughter. How could she lie to me so shamelessly? Did she think that I am a bloody fool? Did she think that I am a simpleton who she can manipulate at will? I had a mind to say a few nasty things to her, but resisted the temptation. She is, after all, my aunt - my father's own sister. But I hold no grudge against her anymore. She was, after all, a mere instrument of fate. I am very happy with Rajkumar. He is an ideal husband for me."

Laxmi stopped again and remarked, "Amrita has found happiness with her husband. Many people thought it unlikely considering the age gap between them."
"Age doesn't make much difference if two people are of the same mind," Purna added, "Why, our uncle Tika is twenty-five years older than his wife and they are living happily together."

Laxmi continued reading, "Needless to say, I also met my cousin-sister Anita whom I had never seen before. She still lives with her parents while her husband is away. Anita is very fair and pretty, with shoulder-length hair, thin as a pencil, and very sweet, too, not at all like what I had imagined her to be. She is the opposite of her scheming mother and seemed to be quite naïve, too. Now I honestly believe that she played no part in her mother's plot. She came to our house many times and showed me around in Dharan. We went shopping together, visited the temples of Budha Subba, Dantakali and Pindeshwori, and went to the cinema to see Hindi and Nepali films. By the time we left for Kathmandu she and I had become good friends. She has a son – a cute little boy of two. By the way, I believe you already know that I am also with a child."

Here Laxmi stopped and said, "How lucky she is! They say that when God starts giving, he doesn't just give in small quantities; he actually pours the stuff through the roof. It must be true."
"It is true. And someday, the gods and goddesses will start giving us, too." Purna said.
"When? When are they going to start giving us?"
"Be patient. We are still young and there is still plenty of time."
"But I am tired of waiting, and so are our parents and neighbours."
"I can understand why our parents are anxious, but as for the others, it's none of their business," Purna said.

Laxmi turned her attention back to the letter. "Now you may be wondering whether I have met Sharan. The answer is yes. When I arrived in England I found out from my husband that his nephew Sharan was also there at the same place. Since he is a young soldier of low rank he hasn't got a 'family permit'. A few days after we arrived, he came to visit us. And believe me, it was amusing. He couldn't look me straight in the eye, and sat stiff and erect on the sofa like the young soldier that he is. You see, he has to talk deferentially to me not only because I am his aunt, but also because my husband is an officer and he is only a soldier, a Lance Corporal in fact, which is much lower in rank. I don't understand much about these army people. These days he calls me aunty. He speaks very little to me and tries to avoid me. Actually, he can also call me elder sister-in-law from his wife's side if he likes to. Now you may be wondering if I have any feelings for him. The answer is No. I am older and wiser now, and Rajkumar is a much better man than him in every way."

"So she's finally got what she wanted." Laxmi remarked with a chuckle.
"What did she want?" Purna asked her.
"Revenge," Laxmi replied.
"How is that?" He asked again.
"Sharan has to call her aunt and speak deferentially to her now." She replied.
"It must be very awkward him to do so," Purna remarked.
"That's the point. And that's for the rest of his life, too."

She resumed reading. "Our third uncle lives in a place called Chichester quite far from here. I can't even properly pronounce these English names; they are so tongue-twisting. And all the *goras* (white people) look the same to me. This place we live is called Chatham. I haven't met him yet, but he has phoned me a few times. He is coming to visit us sometime next week. Rajkumar knows him well because they are both officers. Uncle told me that aunty and children are coming to England to live with him in about three months. When they arrive, we plan to visit them. Aunty was very nice to us in Kathmandu."

Laxmi stopped to take a short break again. "I hope you liked the stuffs that I have sent you. They are not much, but I'll try to send more next time. Please write to me from time to time. Sometimes I feel terribly homesick living among strangers so far away from home, especially when Rajkumar is away on exercises. I hope my brothers are in good health. Please give them my love and regards. May the gods and goddesses bless you always and keep you healthy and happy, and give you a child this year. And please don't forget to convey my love to younger sister-in-law Lalita. Tell her I miss her and I'll write to her next time. Also, please don't forget to give my love to my darling nieces. I hope to see them when I come back in three years.

Your loving sister-in-law Amrita."

"That was some letter," Laxmi said with a happy smile.
"Yes, quite some letter."
"What must it feel like to live in such a wonderful place so far away from home?"
"That's something you'll never know," Purna remarked with a smile, himself wondering what it would be like.
"I am very happy for her," Laxmi said, "She is so nice to me, like my own sister."
"Yes," Purna said.
"Not all sisters-in-law are nice. Some of them are downright nasty. Like my childhood friend Phulmaya's sisters-in-law who were scheming bitches. She used to cry her heart out every time she came to visit her parents. She didn't want to go back because her sisters-in-law and mother-in-law made her life hell. It was so sad." Laxmi said.

"Did you notice that she calls her husband by his first name?" Purna remarked.
"Many young women do these days," Laxmi replied.
"But you do not," Purna teased her.
"I am not that modern. If I start now I'll feel terribly uncomfortable. Besides, I don't think our parents would look kindly at that," she replied.
"Times have changed and the older generation must accept the changes, whether they like it or not," Purna replied, with a line he had borrowed from Milan. "Milan and sister-in-law call each other by their first names. I see no problem with that and I haven't heard father and mother object."
"But I have heard some other people make nasty remarks against Lalita," Laxmi said.
"Some people would remark upon anything," Purna's said.
"Wait, that's not the end. There's some more on the back page," Laxmi said.

She continued reading, "At the end she has written: PS: Oh, I almost forgot to tell you, sister-in-law. When I was in Kathmandu, I learnt that there are doctors called sexologists who can apparently help childless women to conceive. I think you should go to Kathmandu with my elder brother to seek help, if you don't mind my saying so. I am prepared to help you financially."

Both husband and wife fell into a brooding silence. The first and foremost duty of a wife, according to the conventional thoughts, is to produce children, an endeavour in which Laxmi had failed so far. Every day, she silently cursed her 'broken fate', as she called it, and quietly shed voluminous tears of frustration in the depth of the night. She didn't know that in his state of half-sleep Purna sometimes heard her anguished sighs and silently prayed for her. And because of his love for her, he steadfastly refused to consider the *'other option'* shown to him. *As long as Laxmi lives - and I pray that she will live until the ripe old age and will outlive me - I will not consider second marriage. Never!* He was resolute in that.

"We could go to Kathmandu, you know," Laxmi said after an extended silence.
"We could, but where's the money?" He said. "Doctors are very expensive and we don't have that kind of money."
"Amrita says that she is willing to help."
"I can't take money from my sister." He replied.
"She can loan it to us?" She said hopefully.
"Sure she can. But when will we ever be able to pay her back?"
"Then you can get yourself another wife," she half-sulked.
"That's out of the question," he said seriously, "But let me think."
"Think about what?"
"About going to Kathmandu," he replied. "If that will make you happy, then I'll certainly give it a thought. But don't ask me to take money from my sister."

Laxmi didn't push him any further. She knew that his pride prevented him from taking financial help from his sister. In spite of his inborn humility, Purna was, when it came to that, a proud man.

A few days later, Laxmi sat down with a pen and paper to write a reply to Amrita. She wrote:

'Dearest Amrita,

Sweet, sweet remembrance from your unlucky sister-in-law. Thank you very much for your letter.'

Then she stopped and thought for a long time. "It's been such a long time since I last wrote a letter," she muttered.
"Do you know how to write a letter?" she asked her husband.
"I have never written a letter," Purna replied matter-of-factly.

A month later, the day of the nationwide local level elections arrived. Like every other village in the country, the village of Khewang was preparing to elect officials to the village development committee, and every nook and corner of the hills was abuzz with party politics. There were heated debates at the schools, post offices, teashops and resting places. Following the restoration of parliamentary democracy in 1990, the country had split vertically along three main political lines – the democrats under the flag (four large white stars on a red background) of the centrist Nepali Congress, the various communists under the red flag (a white hammer and sickle on a red background) of the mainstream Nepal Communist Party (United Marxist Leninist) and the remnants of the old regime under the red-and-blue flag of the rightist National Democratic Party. Each party claimed that it was the most patriotic, and accused the others of being stooges of one or the other foreign powers – namely China and India, and sometimes the West. The matter was further complicated by the fission within each of the contesting parties since the last mid-term elections in 1995. This political division had bitterly divided many families, with the father supporting one party and his son actively campaigning for another, some with tragic consequences.

On the day of the election Purna woke up early in the morning and went about his work as usual. After a cup of black tea he sat down to weave a bamboo-cane basket, whistling his favourite tune. He was a quintessential example of the voiceless people. He didn't care for politics. He had no idea what he stood for and what he stood against. He did not have any views on any topic other than his own farm and animals. In short, he was blissfully unaware of his rights as a free citizen of a newly democratic nation. And he had no way of knowing that on this fateful day politics was about to define his life.

Milan left early for the school where the polling station for the area had been set up. For the past couple of months, he had been campaigning for his youngest grand-uncle Jit Bahadur, who was standing for the post of ward chairman (a village is made of several wards), as an independent candidate. This was the second time for the old man. He had stood and lost in the previous election, and blamed his failure on the ambiguous election symbol he had been given at the time – a lantern. This time he had asked for and got a rooster. "Nobody can possibly mistake a rooster for anything, not even my myopic-eyed elder sister-in-law," he had declared. At one time a sympathizer of the little known secessionist Limbuan Liberation Front, the old man firmly believed that the indigenous people of the country should unite behind a party that would represent their interest. There was actually a political party that claimed to represent all the indigenous people led by a maverick Magar politician. But citing lack of popular support the election commission had refused to recognize it as a national party. Jit Bahadur was a firm supporter of the idea put forth by a prominent Nepali intellectual that the country should be government along a federal structure, with each geographical area governed by the majority ethnic group indigenous to that area. Thus the Limbus would have their *Limbuan*, the Rais their *Khambuwan*, the Magars their *Magarat*, the Gurungs their *Tamuwan* and so on. This arrangement would help to decentralize power and empower the indigenous people, and bring about true democracy because democracy is about empowering the people. Milan agreed with his grand-uncle. In Kathmandu he had seen and felt how utterly inconsequential and powerless the ethnic people of Mongoloid stock were.

Before leaving Milan said to his older brother, "Elder brother, make sure that you come to the polling station in the afternoon. We must vote for our youngest grand-uncle."
Purna nodded his head and said, "Don't worry, I'll be there."
"And don't forget to bring father, mother, elder sister-in-law and Lalita," Milan said.
"I won't forget," Purna replied laconically, without looking at his brother, and continued to work.

A short time after Milan had left, Ratna quietly slipped out of the house to go to another polling station. Purna saw the boy but didn't call out to him as he seemed to be in a great hurry. Although Ratna was not old enough to vote, he meant to do just that. He was an ardent supporter of the communists and was volunteering for them on the sly. He had urged his sisters-in-law to vote for the communists because "They are the only ones who stand for the poor and oppressed masses." Recently there had been rumours that some young men had joined the Maoists and were secretly planning to disrupt the elections, encouraged by the growing success of the armed rebellion in the dirt-poor mid-western hills. There was a cousin of his who talked of armed revolt but didn't admit to being a Maoist. There were two other young men who spoke in the same manner. And there was his firebrand teacher who filled and fired up his imagination with talks of a '*violent revolution to overthrow the semi-feudal system*'. Thus at a very young and impressionable age he had arrived at the conclusion that the *dictatorship of the proletariat* was the only way forward for the country, and was secretly toying with the idea of leaving home to join the rebel outfit. But much more than communist philosophy (of which his young mind understood very little anyway), he had been drawn by the romance of becoming a heroic guerilla fighter - with a loaded rifle in his hand and the power that comes with it. After all, according to his teacher, his hero Mao Ze Dong had once said, "Political power comes from the barrel of the gun."

That morning Purna's mind was, for once, on politics or what little he understood of it. He was muttering to himself: "Everybody is begging for vote, the Congress, the Communists and everybody else. People who don't bother to greet you at other times come to your house, join their palms ingratiatingly, flash their tobacco-stained teeth and ask for vote. Once they get elected they do nothing. They go to the center and earn loads of money for themselves."

Laxmi arrived with a bundle of green grass. She put down the grass, wiped the sweat off her forehead with the tip of her draper and asked, "What's the matter? Why are you muttering to yourself?"
"Nothing," he replied.
"When are we going to the polling station?" she asked.
"In the afternoon," he replied laconically.
"Who are we going to vote for this time beside grand-uncle?"
"We must vote for our grand-uncle for ward chairman. As for the other seats do what you like."
"But I doubt whether he has any chance of winning."
"I don't think he has. But we've got to vote for him anyway."
"Do you think there will be trouble? People say that the Maoists have been calling for a boycott."
"Let people do what they like. I don't care," Purna replied.

That afternoon all adult members of the family walked to the polling station, except for Narmaya who, though she wanted so much to vote for her brother-in-law Jit Bahadur, had to remain at home because of her broken leg. There was a sizeable crowd at the polling station, and the place had acquired the ambience of an annual village fair minus the hawkers advertising their wares. Along the way, flags of various political parties fluttered proudly in the wind - the most numerous being the red flag of the communists. This was hardly surprising as the eastern hills of Nepal had a reputation for being the stronghold of the communists who called it their 'Red Fort'.

As they neared the school, cadres and volunteers of different political parties accosted them, literally begging for votes on behalf of their respective candidates. Dil Bahadur and Purna politely assured each of them that they'd vote for their candidate. Milan was waiting for them with Jit Bahadur and his other supporters. "I had almost given up hope that you people would come," said Jit Bahadur with a wide grin of relief on his face.
"How can we forget, uncle? We'd have come even if there had been an earthquake." Dil Bahadur reassured him.

After they cast their votes (getting the usual indelible ink mark on the tip of their index fingers lest they return to vote again) they started to make their way back home. Before leaving, Kamala told Milan to return home as soon as the voting was over.
"Did you find the rooster?" Dil Bahadur asked his wife and daughters-in-law as he led the way way along the edge of a terrace.
"Yes," replied Kamala, "but I nearly didn't see it at first. It was almost at the bottom."

"This reminds of me of my poor mother," Dil Bahadur said with a smile, "She'd wanted so much to vote for her brother-in-law. If only her leg weren't broken."

They had not reached very far when they heard several shrill, angry shouts and what sounded like slogans from the direction of the polling station. Greatly alarmed, they turned back to take a look. People were running about excitedly, some of them shouting, "They are trying to capture the booth. Stop them!"
"What's happening? Has a fight broken out?" Kamala asked nervously.
"It looks like it has," replied Purna stretching to take a better look.
"It seems somebody's trying to capture the voting booth," Dil Bahadur added.
"Why would anyone want to capture the voting booth?" Kamala asked.
"To prevent the supporters of other parties from casting their votes, I suppose," he replied, "It is not uncommon in our country."
"I am worried," Kamala said anxiously, "Milan might be in the middle of the fight. He might get hurt. Purna, go and bring your younger brother back."
Without answering her, Purna ran back to the polling station and disappeared into the melee.

As the shouts grew shriller and angrier Dil Bahadur said to his wife, "Stop worrying! The boys will be all right. Let's go home. It's not wise for women and children to stay here. That rowdy bunch will start throwing rocks and projectiles any minute. You might get hurt." Dil Bahadur led wife and daughters-in-law home.

At the polling station, angry and excited supporters of the two feuding sides – Congress and Communists – were in the middle of a heated verbal exchange, furiously flinging invectives and accusations at each other. Each side accused of the other of trying to capture the booth and of being unpatriotic. The Communists accused the Nepali Congress supporters of being India's stooges and selling the country's rivers to India (a reference to a past treaty made with the neighbouring giant during a Nepali Congress government to harness the river waters, deemed by many Nepalese to be grossly unfair to Nepal and advantageous to India). The Nepali Congress supporters on the other hand accused the communists of being China's stooges and of aspiring to impose the failed totalitarian communist system in the country. No political debate in Nepal can be complete without dragging the names of the two neighbours into it. It's a part and parcel of being sandwiched between two giants.

When Purna pushed his way into the hornet's nest, he did not find Milan there. Instead, on both sides of the political divide, shouting at each other furiously, he saw his friends, cousins and uncles – all low-rung workers and volunteers of their respective political parties. Deciding that he had no business to be in the middle of a political quarrel, he decided to push his way out of the crowd. As he was about to do so, a fisticuff suddenly broke out near him. Before he had time to fully grasp the situation, a young man was bleeding from his mouth – his front tooth had apparently become loose – and another young man had his shirt torn with all the upper buttons missing. Instinctively, Purna decided to separate the two combatants as they prepared to exchange more blows. But to his dismay he saw that several fights had broken out all around him, and more angry men were pouring in to join in. The place quickly turned into a battle field.

As Purna was in the middle of the brawl, he couldn't help being pushed and punched inadvertently. So instead of trying to play the peacemaker, he thought it wise to escape and started to push his way out frantically, but suddenly a punch landed on the back of his head and he staggered. He never found out who had landed that punch on him. At that very instant a man suddenly pulled out a dagger from his pocket and collided with him. The six inch long blade sank deep into his chest just below the heart. It happened so fast and so unexpectedly that nobody could tell for sure afterwards who had wielded the knife and how Purna had got stabbed. But people were quick to cite the oft-repeated Nepali proverb: "When two bulls fight it's the calf that gets trampled."

"Aiyaa ...... mother, I've been stabbed," he cried in pain, clutching the handle of the knife sticking out of his chest. His face contorting in excruciating pain, he slowly bent forward and sank to his knees, still clutching the handle of the knife. He remained suspended in that position for a minute and then slowly sank to the dusty earth, blood oozing out of his wound and painting his shirt a dark red.

"Murder, murder! ..... A man has been knifed down, a man has been killed," somebody cried frantically at the top of his voice. Suddenly the combatants of both parties scattered in different directions raising a cloud of dust. The dust slowly settled down to reveal only a few men who had remained behind. Rooted to the earth they were standing on, they were staring at the dying man in utter disbelief. The place had suddenly become quiet and still. The only sound that could be heard was the low whine and kicking of the feet of the mortally wounded man, lying face down, with his blood colouring the light brown earth around him.

Depth of Sorrow

When the quarrel had broken out, Milan had wisely decided to stay out of it. He was involved with neither of the two warring sides. So he had stood apart at a safe distance to watch the spectacle unfold, unaware that his elder brother had returned to look for him. When he heard people cry out, "Murder, murder …. A man has been knifed down," he too decided to leave the area. But as he was running away, he heard someone shout, "It's Purna who's been stabbed." He wheeled around and ran towards the dying man, hoping that what he had just heard was not true.

When he reached his fallen elder brother, Purna was already beginning to lose consciousness, completely soaked in his own blood. When Milan turned him over and took his limp body in his arms he noticed that the knife-handle was still sticking out of his body.

"Elder brother, don't go away. Don't go away. Don't leave us, elder brother. Don't leave us," He implored to the dying man through tears, his voice breaking.
The dying man looked at him with sad and painful eyes and moved his lips to say something but no sound came forth.

"Say something, elder brother, anything. Don't leave us like this. Please live. Don't die. Elder sister-in-law is waiting for you at home. Live for her sake." He said in an anguished voice. He couldn't see properly; tears of grief streamed out thick and fast and blocked his sight.

His face contorting in pain, Purna moved his lips again and whispered with a tremendous effort, "Milan, look after …ahh… father, …. mother …. grandma … ahh….. and your elder sister-in-law."

"Yes, elder brother, I will." Milan cried openly. "But you are not dying. You are not leaving us. You will live."

"Tell your ..... sister-in-law ..... ahh .... that I am ...... sorry ......ahh .....my .... end .... has .... come." With these words Purna breathed his last and lay still. Lifeless. He was dead. Dead at the age of twenty-eight. He died without becoming a father. He died leaving a childless widow behind him. At the time of his untimely death he was still thinking of taking his wife to Kathmandu to seek medical help.
Milan raised his tear-filled eyes and looked at the silent men around him. "Dead. My elder brother is dead," he cried in anguish. "How am I going to tell my father and mother? How am I going to tell my sister-in-law? What am I going to tell them?"

Then suddenly he was filled with rage – rage at the man who had done this and run away so cowardly, and rage at the world that had let it happen. He stood up and bellowed at the top of his voice: "Who murdered my innocent brother? Who? What had my brother done to get killed in this manner? Tell me who did it? I will kill that son of a whore. I will chop his body into little pieces drink his blood. Hey, you coward, whoever you are, come out in the open if you have drunk your mother's milk. Come out and face me if you are your father's son. Let me see if you have the guts to kill me as well."

Dil Bahadur and the women had just reached home when a passerby told them that someone had been killed at the polling station. When they inquired as to the identity of the murdered man, the man said that he didn't know and hurried on. Kamala hoped (aloud) that it wasn't either of her sons. Dil Bahadur wanted to go have a look, but she prevented him saying the killers may still be lurking around.

Depth of Sorrow

Half an hour later, the young son of their nearest neighbour arrived running, panting heavily. "Elder brother Purna has been stabbed. He is lying dead at the school. Brother Milan is looking after the dead body." The boy blurted out in a single breath.

Dil Bahadur found himself trembling and sweating as the women began to sob. His mind became numb, he couldn't think of anything. Without a word, he started to run. He ran as fast as his feet could carry him. He ran as if his life depended on it. He didn't see anybody, he didn't hear anything. He didn't notice Kamala and Laxmi running after him in his footsteps – sobbing continuously, tears of sorrow streaming down their cheeks.

It was a sunny and windy day of a sunny and windy season. Here and there gusts of wind picked up the light brown dust of earth and twisted it into a miniature twister. When the murmuring men saw the dead man's father, they parted respectfully to make way for him. Milan and Ratna were sitting disconsolately by the dead body. Ratna had arrived as soon as he had heard. Jit Bahadur was also there, trying to console the bereaved boys. Dil Bahadur stared at the prostrate body of his dead son. Taking off his cap to reveal his balding crown, he crouched down and squatted beside the corpse, resting his forehead on the palm of his hand – with the most mournful expression on his aging face. It was a tragic sight.

"My son, you have left us so suddenly. I'd never imagined that I'd have to see this day," he whispered in a sorrowful voice. He turned to his uncle and said, "Uncle, what happened to my son? Who did this to him? Why was this done to him? He was innocent. He was not involved in politics. He had nothing to do with politics."

Kamala and Laxmi arrived and threw themselves upon the dead body, sobbing uncontrollably. "Son, my darling son, my heart," Kamala wailed, "Why have you left us? What have you done to deserve this? Why did you have to leave us in this manner? Who did this to you? Who took away your life? Come back, my son. Open your eyes. Don't be cruel to your poor mother. Come back, my son. Talk to me."

And Laxmi wailed simultaneously, "Husband, my poor husband. Why did you have to leave me? Why? How am I going to live without you? What am I going to do without you now? My heart has broken." Turning up to the sky, she bemoaned with tearful eyes, "You merciless, unjust God, why have you taken away a good man from his wife and family? Why? What had he done to you? What wrong had I done that you had to punish me by making me a widow? Don't you have any compassion? Return him to me. Have pity on this poor woman. Make him speak again." Turning back to her dead husband, she implored, "Open you eyes, husband. Talk to me; say something, anything you like. Just say something." The grief-stricken young woman banged her wrists repeatedly and broke her glass bangles. Then she collapsed on her dead husband's chest and fainted.

Kamala turned her attention to her unconscious daughter-in-law and cried, "Somebody please bring water. My daughter-in-law has fainted." In no time at all somebody brought an amphora of water from somewhere and splashed it on the unconscious woman's face.

A short time later the policemen who had been visiting other polling stations in the village arrived hastily. "Oh, brothers policemen, where were you when the murderers killed my son? Isn't it your duty to protect innocent people? What were

you doing when my poor son was stabbed?" Kamala cried when she saw them.
Without answering her, the men in uniform quickly pushed the growing crowd back and told the people not to move the dead body as there'd be a post mortem. The bystanders murmured an agreement that there must be a proper investigation and the culprit must be found and punished.

A short while later a small group of people arrived carrying the four-starred red flag of the Nepali Congress Party, shouting shrill slogans:
"Long live brave martyr Purna!"
"Death to the murderer!"
"Hang the murderer!"
"Communist murderers, leave the country!"
"Down with the politics of murder!"

The crowd, numbering about a dozen men and women, forcibly pushed past the outnumbered policemen who made a feeble attempt to stop them. "Becareful, brothers and sisters! Don't move the dead body," one of the policemen said, "We'll have to inform the headquarters and carry out an investigation."
But the protestors ignored the policemen and proceeded to wrap their flag over the dead body. Dil Bahadur tried to stop them.

"No, no, no," he said, "Please, don't do this. You can't do this. My son was not a member of the Congress Party. He was not a member of any political party. He had nothing to do with politics." But the mob pushed him aside and continued to wrap the body. Some of the bystanders joined the mob and a few who belonged to the communist party tried to put up a resistance claiming that the victim was a member of their party instead. A scuffle nearly broke out but they were quickly put to flight.

Dil Bahadur turned to his uncle and pleaded, "Uncle, please do something. Stop them!"

Jit Bahadur intervened, "Please leave my deceased grandson alone. He was not with any political party. He didn't even care for politics. He only came here to vote for me on my insistence."
But the leader of the group, a firebrand local youth, wouldn't listen to him, "What do you know, old man?" he lashed out threateningly, "Do you think anybody would come to vote for you? You don't have any supporters. You may not have known it, but your grandson was a member of our party. That's why the communists killed him. So shut up and leave this place immediately, otherwise I won't be responsible for the consequences."

Milan, quiet until now, stood up to face the man. "I won't let anybody touch my brother's body," he shouted. "He was not with any political party, do you hear me? Leave us alone."

But one of the frenzied protesters shoved him and in anger Milan shoved him back. A fight would have erupted had the nervous policemen not intervened. Two policemen held a struggling Milan firmly while some men led the other man away.

"Uncle, listen to us. We are doing this for you," the leader said to Dil Bahadur, "We are doing this to give you justice. We'll take your son's body to show to all what heinous crime has been committed by the communist murderers. They are killers, mass murderers. They have killed and murdered millions of innocent people all over the world. Your son's death has not been in vain. He has given his life for democracy. He has become a martyr in the cause of freedom."

Suddenly, a larger group of people appeared carrying the bright red hammer-and-sickle flag of the communists. There were about three dozens of them and all of them were armed to the teeth with knives, khukuris, axes and machetes. They marched straight towards the dead body, shouting shrill slogans:

"Love live our brave martyr Purna!"
"Long live the Nepal Communist Party!"
"Down with Nepali Congress!"
"Hang the Congressee murderers!"
"We won't let anybody do politics over a dead body!"
"We'll avenge this murder!"
"Down with the lackeys of Western imperialists!"
"Death to the stooges of Indian expansionists!"

As the two mobs faced each other angrily, the situation turned explosive. Both sides wanted the dead body. Both sides claimed that the dead man was their cadre. The bereaved family and the outnumbered policemen watched the farce helplessly as the two sides screamed for each other's blood.

"The dead body belongs to us. Hand it over to us."
"No, we won't. It belongs to us."
"He was a communist."
"He was a democrat."
"You killed our cadre. You are murderers. Aren't you ashamed of yourselves?"
"It's you who killed him. And it's you who should be ashamed, not us."

The cacophony of angry shouts, accusations, curses and threats grew louder and angrier. It was only a matter of seconds before it would erupt into another brawl. But at the last moment, the Nepali Congress supporters, being less numerous and unarmed, suddenly got cold feet. They dropped the corpse and fled from the scene, and the communists triumphantly claimed the body. They tore the flag of the Nepali Congress into shreds, burnt it and then replaced it with their own flag. Their leader climbed on a nearby rock and gave an impromptu speech - fiery and inflammatory in content, and filled to the brim with incendiary propaganda, as usual. He claimed that the whole world knew that the dead man was a dedicated member of the Communist Party and that had been the reason behind his brutal murder. He went to on claim that Indian and Western imperialists had a hand in the murder. "This murder was committed by a hired assassin of the capitalist-imperialist murderers. It's a part of their global conspiracy against the international communist movement," he charged.

They then lifted the body and made for the village. The dead man's family watched helplessly as the noisy procession vanished around the corner.
"My son is not a martyr; he is just a luckless victim of an unfortunate circumstance," Dil Bahadur lamented with tearful eyes.
'I'll keep an eye on them," said Ratna and without waiting for an answer he followed the mob.

At dusk that evening, the communists brought the dead body back to his house. Neighbours and relatives came to keep vigil all night. Early the next morning the policemen arrived to examine the body. After a cursory examination they gave permission to dispose the body.

Milan and his uncles and cousins prepared the dead body for funeral. They undressed the cold and stiff corpse and washed it with clean water. Then they dressed it again with the dead man's best clothes. After that they wrapped it with a plain white cloth and carried it to the courtyard where they placed it with the head pointing towards the east and the feet pointing towards the west. Several rupee coins were placed on various parts of the dead man's body - mainly his forehead, eyes, lips and chest.

The communists tried to drape the corpse with their red flag once again, but this time Dil Bahadur stood fast. He was adamant that he would not allow any more politics over his son's dead body. Since the communists had already achieved their political objective they did not insist. By that time the eastern hills had already become rife with the rumour that an active member of the Nepal Communist Party had been murdered by a Nepali Congress killer in cold blood.

The entire neighbourhood gathered for the funeral procession. People milled around silently, exchanging quick, grief-stricken glances. They spoke very little. Limbu mourners mustn't greet each by either words or gesture of hand. No namaste, no hello, no how-do-you-do. Only glances can be exchanged to acknowledge someone's presence. They can, however, converse. Dil Bahadur had wanted to bury his son at the village burial ground in the nearby graveyard hill according to old Limbu custom, but Kamala had opted for cremation by the river bank saying that this was the thing to do in these times. Besides, she had added in a most mournful voice, her deceased son had loved the river which was a part of his life. The others had agreed unanimously.

The corpse was placed on a stretcher made of freshly-cut green bamboo-shoot. Then the weeping family members, relatives and neighbours paid their final respect to the dead man by circling his remains in a clockwise direction. When they arrived at the feet they placed flowers and money on the dead body, joined their palms (with the fingers pointing upwards) in a *Namaste,* and murmured prayers for the deceased man's soul. *May his soul rest in peace!*

After everyone present had taken his/her turn, the priest mumbled his prayers and then declared in a loud and clear but solemn voice: "Let it be known to all present here today that as of this day Purna Bahadur Sambiu, son of Dil Bahadur Sambiu and grandson of Bom Bahadur Sambiu, has died and is no longer a member of his family and of the human race. He must now leave the house where he was born and the place where he spent his entire young life, and find a new home among his forefathers in the afterlife." The older men grunted their approval in unison.

Then at the behest of the priest, Milan, Ratna and two other young men lifted the stretcher upon their shoulders and started the slow march downhill to the bank of the Tawa River. The procession was led by the priest with a naked khukuri in his hand. Some men had already descended to the river bank early in the morning to prepare the funeral pyre.

After the corpse was placed on the funeral pyre, the priest circled the dead body three times chanting his ancient incantation as the somber crowd watched silently. He turned in all four directions to inform the gods, goddesses, spirits and the souls of the ancestors of Purna's death in spite of every effort to save him. He called upon the dead man's forefathers to accept the young man's soul as he was one of them. When the ritual came to an end, a teary-eyed Milan circled the funeral pyre three times, lit a torch and put fire to the mouth of the corpse.

The tinder dry wood quickly caught fire, and within an hour the flames consumed the flesh completely, in front of the eyes of the mourners. Only the residue remained in the form of gray ash which was collected and thrown into the river along with the dead man's clothes. Thus Purna was cremated by the bank of the river where he used to fish every spring and summer. Nothing remained of the simple and quiet young man except memories of him. But even memories do not last forever. They last only as long those who hold the memories live, and when they too die then nothing remains – not even a faint trace that he ever existed. But this is how nature has meant it to be. If the world were to be covered with the vestiges of the past, then there'd be no place for the present and the future.

When the mourners returned from the funeral, each was put through a symbolic cleansing ceremony which involves sprinkling of clean water from a jar over their bodies with a leafed-stem of an herb. Then they were offered refreshment – *rakshi, jand, tongba* and *chiura*, the dry beaten rice that the Nepalese love so much.

The Limbu's mourning period lasts four days for a man and three days for a woman. During the mourning period the family members of the dead person observe certain restrictions. They do not eat meat. Things like salt, oil, ginger, garlic and chili that make the food palatable are strictly forbidden. They are forbidden to play, entertain or worship.

They are forbidden to greet seniors and elders by bowing down or saluting. The chief mourners (the sons of the deceased, in most cases) have to remain in seclusion and are forbidden to speak to people of other races. The Limbus believe that like birth, death is a messy affair and makes the house and everything in it, including its human inhabitants, impure. Therefore, they must go through an elaborate purification ceremony at the end of the mourning period, presided over and conducted by a priest. If the purification rites cannot be performed on the said date owing to economic and other reasons, then it must be performed at a convenient date within the next forty-five days. The purification ceremony is followed by a sumptuous feast for all relatives and guests. In the old days this feast used to be so grand that it used to drive many Limbu families into penury in their zeal to exhibit their wealth and magnanimity.

Now back to mythology once again for there is a story to explain the above as well which the priest relates during the purification ceremony: Kesami and Namsami, the twin sons of a primordial woman, were as different as the hills and the plains. Kesami was a man and Namsami was a tiger. By the time they had reached adulthood they had turned into mortal enemies and vowed to kill each other at the first opportunity. It was an enmity that would only end in the death of one or both. In the footsteps of his forefathers Namsami the man learned to use bow and arrow and became a hunter. Urged by his natural instinct, Kesami the tiger went to live deep in the forest. Then both brothers planned to hunt each other down. One day Namsami went deep into the forest with intent to ambush and kill his brother. He climbed up a tree, made a platform high up in the branches, and waited for the tiger. Kesami arrived shortly afterwards following Namsami's body ordour. There the two mortal enemies faced each other for the last time - Namsami up in the tree with his bow and arrows and Kesami with his fangs and claws staring angrily up at him. Kesami began to climb the tree with his powerful paws, and Namsami shot him seven times with his arrows, narrowly missing each time. Kesami made his way steadily upward and Namsami was left with only one arrow. When the tiger was almost at his feet, Namsami, being a human (and humans being naturally more cunning and devious than animals) quickly devised a deception. He conceded defeat and asked his brother to open his mouth wide so that he could jump into it. The unsuspecting Kesami foolishly opened his mouth wide. At that instant Namsami slammed his remaining arrow into the Kesami's gaping mouth with all his strength and the tiger crashed to the earth and died instantly.

When he was sure that the tiger was dead, Namsani climbed down from the tree, skinned his dead brother and dried the skin in the sun. He then carried it to different places to exhibit it in exchange for food. He went to the north and brought back salt (an allusion to the fact that rock salt was imported from Tibet in the old days). He went to the east and brought back ginger and garlic. He went to the west and brought grains, and he went to the south and brought back meat and money. He did so without the knowledge of his mother, who was deeply distressed by the enmity of her two sons. Upon consuming the food thus obtained, the mother and son became ill. And when the mother found out the truth, she called all the venerable men and women of the land to suggest a way out for them. The venerable men and women consulted amongst themselves and told them (the mother and son) to mourn for four days during which time they were to refrain from eating delicious food, and to perform the purification rites on the final day. The mother and son did as they were told. On the day of the purification ceremony, attended by all the venerable men and women, the mother and son offered their guests a splendid dinner, and the happy guests gave them the permission to consume the restricted food again.

Now, on the day of the purification ceremony, neighbours and relatives arrive early in the morning. They bring with them food and liquor as contribution to lighten the economic burden on the dead man's family. The women help to clean the house and prepare food for the guests, and the men help to prepare the site for the ritual and to slaughter the pig and chickens.

Then the priest performs the ritual to escort the soul of the dead person to the land of his forefathers. The dead man's supposed journey to the abode of his august ancestors takes place in the following way: After constructing an altar and laying out the necessary ingredients (rice, meat and *tongba*, among other things), the priest sits down to perform the ritual surrounded by men and women. In his deliberately slow and low, but melodious voice, he begins to recite the lengthy incantation to invoke the spirits of the dead. First he summons the dead man' ancestors and tells them the reason for his death. He tells them that several attempts were made to save the dead man's life but all had failed, that being the reason for his having to leave the mortal world. When the spirits apparently understand, after a lengthy discussion with him, he then he addresses the dead man's soul and tells him not to wander in the village, forests and hills anymore but to accept his fate and take the food offered to him in preparation for his journey to the eternal land of the afterlife. Now the dead man is reluctant at first because of his attachment to the material world. But the priest keeps on calling him until he finally acquiesces.

When the dead man's soul finally enters the altar room the priest takes the spirit into his body and immediately goes into a trance - rocking violently and mumbling unintelligibly. After sometime he becomes his normal self again and makes the symbolic act of offering food to the dead man which the dead man supposedly accepts and consumes. Then the priest begins the ritual to escort the dead man's soul to the land of his forefathers. It is a lengthy ritual accompanied by hoots and cheers of approval from the old men. The dead man's soul has to pass through many mountains, rivers, valleys and plains, and overcome many obstacles in order to reach his final destination.

Milan sat silently throughout the long proceeding. As he ran his eyes slowly across the craggy and time-worn faces of the old men and women, he saw the ways of the hoary past reflected in their ancient eyes. He realized that to them the dead man's supposed journey to the other world was as real as the earth, the moon and the sun. But to him it was just one of the many archaic rituals that defined his race.

When the ritual finally came to an end, the exhausted priest conveyed the dead man's message to his eager family while leisurely sipping *tongba*, "When I was in trance I talked to Purna. He says that he is sorry he had to leave you so abruptly, but it was not his doing. He says that he didn't want to leave so soon and there were many things he wanted to do. He asks you not to cry for him as he is very happy now in the other world."

The men and women nodded their chins in satisfaction. The priest then added somberly that the spirits had told him that there was going to be another death in the village within the next six months, and this time it was going to be a child.

Parents of small children became afraid. "Let it not be my child," each prayed silently.

The Limbus also believe that if a person dies at a young age (from illness or accident), then that person's discontented soul turns into an evil spirit. According to mythology, the first evil spirit was that of an unmarried young woman who died while helping her brother to build his house. While struggling to erect a heavy wooden pillar her bamboo-comb stuck to her hair fell into the pit. Without thinking she let go of the log and bent down to pick it up. Her brother could not hold the heavy log alone and it crashed on top of her head smashing it into the pit. She died instantly and her soul turned into an evil spirit. Her brother completed the house but because of the evil spirit it was plagued by bad luck. He could rid his house of the evil spirit only after summoning a priest to perform a special ritual to ward off the evil spirit as prescribed by goddess Yuma. Later other young people died in different ways. Some fell off trees while cutting wood. Some fell off cliffs while collecting honey. Some were attacked by wild animals. Some drowned while swimming in ponds and some were swept away by floods when crossing rivers. Some died of illness and some were murdered. Because their wishes were unfulfilled, their frustrated souls turned into evil spirits. The Limbus perform ritual worships at least once a year to ward off these evil spirits.

A few days later a contingent of police arrived from the district headquarters to investigate the murder and took into custody a number of men belonging to both political parties for questioning and later released them all for lack of evidence. People pointed their fingers at different directions depending upon their political allegiance. All of the accused vehemently denied the accusations and the murderer was never caught. The election was annulled and another was scheduled for a later date. When that day arrived, it went off peacefully without any untoward incidents.

With the sudden and violent death of her husband, Laxmi's little world came crashing down. Only at the death of a loved one does one truly feel the frailty and brevity of life, and at such times one sees death and despair around every corner. So wherever she looked she saw nothing but utter darkness. She was not in the habit of making future plans; there had never been any need. The only plan she had was to have children. She had expected to spend her life in the company of her husband till death. She had expected to have his children, grow old with him and die only a few years apart from him. She had never imagined that he would die like this. She had never imagined that she would become a widow at such a young age. It had seemed impossible until it had suddenly happened. But this is what life is – a journey into the unknown, with unexpected twists and turns, death being the only certainty.

The day her husband died she broke the bangles on her hands and stripped herself of her jewelry. She washed away the 'sindoor' (red lead powder) at the parting of her hair in the middle of her forehead that Nepalese women wear as a sign of matrimony. But unlike the Hindu widow who is under societal compulsion to wear a plain white garment and play the grieving widow to the hilt all her remaining life, a Limbu woman is not expected to do so. Her mourning period lasts only as long as that of the other members of the family. Also, a Limbu woman is free to marry after her husband's death if she chooses to. The idea, of course, did not enter the distraught young woman's head at the time. She was too engrossed in grieving for her dead husband. She wept for many days. She lost her appetite for food and consequently lost her weight. "I must have committed an immense sin in one of my past lives to suffer like this in my present life," she lamented to whoever lent her a sympathetic ear.

During these darkest hours of her life, Lalita provided the much needed psychological support. Laxmi knew that Lalita was the stronger type and took comfort in the latter's consolation. Her mother-in-law also treated her with compassion telling her, "Daughter-in-law, you are like our own daughter and we'll be there for you no matter what." Amrita wrote her a long, tearful letter from England. "You, elder-sister-in-law, are like my own sister," she wrote, "Your happiness is my happiness and your sorrow is my sorrow. When you came to our house, I was just a little girl. I grew up playing with you and sharing your pain and happiness, as you shared mine. Do you remember those idyllic days when we used to go to the woods to collect grass and firewood and pick mushrooms, wild berries, walnuts and hazelnuts? Those were the happiest days of my life."

For many days after Purna's death, there was a mournful quietness about the house. Nobody said much. There was not much to be said. But time is a great healer. It moves at its own deliberate pace covering its old tracks. Today's heartbreak becomes tomorrow's memory. The best thing about memories is that they are more bitter-sweet than hurtful.

As she embarked upon the process of recovery, Laxmi stopped crying and began to think of her future. What were the options available to her? Married at the age of sixteen, widowed at the age of twenty-five and without a child to show for the marriage. Her future had died with Purna. *What am I going to do now? Do I still have a purpose in this life? Do I still have a rightful place in this house? If not, then where can I go?* She asked herself repeatedly and came up with blank. At one time she even contemplated going back to her maiden home, but argued against it when better sense prevailed. *What have I got there? My parents have already washed their hands off me. If I go to them they would still take me back out of love, but I would only be a burden on them. My brothers have wives and children of their own to support, and the sisters-in-law might not be so accommodating. It's not their fault, it's just the way human relationships work*, she thought. An unattached adult daughter or sister in the house (whether a spinster or a divorcee or a widow) is viewed as a liability. Unless she is wealthy or happens to be the breadwinner of the family, there is no respect for her. This is truer for a childless widow.

And so, Laxmi continued her sad and empty existence, continuing to fulfill her duties as the obedient daughter-in-law. The neighbours and relatives sympathized with her for the moment and consoled her with sympathetic words, but she knew that the goodwill would not last. She knew that the day was not far away when some of the more superstitious and malicious among them would start accusing her of being the cause of her husband's death. *She is jinxed and he who marries her will meet the same fate as her dead husband*, they would say. They would even call her a *husband-eater* behind her back. She was not a stranger to such malicious tongues. She had closely watched and felt the pain of humiliation. A childhood friend of hers had had the misfortune to lose her mother shortly after birth. Hurtful remarks such as 'mother-eater' were intentionally and unintentionally hurled at her and she used to be so distraught by the careless and cruel remarks of adults and children alike that she used to hide and cry in shame.

In the eyes of the superstitious Nepalese, to be jinxed is to fall as low as the so-called untouchables – *Kami* (gold / iron smith), *Sarki* (shoe / leather smith) and *Damaai* (tailor / weaver) – who are supposed to be jinxed all their lives. They are the poorest, the most oppressed and the most powerless class of people in the society. They are bullied, insulted, jeered at, spit upon, kicked and beaten for no apparent reason, and at the end told that it's their fault. Even in these modern times, some conceited high-caste people still go so far as to wash immediately if they happen to lay their eyes on the face of an untouchable the first thing in the morning. They expect (and forcibly demand) the untouchables to treat them with utmost respect and be obsequious to them at all times. These same self-important high-caste people, however, happily wear the clothes sewn by the hands of the tailors, walk in the leather shoes made by the hands of the shoe smith, and adorn their faces and bodies with the gold and silver ornaments made by the hands of the goldsmiths. There is no dearth of racist bigots in the world; it's just that they refuse to acknowledge that they are racists. And with them around, it is the fate of the poor and the downtrodden everywhere to suffer.

But life must go on, however bleak the future may seem for at the other end of a proverbial dark tunnel there is always a proverbial bright light of hope. *If it is in my destiny to suffer, then I'll do so with courage and dignity. I am not going to complain about anything and against anybody, not even against the pitiless gods who have let me down so cruelly,* Laxmi made a silent pledge and trudged on with life. So with every rising of the sun above the eastern horizon, she filled her days with work. And with every setting of the sun beyond the western horizon she lay silently in her bed - the same bed that she used to share with Purna in happier times - staring at the dark ceiling, feeling utterly alone and helpless in the all encompassing darkness.

Purna's death altered the situation completely for Milan. Now all the duties and responsibilities of his deceased elder brother fell upon his unwilling shoulders. It was quite the opposite of what he had in mind. Even after the Malaysian fiasco, he had secretly nurtured the dream of returning to the city someday because that that was where his heart really belonged.

That was out of the question now. He was expected to quietly slip into his dead brother's shoes. It was his duty to do so. And he made up his mind to do just that and face the challenge that life had thrown at him. Whereas previously he only helped his father and brother in the farm, without involving himself in the decision making process, he now turned himself into a fulltime farmer. The transformation was not easy, though his father was there to teach him. He still wore his jeans and T-shirt and even his sunglasses in the fields, prompting the men and women to smirk and laugh behind his back, "There goes the city boy."

Four months after Purna's death, the arrival of a piece of good news from England helped to bring the smile back on everybody's face. Amrita had given birth to a healthy boy. She had sent some colour photographs of the infant with herself and her husband - both beaming with happiness. She looked happy and contented. She had also gained weight and looked every inch the full-fledged woman that she had grown into. After a long time the women had the opportunity to fuss effusively over something and they did so with impunity. Happiness is infectious and it quickly spread to the men as well. Even the sad and forlorn looking Laxmi laughed merrily. She was happy for Amrita.

The various rumours and conspiracy theories surrounding Purna's murder slowly died out and life returned to normal. But not quite. There were signs of uneasiness in the hills. The countryside was becoming increasingly restless, and even a man as apolitical as Dil Bahadur could sense the growing unease. Political instability resulting from constant bickering for power among the top echelon leaders of the ruling party in Kathmandu and chronic poverty in the country were pushing the disillusioned people to the brink. The armed rebellion started by a handful of Maoists in the 'dirt-poor' mid-western hills with a handful of rusted rifles and muskets had quickly taken root and spread to other parts of the country in spite of (and some say because of) successive police actions named rather romantically as 'Operation Romeo' and 'Operation Kilo 2 Shera'. These brutal police operations were highly successful in killing and uprooting a large number of rebels and civilians. However, they were also successful in driving the terrified rural folks into the arms of the rebels. There were ominous looking dark clouds on the horizon.

That year Maoist cadres began to trickle into the eastern hills. At first they came stealthily and without arms in small numbers. They held clandestine meetings and called upon the people to overthrow the old system by exterminating the oppressors and exploiters starting from the grassroots. They exhorted the people to rise up against economic exploitation, political repression and social injustice. Not surprisingly a large section of the poverty-stricken rural populace turned a sympathetic ear to their cause.

The call to arms by the Maoists is not entirely unjustified. But it is not entirely justified either. It is justified to the extent that the rebels want to root out feudalism, social injustice and rampant corruption in the society. After two centuries of peace, stagnation, corruption and grinding poverty the country had become ripe for revolution. Every forest needs a fire from time to time to rejuvenate itself. The old and decaying trees take up space and resources; they block the sunlight and monopolise the resources, and thus impede the growth of the young plants. Their continued existence endangers the very existence of the ecosystem. But nature has a cure; it puts the moribund forest on fire. After the fire has settled down new life sprouts out of the ashes of the old. It's the same with human societies. While peace is desirable and is one of the ultimate goals of mankind, the bitter truth is that wars are an integral and essential part of human evolution. It is through conflicts that human civilizations have risen up to such dizzy heights. If humans had always lived in peace, they wouldn't have been much different from apes. There would have been no Mesopotamia, no Egypt, no Greece, no Rome, no China and definitely no global modern civilization. Humans would still be digging out roots and running scared of predatory animals. Therefore, peace at the expense of progress is neither desirable nor justifiable.

There has been no time in human history when there has been total peace. Wars have given human societies a sense of purpose and an impetus to move forward. If one turns the pages of history, one finds that peace is in fact an interlude between wars. In fact, prolonged peace is bad for the health of human civilization. In times of prolonged peace every human society drifts into corrupt hands, and it takes a war to ultimately rid the society of its evils. Human civilization has progressed so far because humans have consistently engaged in warfare – against their rivals, against their competitors, against their tormentors and against their oppressors. They have made war for the pursuit of wealth and for the control of resources. They have made war for the sake of conquest and glory. They have made war to build and expand empires. They have made war to free their homeland from foreign rule. In modern times they have made war for the cause of *liberty*, *equality* and *justice*. And they have also made war for the sake of peace. This is the reason the two world wars of the 20th century were called the wars to end all wars. That they didn't succeed is a testimony to the fact that war is integral to the human character.

History stands testimony to the fact that every great political upheaval gives rise to a new political system which helps to bring about peace and propel the nation forward for a period of time. But the dynamism and purpose of the system doesn't last for ever. Slowly and surely corrupt and opportunistic people wriggle their way into the core of the system and eat it from inside out, like parasites. Corruption brings stagnation and decadence. If the guardians of the system are unable to see the writing on the wall on time and bring about the necessary changes, which seems to be more often the case, then widespread discontentment among the less privileged sections of the society eventually leads to rebellion. Every nation has to go through this cycle of war and peace to move forward.

A brief look at the history of neighbouring China - worth citing here as it is the oldest (and perhaps the most advanced) living human civilization - provides ample proof to support the above. In the ancient days the Shang, Chou, Ch'in, Sui, Tang and Sung dynasties rose and fell one after another in succession. Each dynasty rose on the ashes of the preceding dynasty after a period of warfare, led the country through a period of peace and prosperity, and then became corrupt and decadent. In the medieval period, the Mongol Yuan dynasty ruled China for more than two centuries and when it became corrupt and decadent a peasant-turned-monk-turned-rebel led a successful rebellion to chase the Mongols out of China and established the Ming dynasty. But when the Ming dynasty itself became corrupt and decadent after two and half centuries of rule, the Manchurian Qing dynasty took over after a protracted period of warfare. The Manchus themselves became corrupt and decadent after three centuries of rule, and their rule came to an abrupt end when Dr. Sun Yat Sen led a successful revolution against them. But the new republic did not go according to the revolutionary leader's plan. The country fell into anarchy with half a century of vicious warlordism, until the victorious communists led by Mao Ze Dong established control. Each dynasty brought the country peace and prosperity in the beginning. Then it slowly became corrupt and fell into decadence. The present communist system will serve the Chinese people for the next two centuries at the most (it most probably will not last that long) and then when it falls, as it surely will because of its rigid nature, a period of chaos will reign again. And at the end of the chaos a new system will emerge.

The people's war in Nepal is following established patterns. Following Prithvi Narayan Shah's quarter century campaign of conquest, a new political system emerged that took the country to great heights for the next half a century. During those heady days of Nepalese imperialism the Nepalese empire grew into twice its present size and had it not been for the British it would have swallowed a sizeable portion of present-day India. After the country's expansion was checked, the royal court fell into the hands of ambitious but corrupt and incompetent courtiers who feuded amongst each other constantly, paving the way for the bloody rise of Junga Bahadur Rana. Under the Rana family rule, a century of peace and stagnation followed until they were toppled by a popular revolt in which the titular King sided with the people. But the downfall of the Rana regime had, perhaps, less to do with the revolt at home than to pressure from the newly independent India. Because of this, their power base was never properly removed and the root causes of the country's backwardness were never properly addressed. Under the subsequent partyless system imposed by the authoritarian King Mahendra after a brief experiment with democracy, feudalism and corruption took deeper root. Thus, by the time people's discontentment spilled out into the streets of the country's urban areas in 1990, the long-suffering people had been clamouring for drastic changes that had been long overdue.

But the restoration of democracy did little to quench the people's thirst for change. Sure, it changed the way the government was formed, but much of the needed reforms never took place. Once again the root causes for the country's backwardness – feudalism and political marginalization of a large segment of the society - were ignored. The traditional 'haves' (the feudal class) continued to wield the baton of political power and have the country's resources at their disposal while the traditional 'have-nots' continued to be left out in the cold. Thus, as far as the poor masses were concerned democracy had brought practically no change. The 'have-nots' were anxious to break free of the shackles of poverty and servitude, while the 'haves' desperately wanted to cling on to their cozy past. A new political thinking was urgently needed to move the country forward into an era of justice, peace, growth and prosperity, in that order. That never happened and as a result conflict became inevitable.

But sadly there is more to the Maoist rebellion than meets the eye. It has hidden dimensions that the common man is unable to see. As much as the people's war is about rooting out corruption and social injustice, it is also about the raw ambition of a small group of men educated on hardline Marxist philosophy. The Maoists do not only want to overthrow the monarchy and 'liberate' the oppressed masses, as they claim, their ultimate goal is to impose the out-dated 'dictatorship of the proletariat' upon the people by creating an environment of fear. They aim to grab absolute power in the name of the people and turn the country into another laboratory to test Marx's failed theories. Some people never learn from the lessons of history, and a whole generation of people has to suffer because of their stubbornness. And to this extent their rebellion is not justified. Stuck in a time-wrap they aim to impose a totalitarian one-party rule by eliminating all opposition to their dogmatic ideology. The only way that can be achieved is by exterminating and exiling all of their detractors. But it seems their dream doesn't end there. Like the now decimated Talibans of Afghanistan, they have dreams of conquering not only their own country, but also of exporting their ideology to neighbouring India and then to the rest of the world.

So along with the greedy landowners and devious money lenders who are their natural enemies, those who believe in freedom and democracy have also become their prime targets. The various literatures published by the rebels and their supporters prove conclusively that they have borrowed more than a leaf from Cambodia's Khmer Rouge, the ultra-leftist outfit led by the notorious Pol Pot, whose utopian dream of creating a perfect agrarian society resulted in the mass murder of millions of his compatriots in the 1970s and turned the peaceful Buddhist nation of Cambodia into one of the worst killing fields history has ever seen. In their usual diatribes against the capitalist-imperialist West, the Maoists have labeled the Killing Fields of Cambodia as nothing more than a fictional product of the Western capitalist-imperialist propaganda machine. Judging by their *modus operandi*, Pol-Potists would have been a more fitting name for them. When the eminent 19th century philosopher Karl Marx wrote his revolution in the pages of *Das Capital* that was to change the lives of billions of people all over the world, he never foresaw the rise of brutal and ruthless tyrants like Stalin and Pol Pot in the shadow of the new system he proposed.

For the international leftists, the rebellion is also about settling of old scores. The fall of communism in the former Soviet Union and its satellite states in Eastern Europe in the early 1990s left the international communist movement in tatters. The badly shaken and disillusioned leftists nurtured a deep hatred of the free world and its apparent leader the United States of America. Time and again they have tried to drive a wedge between the free nations of the world. Mao was once reputed to have said: "My enemy's enemy is my friend". Taking that line (of wisdom) to their heart, they have found common cause with all sorts of rightist and leftist extremists whose one common goal is the downfall of the free world. Thus they have rallied behind extremist organizations like the International Revolutionary Movement (known by its French acronym RIM) which openly advocates the violent overthrow of elected governments in countries across the world. After having failed in Peru, RIM has concentrated its full effort on Nepal in its bid to turn the country into the next frontier in their fight against the free world. The Western media (the section that is aware what's happening in this Himalayan backwater) mistakenly believe that Nepal (because it is one of the most backward countries in the world) is still fighting the remnants of the previous century's war. They couldn't be more wrong. International communism is attempting to make a comeback, and with the way things are going in Nepal, they might yet succeed. When that happens they will be in for a big surprise.

But talk of freedom and democracy doesn't make much sense to half-filled stomachs and half-covered backs in the face of the lure of free food, clothes and shelter for all. The rebels had shown them a dream, and hundreds of impoverished rural men and women were flocking to the militant outfit in pursuit of that dream. That year confrontations between the guerillas and the police increased drastically - both in regularity and ferocity - and occupied headline news on the national and international news media. Even though the rebels suffered higher casualties than the police in every confrontation, they were able to claim strategic victory because once the policemen returned to their posts they were quickly able to reoccupy the villages. The rebels had one big advantage over the security forces – anonymity. Anytime the situation got too hot to handle, they could easily discard their weapons and pass off as innocent civilians.

At about this time Milan's younger brother Ratna began to feel angry and restless. A robust-looking lad of fifteen, he was fed a constant diet of revolutionary ideas by his leftist teacher whose fiery rhetorics had had the desired effect on his impressionable young mind. He constantly seethed with anger - felt his blood boil, literally - at what he perceived as the wanton acts of injustice perpetrated in the name of culture, tradition, religion and freedom. He wanted urgently to do something – to eliminate the oppressors and exploiters, to cure the society of its evils, to rid the country of the parasites that were sucking it dry from inside, and to sacrifice his life for the noble cause, if necessary. But until the right time came, he had to keep his feelings concealed. He knew that his apolitical father and liberal-minded brother would not approve of his radical views. One day he and two of his friends secretly took an oath to join the guerillas by nicking their fingers with a knife, and making a solemn vow that when the right moment came they'd run away from home to join the rebel outfit.

Sometime after this, late on a quiet afternoon a group of Maoists walked into the village. Milan wasn't at home that day; he had gone to see a friend in a nearby village. The sun was on the last leg of its solitary race to the land beyond the western hills and Dil Bahadur had just finished washing his hands after feeding the pigs when he saw a file of men and women walking purposefully towards his house. There were about two dozens of them. They were carrying guns slung easily across their shoulders and knapsacks on their backs. He instinctively knew who they were - Maoist guerillas who had wrought so much havoc in other parts of the country. Suddenly his heart began to pound furiously and his hair stood on end. He was afraid. He had heard many stories of their atrocities. "Maoist guerillas!" He muttered under his breath, "I pray that they won't stop by my house."

But that's exactly what the guerillas had on their mind. They walked straight into his courtyard. A lean and sturdy looking man with a dark complexion, sharp nose and deepset eyes sauntered towards him authoritatively. It was obvious that he was the commander of the group. After eyeing Dil Bahadur from head to foot and mentally sizing him up, the guerilla commander, who was about thirty, said softly and politely, "Father, we are passing through your village. My comrades have covered a great distance today and they are tired and hungry. We are looking for a place to spend the night and something to eat as well."

Before Dil Bahadur could think up a reply, the commander turned to his subordinates and said, "Comrades, we'll spend the night here." The other guerillas immediately headed for different corners of the courtyard, put down their knapsacks and guns and asked the womenfolk for water to drink and wash.

"Yes," Dil Bahadur meekly breathed out his reply, "You may stay the night." He didn't have the courage to say no. He had heard that the guerillas spoke politely and respectfully, but took what they wanted by force.

"I see that you have two houses; we'll use one with your kind permission," the commander stated. Dil Bahadur was sensible enough to understand that it was not a request; the man was implying that he'd take whatever he needed by force, if necessary. It didn't matter whether his host agreed or not.

"That's all right with me," Dil Bahadur replied, feeling utterly powerless, "My son and daughters-in-law live in the two small rooms on the first floor; you can use the ground floor."
"Thank you. All we need is a roof above our head for the night. We'd be glad if you could kindly arrange to provide us with food and water as well. You will be doing the country a great service. We are fighting this war for people like you," the man said.
"Take what you need," Dil Bahadur heard himself say, "Everything I have is yours."
"We won't need much. We need water, firewood, rice and meat, if there is any. I can see that you have a fully grown

goat. That will serve us fine," the man said looking at the big, bearded goat tethered nearby with approving eyes.

Dil Bahadur had fed and cared for the goat for three years. It was his prize goat; the biggest of the four he had. He had kept it for some special occasion. He couldn't part with it so easily. "I've got a few pigs," he suggested carefully choosing his words, "perhaps your men would like to have a pig instead." "No, we'll take the goat," the leader replied, "some of us are Brahmans and do not eat pig."

Dil Bahadur did not have the courage to protest and that settled the matter. They would have his goat that night and thank him profusely in the morning.

Meanwhile the other rebels had quenched their thirst and splashed cold water on their faces, hands and legs to wash off the sweat and dirt. Dil Bahadur noticed that they addressed each other as 'comrade', and spoke politely and respectfully to each other as well as to their hosts. *Can these be the same people who murder and pillage so viciously? They are so polite and respectful. They don't at all look the barbaric type.* In spite of having to lose his prized goat, Dil Bahadur began to doubt the authencity of the rumours he had heard.

After a short rest, the rebels constructed a stone-oven at one end of the courtyard, inserted some dry firewood in it and started a fire. They put a large bowl of water on the stove. Then they slaughtered the goat (by beheading it with a khukuri) and poured the boiling water on the carcass to make it easy to pull out the hair. The Nepalese do not skin their animal carcass; they like to eat the flesh with the skin intact. Also, they do not throw away the blood. They collect it in a pot and later add the clotted blood to the meat while cooking the same. As they waited for dinner the guerillas chatted away happily about the ongoing confrontations in other parts of the country, lavishing generous praise on their comrades for their bravery. Some of them sang the 'people's songs' while others took turns to stand sentry with their guns at the ready.

After dinner, the rebel commander summoned the entire family of his host to his presence. Dil Bahadur had heard that Maoist commanders went about by their aliases to conceal their real identities. This particular commander went by the *nom de guerre* Comrade Prakash. He gave a long inflammatory speech on the need for every countryman - especially the peasant - to rise up against oppression and exploitation. "There is no real democracy in this country. Real democracy can exist only under the people's rule. The so-called democratic government in Kathmandu is a sham; it doesn't represent the grassroots; it represents only the capitalists, feudalists and lackeys of imperialists, and caters to their interest only......... We are fighting for your sake, to liberate you from bondage and slavery. Therefore, every young and able-bodied man and woman must participate in the people's war because it's your patriotic duty to do so...... Believe me, the victory of the people is certain and imminent. The old system is doomed, it has no future. The People's Liberation Army is moving towards victory every day, but you must also be ready to make the sacrifices........"

Afterwards Ratna sat with the rebels by the fireside and listened excitedly till late into the night. He knew that the day he had been waiting for had finally arrived. Tomorrow morning at sunrise he'd leave with the rebels in pursuit of glory. He would make a name for himself in the battlefield. He would become a feared and respected guerilla fighter. He'd liberate the masses of his country from oppression and exploitation. That was the true calling of his life.

In bed that night, Dil Bahadur whispered his apprehension to Kamala. "I am worried," he said in a voice filled with anxiety.
"But they seem nice enough," said Kamala, "They are very polite and respectful."
"There's no doubt about that," said Dil Bahadur, "and as long as we listen to them quietly and fulfill their demands, they will not harm us. After all, they say that they are here to liberate us. But I am afraid of the police."
"So am I," remarked Kamala, "when they find out that the guerillas spent a night here they won't be so accommodating."
"And sooner or later they are bound to find out," said Dil Bahadur in a resigned voice. "People must have seen them and they will talk."
"There's nothing we can do about it," said Kamala, "though we can always tell them that the Maoists compelled us at gunpoint."
"True. And they did in a way. With luck the police might take us at our word. But I am worried that the Maoists might make it a habit to stay at our place every time they pass through the village. It will be very difficult to explain the second time. You know how suspicious and jittery the policemen are these days."
"I am even more worried that they might decide to make a permanent base here in the village. If they do, this village will turn into a battlefield."
"They'll have to attack the police post for that."
"They will, sooner or later. There is no doubt about that."
"And it's always the innocent who suffer," Dil Bahadur concluded philosophically. In every conflict it's the innocent that gets caught in the middle. He had seen it first hand as a young man three decades earlier. After King Mahendra had

banned the political parties in 1960, a rebellion had broken out in the country. The outlawed parties – the Nepali Congress and the communists – had burned bridges and attacked police posts in the countryside, and the government had sent in the army to quell the rebellion. Dil Bahadur had witnessed the army pursue and shoot to death a man in front of his very eyes.

The following morning an excited Ratna got up earlier than usual with a mind to follow the guerillas as they prepared to leave. But when he saw his mother's face he began to have second thoughts and at the last moment he decided against it. Something held him back; he didn't know what. Perhaps it was his love for his mother, he thought. Or perhaps he didn't have the guts.

When the tiny silhouette of the last of the guerillas disappeared above the hill, Dil Bahadur breathed a sigh of relief, wondering aloud what the policemen had been doing all this time. They must certainly have heard of the arrival of the guerillas. Either they were too lazy or too scared to investigate. Perhaps they got the fright of their life seeing how hopelessly outnumbered and outgunned they were. But he knew that once the rebels were gone, they would come. And he was right. At midday two policemen arrived at his doorsteps to query him regarding a group of suspicious looking men the previous night. Dil Bahadur told the policemen truthfully that they were Maoist guerillas and that he was forced to give them shelter at gunpoint, against his wish. After a lengthy interrogation the policemen seemed to be satisfied and left amiably, asking him to report to them if the guerillas appeared again.

That was the first visit by armed Maoists, but not the last. In a year they would set up a permanent base in the village. They would parade in the school ground, sing their 'people's songs', collect donations from the villagers, force the villagers to watch their cultural programmes, and publicly flog and execute the 'enemies of the people'. But that was for the future. This was just the beginning of that future.

Throughout that year groups of armed Maoists passed through the village stealthily, usually at night, at least once a month. But they did not make any attempt to attack the police post or set up base there. Everyday on the radio there were reports of bloody skirmishes in other parts of the country resulting in massive casualties. But the village of Khewang remained peaceful. The Maoists and the policemen, who knew about one another's activities, kept a safe distance from each other.

And nobody died in the village that year - not even a child. But as the year progressed, the activities of the Maoists went on increasing alarmingly to the growing helplessness of the handful of policemen stationed in the village. Then the village became rife with rumour that the guerillas had set up a training camp in the jungle above the village and that they were training in guerillas warfare tactics. Some whispered that gun shots could be heard, but nobody was sure and nobody dared to go up to investigate. Their fear was compounded by unsubstantiated rumours that a large contingent of police force was coming to search and destroy the Maoists. To each man his own life is more precious than anything else, in spite of his claim to the contrary. It is so because at the core of existence is the survival instinct and in the face of danger that instinct takes precedence over everything. Then life seems like a flickering candle ready to be extinguished by the slightest whiff of wind.

For better or worse, the winds of change had finally arrived in the eastern hills of Nepal, albeit with an ominous cloud. Nobody knew where it would lead to, but change was definitely in the wind and the pillars of the 'old system', as the Maoists called it, was beginning to shake from the core. Change is an inherent trait of nature. Nothing lasts for ever; nothing remains the same for long. Everything must undergo change. It is the same with tradition and culture which are, after all, products of time, geography and circumstance. What a community does at any point of time to satisfy its material and spiritual needs is culture, and the way that they have been accustomed to doing certain things is tradition. With change in time and circumstance, they must undergo change. This is a continuous process and any community that resists change and tries obstinately to hang on to the ways of the past is doomed to perish. And if change is not allowed to take place peacefully then it will take place violently, as was happening in Nepal's case.

Culture and tradition are good only as long as they do not hinder progress. Once a certain aspect of culture (and tradition) stands in the way of progress, it should either be modified or discarded completely. Useless relics of the past have little use in the world of the present and the future, except to adorn the walls of the museums with. Of course, people must study and take lessons from history because it helps them to determine the right course for the future, but they mustn't strive to live in the past. They must continuously move forward. As the most advanced form of life on earth, it's a responsibility entrusted to humans by nature.

A few months after the first visit by the Maoists, Milan learnt from the village grapevine that his younger brother Ratna, who often went missing inexplicably, had taken a vow to join the rebels. This explained the boy's strangely restless behaviour and frequent disappearances, and he became alarmed. He had known for a long time where his younger brother's political sympathy lay. But he had not imagined that the boy would join the rebels. Milan had nothing against the Maoists. He himself believed that the archaic and feudalistic social system that was the root cause of the country's backwardness had to be dismantled. But unlike his younger brother he believed that transition had to take place by peaceful means through democracy and not by violence and terror. Even after his ordeal in Malaysia and his elder brother's murder, his faith in the tenets of freedom and democracy had remained intact. But the real reason for his alarm was that he feared for his younger brother's safety.

He contemplated for a few days as to the best course of action to take – whether to tell his father or talk to the boy himself first. After consulting with Lalita he decided on the latter course. One quiet and lazy afternoon, he summoned the reluctant boy to his room and said, "Ratna, I hear that you are planning to join the Maoists. Is that true?"
"No," the boy lied. "Who told you?"
"Don't lie to me," Milan said sharply, "I have ways of knowing. You can't hide anything from me."
The boy didn't reply. Milan tried to search his eyes but the boy avoided eye contact.
"I don't want you to have anything to do with them." Milan said.
"Why not?" Ratna retorted, meeting his eyes defiantly. "What's wrong with fighting against injustice and exploitation?" There was a flicker of antagonism in his voice.
"Nothing! I too am against injustice and exploitation. But I am afraid that you might get hurt."

"You don't have to worry about me. I can take care of myself," Ratna said antagonistically, with a sudden flash of anger in his eyes.

Milan lost his temper. "Don't talk back to me. I am your older brother, you know." He scolded the impudent boy. "You are too young for politics and war."

"I am old enough to do what I like. Nobody can stop me," the boy retorted angrily, "I am going to fight to rid my country of the parasites that are sucking its life-blood."

"You don't know what you are talking about. Propaganda and rhetorics have poisoned your impressionable young mind. I am not going to let you join the guerillas."

"Who are you to stop me? Nobody can stop me. Not even father," The boy retorted angrily and stormed out of the room.

"Just you wait. I'll tell father and you will see," Milan shouted after him.

"Tell him. I don't care," the boy shouted back as he descended the wooden steps angrily.

Milan thought long and hard and decided not to inform his parents as it would only add to their distress. A few weeks later he again found an opportune moment to try to talk some sense into the boy.

"Our parents are simple and honest folks, Ratna. They don't understand this dirty game called politics."

"That's why their generation has suffered so much, older brother," the boy retorted.

"I am surprised at the way you talk. Do you also understand what you say or do you just repeat like a parrot the words that your comrades have put in your head?"

"I am not a child any more, elder brother," replied the boy with annoyance, "I am almost sixteen, and I know and understand more than you think I do."

"No you don't. You don't know anything; you just think that you do. If you go down this path your life will be ruined. You will get killed, you know. There is no way your Maoists are ever going to win this war. The government still has not mobilized the army, and when it does your rebels will be crushed like insects. Our parents have already lost one son; they won't be able to cope with the loss of another."

"I will not die," Ratna declared, "And the Maoists are not going to lose the war. They are marching towards victory every day. They have attacked police stations all over the country and killed scores of policemen. Our struggle will be long and bloody and many people will have to sacrifice their lives, but in the end the People's Liberation Army will prevail."

"So you have made up you mind to join the guerillas?"

"Yes, when the right time comes, I will," the young hotheaded revolutionary-in-the-making made plain his intention.

"You are only thinking of yourself. Don't you think your joining the rebels will jeopardize the safety of out family?"

"I am sorry, older brother, but that's a risk I am willing to take for the sake of my country."

"What about us? What about our parents? How can you expect them to make sacrifice for a cause they do not believe in. You are being selfish, utterly selfish," Milan scolded his brother.

"No, I am not, older brother. I am not being selfish. It's you who is being selfish, because all you want is to become rich and live a life of comfort in the city. That's what you want, isn't it?"

This angered Milan greatly but he chose not to counter the accusation. He knew that it was true, to an extent. He could have told his younger brother that, yes, he wanted to get rich, but not by unlawful means, but he decided against it. The boy

wouldn't have understood. As far as the boy was concerned there were only two kinds of people on earth, the rich and the poor. The rich were the hated class enemy – to be exterminated and wiped off the face of the earth. "Your young mind has been poisoned by all the propaganda that you hear every day. But that's fine with me. I don't care what happens to you anymore. It's your life after all, not mine. It was my duty to caution you as your older brother and that I have done. But just don't leave home for at least a year."
"Why?"
"Because mother still hasn't fully recovered from the shock of elder brother's death. Your leaving home so soon will be too painful for her to bear."
The boy thought for half a minute and then said reluctantly, "All right. I won't leave home for a year. I give you my word. But after that I will be free to do as I like."

A few months later Lalita became pregnant again. This time around it was not an accident, unlike the first and second times. She had planned it, and even quarreled for it with Milan who had been reluctant at first. "We already have two flower-like daughters," Milan had said, "We don't need any more children." But she had insisted, telling him that she had to have a son because that's what everybody expected of her. She was well aware of the pressure that was building for her to produce a son. Her mother-in-law had confided to her one day, "I had much hope from eldest daughter-in-law initially but she turned out to be barren. I don't blame her for that; it is her destiny. Now that my eldest son is no more she won't ever become a mother. You too have given us only two granddaughters. We need a grandson in the family to carry forward your father-in-law's bloodline." Narmaya, her great-grandmother-in-law, had added: "I have become old and weak. I don't have many more years to live. It is my fervent wish to hold my great-grandson in my withered arms before I die."

But Milan was against it. He had argued, "In these modern times, we mustn't have more than two children. As it is, the earth is already overpopulated."
"Do you want your bloodline to come to an end? And who is going to look after us in our old age?" she had retorted.
"Why do people worry about their bloodlines? I don't see any point in that? Who will remember you a hundred years after your death? Nobody, not even you direct descendants, unless, of course, you yourself become famous. I don't know any of my forefathers beyond my grandfather."
"If we have no sons then one day when you are over forty you will suddenly realize that you need a son and you will bring home a young wife."
"No, I won't."
"Yes, you will. I know what men are like."
Seeing how adamant Lalita was, Milan had agreed reluctantly.

This time around Lalita was determined to deliver the baby at her parents' home in Yangnam. It was her mother's wish and Milan had no objection to it. It is natural for a woman to want to deliver at her maiden home because she believes that she can get better care there, which, of course, is not true in every case. But one's belief is like a big, immoveable rock; it cannot be moved or shattered easily. So she planned to depart for Yangnam two months prior to the delivery.

Everyday she examined her reflection in her hand-mirror as she meticulously oiled and combed her silky black hair. She hadn't failed to notice that after giving two births she had gone through some clearly visible, and quite unflattering, changes.

There were patches of dark skin on her cheeks, her once tout and inviting breasts sagged under her blouse, and a thin wad of fat had begun to accumulate on her formerly slender waistline. She realized with some consternation that her once svelte figure was going round and plump. "I am definitely not as pretty and attractive as I used to be," she whispered to herself. "I hope Milan still finds me sexy and desirable."

She recalled in her mind the days when she had fallen in love with him. She remembered how having little else to do she used to spend much of her time in front of the life-size mirror grooming and admiring her reflection. Those heady romance-filled days were long gone, and she knew that she was getting older and less pretty. But on second thought she didn't care. She was happy. She was going to have a son.

The first anniversary of Purna's death passed quietly, without any untoward incident. A week after that Ratna stole away from home early in the morning without informing anyone. When he didn't return home by nightfall, Kamala began to worry. But she took comfort by telling herself that he must have gone to a friend's or a relative's place as he quite often did. Although Milan suspected the real reason, he kept his mouth shut. *The boy might yet return*, he told himself. But when the boy didn't return the next day, Kamala became frantic. She nagged her husband and son to go look for the boy. It was then that Milan decided to tell the truth. Dil Bahadur and Kamala were stunned at first and admonished him for not telling them earlier.
"Why didn't you tell us? You should have told us," Kamala chided him.

"I am truly sorry, mother. I thought it would only distress you."
"If I had known, I'd have stopped him."
"You couldn't have, mother. I tried. I did my best to dissuade him, but he was stubborn and quarreled with me."

At length Milan was able to convince them that nothing would have made the boy change his mind. Nevertheless, at the behest of Kamala, the father and son went out in search of the boy, asking everyone if they had seen him.
"I think I saw him walking past my shop yesterday morning," the woman at the teashop said scratching her head, trying her best to remember.
"He was in my class yesterday morning, but I noticed nothing unusual about him," Ratna's Math teacher said.
"I saw him going uphill with a stranger," another woman said. "He seemed to be in a hurry," she added thoughtfully.

Finally, one of Ratna's classmates told them that Ratna had gone to join the guerillas. Milan said that he had guessed as much. They returned home tired and dejected. Milan didn't need to convince his father that his younger brother had gone to the rebels.
"He was a hot-headed boy, but I never expected him to do that," said the old man sadly, as he exhaled a puff of nicotine-filled smoke.

When they returned home without the boy, the flicker of hope in Kamala's eyes died. Her face turned ashen with shock and grief and she became frantic.
"Where's he? Have you found him?"
They shook their heads sadly in denial.
"Has he gone to them?" she asked again.

"It looks like he has," Dil Bahadur replied letting out a long sad sigh.
"I have already lost one son. Now another's gone. I can't bear the grief anymore. What have I done to deserve this? Why doesn't God have pity on me?" She lamented mournfully and began to cry.

Dil Bahadur could think of no words to console his aggrieved wife. He sank down on his favourite stool, took his cap off, and sat still with his hand on his forehead, deep in his thoughts.
"Purna's mother, don't cry," he said at length. "He'll be all right."
"No, he will not. He will not be all right. The Maoists will send him to fight the police, and the police will kill him. They will shoot my son dead and leave his body to rot in a far off place. My poor son! My poor innocent son! He is not even sixteen. He doesn't know anything. Why did the accursed Maoists have to start this accursed war? Why did they have to take my son away from me?"
"They didn't take our son away, Purna's mother," Dil Bahadur said, "He went of his own free will."
"It's the same to me," Kamala replied through tears, "He went because they started this war. He's gone. My poor son is gone. Gone for ever. I will never see him again."

In the month of March the sun once again crossed over into the northern hemisphere heralding the arrival of spring. This crossing over, called vernal equinox, is calculated precisely every year by Hindu astrologers in their two millennia old calendar, without the aid of modern alstronomical paraphernalia. This day is celebrated by the Nepalese by eating yams of all shapes, sizes and colours. With the arrival of spring the hills once again became alive with the blooming of flowers, chiefly among them rhododendron, poppy, magnolia, primrose and poinsettia, and the sounds of birds chirping merrily among the young leaves of the trees that fluttered playfully in the gentle breeze. Then, inevitably, spring gave way to monsoon which brought torrential downpour with abrupt lightening and thunderstorms. When the rains subsided, Milan accompanied Lalita to her parents' house in Yangnam with his little daughters. As they were about to depart Kamala said to Lalita: "Daughter-in-law, take good care of yourself and come back with a son. You know that it is our fervent wish to see a grandson from your womb. You have already given us two lovely grand-daughters who are the light of the family, and we are thankful for that. But as you yourself know daughters are a few years' guests only; they grow up and leave the home of their birth never to come back again. Sons are the ones who inherit and take care of the house. They are the security of old age."

The trail was still wet and slippery, and the still swollen rivers roared with only slightly diminished vehemence. There was only a month and a half to go before delivery, but in spite of the heaviness about her, Lalita walked sprightly and cheerfully. Her mother and sisters were delighted to have her back once again. This was Milan's second visit there and to his utter relief and amazement he found that this time around his father-in-law was better disposed towards him. *Perhaps it's Lalita's pregnancy*, he thought. *Or perhaps it's just the time*, Milan thought with an amused smile and a contented expression on his face as the old man warmly welcomed him calling him 'my son-in-law'. In the evening, the old man accompanied him to dinner, and after that the two sat down to have *tongba* in the verandah. Caressing his mustache lovingly, the old man talked effusively of the trials and tribulations of life, as older men are wont to do, and regaled him with amusing anecdotes from his young days, guffawing loudly every time he recalled something funny. Milan was surprised to find that he felt at ease with the man who had once seemed like an ogre to him. His own father, who was a good man, no doubt, never talked to him in such an open and frank manner. Before he was shown to his bed that night, he had changed his mind about the old man in spite of the insult that the latter had thrown at him during his first visit four years earlier. "It seems the old boy is not that bad, after all," he whispered to Lalita when they were alone, brushing her breasts gently with his hand.

"It's not him that's changed, it's the circumstances. He is the same as ever," she replied as she grabbed his crotch coquettishly.
"Now you are being philosophical," he teased her.
"I have become just a little more mature," she replied with a mischievous wink and pressed her breasts closer to his chest.
"But your father has still not forgiven you," he said searching her eyes and running one hand over her bloated belly and the other on her breast.
"No, but it's as good as that because I know that deep inside his heart he's forgiven us, it's just that he hasn't been able to express it verbally."
"After tonight, I am inclined to agree with you," Milan replied with a smile. He felt happy. "The last time I met him he was a tiger."
"I think you said he was an ogre," Lalita laughed heartily.
"So I did," he replied, "but now he's transformed himself into a human. I just hope that he won't change back to his old abusive self."

After staying two more days in Yangnam, and enjoying the newfound hospitality (he was feted generously and there was pork and tongba everyday on the menu), he returned home alone promising to Lalita that he'd come as soon as she sent for him. Before leaving he gathered his little daughters in his arms and whispered, "Be good. Don't bother your grandfather and grandmother too much. Daddy will be back to get you in a month." He kissed the girls on their cheeks and forehead.

The month passed at a snail's pace and not a single day went by without Lalita and his daughters coming into his thoughts. He missed them. But when his eyes fell on the sad and emaciated figure of the woman who was his widowed elder sister-in-law, withered by grief, he forgot his own sadness. His pain was nothing compared to hers. *Those cheeks were once rosy, those breasts were once full and alluring, and those buttocks were once round and tempting. There used to be a shy smile on that sweet face. Where have they all gone? Now she's just a pathetic shadow of her former self, so utterly forlorn and gloomy.* He thought sadly. It broke his heart to see her like that.

Laxmi went about her work so quietly that sometimes it seemed that she didn't exist at all. Like her dead husband she never complained of the injustices of life. Not even once. He wondered how much she must miss him. And he realized with a pang that he missed his elder brother, too, and he was suddenly overcome with a melancholy feeling that he could not understand.

One day when she was serving him dinner he remarked casually: "Elder sister-in-law, it must be so hard for you."

She looked at him with her round, sad eyes, still holding the serving spoon in her hand, and said, "Please don't remind me of my misfortunes, brother-in-law, it makes me miserable."

"I am truly sorry," he apologized. "I hate to see tears in your eyes, older sister-in-law, I really do."

"I have no more tears to shed, they have all been spent. And please don't pity me. It makes me feel worthless. If it is my destiny to suffer, then so be it. Don't you know that a woman's birth is a loser's *karma*?"

"Don't say that, sister-in-law. You are as good a woman as any man can ever have for a wife. My late brother was really fortunate to have you."

"Some people say that your elder brother died because of me. They say that I am jinxed."

"Don't pay attention to those superstitious people, sister-in-law. They'll say anything to hurt you, but you know that's not true." Milan replied indignantly, his ire directed at the spiteful people who wouldn't let a poor widow live in peace. Laxmi went back to her pots and pans without replying. That was where she found solace and security.

As Lalita's delivery date came nearer, Milan found himself in an increasingly anxious frame of mind. Sensing his anxiety, his mother said (it seemed she had an intuition for such things): "Don't worry. She'll be all right. She's not an inexperienced young girl; she's already given birth twice. She is strong and healthy. She'll be fine."

When his eldest daughter was born he was too young and naïve to worry. When his second daughter was born he was far away in Malaysia and insulated by the vast distance. Now he was mature and within reach of his wife and daughters, yet not quite so near. That was the reason for his anxiety.

Early one morning on the day of Lalita's delivery according to her calculations, Kamala said to her son as she handed him a hot mug of black tea, "According to my calculation, today is the day." She had predicted quite correctly the previous two times. The first one she had missed by only one day and the second had been on the exact day.

"Yes, mother" he replied, "You told me so."

"Last time she had it quite easy," Kamala said. "Her labour lasted less than an hour and she gave birth without much pain. You were not here then. She was up and about within a week."

"So I have heard mother," he replied.

"We took good care of your wife," Kamala added.

"I am sure you did mother," Milan replied, "She is your daughter-in-law."

"I hope her folks are taking good care of her," said Narmaya, who had just arrived from the toilet with an empty bucket. She had heard the last part of their conversation. In the old days there didn't used to be toilets in Nepali houses. People relieved themselves in the thickets and woods at daytime. As night swallowed the hills, they came out and relieved themselves at the sides of the foot trails. After the act of defecation they wiped their rear end with whatever they could lay their hands on in the darkness - leaves, rocks and anything that could be grasped with one hand. If someone chanced upon the defecator, it was the intruder who had to back off politely. Thus the Nepali proverb: "........ more shameful to the one who sees than to one who defecates." Then in the next few days the hot sun dried the golden stuff into an unshapely dark-brown cake that attracted a swarm of constantly buzzing green flies. The ever so familiar odour forced the unfortunate wayfarers to cover their noses with their hands or handkerchiefs, spitting out in disgust. If anyone was unlucky enough to step on the unsightly dark brown cake, he/she cursed the originator with these words: "May the butt of that accursed son/daughter of a whore be infested with maggots!"

Modern toilets were introduced in the hills of Nepal only in the 1960s. They used to be, and still are to a large extent, mostly makeshift affairs of creaky wooden planks with a round hole above a hastily dug pit, a sheet of tin for a roof and an old dirty sheet of cloth for a door. But some people, it seems, still prefer the open toilet under the stars.

Narmaya, however, had come to appreciate the usefulness of the toilet ever since her sons had built one near the house. It was full of slits (which let in the warm sunlight in the morning) and without a proper door, just a piece of dirty old cloth in its place to cover the entrance. But it was good enough for her, and for the rest of her family. If someone came whistling to relieve himself/herself when another person was already inside, the one already in the act would cough out loudly to inform the newcomer of his/her presence, at which point the newcomer would either wait at a respectful distance or go somewhere else to relieve himself/herself. Narmaya had got used to washing her rear end with half a bucketful of water like everybody else. She still limped at a painfully slow pace. *Poor old grandma*, Milan thought, *it looks like she is never going to recover fully. She'll take that limp to her grave.*

"Sure, grandmother," he replied giving her a sympathetic look. It saddened him to think that she who used to roam the village freely before the mishap was now confined to the premises of the house, waiting patiently for others to visit her.

After tea he went to see his childhood friend Chudamani, a school teacher who was a vocal critic of the Maoists. This young man, a Bahun by birth and one of his closest friends, had already been threatened by the local Maoists, but he didn't care. Milan returned home late for lunch. Later in the afternoon he sliced firewood at Laxmi's behest. He didn't stop even when it began to drizzle. The monsoon was on the wane and it would completely stop raining in a few days. The wood was damp and infested with a multitude of creeping, crawling insects. At each stroke of the axe they were unceremoniously dislodged from their hitherto safe haven and ran in all directions hunting for cover. Milan paid scant attention to the plight of the newly homeless creatures. His thoughts were preoccupied with the thoughts of Lalita. *She must have given birth by now. I hope she didn't have to go through too much pain.*

He wished she were at home with him instead of with her parents in Yangnam. After more than a month's separation he was anxious to touch her, to caress her, to stroke her, to lie beside her soft, warm and inviting body. It had been many months since he had last made love to her, what with her pregnancy barring the way. He knew that some men continue to have sex with their wife until the penultimate day, but he had stopped in the fourth month, not because of any religious conviction (he had none), but because of consideration for her. Now he was eagerly anticipating the day when he would be able to resume his sex life. But that was still some months away. As darkness prepared to engulf the hills, he wiped the sweat off his forehead with a swipe of his hand and muttered, "I guess it's time I went to fetch them. In fact, I should go tomorrow. Yes, I will go tomorrow." He collected the sliced pieces of wood and arranged them in neat rows at the side of the house. After that he washed his hands and legs and went into the kitchen where his sister-in-law had prepared a jar of *tongba* for him. He took one saying, "Is this mine?"

"Yes," Laxmi replied without looking at him. She was busy cooking spinach curry in the smoke-filled kitchen. The toxic smoke spewing out of the mud-stove hurt his eyes, but he didn't flee. Lack of proper ventilation kills uncountable Nepalese women every year from respiratory-related diseases such as bronchitis and tuberculosis. The problem is with the traditional design of the stove. It is unscientific, inefficient and spews smoke like a brick kiln. But people are so resistant to change that they refuse to do anything about it, even when shown a better way.

"Today is the day," he said to his sister-in-law pulling a bamboo stool.
"I know" she replied, "Don't worry, everything will go well."
"I am not worried," he replied, "I am just a bit excited and nervous." He took a long sip.
"Even after fathering two children?" she said, half-teasing him.
"Yes, even after fathering two children. It sounds funny, but it is true," he replied in a serious tone of voice.

The two sat silently for a long time, Milan sipping tongba and Laxmi cooking curry. The smoke made them cough sometimes. Then Laxmi said all of a sudden, "I'll never know what it feels like to become a mother." Milan was taken aback by this unexpected frankness from his usually reticent sister-in-law. He searched her face and realized that she was making an attempt at humour.

But he couldn't think of the right words to say to her. "You are still young and pretty, sister-in-law," he blurted out after some thought.
"Am I? No, I am not. I know you are only flattering me. I feel old and ugly," she replied somberly.
"You are not old and ugly, sister-in-law. You are young and pretty. And if you will forgive my saying so, you can marry again. There is a life ahead for you if you want it."

"Don't utter such words. It's a sin even to talk like that," she replied.

"There's no sin in a widow remarrying, sister-in-law. Not according to our Limbu culture. It's only the Hindus who forbid their widows to remarry. And just look at the injustice of it. A man can remarry the very day his wife dies if he wants to and nobody lifts a finger at him, but a woman is expected to live the miserable life of a widow for the rest of her life. It is totally unfair and unjust."

"But aren't we Hindus, brother-in-law?" Laxmi asked.

"Well, not really," he replied, "We are not Hindus. The government counts us as Hindus to falsely show in the census that more than eighty percent of Nepalese are Hindus. After that they forget us. They do this with impunity because we do not speak up."

"You should be a politician," Laxmi teased him with a chuckle.

"Me? A politician? Never." He laughed. "I just know a few things because I went to college in Kathmandu. I didn't do well because I was too preoccupied with becoming a *lahooray*, but I had the opportunity to mix with many political-minded young men. I learned quite a few things from them."

He stopped to contemplate for sometime. Then he continued, "You see, Limbu women are not restricted like the Hindu women. They do not have to treat their husbands like God, and they can remarry if they want to and even married women can leave their husbands if they are not happy with their marriage. They can do so without fear of harassment and ostracism or being called slut and whore. Do you know that an aunt of ours – a cousin of our father - has already dumped three husbands and she's now happily into her fourth marriage? And she's got at least one child by each of her husbands."

"Yes, I know. But mother says that's shameful."

"Maybe, but who cares? Does she care what people say? She doesn't give a damn, and why should she? It's her life. She can do what she likes with it."

"Are you trying to marry me off and chase me away, brother-in-law?" she teased him, laughing. But he knew that there was pain underneath that laughter.

"No, sister-in-law," he replied seriously, "How could I even think of such a thing? You are a part of this family and you have as much right in this family as anyone. I am sorry if I offended you, but I was just reminding you of your rights as a modern woman. If one day the right man comes along in your life then you should marry him. But if you choose not to, then you have my assurance that you will get your fair share of the property."

"Oh, brother-in-law, I didn't mean it that way. Please don't talk like that. You are too kind to me." She said in mock exasperation.

"I am not kidding, elder sister-in-law. I am serious. I really mean what I said." He said with a somber expression.

"I guess it's a woman's lot to suffer," she said with a resigned voice after some time.

"No, it is not, elder sister-in-law. Not anymore. The times have changed. If you have the will to stand up for your rights, then you can bring changes."

"But this male-dominated society won't let us do anything. Why only men, even women stand in the way of women who try to move forward."

"Sadly, that's true. That's why women will always be slaves in this part of the world," Milan said philosophically.

After a few minutes of silence Laxmi said, changing the subject, "Are you still thinking of migrating to the city, brother-in-law?"

Milan reflected for a long moment and said, "It doesn't matter anymore. I have this house to look after, and grandma, father and mother will never agree to leave. They belong here as the hills and the forests and the streams and the rivers belong here. They will never be happy in the city."

"That's true. But what about your own dream?" She asked sympathetically.

"I guess it will remain a dream forever," He replied with a wistful note in his voice. Laxmi noticed that familiar faraway look in his eyes.

"If only your elder brother hadn't died," She said.

"It's not his fault," he replied.

But silently he agreed with her, *yes, if only he hadn't been killed. If he were still alive, I'd be free to pursue my dream.*

Laxmi was loath to admit to herself, but the conversation with Milan had somehow uplifted her spirit. She felt light, happy and liberated. She hadn't felt like this in a long time. And in a very strange way she felt inspired by a surge of new hope. *Perhaps someday things will change for the better. Perhaps life has better things in store for me.* But still she wasn't ready to consider remarriage; she was too faithful to Purna for that. That night as she lay in her bed alone, as always, staring at the ceiling before sleep transported her to the land of dreams she told herself that she was not going to remarry. "My heart belongs to my husband, even if he is no more," she whispered in the dark. But the more she thought, the more she found her conviction faltering. *Milan is right,* she thought at midnight. *There is more to life than pain and suffering. I have to leave the past behind. I have to rise out of this depth of sorrow. There is a life to live, and may be someone out there to share that life with. My dead husband loved me, and his soul will be happy to see me happy.*

᠅

An hour before noon the next day two young men arrived hastily. One was wearing jeans trousers and red chequered shirt and the other was wearing the fake British army camouflage (complete with boots) that was so popular in those days with the young men of the hills who wanted to look macho. Both wore dark sunglasses. When they walked into the courtyard, Dil Bahadur was resting on a straw mat smoking his *khosela*. He wondered who they were; he had never seen them before.

The boys greeted Dil Bahadur politely addressing him as 'father' and introduced themselves. One turned out to be Lalita's younger brother Suman and the other his cousin. Milan had just had his morning meal and was going through an old novel in his room when his father called him. He looked out of the window and when he saw the two boys he came out hurriedly with a puzzled yet expectant expression on his face.

The boys greeted him with the customary Namaste, and he did likewise in return.

"Where's Lalita?" He asked them.

"Brother-in-law," Suman said, "There's been an emergency and we've come to fetch you."

"What has happened? Is anything wrong?" Milan asked. *Something has gone wrong, otherwise these boys wouldn't be here,* he thought with a cold feeling in his heart.

"Elder sister has been taken to the district hospital in Phidim Bazaar." He replied.

"Why? What has happened to her?" He was almost frantic now.

"She has had some complications," the boy replied.

"What complication?" he asked sharply.

"I am not sure what, brother-in-law. They asked us to fetch you as soon as possible, so we came running," Suman replied.

"Has she given birth?" Milan asked.

"Yes."

"When did they take her to the hospital?"

"Early yesterday morning, at the same time we left."

"Are you sure she is all right?" he asked again anxiously. He was beginning to imagine terrible things.

"She was all right when we left. They said it's only a minor complication. She has lost some blood. Nothing to worry about really. She wished to see you, that's why we came as fast as we could."

Milan hurriedly explained the situation to his alarmed parents and went to his room to get ready to leave. When Gorimaya served the boys milked tea and fried eggs they eyed her with unfeigned interest. She was a comely girl of thirteen - slim and petite with a wasp-like waist, a pair of apple-sized breasts under her shirt, straight black hair tied in a neat plait and a shy half-smile on her delicate pink lips. *This must be Gorimaya of whom my elder sister talks so much. She is indeed very attractive.* Suman thought as his heart raced. At age sixteen he was highly susceptible to the attraction of young girls. On her part Gorimaya was acutely aware of the boys' attention although she pretended not to look at them directly. But she had already scrutinized them from her bedroom window. *That one on the left resembles my sister-in-law somewhat*, she thought. *He must be her younger brother Suman. Not a bad looking boy, though not as good looking as his sister,* she thought.

After allowing the boys to rest for an hour - the boys had started at 3:30 AM that morning - the threesome started the journey shortly after noon. Along the way Milan asked the boys a torrent of questions pertaining to Lalita's well-being. The boys answered as truthfully as they could. Their answers, however, did little to allay his fears. *Something has gone wrong. Terribly wrong. They are just not telling the truth.* He kept repeating to himself silently. Afterwards, as the trio walked briskly and wordlessly Milan's mind was hounded by one dreadful scenario after another. He imagined Lalita in excruciating pain in a hospital bed crying out for him. Then he saw her giving birth to a healthy little baby and then lying contentedly afterwards, waiting to show him the baby. Then he imagined her giving birth to twins or even triplets, that being the cause of the complication. Finally, and with unmitigated dread, he saw her lying on the hospital bed – cold, still and lifeless. This thought nearly brought tears into his eyes. *No, that cannot be*, he reprimanded himself, *how can I even imagine such a terrible thing?* But the thought just wouldn't go away. Again and again he tried to fight the apparition of his fear in his mind, but he found himself losing the battle. *Please, let nothing happen to her. If anything happens to her I'll be ruined. She is my love, she is my life. I won't be able to live without her.*

Stop thinking, he commanded himself. *Stop thinking! Stop!* But thought is an obstinate creature. If it were a living being then it would be a wild horse. You just cannot tame it easily. The more you want it to stop, the more it gallops. For it the whole universe is like an infinitely wide and empty plain where it can run amok in any direction at will. The threesome walked quickly, oblivious to the stunningly beautiful sights and sounds of nature that surrounded them, each lost in the depth of his own thoughts. Milan thought ceaselessly of Lalita all the way while the two boys thought of the pretty girl they had left behind without proper introduction. *I think I should visit my sister's house more often*, Suman thought with dreamy eyes.

Shortly after sundown they reached the village of Medibung where the unpaved motorable road had only recently arrived. This was the village of Amrita's husband, but Milan didn't have time to greet her in-laws. They spent the night in a lodge, labeled 'Hutel and Resturent' on a crude signboard, and caught a truck to the town of Phidim early the following morning. The dreary-looking Indian-built contraption roared and spewed toxic black smoke as it laboriously made its way southward along the dusty, pothole-filled uneven road that winded its precarious way up and down the slopes. Up and down - several hairpin-bends downhill to the river bed, where the driver's helper poured a gallon of water into the radiator, and then several hairpin-bends uphill again only to start another downhill ride.

They reached the red-earthed town of Phidim shortly after midday. Sprawled on a plateau that rises above the River Pheme, Phidim Bazaar is quite a large town by the hills' standard. It is the administrative center of Panchthar District. With a number of shops, hotels, lodges and restaurants that are lit dimly by yellow electric bulbs at night (the result of a small hydro-electric power station nearby), and several government offices, a hospital, district police headquarters, an army barrack nearby and even a shop that somewhat resembles a modern department store, the town of Phidim has a semi-urban look and feel about it. The plateau is surrounded by higher hills on all sides except the south-west, and at night the dim lights of Myanglung Bazaar, the administrative center of Terahthum District several kilometers to the west, and the village of Yangnam in the north, twinkle like groups of distant stars. But when Milan alighted from the truck he cared for none of these. He hastily led the way towards the nearby district hospital where the resident doctor rarely showed up for work, though he never forgot to collect his salary.

As soon as they entered the hospital premises he sensed that something was wrong. At the deserted reception they met a young nurse who, after Suman had described his sister, pointed them towards the woman's ward with a sympathetic look in her dark eyes.

At the door Milan met Lalita's uncle, a middle aged slitty-eyed little man with a potbelly, and asked him, "Where is she? Is she all right?"

Without uttering a word the man opened the door and ushered him inside. As soon as he entered the ward, he heard the sobbing and weeping of women around a bed in a corner past the tall but slightly stooped figure of his father-in-law. He instantly knew what had happened and froze. His father-in-law said in an anguished voice, "It's too late, son-in-law. You have arrived too late. She has left us all and gone to heaven."

Milan felt the floor slide under his feet. He felt weak and his knees trembled under the weight of his body. For a brief moment he saw only darkness before his eyes. He swayed and leaned against the wall to support himself.
"Dead? My Lalita ..... is .... dead?" he asked as if in a dream. It felt so unreal, so unbelievable, and so far-fetched.
"Yes, son-in-law. She is dead. She's gone. She's left us all." The old man replied haltingly in the most sorrowful voice. He looked broken.
"When? When did she die?" He heard himself ask.
"Half an hour ago. She was asking for you before she breathed her last." The sorrowful man replied.
"How? How did she die?"
The old man didn't reply. It was his wife who did, taking a break from her sobbing. "It was a breach delivery, son-in-law. The baby came out the wrong way – feet first. It was a difficult

birth. We managed to pull the baby out, but she bled to death. We rushed her to the hospital as soon as we realized that her life was in danger, but we were too late. It's my fault. I was unable save my daughter's life. I am a sinner, son-in-law. I couldn't save my darling daughter. I couldn't save her for you. I have committed an unforgivable crime," she wept loudly and openly.

Milan stared at the dead body of his wife lying prostrate on the bed past his tearful father-in-law, past his wailing mother-in-law and past the rest of the people assembled there. He began to walk towards it as if in a trance. *This isn't happening. It's only a bad dream – a terrible nightmare. It is not happening. I am going to wake up and everything is going to be all right.* Somehow the whole thing seemed surreal to him. He felt as if he was in a terrible dream and would wake out of it any minute. *How could my Lalita be dead? No, she is not dead. She is in a deep slumber. She'll wake up when I call her name. She will open her eyes and smile sweetly at me when I touch her. Wake up, my heart, there's nothing wrong with you. You are fine. It's time to go home.*

Before he reached the death bed, a woman stood up and handed him a baby. "The child is safe," said Lalita's aunt.
"My child? It survived?"
"Yes, son-in-law," the thin-faced middle-aged woman replied, "The poor child has survived". Without thinking he took the infant into his arms and stared at it through a film of tears. "It's a boy," the woman added. With the infant in his arms, he moved towards Lalita and gazed down at her face. Even in death she looked serene and beautiful. For a moment he thought that the others were lying to him. She looked so alive, as if she would wake up any moment, smile at him sweetly and start talking. He gently ran his fingers across her cold and

lifeless face, and then sank to the floor beside her on the bed. The aunt who had handed him the infant hastily retrieved the child from his arms. He hugged Lalita's body tightly in his arms as a torrent of tears flowed down his cheeks, and then he began to sob.

"Lalita, my love, what have you done?" he whispered in an anguished voice. "Why did you leave me like this? What am I going to do without you? How am I going to leave without you now? What am I going to tell my daughters when they ask for their mother? What am I going to tell my father and mother when they ask for their daughter-in-law? Don't you know that you are too young to die? Remember the promise we had made to each other? That we will live and die together. But you didn't fulfill your promise. You are so cruel, so heartless. You have betrayed me. You have left me to face this life alone? Why? Why? Answer me, my love."

Early the next morning Lalita's dead body was wrapped in a pure white cloth and carried down to the bank of the Pheme River on a green bamboo stretcher. The procession included relatives and friends in the town of Phidim. As the yellow flames consumed the dead body in front of the sorrowful eyes of the disconsolate family members, Milan's father-in-law stood beside him and whispered, "Son-in-law, please forgive me for my sins. I have been a fool, a bloody fool. I never took the trouble to tell my daughter that I had forgiven her. But I want you to know that I had forgiven you and her a long time ago."

"Father, I have known that all along," Milan replied, "So did Lalita. No matter what, she always loved you and cared for you. And there is no need for you to ask for forgiveness

because you have done no wrong. I would have reacted in the same manner if I were you."
"What hurts me so much, son-in-law, is that I never took the trouble to tell her ..." The tearful old man almost choked on his words; such was the depth of his remorse.
"She knew, father, she knew that you had forgiven her," he replied.

Afterwards, Milan desolately trudged behind his father-in-law as the mournful group made the mostly uphill journey on foot to Yangnam. Nobody spoke. They walked in silence with grief drawn across their faces, each remembering the deceased in his/her own way and the part that she had played in his/her life. The infant changed hands several times and broke the silence from time to time by letting out a shrill cry, and quiet again after his grandmother fed him powdered milk from a milk-bottle she had bought in Phidim Bazaar.

When the slow-moving group reached the village at dusk, a happy and excited Kalpana ran out into the courtyard.
"Father, father" she cried out happily, "Look my father has come."
Her younger sister Samjhana tottered towards him with a happy smile on her cute little face. Milan took the girls in his arms and planted kisses on their tender cheeks.
"Where is my mother, father?" Kalpana asked innocently, looking at the trail expectantly.
Milan couldn't find the right words to say to his little daughter who wouldn't understand. She was so innocent. At length he found his voice and said, "She has gone far away, my daughter. She has left us."
"Where has she gone?" the little girl insisted.
"To a place where you and I cannot go, daughter."

"Where is that place that we cannot go, father? I want to go there, too."
"I don't know, daughter. It's far, far away."
"When is she coming back, father?"
"She is never going to come back, darling. She's gone for ever."
"Why isn't my mother coming back? Is she angry with me and my sister?"
"No, she is not. She is not angry with you, my child. She always loves you."
"Then why has she left us? Why isn't she coming back? She told me that she'd come back as you as you arrived."

And then he couldn't hold back the tears any longer and wept without inhibition, pulling the little girls tightly to his chest. They were too young to understand but seeing him cry, they too began to cry. Another dream had failed him. Here, in this harsh and beautiful land supposedly blessed by the gods, dreams die every day.

There was a mournful quietness about the household once again - a quietness pregnant with deep sorrow. Two deaths within a span of two years had shattered the spirits of those still living. When death starts stalking it returns again and again to reap its grim harvest, the Nepalese have a saying. But they also counterbalance that by saying: *The dead are dead, nothing can be done to bring them back, but the living must go on living*. So they went about their work quietly, speaking as little as possible. The mournful silence was disturbed from time to time by the squeal of the newborn infant demanding nourishment and the sob of his orphaned older sisters crying out for their mother. It would be a long time before happiness would return to the twin houses again.

A day after the heartbroken Milan returned home with his three children, Kamala took her newborn grandson to Laxmi's room and placed it gently in the latter's arms.

"Daughter-in-law," she said, "I submit this poor little orphan in your care. Poor child, his unfortunate mother died at a young age while giving birth to him. He will carry that stigma with him for the rest of his life. Like you, she was like a daughter to me. But nobody can prevent the hand of fate. Not even the gods themselves. What's written at the time of birth cannot be altered. It was written for her to die young, so she died young. This child is yours now. Take care of him. Look after him. Bring him up as your own son."

"But what does brother-in-law .....?" Laxmi started.

"He agrees with my decision," Kamala cut her short hastily.

Laxmi took the infant in her arms and laid it gently on her lap. She gazed silently at it for a long, long time. Then slowly teardrops ran down her cheeks and fell soundlessly on the infant's soft cheeks, one harmless drop after another. She wiped them off with her fingers as the pink little child thrashed about its tiny arms and legs. *To gain something in life, one has to lose something.* She thought sadly. *But what great losses! What irreparable losses! First, I lose my husband and then my brother-in-law loses his beautiful young wife. And then I get her child. Poor Lalita, she was so beautiful and vivacious.*

She turned her attention to the infant. "Poor child," she cooed softly to the baby with tearful eyes, "How luckless you are - orphaned the day after you were born. But don't you cry, my little darling, because I am here for you now. I will always be with you. I will never leave you for even a moment. From this moment I am your mother and you are my son. Even though I am not your mother by birth, I will be your mother by *karma*. I will feed you, wash you, sun-bathe you every morning and massage you with mustard oil, and rock you to sleep in your cradle singing lullabies every night. Just you wait and see! I will give all my love to you. I will take good care of you and bring you up as my own son. When you are able to talk you will call me 'mother' and I will call you my son. My own son!" She lifted him up, pressed him to her breasts and then kissed him all over his delicate face.

Afterwards, when the child was peacefully asleep, someone gingerly knocked her door and when she opened she found Milan standing there. "Elder sister-in-law," he said, "I just can't imagine what I would do without you. To me you are like an angel. I can never thank you enough."
"I am only doing what needs to be done, brother-in-law. This is the least I can do for you," she replied and then added a moment later, "You and I are family, aren't we?"

He nodded in agreement. *Yes,* he thought, *we are family. She and I. The two of us. We are the same age and we live under the same roof. She's lost her husband and I my wife. But the similarity ends there. She is so mature and responsible, and I? I still feel like a wide-eyed eighteen year old boy. I sometimes suspect that I act like one, too.*

It was the year 1999 AD (Nepali year 2056 Bikram Sambat). After five years of political instability with one ineffective coalition and minority government after another in the capital, the parliamentary elections arrived once again. The people were given another chance to elect a majority government to right the previous wrong. Too grief-stricken, Milan abstained from voting; so did other members of his family. Dil Bahadur, Kamala and Laxmi had haunting memories of the election that were too painful. This time around there was no violence in the village. There were calls by the Maoists to boycott the elections once again, accompanied by threats of violence and sabotage. But the elections went largely peacefully throughout the country. The Nepali Congress, a left-of-centre democratic party, an old horse in Nepali politics (the oldest, in fact), once again emerged victorious and formed the government. The people let out a sigh of relief, but it was short-lived. The country was soon wracked by an internecine power-struggle within the ruling party. Taking advantage of this downside of democracy, the Maoist jauggernaut continued to grow and roll and trample the countryside. Thus, while the short-sighted politicians squabbled in Kathmandu, the rebels drastically escalated their attacks on police posts throughout the country, killing scores of policemen (who were poorly equipped and untrained to fight the insurgency). At the same time, they increased attacks on those deemed 'enemies of the people' – landowners, moneylenders and all those who dared to express their disagreement with their political ideology and modus operandi. Every day stories of vicious and gory killings occupied the headline news in the national news media. Many of their victims were flogged and shamed in public; some were taken to the jungle and tortured mercilessly and then executed in the most brutal manner – sliced, hacked or impaled to death, and their bodies mutilated in the most barbarous manner. The rebels rarely wasted their precious bullets on their 'worthless' victims, preferring to hack them with khukuris and knives. Taking lives meant nothing to them; it was the propagation and imposition of their political ideology that was of paramount importance.

But something good comes out of everything. Every dark cloud has a silver-lining, and even evil has a good face. In the remote villages greedy landowners were put to flight and their lands and houses confiscated and occupied by the rebels, and sometimes distributed to the people. Devious moneylenders had their bills confiscated and torn to shreds. But the well-to-do and those with sons and daughters employed in the cities and foreign countries were politely requested (at gunpoint, of course) to make donations amounting to hundreds of thousands of rupees. Many paid up without a squeak and others took flight. There's nothing dearer to a one than one's own life.

Part IV
Reign of Terror

Reign of Terror

Nine months after the national elections, the security situation in the country went from bad to worse. The handful of terrified policemen stationed in Khewang followed the examples of their colleagues elsewhere and packed up their belongings and quietly left for the safety of the district headquarters after a string of threats of attacks (that failed to materialize) by the Maoists holed up in the forest above the village. With the police gone, never to return again, the village fell into the hands of the rebels without a fight.

The following morning a large contingent of armed guerillas marched triumphantly into the village. They walked in a single file, with their rifles and muskets slung easily across their shoulders. Many of them wore the green Maoist uniform complete with a matching green cap with a lone red star on it. They headed straight for the office of the village development committee where they hoisted their red 'hammer-and-sickle' flag and set up base of operation.

When the guerillas were taking over the village, Milan was helping his father castrate a couple of squealing piglets. They had already finished work on the first piglet which was grunting painfully nearby and were now onto the second animal. This time the father and son changed places. Dil Bahadur pinned down the piglet firmly holding it by the legs and snout, and while the poor creature let out an ear-splitting squeal of pain, Milan carefully slit its scrotum with a shiny new shaving blade. This was the first time for him and his hand turned red with the blood that spurted out from the cut. He carefully plucked out the balls one after another and put them in a saucer. Then he sewed up the wound with a needle and string. After that he applied a thick paste of turmeric powder in mustard oil on the wound. It took him roughly half an hour to perform the operation, with his father instructing him at every step, and throughout the operation the piglet screamed incessantly. With the operation over, Dil Bahadur let the piglet go. But the poor thing didn't run away immediately, it continued to lie, grunting in pain. After two minutes it slowly pulled itself up and trotted away, squinting fearfully at its tormentors, who were by now busy washing off the blood on their hands and legs.

After setting up their base the new masters of the village dispersed into small groups and went about the village exerting their new-found authority. They knocked on every door and instructed the people to gather at the high school premises in the afternoon, threatening dire consequences for anyone who failed to show up.

When four young guerillas stepped haughtily into their courtyard, the father and son had just finished washing. Dil Bahadur noticed that one of them was only about fourteen years of age and he couldn't help remembering his own son, Ratna. *He must be doing the same thing these kids are doing in some far off corner of the hills, if he is still alive*, he thought with a tinge of sadness. There had been no news of the boy since the day he had left home a year and a half earlier. *The poor clueless parents of these boys must be going through the same pain that we are going through.*

The young guerillas carried old and worn out guns, loaded and cocked, and strutted with the arrogance of victors. *What battle have they won?* He asked himself. The next thing that entered his mind was '*It's dangerous for boys to handle lethal weapons.*' He realized too late that he had thought those words aloud.

The young guerillas looked at him sharply and said, "What did you say, father?"

"Nothing. I said nothing," Dil Bahadur stammered. One has to be careful. Kids with guns can be infinitely more dangerous than adults with guns.
"You are lying, old man. I think I heard you say something about guns being dangerous in our hands?" the oldest among them said harshly. He was apparently the leader of the group.
"Me, too," added another belligerently.
"I am sorry, please forgive me." Dil Bahadur apologized, with beads of sweat appearing on his forehead.
"We know very well how to handle guns, father," the youngest of them added. "Would you like a demonstration?"
"No. I believe you do," the old man replied fearfully.
"Good," said the leader of the group. "Now listen. All villagers are to report to the high school premises at three o'clock in the afternoon. Anyone who fails to show up will be dealt with according to the laws of the people."
"What for? And what exactly is the law of the people?" Milan said sharply, with undisguised scorn in his eyes. He was losing his patience at the arrogance of the boys.
"Don't ask questions, brother. Just do what you are told to do," the leader of the group hissed threateningly.
Milan was about to open his mouth again, but his father whispered sternly to him, "Hold your tongue!"
"We will come. All of us, except my old mother who's got chronic pain in her legs and cannot walk that far," Dil Bahadur said.
"If she is unable to walk then you and your son can carry her, can't you?" the guerilla said.
"Yes, we can," Dil Bahadur replied.
"Good!" the boy said.

After they disappeared round the corner, Dil Bahadur turned to his son and hissed, "Do you want to get killed?"

"But father, they can't just walk into our home and tell us what to do. We are not criminals; we are law-abiding citizens of a free and democratic nation," Milan said.

"You may be. But it means nothing to them. Can't you see that? If you are so foolish as to stand up to them, they will kill you without thinking twice. I don't want to lose the last son I have left," Dil Bahadur said.

"This is not right," Milan shook his head angrily. "Who the hell do these Maoists think they are? Why must I take orders from them?"

"Because they've got guns in their hands and you haven't. That's why," Dil Bahadur replied and walked away.

Well before three in the afternoon the whole village gathered at the school premises as ordered. The place was resplendent with the colour red. Red banners and red flags fluttered everywhere. The Maoists, most of them strangers to the village, strutted confidently in their green uniform. Many wore red bandanas on their head which gave them an air of menace. Some were busy controlling the crowd while others were getting ready for the march past. Among them Milan noticed the firebrand school teacher Kishor, Ratna's Nepali language teacher and his chief political mentor. He was one of the five sons of an impoverished Bahun who lived at the upper part of the village. This sharp-featured, emaciated little man with a goatee and thick black-framed glasses was apparently the ideologue of the group. His zeal for the cause he was fighting for smouldered plainly in his piercing dark eyes. Another Che Guevara eyes, Milan thought, this one behind the safety of glasses. When the former school teacher saw Milan, he walked over to him and said in mock-friendliness, "Milan-jee" ('jee' being a term of respect added after the addressee's name), "I am glad you have come."

"I had no choice," Milan replied with a forced smile. The teacher ignored the whiff of sarcasm in his voice and said, "We must all unite to liberate the people from slavery. I hope you will join us someday. You will make a terrific fighter, you know."

"I am sorry but politics is not my cup of tea," Milan replied.

"Who said anything about politics?" the revolutionary said with a smile. "We are here to free the impoverished masses of this country from oppression and exploitation. It's every man's duty to fight against injustice, don't you think so?"

"It sure is but …."

"Never mind," the former school teacher cut him short, "Your younger brother is doing very well. You probably haven't heard, but he's become a sort of a hero."

"Where's he? Where's my little brother?" In spite of the gravity of the situation, Milan's eyes suddenly lit up with hope. His father and mother would be tremendously happy to hear of the boy. Any little piece of news would do.

"I can't tell you that. But I assure you that he's doing very well. Be seeing you around." Comrade Kishor lost interest in him and walked away.

Then Milan noticed Tej Bahadur looking at him. This quiet young man from the nearby village of Tellok, and whom Milan had known since childhood, had left his young wife and five year old son to join the rebels. He nodded and smiled at Milan and Milan did likewise. The man, however, did not make any attempt to approach him. Neither did Milan.

The commander of the rebels was a tall and tough-looking young man who went by the *nom de guerre* Comrade Prakash. He had dark skin, a long aquiline nose and deep-set eyes on a bony face. Milan thought it ironic that for a political outfit that professed to champion the cause of the downtrodden, the bulk of its leadership was made of Bahuns, the dominant 'high-caste' ethnic group in the country. "This war, I suspect," he whispered to his father, "is not really about us. It is between two classes of Bahuns and Chhetris – the richer ones in the urban areas and their poorer cousins in the rural areas. Have you noticed that the Maoist leadership is composed almost entirely of them?" His father didn't respond, but he added anyway, "On second thought, it's always been that way in this country and it will continue to be so for the foreseeable future."

Looking first at the rebels swaggering confidently as if they had just won a great victory, and then at the pinched, frightened and suspicious faces of the villagers, Milan for the first time came to grips with the gravity of the people's war. He was suddenly struck by a cold, hard realization that the war had arrived at his doorsteps and it was there to stay. Suddenly, the future looked dark and ominous, and he was overcome with a feeling of dismay. Until now he hadn't thought much of the Maoists, believing that the rebellion would die out of its own accord or would be easily crushed by the government. Watching this triumphant war party now and having seen the determination in their eyes, that didn't seem likely. *These rebels are prepared to kill and die for what they believe in. Their own lives and the lives of innocent people mean nothing to them.*

The program began with a parade by a disciplined group of gun-toting guerillas to the loud beat of drums. There were many young women among them and some of the boys were as young as thirteen. "At ease! Attention! At ease! Attention! Forward March ...... Left, Right, Left, Right ...." The guerillas marched smartly in perfect unison from one end of the field to the other end and back to the beat of drums, and the rag-tag army suddenly transformed into a formidable force in the eyes of the spectators. It was easy to see that they had plenty of practice in the jungle. The purpose of this display of raw military might was two-folds, Milan concluded. The first was to impress upon the people that they were going to win this war and the second was to put fear into the hearts of their detractors. When the parade came to an end, the crowd broke into a thunderous applause as they had been instructed to do. Milan reluctantly joined in. He knew that everyone was being watched with sharp, hawkish eyes.

Comrade Prakash, the area commander, climbed up the makeshift wooden stage with a grin on his face. After a brief introduction, he embarked upon a long and incendiary speech. The gist of his speech was as follows: "The present government does not represent the people. It only represents the big landowners and aristocrats who are mere stooges of Indian expansionists and Western imperialists.......... The so-called democracy we have in this country is not true 'democracy', it is an anachronistic system imposed by foreign powers for their own selfish ends........... We'll give you true democracy because only Maoism can bring true people's democracy by eliminating the enemies of the people......... The root cause of the country's problems is the monarchy and the feudalistic social system that it represents. Since the palace still commands the loyalty of the army and police, real power lies with the King and not with the elected government. Therefore, the main goal of the people's war is the overthrow of the anachronistic monarchy.......... Oh, poor and oppressed brothers and sisters, we are fighting to liberate you from slavery. We are sacrificing our lives so that you can be free. The word 'Maoist' means a poor person, therefore you are all Maoists and this war is your war. So join the People's Liberation Army and fight alongside your comrades in this glorious campaign of liberation..........The people's war has now reached a critical phase. We are beating back the forces of the 'old system' everywhere. Despite their claim to the contrary we now control almost the entire rural area. We are on the verge of victory. No one and nothing can stop us .... Under the people's government all exploiters, swindlers, thugs and other enemies of the people will be tried by the people's court according to the people's law ....The corrupt and inefficient judiciary of the 'old system' takes years to give justice and lets the guilty party go unpunished. That will not happen under Maoism. People's justice will be swift and terrible. There will be no mercy for the enemies of the people; they will be executed immediately ...."

During the speech the young guerillas, most of them school dropouts, cheered and clapped every time he uttered something that was to their liking or, more correctly, something they had been conditioned to like. Rest of the audience meekly followed suit. Most did not make much sense of the comrade's speech, but they clapped vigorously anyway. Like sycophants, being acutely aware that sharp and cruel eagle-eyes were fixed upon them. When absolute power is concentrated in the hands of a few, even honest people are forced to resort to sycophancy to save their skin. These were uncertain times and one could never know what might happen next. One might be branded a public enemy for the slightest offence and beaten up or even executed in the most brutal manner. When one man goes insane, the world can ignore him. When the whole world goes insane, one sane man ignores it at his own peril.

Near the end of his speech the area commander announced the dismissal of the elected village committee and the entire hill reverberated with the sound of thunderous applause.

When confronted with brute force, most people turn out to be cowards. Their self-preservation instinct takes control of their conscience and the only thing that they can think of is how to save their own skins.

After the last sound of applause died out, the guerillas proceeded to mete out 'people's justice' to the captured 'people's enemies'. The unfortunate men, there were three of them, were dragged out and paraded in full view of the public. They were branded public enemies and their crimes read out one by one. Even from a cursory glance, it was obvious that they had already been given the preliminary treatment. The first to face the 'people's wrath' was a young school teacher named Chudamani Dahal. A supporter of the ruling party, this young man was an outspoken critic of the Maoists and the rebels had threatened him with dire consequences. Days before the Maoist takeover of the village, Milan had advised him to flee, but he had refused. Milan considered him as one of his closest friends; the two had grown up together running up and down the hills until Milan had gone to Kathmandu.

Chudamani walked with his head held high, unafraid and defiant. Even when the guerillas (many of whom would have been his students had they been of the village) shoved him roughly and jeered at him, he stumbled and picked himself up defiantly. Milan was profoundly impressed by the courage shown by his friend. Of the other two 'public enemies' one was an elected ward chairman and the other a drunkard who gambled by day and tormented his long suffering wife and children by night. Both frightened men shuffled meekly, trembling in fright, with their heads hanging in shame.

Comrade Prakash sauntered towards the three captives. At that moment, in that remote corner of the world, he was the man with the last word. He knew that and held his person with an unmistakably arrogant air of authority. There is nothing sweeter and more intoxicating than the power to decide the fate of fellow men. Countless men and women of ambition have conspired, fought, killed and died for it. Apparently, this man reveled in power – the kind that comes directly from the barrel of the gun.

After he had finished inspecting each man carefully with contemptuous eyes, he said to them: "It gives me great pleasure to punish scums like you for the crimes you have committed against the people. Today, I'll see to it that justice shall be done and no mercy will be shown to you."
"What crime?" asked Chudamani boldly, without a hint of fear in his voice, "What crime have I committed?"
The other two trembled in fear, sweating profusely.
"Who told you to speak?" The area commander bellowed and slapped him squarely in the face. Chudamani staggered back and nearly fell.
But he quickly regained his composure and staring back at his tormentor insolently, said coolly, "I am a free citizen of a free and democratic country. I don't need anybody's permission to exercise the rights guaranteed to me by the constitution of my country." There was an audible gasp from the crowd. *What is the fool doing? Does he want to get killed?*

Comrade Prakash glared angrily at the *insolent* school teacher. He was clearly surprised at the latter's audacity. "So you think you are smart? You think you know everything?" he spat out clenching his teeth, his dark face turning darker with mounting anger. "I'll make an example of you. Oh, I will, and by the time it ends you will be begging for mercy," he rasped. Chudamani did not reply; he placed a steady stare in the guerilla commander's eyes. Then for a long moment, the two men stood facing each other, each trying to out-stare the other. *These two could have been brothers*, Milan thought as he compared the two - *both of them dark, tall, lanky, proud and defiant. One fired up and demonized by his political ideology and the other unyielding in his faith in freedom.*

Comrade Prakash turned to the murmuring crowd and raised his hand. Immediately, all sounds died out. Not a voice, not even a squeak, not even a cough, and not even the nervous rustle of feet could be heard.

"Brothers and sisters," he cried out at the top of his voice, so that even those at the furthest corner could hear him clearly. "Before you today stand three criminals - the hated enemies of the people. These are the parasites that have bled our motherland dry. Therefore, we have brought them before you today in this people's court to face the people's justice."

Pointing at Chudamani he said, "You all know this school teacher. He has been spreading vicious lies and rumours against the just and noble people's war. He talks of freedom and democracy, but in reality he serves the feudalists and imperialists. The 'freedom' he so zealously talks of is not real freedom; it's a ploy by the Western capitalist-imperialists to recolonise the impoverished countries. The 'democracy' he talks about is not real democracy; it is a cruel ruse by the rich to further exploit the poor. Time and again we have warned him not to speak against the revolution, but he has deliberately turned a deaf ear. Therefore, we have been forced to bring him before you today to face the people's justice."

At a hand signal from him, a big, swarthy rebel stepped out into the open. Even at a single glance it was clear to one and all that he was the sort who has far more brawn than brain, and was mighty proud of it. He made an act of spitting twice into his each of his palms, rubbed them together, and then picked up a freshly-cut bamboo staff lying nearby. There were several of them lined up in a neat stack there. He held the staff firmly with both hands and walked towards the school teacher with slow and deliberate steps. He stopped at a distance of a meter from his intended victim. Chudamani looked straight into the swarthy fellow's pitiless eyes. He did not flinch. If he was afraid he showed no sign that he was. He calmly waited for the inevitable.

"Get ready, you son of a whore," the swarthy man hissed, his voice filled with hatred. He swung the staff high up above his shoulder and with a swift and powerful motion brought it crashing down on the backside of the school teacher's legs. There was a sharp report as bamboo-cane met flesh and the school teacher winced in pain. But he did not cry out. The swarthy man struck again and again, one swift and powerful blow after another. "Two, three, four, five, ..." Milan found himself counting under his breath.

After enduring fifteen strokes without a sound - with clenched teeth and tearful eyes - Chudamani could withhold no more assault on his body and finally let out a howl. It echoed back from the school building and the hills and fell on terrified ears, piercing their very soul. But the swarthy man didn't stop; he went on striking. He stopped after the twenty-fifth stroke and carefully examined his weapon. Finding that it had fractured longitudinally, he threw it away and moved to pick up another. But another guerilla signaled to him his intention to take over. The second man, a slender but tough-looking boy of not more than sixteen, picked up a fresh bamboo-cane staff from the stack and proceeded to strike Chudamani on his back. "Twenty-one, twenty-two, ..." Milan resumed counting. After the thirtieth stroke, Chudamani staggered and fell face down on the ground, but two rebels wearing red bandanas on their heads quickly ran towards him, caught him by his arms and propped him up. Then the beating continued. "Thirty-one, thirty-two, ……….thirty-nine, forty." Milan went on counting.

"That's enough for now," Comrade Prakash said and the boys who had been holding the school teacher let the limp man slip from their hands. Chudamani slumped on the dusty ground and did not move. His back and legs were painted red with his own blood. Everyone waited with bated breath. They were all thinking the same thoughts. *Is he dead? Have they killed him?*

But as the crowd watched silently, the fallen man stirred. Slowly, very slowly, and with a huge effort, he moved his arms and legs. Then he raised his head and pulled himself up with a tremendous effort and sat on his knees. He spat out a blob of dust mixed with saliva and blood and remained in that position for an extended moment.
"You will never win," he said to the area commander, "Never!"
"Shut up! You insolent son of a bitch …." the swarthy guerilla bellowed at him.

Comrade Prakash signaled to the man to be quiet and said to Chudamani, "Confess your crimes and apologize, and I'll let you walk away a free man."
"I haven't committed any crime," Chudamani spat back.
"You have been going around telling lies about the people's war and spreading vile rumours against our leaders," Comrade Prakash charged.
"I was only speaking the truth," Chudamani replied.

"Don't talk back to the Comrade, or else I'll cut off your tongue," the swarthy man threatened him crossly.

"Take him away. Make sure he doesn't escape. We'll deal with him later," Comrade Prakash instructed his subordinates, who caught the wounded man roughly by his arms and hair and dragged him away.
"You know we don't like to waste bullets on scums like you," one of them said.

After Chudamani had been dragged to a corner, Comrade Prakash said to the swarthy man, "Now let's take care of the other two."

When their turn came, the terrified ward chairman and the drunkard sank down on their knees and whined for mercy with tearful eyes. But the guerillas were in mood for leniency and proceeded to mete out the punishment. Their shrill screams and heart-rending cries rang into Milan's ears long after the beating was over.

After the two were released the cultural program began in earnest. Maoist cadres of both sexes sang the 'people's songs' and danced the 'people's dance' to the beat of the 'people's music'. (The Maoists denounce all other forms of entertainment as feudalistic, reactionary and decadent.) Then they staged a play which demonstrated how the exploiters and swindlers took advantage of poor villagers and how in the end they would be punished by the People's Liberation Army for their crimes.

The show lasted until sunset. There is no business like show business, as the Americans like to say, and the master propagandists that the Maoists are, they are masters of this art in their own way. By the time the show ended, they had captured the hearts and minds of a large number of villagers. At the conclusion of the program the villagers were told to go home quietly and not to get involved in any activities contrary to the spirit of the revolution. Before leaving Milan stole a quick glance at the furthest corner of the ground where his friend was detained, and noticed that he was tethered to a wooden post, his hands tied behind his back. *They are going to execute him,* Milan thought. *There is no doubt about that. Was he foolish to defy the Maoists? He probably was not. Men like him are different from the rest of us. He is fearless; the rest of us are cowards. We do not have the courage to stand up for what we believe in; he has the guts to die for his belief. The rest of us flow meekly with the current, men like him create their own currents. That's what makes him different.*

The public humiliation of the school teacher was but one of the many terror tactics employed by the Maoists to force the people into submission. On the way home Milan concluded that though the cause taken up by the Maoists was not wholly unjustified, they had to be resisted because of their aspiration for absolute power. And he was right in feeling that way about the Maoists. Any individual or a group of people or a political party that aspires for absolute power must be opposed for that is the greatest injustice of all. That they want it in the name of the people makes very little difference; even the biggest of tyrants do so ostensibly in the name of the people. From Adolf Hitler to Joseph Stalin to Mao Ze Dong to Emperor Bokasa to Idi Amin to Pol Pot to Saddam Hussein, to name but a few - all of them have wielded absolute power in their respective countries in their respective times and wrought death, destruction and untold miseries to countless people. And ironically, they have all done it in the name of the people. They may have had the best of intentions at the beginning, but power is a great corrupter and it corrupts all who wield it. The Maoists are very patriotic and have good intentions for the country; there is no doubt about that. But good intentions alone do not make the world a better place, for intention and deed are two different things. As someone aptly put it, some of the greatest crimes in history have been committed with the best of intentions. So while it is not wrong to fight against injustice, it is wrong to shed blood to replace one set of injustice with another set of injustice. There are better ways of loving one's country than eliminating those countrymen that disagree with one's ideology.

There was a hushed silence in the village from that day. The environment of fear was so pervasive that people spoke in subdued voices. Even the womenfolk who chattered and gossipped endlessly at the village spring now talked in whispers. Everyone looked at everyone else with suspicion. *Is he/she going to tell on me? Is he/she going to falsely accuse me of being a collaborator? If I say this or that, will the Maoists brand me public enemy and flog me?* It also came to light that in the immediate aftermath of the takeover many men and women had joined the Maoists ranks – a few willingly and the rest out of fear. Those who had not done so lived in constant terror, and glanced left and right before speaking. Even walls have ears, the Nepalese have a saying. How true it sounds at such perilous times!

Three days later the beheaded and badly mutilated body of the school teacher was found near a stream west of the village. The severed head ("I didn't know it looked so impersonal and unsightly when detached from the body," Milan remarked to his father) was lying a few feet from the near-naked torso. A swarm of green flies buzzed constantly as they darted over the swollen corpse. It was obvious that the dead man had been severely tortured before execution.

A week after the brutal murder of the school teacher (which nobody mentioned openly), the Maoists announced the formation of the people's local government. To demonstrate that they were not imposing it forcibly upon the villagers and that the villagers themselves had taken the initiative in its formation, they nominated an unwilling Jit Bahadur to the post of chairman. When he showed hesitation, they made threats of dire consequences. Carry a loaded gun and speak politely, that's how the Maoists operated. Fearing for his life the old man quietly acquiesced. Dil Bahadur was also made a member, he being one of the 'grassroots'. The utterly bewildered man didn't even let out a squeak in protest. He had seen enough violence not to speak. The first act that the new village committee passed was for every house to fly the red flag of the Maoists atop the roof, which was promptly translated into action. The flags were magnanimously provided and hoisted by the guerillas themselves. They were a proud symbol of the people's victory.

Now fast forward. A year later the village was in the full grip of the Maoists. The policemen did not return. This was, in part, owing to the remoteness of the village and the treacherous trail that led to it. In the meantime the Maoists had implemented several so-called 'people-orientated programmes'. They had banned the singing of the national anthem (which consists of half a dozen lines in sycophantic praise of the King) in the schools. They had revised the school curriculum to incorporate 'people's education', and everything deemed reactionary was replaced by communist ideology.

They had turned the high school ground into a permanent parade ground, where the ever-growing army of grim-faced and green-uniformed gun-slinging young men and women marched smartly to the beat of drums with grandiose dreams in their impressionable young minds. *We'll conquer all - today these remote mountains, tomorrow the whole wide world.* The same venue was used at regular intervals for the 'cultural programs' that every villager had to attend. They had seized the lands of the absconding landowners. They had banned gambling and consumption of alcohol, though people still took a swig or two on the sly behind closed doors. They kept strict vigilance on the coming-in and going-out of the people. Insiders had to take their permission to go out and then return within the stipulated timeframe. Outsiders had to show their identification to enter the village. They called it their visa system, whatever they understood by that term.

Every coin has two sides, as the saying goes, and every action has up side and down side. First the up side: Fraudsters and swindlers (and there are a few in every place) were punished and chased out of the village. Devious moneylenders had their bills torn to shreds, and those who owned more than a fair share of land had their land confiscated.

Now the down side: Loss of freedom. Rule of fear. Forcible recruitment of young men and women into the militia and consequently exodus of the same from the rural areas. Young men and women unwilling to join the rebel militia ran away to the towns and cities and from there to India in search of lowly-paid menial work. Thus, thousands of able bodied young men and women who should have been tilling their farms and engaged in other productive work were forced to become rickshaw-pullers, watchmen, dishwashers, pimps and prostitutes in the filthy and seedy streets of Indian cities. As a result manpower to tend to the farms and animals became scarce. True, Maoist cadres sometimes came and helped for free with much fanfare. But even a layman knows that farming is not about one day's worth of work. It's not even about a week's worth of work. It's a year-round job requiring many hands and constant attention. In the meantime the rebels lived off the sweat of the poor people. They had to be fed and quartered at any odd hour they chose to appear at the doorsteps. Anyone unwilling to accommodate their demand was immediately accused of being in league with the 'enemies of the people'. Worst of all, one had to take the permission of the Maoists for every little thing – even to observe one's own tradition such as birth rites, death rites and wedding ceremonies - things that people had taken for granted since times immemorial. Thus, fear stalked in every nook and corner of the hills. People were afraid to speak up; they were afraid to complain. Not only the walls but even the open sky had grown ever watchful eyes and ears.

Nothing affects the human psyche more than fear. It does strange things to people. It makes them do things they wouldn't even think of doing in normal circumstances. Right becomes wrong and wrong becomes right, and instead of speaking out against the perpetrators of terror, most people choose to join them to save their own skin. On the other hand, power has the tendency to corrupt and dehumanize even the humblest of men. The guerillas, most of them barely able to read and write, could not be expected to be much above that. Drunk on a liberal dose of raw power that came directly from the barrel of the gun, they quickly resorted to settling any dissent or insubordination with violence. That was the only language they had been taught; that was the only language they understood. People were routinely threatened, assaulted, dragged before the 'people's court', beaten up, tortured and sometimes murdered for the slightest offences, all in the name of the people. In the meantime in other parts of the country, the rebels had drastically increased attacks on the police. Ambushes and skirmishes took place almost every day. It was getting on time for the increasingly beleaguered government to send in the army.

The brutal murder of his friend had deeply angered Milan. It had thoroughly shaken the foundation of his belief in the goodness of the human heart. But much of the time he was preoccupied with the thoughts of his dead wife. He missed her dearly. Her absence hurt him like a constant ache in his heart. She was not only his wife; she was his lover, his life partner and his soul mate. She fit his hand like a glove, and he hers. She was beautiful, robust and sexy. She loved him, as he loved her and he was devoted to her, as she was to him. Her death had cut a deep hole in his consciousness, and he knew what it was. Emptiness. That's what it was. Sometimes that emptiness threatened to swallow him up and drag him into a dark pool of misery. "I should not have left you alone, Lalita. If I had been by your side, you would not have died. It's my fault. It's entirely my fault. I am to blame for your death," he reproached himself everyday.

Although people repeatedly advised him to marry again and move on with life ("A new wife will rejuvenate your life," they said to his skeptic ears), he had absolutely no thought of doing so. To him the very idea was unthinkable; it would be an act of betrayal to his dear departed wife and her memories. "Lalita, I will never be unfaithful to you. I will keep you alive in my heart and cherish your memories and love you for as long as I live. I will remain true to you until my dying day," he whispered into the darkness of the night in his lonely bed. Like

Laxmi, he had acquired the habit of staring at the dark ceiling in the dead of the night.

That year Amrita and Rajkumar came back from England on a six months' vacation. She wrote from Kathmandu expressing her desire to come to the village. She had sorely missed her parents and sister-in-law and was anxious to see them. After consulting with his father and mother, Milan sent her a reply urging her not to come as the situation was not favourable. He warned her that if she came the Maoists were sure to ask her husband for 'donation' amounting to hundreds of thousands rupees, if not in Khewang then certainly in his own village Medibung. If they failed to comply the rebels would hold them hostages until their demands were met. This had become a regular occurrence in the rural areas and even in the smaller towns and bazaars across the country. In the villages the Maoists appeared in person to demand payment, with a friendly smile and polite words on their lips and loaded guns in their hands. In the towns and bazaars they sent threatening letters. Nobody was immune, nobody was safe. Not even government officials. The Maoists worked out how much each man earned and then stipulated the amount. Nobody dared tell the comrades to their face that they were collecting 'extortion money' and not 'donation money'. The government, on its part, sat with its hand tied, too powerless to take any action. In fact, even highly placed government officials were rumoured to have made payments to the Maoists. Not even foreign tourists were spared. They were made to give voluntary donation, at gunpoint, naturally, and given hand-written receipts in exchange for their trouble.

Amrita and Rajkumar spent their vacation shuttling between their houses in Kathmandu and Dharan. She found someone to carry her presents to Khewang (there were always a few people who traveled to and from Kathmandu and Dharan). At the end of their vacation they went back to England to live a life insulated from poverty, hardship and fear. Things look quite different from a safe distance.

In the meantime in Kathmandu the ruling party changed its prime minister once again. Not that it mattered much to the people. 'Every holy man that shows up turns out to be a fake', the Nepalese have a proverb, referring to the ash-painted, half-naked Indian fakirs who roam the hills begging for alms. To the people driven to pessimism, the new prime minister was no different from his predecessor, and his successor would be no different from him. They were all the same; there were no great expectations of any of them.

By this time, across the length and breadth of the country (all 800 kilometers by 150 kilometers of it as the crow flies), there was one word on everybody's lips – peace. This is the universal paradox of human societies – when there is peace people do precisely the things that precipitate war, and when there is the war they clamour for peace. And they start looking for scapegoats. The only problem was that the country had fallen so deep into the quagmire that peace by this time had become an unattainable goal. Since both warring sides were unwilling to lay down arms, the only way peace could be achieved was for one of them to achieve total victory over the other. The Maoists were determined to do just that, by any means, no matter how long it took and no matter how many lives were taken. People's lives didn't matter to them; it was only the propagation of their dogmatic ideology that mattered. Hardcore Maoist ideologues were determined to prove that despite the setbacks of the late 80s (when the Iron Curtain had fallen in Europe), communism still had relevance in the modern world and was, in fact, the way of the future. They

Reign of Terror

justified their 'killing' by claiming that it was not them that had started the war in the first place; the rich had been killing the poor for centuries; which has some truth in it. The government, on its part, was equally determined to crush the insurgents, though so far it had refused to deploy the army, which was under the constitutional monarch's control anyway. The august makers of the democratic constitution had for some reason left the army under king's direct control. In any case, the army's traditional loyalty to the king was such that they wouldn't have moved a finger without the king's consent and the popular King Birendra, who in the eyes of the people was the only one who had truly fulfilled his constitutional duties, was unwilling to deploy his army against his own subjects.

Although peace reigned on the surface, life would never be the same again for the people of Khewang, or of any other village in the hills of Nepal, for that matter. If one quietly submitted to the idiosyncrasies of the rebels' political ideology and became a dumb sheep in the flock, he/she was left alone. But if anyone dared to let out so much as a squeak against them or their policies, he/she was immediately silenced with threats of violence. To the uneducated mind the swift and merciless justice of the Maoists was highly impressive. A lawsuit that took years to settle in the courts took only a matter of hours, and the guilty party was punished immediately, with death in many cases. Once accused by the Maoists it was hard to prove one's innocence because in their legal system a person is considered guilty until proven innocent. It is no wonder that the highly impressed villagers, many of whom understood justice only in its crudest form ("An eye for an eye"), began to praise the rebels for bringing peace and justice to the rural areas.

Narmaya, who was approaching her eightieth birthday (and whose fractured leg was never to be fully healed) spent her days in the company of her grand-daughter and three little great-grandchildren. The presence of the Maoists made little difference to her - her only complaint being that she could no longer have her daily dose of *tongba* openly. In retrospect, her life had been one of ignorant bliss. Although she had lived through a significant part of the country's modern history – from the fall of the Ranas to the advent of democracy to the seizure of power by the King to the restoration of democracy to the ongoing Maoist rebellion - she had barely been aware of any of the above political events. These were things that were out of her field of interest.

Four years after the death of her husband, Laxmi had fully recovered from the cruel blow that life had given her. She had accepted her lot as *fait accompli* – inevitable, like death - and consigned her past to the deep recess of her memory and got on with life. She no longer grieved for her dead husband ("No amount of grieving will bring him back," she had reasoned correctly), though he still came into her thoughts occasionally, but without hurting. In the days following his death, she had waited for his apparition to come to her in the dead of the night, as she had been told it would. She hadn't been afraid of the thought of meeting his ghost. But much to her disappointment no such thing had happened. Now it didn't matter to her anymore.

She had, in fact, found happiness. The children had given her life a new meaning and a new purpose. They had rejuvenated her life. Ever since Lalita's death, she had immersed herself in the care and upbringing of the children. She had named the little boy Santosh, meaning contentment in Nepali. She never left him alone; she played with him, ate with him and slept with him. In the meantime the boy's elder sisters had also attached themselves to her and tacitly adopted her as their surrogate mother, much to her pleasure, and she had reciprocated their feelings. She was happy to be their mother. Thus preoccupied with the upbringing of the children, she no longer felt alone and miserable. In the children she had found her happiness, and in their future she saw her future. She fed them, bathed them, washed their clothes, prepared them for school and took them to bed at night. In short, she lived for them and her whole life revolved around them.

Kamala had not failed to notice the change in her daughter-in-law and one day confided to her husband happily.
"Have you noticed the change in our eldest daughter-in-law?" she asked him.
"Yes," he replied, and then added pensively, "Poor daughter-in-law, misfortune always strikes the good-of-heart. But I am happy that she is happy now."
"If only we could find a good man for her," she said thoughtfully.
"I don't think she wants to get married. She seems to be very happy as she is," he replied.
"For now she is. But when the children grow up, she'll be alone and miserable once again." Her intention was not to remove her widowed daughter-in-law from the scene; she was not clever enough for that. She genuinely wanted Laxmi to be happy.

Kamala was also concerned about her two sons. She had got over Purna's death, but she was irked by Milan's continued insistence on remaining a bachelor even after repeated advice by all and sundry to the contrary. And Ratna's complete disappearance was a cause for constant grief. The boy was not among the guerillas in the villages; he hadn't been seen anywhere in the neighbouring villages. The local Maoists insisted that he was alive and well, but they steadfastly remained tight-lipped about his whereabouts. And so Kamala worried constantly. One night, as in many other preceding nights, she suddenly woke up, sweating and shaking, shook her husband out of his slumber and said in a frightened voice, "Purna's father, I just had a terrible dream."

"What have you dreamt of now?" the irritated man grumbled. He hated to be woken up in the middle of the night. But Kamala was unperturbed by her husband's irritation. She believed in her dreams. She believed that a dream, whether good or bad, was a premonition of things to happen. She was not alone in this belief. Most Nepalese, especially the womenfolk, believe in the power of dreams, though they have differing views. While some believe that whatever one sees in a dream will translate into real life, some are of the view that the exact opposite happens. For instance, if someone dies in a dream it means that that person will either die in the near future or will have a long life, depending upon what who you ask. If one manages to kill a snake in dream then one is likely to vanquish one's enemies, but if the snake chases or bites him/her then the opposite is likely to happen. Kamala's dreams were a regular occurrence and she always made it a point afterwards to relate them to whoever she found willing to listen, and ask for interpretation, and if none was forthcoming then supply her own. She had learnt to interpret her dreams from her mother, who had learnt it from her mother, who in turn had learnt it from her mother and so on. But Dil Bahadur was skeptic about the interpretation of dreams; he himself rarely remembered his dreams.

"I saw Ratna walking hand in hand with his dead brother. They were going away from the house. I called after them but they didn't seem to hear. They didn't even look back, they kept walking away. What does it mean?"

"Why do you women have to interpret every dream? It means nothing. It's just a dream. It means that you worry too much. That's all. Now go back to sleep."

"I think it's a premonition," she persisted.

"Maybe, maybe not," he replied laconically. "But I can tell you this. I know deep down in my heart that Ratna is all right."

"How do you know? You haven't heard from him since he disappeared. Have the Maoists told you anything?"

"No, but if anything had happened to him then we would certainly have heard. I am a member of the local government. The fact that we haven't heard anything proves that he is all right."

"But I am worried sick. Why can't you men have more compassion like us women?"

"It's not that I am indifferent," Dil Bahadur said, "But there's nothing we can do about it."

"He is eighteen now. If he had not run away to the Maoists he'd have passed high school by now," said Kamala wistfully.

"Stop worrying about something that's not under your control," Dil Bahadur chided his wife and turned to the other side. Night time was the only time she could have intimate conversation with him. At day he was busy with his work and meetings (that he had to attend now as a member of the village government) and she didn't get much opportunity to talk to him.

Although Dil Bahadur was deeply concerned about his missing son, naturally, he also had reasons for consolation. The fact that his son was a guerilla fighter was not lost on the local Maoists, and it had given him a certain amount of leverage.

The *comrades* spoke to him respectfully and the younger ones addressed him as father. This pleased him immensely. And much to the growing annoyance of Milan, he had even begun to regard the Maoists as liberators, though in his heart he was not yet a full convert to their cause. Democracy didn't make much sense to him, but deep in his heart he was still loyal to the King.

Kamala nudged him again and said, changing the topic, "I worry a lot about Milan, too. Ever since his wife died he has lost his jest for life. He talks very little and doesn't mingle with his old friends. He can't go on like this for ever."
"He'll get over his grief," Dil Bahadur replied. "It takes more than a couple of years to heal a wound as deep as his."
"But some men ….."
"Some men take a new wife less than a week after their wife's death," Dil Bahadur cut her short. "We see a few of them everywhere. They do not care for their wives and children. To them wives are nothing more than objects to be acquired and discarded at will to satisfy their sexual desire. Milan is not one of them. He truly loved his wife and was devoted to her."
"Exactly," replied Kamala, "He was devoted to his wife and that's the problem. Even after her death he is still devoted to her. He doesn't seem to realize fully that she is dead, gone for ever. No amount of grieving will bring her back. He cannot go on pining for his dead wife for ever."
"You worry too much. He'll get over it."
"He won't if he goes on like this. Don't you think it's time he got married again?" She persisted.
"Yes. But I think it's better for us to leave that decision up to him. Let him make up his own mind in his own time. Besides, it is difficult to find a young unmarried girl for a widower with three children."

"He is still young and good looking. There'll be plenty of girls for him," Kamala protested.

"He may be young and good looking, but the fact is that he is also a widower with three children. And I am afraid only over-the-hill spinsters will be willing to marry him," Dil Bahadur replied apprehensively.

"Shall I talk to him again tomorrow? Do you think he'll listen this time?" Kamala asked.

"How many times have you talked to him? Has he ever listened to you? But since you insist, you may go ahead. Do what you like. But I don't think he will listen. That boy has a mind of his own, he has. He is not a sheep that follows the flock blindly. Now go to sleep and stop troubling yourself too much," Dil Bahadur replied and in a matter of minutes was asleep.

The next day, Kamala broached the topic with Milan.

"Milan, my son," she said, "It's been two years since daughter-in-law died. She was a good woman and a good wife to you. But you cannot go on grieving for her forever. The dead are dead, but the living must go on living. Life must go on, no matter what. Don't you think it's time to lay the past to rest and move on?"

Milan listened quietly. *Here it comes again*, he thought. It was the umpteenth time she had brought up the topic. Laying the past to rest, according to his mother, as he understood it, was for him to find another wife. But he didn't want to think of another woman. Not yet. It was too early. Remarrying so soon after Lalita's death would be a betrayal to her and her memories. He couldn't possibly do that. He loved her and he would always remain true to her. Sometimes he thought that she hadn't died at all, but gone to some other far away place, like he had told his daughters after her death. Sometime before the birth of their first child she had said, "Milan, listen to me. If in case I die I want you to marry again. I don't want you to grieve over me all your life. I want you to be happy, with or without me. All I want is for you to remember me sometimes." He had told her not to talk like that. At that time the thought of her dying had been unthinkable. In retrospect, he now realized that her words had been prophetic.

"Son," Kamala continued, "both your father and I are getting old. You know that you need a family …."

"But I already have a family, mother," Milan cut her short. "I have three lovely children who are fast growing up."

"But you don't have a mother for them. They need a mother."

"They already have a loving mother in elder sister-in-law," he replied, trying to cut the conversation short.

"She can't always be a mother to them. They need a real mother - a mother who is their father's wife."

"Their real mother is dead, mother. No one can replace her," he replied.

But Kamala was persistent. "Think about it, son," she said, "if not for yourself then for us, your poor father and mother."

A long silence ensued.

"Will you do that for us?"

"All right, I'll think about it," he said grudgingly, "but not now, mother."

"When?" she asked hopefully. It was finally working, her persuasion.

"Give me a year or two."

"If you give me your word then I am prepared to wait, but not a day longer than a year."

"Two years," he pleaded.

"No, not more than a year," she insisted.

"All right," Milan said reluctantly.

"Is that a promise?" She asked.

"Yes, mother," he replied laconically. He had no intention of fulfilling his promise.

Kamala was satisfied. That was a start, at least. *Once a new woman enters his life he will be happy again,* she thought. She desperately wanted to see him happy. She was convinced that a woman - the right sort of woman – was the best thing that could happen to a man. She also knew that his future wife had to be comparable to, if not better than, his dead wife. She intended to find one just like that. So, starting that day she began to think of a suitable girl. *I'll find him a wife with all the thirty-two good qualities*, she thought happily. Tall, fair, slim, pretty, modest, good-natured, with a sweet voice, obedient, respectful, hard working, good cook, virgin and a good family background were some of the qualities she could think of. She didn't have the faintest idea what the rest were, but she didn't care.

A year later in the thick of the monsoon season, on the first day of June in the year 2001, a terrible thing happened in Kathmandu. At a weekly family gathering of the royal family, the heavily inebriated crown prince slaughtered his entire family, including himself, over a marriage dispute with his mother, the Queen. "He looked like the Terminator himself," is how one of his royal aunts, who survived the massacre unscathed but badly shaken, described him later. According to eyewitnesses this is how the event unfolded.

The thirty year old Crown Prince Dipendra arrived at 7:30 PM in the evening at the royal banquet hall (one of several) in the century old (but modern-looking) Narayanhity Royal Palace, which sits inside a large walled compound smack in the middle of the city of Kathmandu. As soon as he entered the hall he started to play billiard by himself. While at it, he gulped down a few pegs of whiskey. He looked sober and cheerful, and there was no cause for anyone present in the hall to suspect anything untoward. After some time he asked his aide-de-camp to bring him his 'special cigarette' which, according to the ADC's later testimony, was laced with hashish. He had started puffing the stuff a year earlier, it was later revealed. By the time King Birendra and Queen Aishwarya entered the hall at 8:15 PM, he was fully inebriated. The King and Queen headed straight for the adjoining room where the Queen Mother (the King's step-mother; his own mother had died a long time back) was waiting for them. In the meantime, noticing that the Crown Prince was swaying - finding it difficult to hold his self upright - his younger brother Prince Nirajan and some royal cousins helped him to his bed chamber which was not far away. Once there, he dismissed them and sprawled on the floor in a drunken stupor. Sometime afterwards the royal maid heard him stagger to the bathroom and throw up. Then he made two calls on his cell phone to his girlfriend, the last time to tell her that he was going to bed and that he would see her the next day. But instead of going to bed he changed into army combat (camouflage) gear and headed for the reception hall with not one but three guns on him. Later, there was speculation as to whether he was really drunk or just feigning drunkenness.

At about 9:00 PM the fully armed Crown Prince suddenly appeared at the doorway of the L-shaped banquet hall where he had earlier played billiard. As it was common knowledge in the Palace that he was a crack shot and playing with guns was his hobby, those who saw him saw nothing sinister in that. They thought that he was playing a prank. But without uttering a single word, he fired 'rat-tat-tat' at the King, his father, who was standing near the billiard table talking to some guests with a glass of whiskey in his hand, with a 9mm caliber MP-5K submachine gun. The utterly astonished king said, "What have you done?" and slowly sank to the floor. After watching the King fall, the Crown Prince withdrew from the hall and discarded the 12 bore SPAS 12-L French SPA gun that he was carrying. Then he entered the hall again and fired again at the mortally wounded monarch with a 5.56 calibre Colt M-16 A2 rifle. At this point his youngest uncle Dhirendra, who some years earlier had voluntarily given up his royal title following a family quarrel, tried to intervene. But the unfortunate man had no chance. He was shot point blank in the chest. The force of impact lifted him up and threw him a few feet back and he died instantly, in front of the eyes of his three utterly shocked daughters. Then without taking a break the Crown Prince shot at the young husband of his sister. The young man, fortunately, survived the attack.

He backed out of the hall again, and then again quickly returned to continue the killing spree. This time he shot his sister, Princess Shruti, a young mother of two infants. The young princess was tending to her wounded husband when she was cut down by the bullets. After slaying his only sister, he turned his attention to his three aunts (the King's sisters) and shot them one after another, two of them fatally. Then again he walked out of the hall. Recovering from the shock, Queen Aishwarya (his mother) and Prince Nirajan (his younger brother) followed him into the garden, apparently to reproach him for what he had done and to stop further bloodshed. But the insane Crown Prince was in no mood to listen to their pleas. He did an about turn and shot his mother point blank in the face (the dead queen's faceless head had to be covered with a mask during the funeral procession as it had been completely blown away) and then pumped several bullets into his younger brother. Thus having slaughtered every member of his immediate family, he tottered a short distance to the garden pond and shot himself in the temple with a revolver.

In this carnage, dubbed the 'Royal Palace Massacre', and broadcast by the news media all over the world, eleven members of the Nepalese royal family including the Crown Prince lost their lives. The Crown Prince lived for three more days. By a strange quirk of fate and the peculiar Nepali law of royal succession, the Crown Prince who had committed homicide, patricide, matricide and regicide all at one go, was declared king while he was lying comatose in the army hospital. He never got to know of his accession to the throne. After his death, his second uncle Prince Gyanendra, who was absent at the family gathering, was declared king.

As soon as the terrible news spread across the country, like a wildfire, there was massive outpouring of grief for the slain king and queen. The streets of Kathmandu filled with weeping men and women. Inevitably, grief was replaced by anger, and massive riots not seen since the uprising of 1990 hit the streets of the country's cities. This was quite understandable as the dead King had become massively popular by his steadfast commitment to democracy after agreeing to become a constitutional monarch. Conspiracy theories abounded, naturally. "How can a (Nepali) son kill his own father and mother?" the deeply shocked people lamented, as if Nepalese sons were not capable of doing so. "This is not possible. The Crown Prince is an innocent victim of a deadly conspiracy. This is premeditated murder," they shook their heads, pointing accusing fingers at different directions, including foreign powers, depending upon their political allegiance. Even the anti-monarchy Maoists did not fail to utilize the outpouring of the people's grief and anger to their own advantage by labeling the slain king a 'patriotic king'.

"The prophesy has come true," the superstitious Nepalese people declared with finality. Nobody knows who had first made the prophesy and for what purpose, but every Nepali seemed to know that the dead Crown Prince would be the last of the Shah dynasty to rule the country. But they were once again proved wrong. With the twelfth king of the Shah dynasty firmly installed on the Nine-headed Serpent Throne, the prophesy hadn't come true. The dynasty hadn't ended. It didn't even look like it was going to end any time soon. But people believe only what they want to believe and deliberately ignore the facts laid bare in front of their eyes. The fatalistic-minded Nepalese readily believe in superstitions (and the supernatural) without so much as a question, but accept the facts only grudgingly. In the early nineties several thousand people in Kathmandu flocked to the ubiquitous temples of Ganesh (the elephant-headed-pot-bellied-wish-fulfilling Hindu god) to spoon-feed him with fresh milk after a rumour spread (from India, where else?) that the deity's idols had mysteriously begun to sip milk. Even after scientists had examined and explained the cause of the phenomenon, many steadfastly held on to the belief that the idols had really sipped milk.

In the days following the massacre, the question on everybody's lips was, "How was the heavily drunken Crown Prince able to aim so precisely and slay only his immediate family members when more than two dozen people were present in the hall at the time?" There were no answers good enough to satisfy them. But all eyewitness accounts confirmed that it was indeed the Crown Prince who had done the killing. The reason: his choice for bride, a beautiful young lady (herself of blue blood) he was having a relationship with, was for some reason (perhaps owing to her being either a politician's daughter or being of Indian blood from her mother's side) unacceptable to the King and Queen who apparently had their own choice. This had led to several family disputes and heated rows leading to the tragedy. It was rumoured that during one of the rows the enraged Queen had allegedly threatened to disinherit him after he had kicked his sister.

The reaction of the common folks of the older generation like Dil Bahadur, who were at heart staunchly loyal to the monarchy despite being forced to become a member of the people's local government installed by the anti-monarchy Maoists, was "What have the times come to? How can common people like us feel secure when even the King is not safe inside his palace?"

For the young men and women, many of whom had shaved their head in the aftermath of the massacre as a show of respect for the dead King, a new realization was dawning. "Perhaps we should heed the call of the Maoists and take this opportunity to do away with monarchy altogether, and turn the country into a democratic republic." Milan expressed this sentiment to his father who was quick to disagree. "The country cannot exist without the king," replied the old man, repeating the cliché that had been filled into his ears as a young man by the proponents of the now defunct Panchayat System. This sentiment had won the day for the royalists in the national referendum called by King Birendra in 1981 after a violent students' revolt had come close to toppling the party-less system the previous year. The Nepalese people were given a choice between multiparty parliamentary democracy and a reformed party-less Panchayat system (a cleverly crafted name for the king's direct rule). The royalists shrewdly preyed on the sentiments of the older generation and spread the rumour that once they won the referendum the democrats and communists together planned to overthrow the monarchy.

"There will be utter chaos without monarchy. The country will fall into the hands of either the Indians or the godless communists," they warned. This hypothetical scenario was unacceptable to the people to whom the king was not only a reincarnation of God Vishnu, one of the trinity of Hindu Supergods, but also a venerable father figure. The royalists also preyed on the xenophobic mindset of the older generation to whom the perceived threat of expansionist India was, and still is, very real. And as a consequence they had voted overwhelmingly in favour of reformed party-less Panchayat System which would, in fact, leave the executive powers and the sovereignty of the nation intact in the King's hand.

As the monsoon rains dissipated and the pleasant and festive season of autumn arrived, Kamala realized that the time to talk to her son again had arrived. She had spent the year counting the days on her fingers and clandestinely sending out feelers for suitable brides for her son. One quiet afternoon she went to her son's room. Milan was lying on his bed reading an old book. Reading books, magazines and novels during his spare time was a habit he had picked up as a student in Kathmandu. Kamala's eyes fell on the framed colour photograph of Lalita on the sparse wooden table. There was an alluring smile on the young woman's face which captivated her for a while. Then she ran her eyes to the other smaller pictures fixed to the wall by nails – some with only Milan in them, some with Lalita alone, some with both of them and others with their daughters – standing, sitting, holding hands. Smiling cheerfully. Portraits of a happy family – except that the wife was no longer alive.

"Milan," she said softly, her eyes still fixed on the pictures.

"Yes, mother," Milan put aside the book and sat up. "What is it?"

Kamala sat on the bed and said: "Son, a year has passed since you gave me your word. Remember? Now I want you to make good that promise."

Milan sat up straight, ran his fingers across his hair pensively, and replied, "Mother, I am still not ready. Give me some more time."

"If you go on procrastinating you will grow old before you ever become ready."

"Mother, please give me some more time."

"How much more time do you need, son? It's been four years since she died. Surendra's mother says that her older brother in Yamphudin has a marriageable young daughter. She is a pretty girl of twenty-two." Surendra was another one of Milan's many cousin-brothers.

"Mother, have you been going around looking for girls for me?"

"I am your mother, son, and it is every mother's fervent wish that her grown-up children marry and make a happy and stable life. Lalita was a good woman and she gave you three lovely children. But she is dead. She is not coming back. It was not your fault that she died. It was written for her to die young, so she died young. If you go on living alone like this, your life will be miserable."

"I am not miserable, mother." He protested.

"Yes, you are. Have you looked at your reflection on the mirror lately? You neglect to shave the hair on your chin and lips. Look at the walls and tables in this room. They are filled with memories."

Milan touched the hair on his chin and ran his fingers on the mustache running across the length of his upper lip. He knew she was right. It had been two weeks since he had last used the razor blade on his face. After Lalita's death he often forgot to shave, and his room was filled with pictures of his dead wife. He had even drawn one with his own hand and though it was far from being a prize winner it resembled her quite well.

Kamala continued, "Surendra's mother told me that her brother might be willing to give you his daughter. She says that the girl is pretty, well-mannered and hard working. What more could a man want in a woman? Now if you will agree, I'll talk to her. After that you can go with your father to see the girl."
"Let me think about it, mother," he said.
"No, there's no time to think. I am going to talk to Surendra's mother this afternoon," she said.
"No, don't do that, mother. Give me a day or two to think it over."
"All right! But I want your answer in two days."

Kamala waited for two more days and when Milan failed to come to her with an answer, she confronted him again.
"You said you'd give me your answer in two days. I am still waiting."
"Yes, mother. I have been thinking."
"And what exactly have you been thinking?"
"I have been thinking, yes, you are right that I've got to marry again. Yes, you are right that I cannot go on living with my memories."
"Then what's the problem? Is it that you don't like the girl I have talked about?"
"It's not that mother. How can I like or dislike her when I haven't even seen her? Mother, I have thought long and hard about it."
"Go on!"

"I have thought ..... and thought .... and thought, mother. And I have decided that ......" He found it difficult, almost impossible, to express his thought. He suddenly blushed and his cheeks turned red as his mother waited for him expectantly, with a quizzical expression on her face.

"Mother, there is only one woman who I can ..... I mean who is suitable ...... I mean who can understand ..... I mean can be a good mother to my ......"

"Go on! I am glad to know that you have a girl on your mind. Tell me who she is."

"She is not any other girl ....she is my .....my .... my elder sister-in-law," he blurted out as his mother stared at him dumbstruck, "I mean we are the same age and live under the same roof."

Kamala was too stunned to say anything for close to a minute. The possibility of uniting the two in matrimony had never occurred to her. She let the idea sink into her head, gave her brain time to chew it and digest it.

"You want to marry your elder sister-in-law?" she asked slowly, almost incredulously, at the end of the long pause.

"Yes, mother," he replied, "If I have to marry someone then it's got to be her. She is the only one."

"Are you sure?"

"Absolutely," he replied with conviction.

"But you two are as different from each other as day and night," she said searching his eyes for any sign of doubt.

"That's true. But I still believe that I can be happy with her, and she with me. Besides, it will be best for the children."

"Does she know anything about this? Have you talked to her?"

"No, mother, she doesn't have the faintest idea. And I am too inhibited to tell her."

"You should tell her."

"No, mother. I think I'll leave that to you."
"But you know that she cannot have children."
"Who needs any more children? I've already got three. Do I need any more?"
"I don't know."
"Will you talk to her, mother?"
"Yes, I will."
"Mother, promise me that you won't tell her that it was my idea."
"Then whose idea is it?"
"Yours."

Kamala gave her son a long, sympathetic look and said, "You are scared, aren't you? You are scared of what she might think of you. Don't worry. I'll talk to her. I'll tell her that it's my own idea, and that you have got nothing to do with it. But if she refuses, I won't force her."

When Dil Bahadur heard from Kamala later that day he said, "It's not unusual for men to marry their elder sister-in-law. Why, I remember that when Pharka Bahadur's father died some thirty years ago, his mother started living with his younger uncle in less than a year and without even getting married, too."
"So what do you suggest?" Kamala asked.
"I don't see any problem provided that they both agree. In fact, the way I see it, it will solve three problems at once – his, hers and the children's. But do you think she will agree?"
"I can't say, but I hope she will after some persuasion. The only problem with her is that she is infertile."
"But he doesn't need any more children. He already has two daughters and a son."

The next day, Kamala found an opportune moment to talk to Laxmi when both men were out of the house.

"Daughter-in-law," she said, "the untimely death my son and your husband has made you a widow at an age when a woman wants to enjoy her life. We - your father and I - worry about you constantly because you know that you are like a daughter to us. We would be happy if we could do something to bring happiness into your life."

Laxmi listened quietly and said, "I am not miserable anymore, mother. The children have given me all the happiness I need. There is nothing more I want."

"But still," Kamala went on, "you could have a much better life if we could find you a life partner. That would make us happy, too."

Laxmi didn't understand why her mother-in-law was bringing up this topic now. But she realized that there was something to it and listened quietly but inquisitively.

"I have one such person in mind ..... if you don't mind my saying so," Kamala said carefully.

"No, mother, I won't mind. But I don't want to marry and leave this house. Please don't send me away from my children."

"You won't have to leave us, daughter-in-law."

"How can I stay here when I am married to another man?" She looked sad.

"I said you won't have to leave this house....."

"How's that, mother?"

".... if you marry Milan."

"Milan? Marry Milan?" She stammered. Her reaction, as expected, was utter bafflement. She panicked. Her cheeks turned crimson. She had never thought of Milan in that light. He was certainly an attractive young man, but until now he had been nothing more than a dear brother-in-law to her.

"Yes, Milan, your brother-in-law," Kamala said.

"But I can't marry him," she blurted out, "he is my younger brother-in-law."
"You can if you want to," Kamala persisted. "There's nothing that says you can't marry your younger brother-in-law. You two are the same age. Besides, it will be good for the children. Think of the children, daughter-in-law. Think of them. They need a real mother - a mother who is their father's wife."

Laxmi didn't answer. She was still trying to digest the significance of the proposal. Somewhere in a corner of her mind she agreed that the union would be good for the children. They would have proper parents. But still.... Somehow, it seemed so inconceivable to her. Milan? She had always thought of him as a sort of brother, platonically, and not as a possible husband. For other women, yes, but for herself, no.

"And it would make your father and me happy, too, for the sake of both of you and the children. Think about it, daughter-in-law," Kamala said. *Surely, Laxmi is old enough to understand her hopeless situation*, she thought. *Marriage to Milan would be the best thing to happen to her. In fact, it's the only way out for her.* But she did not utter those words.

That whole day Laxmi's troubled mind dwelt on the subject and at the end she arrived at the conclusion that she had no reason to have misgivings with Milan as a prospective husband. Nevertheless, her conscience kept tormenting her because deep in her subconscious mind, she was still loyal to her dead husband.

Milan had prudently made himself unavailable that day. Unknown to anyone else he had given a great deal of thought over the past year to getting married again, and considered the young women suggested to him. But for reasons he himself had not been able to understand, his eyes had come back to rest on Laxmi every time. She was the same age as him, good-looking, polite, reserved, shy, well-mannered and hard working. Above all, she loved his children as her own. He didn't even want to imagine what might have happened to them if she had not been there to take care of them. What better mother for his children could he expect than her? The more he had thought of her the more he had liked her. Did he love her? He did, in a way, but not the way he loved Lalita. Nobody could take her place. Was he sexually attracted to her? Although he hadn't touched a woman since his wife's death, lust had played no part in it. He couldn't think of Laxmi in sexual terms. In fact, his liking for her had been accompanied by guilt, her being his elder brother's wife. Even though Purna had been dead these past five years, it was, to him, tantamount to stealing his brother's wife. Every day he asked himself the same question, "Is it ethically right for me to marry her?" For a long time he had come up with no definitive answer. Sometimes, he came up with a yes, and sometimes no. Finally, considering all, 'yes' had won. They lived under the same roof, went through the same grind wheel of life and had suffered similar blows of fate. But did she have the same feeling towards him? Did she have any feelings for him at all? He had seen no indication to that effect from her. She behaved towards to him as she used to when her husband was still alive. But then there had been no indication from him either.

The next day, Laxmi confronted him alone. He couldn't decipher by the expression on her face whether she was happy or sad or angry.
"Brother-in-law, are you aware of mother's intention?" she asked him. He was caught by surprise. He hadn't expected his

usually reserved sister-in-law to confront him in such a bold manner.

"Regarding what?" He stammered, feigning ignorance.

"You know what I am talking about," she replied. She was certain he knew what she was talking about. *Mother must have talked to him before she came to me,* she thought.

"Yes, I am." He replied uncertainly after a long pause. He added nervously, "I mean mother was saying something like you and I ….you know the two of us ….. suit each other perfectly. Or something to that effect. At least that's what I got to understand."

"And do you agree?"

"No, I don't…" he stammered, "Well, yes I do…… I mean you are a fine young woman, elder sister-in-law, as good a woman as any man could want for a wife."

"Brother-in-law, you know that I am a luckless woman cheated by fate. I have nothing to offer you. Nothing. Do you know what people whisper about me behind my back? They say that I am jinxed. They say that those who associate with me will suffer misfortune, like your poor elder brother."

"You must not listen to what people say. They will say anything to hurt you," he replied.

"Tell me, honestly. What do you see in me?" she asked him, locking her eyes with his. It suddenly occurred to him that this was the first time their eyes had locked into each other's. *She has beautiful, dark-brown, watery eyes,* he thought. That's the only thing he could think of. For a moment Milan found himself too inhibited to speak. Then he gathered his courage and replied, "Everything that one needs in a woman."

She blushed deeply, uncomfortably. "That's not true," she said looking away, "You know my shortcomings."

"That doesn't make you any less of a woman."

"Brother-in-law, tell me honestly again. Do you think it's the right thing to do?" She looked him straight in the eyes again, searching his mind, his very soul, he felt.

"I think it is, provided that you are not unhappy with it. Mother seems to think so. Besides, it will be for the benefit of the children. I am their biological father, and you are their mother by *karma*. In fact, to my little son you are the only mother he's ever had."

Two months later Milan and Laxmi were married with a simple ceremony attended by relatives and neighbours. A day after the wedding Laxmi moved out of her room and moved into Milan's room with her son. The two little girls, Kalpana and Ganga, too scared of the dark to sleep by themselves, moved to their aunt Gorimaya's room, which she formerly used to share with Amrita and Ratna. Still guilt-ridden at taking his dead elder brother's wife, Milan made himself a bed on the floor without a word and left the bed for Laxmi and his little son. Laxmi didn't object. In fact, she said nothing. By an unspoken accord the two started their conjugal life by sleeping separately. In fact, they would continue to do so for the next nine months – he on the floor and she on the bed. That night, before falling asleep Laxmi silently prayed for her dead husband's soul and told him that it was finally over between him and her, and begged for his forgiveness. "I did it for the sake of the family and the children," she said to him. She knew that wherever he was he would understand like he used to when he was alive.

At about this time the Maoists started their nationwide campaign to 'Establish a Base Area'. They intensified their attacks on police stations and government offices. And they intensified the drive to forcibly recruit young men and women into the People's Liberation Army. They abducted school teachers and their students, many of them barely in their teens. 'One person from one household,' became the slogan as they coerced each family to contribute one individual from each family to their cause. With this the exodus of young men and women from the countryside began in earnest. Unwilling young men and women in their thousands escaped from their villages to the towns and cities. A large number of them made their way to India to find lowly paid menial jobs rather than join the militia and certain death.

At the end of the monsoon rains that turned the scarcely-maintained, pothole-filled narrow streets of Kathmandu into muddy pools, there was yet another change of government. This was the tenth government in as many years, and the third after the last election. The new prime minister, who was serving for the second time, and who had ousted the prime minister of his own party for failing to solve the Maoist problem, who in his turn had earlier ousted the prime minister of his own party citing the same reason, immediately announced a ceasefire with the rebels. The Maoists on their part accepted the proposal for peace talks and all hostilities stopped. With the ceasefire, there was peace in the country once again. It was, however, cosmetic only because the Maoists continued to organize, recruit, threaten and extort. "The peace talks are just one of the several phases of our ongoing war," they declared, perhaps to pacify the extremists within their own ranks. It later transpired that they had utilized the ceasefire to reorganize themselves and to replenish their badly depleted arms and ammunition.

This temporary cessation of hostilities brought someone unexpectedly back home. Two weeks after the announcement of ceasefire, Ratna walked home unannounced to the utter surprise and unmitigated delight of everyone. He had no weapons on him, having left them behind. The return of the long lost son brought tears of joy in the aging eyes of Dil Bahadur and Kamala. Ratna greeted his parents warmly and respectfully, assuring them that he was back for as long as the ceasefire lasted. "I've come back in peace," he announced, "but I'll go back to fight if the talks break down." They didn't reproach the young man; neither did he offer any apologies. His running away from home was not mentioned.

He had become a different man from the one who had left three years earlier. He had left home as a boy; he had now returned as a young man of twenty – bigger, stronger, darker, leaner and more confident, and a veteran of many battles. He looked more mature than his years and walked with the confidence of a victorious warrior. And in his eyes burned the fire of revolution – the Che Guevara eyes that had sharpened with use – cold, piercing and ruthless. All except the poor were class enemies – to be hunted down, slaughtered and wiped off the face of the earth.

On the day of his young son's return, Dil Bahadur slaughtered two of his prized roosters for dinner and Kamala prepared the food with her own hands that night. For her the return of her son was akin to finding a precious treasure. Throughout the day and the next she alternately laughed and cried with joy and shed copious tears of happiness, for she was truly happy after a long period of time. "God, please make this ceasefire last for ever so that my son will not have to go back to the cruel war," she prayed fervently.

In the first week Milan's relationship with Ratna was very cordial. He was happy that his long-lost younger brother had come back home, and Ratna, on his part, was happy to see his elder brother once again. As each knew that the other was opposed to his political ideology – one a staunch believer in freedom and the other on the warpath against it – the two avoided any mention of politics. But the next week, something that had to happen did happen; there was simply no other way. The Nepalese have a proverb to explain this as well: "When two people share the same bed they are bound to kick each other sooner or later." As they sat down to a cup of black tea after supper one night, Dil Bahadur tried to unravel his son's life in the guerilla outfit. Ratna, as usual, was evasive on the questions regarding his whereabouts and what he had done, but passionately embarked upon a long discourse on the theoretical aspect of the people's war. "The People's Liberation Army is winning on every front. It's only a matter of a few years before we will take over ......" he declared confidently.

"Not so fast," Milan interrupted him. "You still haven't fought the army. If the government deploys the army, they will decimate you."
"We are ready take on the King's army, anytime, anywhere. And mind my words, we'll defeat them, too," Ratna said with a flash of anger in his eyes and a hard edge in his voice. It was obvious that he didn't like it when anyone tried to demean the people's war.

Dil Bahadur got up and climbed up the stairs, saying "I am not interested in this political debate of yours. I am going to bed now and you boys better do the same."
But the two brothers made no move to do so and continued to argue.

"If you are winning on all fronts, and if you think you can beat the army, then how come your leaders are sitting down for peace talks with the government?" Milan asked.
"The peace talks are just a part of our ongoing campaign to put the pressure on all fronts. War is not fought just with guns, older brother, it is also fought with talks. It is fought on several fronts and in several phases. This is just a phase in our struggle. The people's war will stop only after we have completely vanquished our enemies. And it is the patriotic duty of every Nepali to take part in the revolution," Ratna said.

At the mention of patriotism, Milan's temper suddenly flared up. *Why is it that extremists everywhere think they have a monopoly on the word patriotism? Every damn extremist one comes across claims that he is the only one who truly loves his country and the rest are stooges of foreigners. The truth is that they are the ones who are the real enemies.*

"So you think you are the only one who loves this country, do you? I love my country too, but in my own way. You see, unlike you, I don't go around killing my own brothers and blowing up the infrastructure of my country in the name of patriotism. Look what you have done to this country. You and your patriotic comrades have destroyed everything in your ideological insanity. Everything! There's nothing left for young people like us anymore. Nothing! Everything is gone, everything has been destroyed and everyone is trying to get out. We were doing all right after the restoration of democracy; the economy was picking up, trade deficit with India was decreasing and people were finally getting used to breathing the sweet air of freedom until your stubborn leaders decided to start this war. Do you know what I think of you?

Do you? I'll tell you. You are nothing more than terrorists; it's as simple as that," Milan said crossly.

"We are not terrorists ....." Ratna retorted angrily.

"Yes, you are. If you aren't then who is? Look at the way you operate, look at what you have done to this country."

"What is terrorism? Define terrorism," Ratna challenged him.

"Something as obvious as terrorism needs no definition; it's like asking someone to define life. You threaten, assault, torture and murder innocent people, and then run for your holes in the forest like the cowards that you are. You abduct and hold people for ransom. You plant mines and bombs to kill and maim indiscriminately. You send threatening letters to people and sneak into their house at night to rob them or kill them, whichever suits your purpose. Everything you do is designed to strike terror into the hearts and minds of the people."

"It's not terrorism. It's war. It's for a just and noble cause ..." Ratna interrupted him.

But Milan went on without listening to him: "You can justify any act of terror on the grounds of ideology, religion, culture, patriotism and whatever you choose to justify your heinous crimes with. Your leaders might even find frenzied supporters chanting their names in the streets, wearing T-shirts with their face on them and pledging to die for them. But that won't prove them right. In the long run people will see the truth. They will separate the right from the wrong because they have the capacity to do so. History is not made of one day, younger brother; it's not even made of one year. Even a decade is but a very short period in a nation's history."

"We'll see who will be proved right, elder brother. Just wait and see," Ratna said and stood up stretching himself to his full height.

"Sit down, I am not finished yet," Milan shouted. Ratna sat down, slowly and reluctantly.

Milan continued, "And listen! Not all those who disagree with you, who dare to think differently from you and who dare to defy you are unpatriotic. Neither are they stooges of the so-called imperialists. We love our country as much as you do, if not more. But we do it in a different way. It's you who is being unpatriotic. In your zeal for your revolution you have destroyed everything. Now we have nothing, absolutely nothing. Our economy has gone down the drain; business and industry are at a stand still and we are poorer than we were before. People have lost the spirit and the will to move forward. There's nothing left for young men like you and me. Nothing! Do you understand? No prospect for employment, no environment to start business, not even to do something as mundane as farming. Young people like us who should be engaged in productive work are either killing other young people, like you, or have left the country to become servants to foreigner. All thanks to pig-headed revolutionaries like you who love their country so much that they destroy it like there was no tomorrow."

At this scathing insult to his political ideal, Ratna abrupt stood up clenching his fist and glaring angrily at Milan.
"Older brother, hold your tongue or I'll....." he yelled furiously, with a dangerous glint in his eyes.
Milan stood up to face his younger brother, rolled up his shirt-sleeves, clenched his fists and yelled back, "Or what? What will you do? You'll fight me? You will fight me, will you? All right, let's see you do it. You are not the only ones who can beat up and kill people; I can do that as well you can if I want to. Common, hit me. Let's see if you can punch as hard as you can shoot."

The two brothers glared at each other angrily, with the same thoughts in their respective minds. *If he strikes me I'll kill him. I will. I don't care whether he is my brother or not.*

Hearing the angry exchange outside, Dil Bahadur came out of his room and shouted from the narrow balcony, "Shut up both of you! Shut up and go to your respective rooms this instant. I don't want to hear any more argument in this house."
"Father, you should warn older brother. You are a member of the village government," Ratna said to his father harshly.
Dil Bahadur looked at his sons and said sternly, "I want to have nothing to do with politics in this house. Now go, both of you."

Milan was angry because the Maoists had murdered his childhood friend whose only crime had been to speak up against their atrocities. He was angry because he felt his freedom stifled. On top of that he had to give them 'donation' and provide them shelter. Only recently the Maoists had calculated how much he earned from his cardamom farming, which he had started two years earlier, and asked him to hand over a sizeable percentage of that. Of course, they had done that with extreme politeness, but courtesy means nothing when it is backed by guns. He had quietly paid up, there being no other options available. *This is my village and some strangers arrive slinging their guns like bandits and mouthing some crude slogans, take over the place by force, and then tell me what to do and what not to do. In my own country I have to take permission to do things that I have taken for granted, even to go from one place to another. Am I a prisoner? Am I a criminal? Is this not my country? Does it only belong to some gun-toting revolutionaries who think they can destroy it with impunity?*

Ratna was angry because that's what the people's war has done to him. After fighting the police on and off for the past three years, he had built up a pool of rage inside him. Hurting people meant nothing to him. He did it routinely and without any remorse. He did it with knives, guns, improvised bombs and even bare hands. He wanted to destroy, destroy, destroy – destroy everything that was in the way of Maoism. His commander and mentor Comrade Jeevan had told him time and again, "In the course of the revolution a million people will have to sacrfice their lives. It is inevitable and necessary. It's a sacrifice the country will have to make. All vestiges of the old system must be destroyed completely in order to build a new society based on equality. The year we start anew will be called the Year Zero." The idea had appealed to him immensely. Yes, the Year Zero. The year when all vestiges of the old order will be destroyed beyond repair. The year when everything will start anew. But until then there were more class enemies to kill, more policemen to fight, and more public property to damage and destroy. And now that his own brother had stood in his way (*"Why doesn't the fool understand?"*) or so he believed, he was ready to come to blows with him, even kill him if it came to that. If his father had not intervened, he'd have struck out. He was ready to do that; he was that much angry.

But he held back. It took an enormous will power, but he managed to hold himself back. He lowered his voice and said, "Just be careful what you say, older brother. This village, like the rest of the countryside, is under the control of the *people*. I won't report you to my superiors because you are my older brother, but if my comrades hear anything about it from other sources, which they are bound to if you go on behaving like this, then don't even think of remaining in this village. Even walls have ears, elder brother. Never forget that."

"Are you threatening me? Are you? Go tell them now. I am not scared," Milan shouted and took a threatening step towards his younger brother. He had never been so angry in his life.

Dil Bahadur clambered down the stairs and stood between the two. "That's enough, you two. Now go to bed," he bawled angrily. Seeing how infuriated their father was the two quietly departed.

From that night the two brothers stopped talking to each other. This was symptomatic of a country divided vertically along political lines - the Maoists and their supporters on one side, and the rest of the country on the other side.

A month after this Amrita and Rajkumar returned to Nepal upon the latter's retirement from the British army. They stayed in Kathmandu and did not travel to the hills because of the Maoist problem. Instead, Amrita sent a letter to her younger sister Gorimaya, who had just completed high school, offering to provide for her higher education in Kathmandu. Gorimaya, who wished to study nursing, happily accepted the invitation. Seeing how the Maoists were recruiting young people, Dil Bahadur and Kamala agreed that it would be best for her to leave the village. Milan accompanied her to Kathmandu and returned two weeks later.

The peace talks lasted three months. Several rounds of talks in a tourist resort in the outskirts of Kathmandu valley ended without yielding any results. How could they when the rebels were openly claiming that the peace talk was just a phase of their ongoing war? While the government wanted to rebels to lay down their arms and join the political mainstream, the rebels wanted the formation of a 'constituent assembly' to draft a new constitution that would give 'real democracy' to the people, which was a very noble goal, indeed. But anyone who knew the Maoists knew very well that 'real democracy' was just one of their euphemisms for the 'dictatorship of the proletariat'. This was unacceptable to the King, the parliamentary parties and also to the people who believed in the democratic process. Although the people were disenchanted with the politicians, they were not disenchanted with the democratic process, contrary to what the Maoists and their supporters insisted.

A week before the break down of talks and resumption of hostilities, Ratna was summoned by the local area commander and told to report for duty at an undisclosed location. That same day he hastily bid farewell to his elders. He refused to tell them anything other than that he had to go because of unforeseen circumstances, but he assured them that he would be back as soon as the situation improved.
"But isn't the war over?" Kamala protested.
"It won't be over until we achieve total victory, and we still haven't gone halfway, mother," he retorted.
Kamala began to cry. "I love you so much. When you left I cried and cried, and when you came back I thought it was for good and thanked the gods for returning you to me. But now you are going away again. Why can't you leave the fight to the others? Do you really have to go?" she implored.
"Mother, please do not to try to block my path with your tears," Ratna replied impatiently.
"A mother cries because she feels. She feels for the child that she carried in her womb for nine months and brought into this world through pain and then brought up through sweats, tears and toil."

"Mother, I love you, too. But right now the only tears that can move me are the tears of my motherland. I hear her cry every day. She is asking for my blood. I must go. Please do not block my path with your tears."

Dil Bahadur didn't try to stop him. "Do what you like. But for the sake of all of us make sure that you stay safe and come back home when the war is over," he said. He had resigned himself to the fact that his son was already lost to the war.

As for Milan, after he had nearly come to blows with his younger brother (Laxmi had later chided him for that), he didn't care one way or the other. "It's his life. If he wants to get killed, then that's not my problem," he said to Laxmi.

But Laxmi disagreed with him. She tried to stop her younger brother-in-law.
"Ratna, must you go?" she asked when he came to say farewell.
"Yes, I must," he gave her a short reply.
"Why must you go?" she asked him.
"For the revolution. For my motherland," he replied.
"Think of father, mother and the rest of us. Think of the pain through which you have put every one of us. Think of your mother's tears. If you want to take the advice of your poor elder sister-in-law, then don't go. Stay," Laxmi implored.

"Elder sister-in-law, it's not that I don't love my home and my parents and you. But you know as well as I do that I must go. There is no other way. I have joined the revolution of my own free will; nobody dragged me into it. Now if I desert my comrades they will brand me a traitor and hunt me down. I'd to the same to any deserter. Besides, right now, it is more important for me to think of the pain of my motherland than of my own mother."

Laxmi didn't see any benefit in pursuing the matter. He wouldn't listen to anyone. The war was not out there, it was deeply embedded in his head and in his heart. It was coursing through every artery and vein of his body.
"If you must go, then go. You have my prayers and blessings. And come back safely. When I came to this house, you were but just a little child. I have fed you, washed you and watched you grow up. To me you are like my own little brother," she said sadly.
"Elder sister-in-law, I am not only like your little brother, I am your 'real' brother. I have always looked upon you as a sister. And believe me when I say this, I am fighting this war for the likes of you – to free you from slavery, to give you justice, to give you freedom. Don't be afraid for me. I will not die. I am too young to die. I will come back. I will come back with victory. I will come back with a new dawn in these hills," Ratna replied with dreamy eyes.

"I am not too sure about that, Ratna. I am not even sure that you are fighting for a just and noble cause. Milan says that the war is not good for the country. He says the only way the country can make progress is through freedom and democracy. But I don't understand such things; I am just a poor uneducated woman who can barely read and write. There's been so much fighting and bloodshed. So many people have been killed, so many women have been widowed, so many children have been orphaned and so many homes have been destroyed. This is all I know. I hope some day there'll be peace in this country once again. Until then I guess each one of us must play the role that he or she is fated to play. And since you are so determined to play the role you have chosen for yourself, my blessings are with you," Laxmi said sadly and bade him farewell.

A week after leaving home Ratna found himself near the hill town of Salleri, the administrative center of Solukhumbu District, about a hundred kilometers to the west of Khewang as the crow flies, across the River Arun which separates Limbuan from Khambuwan (the ancestral land of the Rai people).

Ratna, along with about two thousand other rebels and villagers, was preparing to storm the district headquarters and army barracks later that night. Three days earlier in the far western district of Dang the guerillas had made a massive and daring attack on an army barrack killing over eighty soldiers and capturing several truckloads of arms and ammunition. This was the first attack by the rebels on the army. Both the government and the army were completely taken by surprise as the peace talks were still in progress. This was owing to a serious miscalculation on the part of the complacent government which was touting that the talks would be a success and lasting peace would be restored with the constitutional monarchy and parliamentary democracy intact. They had failed to see that the militant faction of the Maoists had already deemed the talks fruitless and a gross waste of time. Also, having got ample time and opportunity to reorganize themselves and replenish their arms and ammunition during the lull, their impatient foot soldiers were gearing for battle once again - this time not against the poorly trained (on counter-insurgency tactics) and ill-equipped police force, but against the formidable Royal Nepal Army. It was only logical that to win the war, sooner or later they would have to take on the army and defeat it. That was the only way, otherwise the stalemate would continue for ever. This unprovoked attack on the army was the last straw for the government. The next day the government announced an end to the ceasefire, sent the army after the attackers and prepared to impose a nationwide state of emergency.

Though largely ceremonial and inactive in recent days, the Royal Nepal Army had time and again proved itself in the battlefield in the past - the invasion and plunder of Tibet in 1791 AD, the war with East India Company from 1814 to 1816 AD, the invasion of Tibet again in 1855 AD, assisting the British to quell the Indian Mutiny in 1857 (Junga Bahadur Rana had himself led a 12,000 strong force and returned with 4000 ox-cart loads of loot), to quell the armed rebellion of the early 1960s, and most recently the Khampa Operation in the mid-1960s to rout the fearsome Tibetan Khampa guerillas who had been fighting Chinese rule from Nepal's soil endangering Nepal's sovereignty from Red China.

Thus, a week after leaving home and three days after the carnage in far western Nepal, Ratna found himself checking and cleaning his rifle, a well-oiled three-naught-three captured earlier from a police post. His heart fluttered constantly in anticipation of the impending battle. As dusk approached the guerillas, nearly half of them women, emerged from their hiding places in the surrounding villages and began to congregate at the outskirts of the town. Like many of his comrades Ratna did not expect to come out alive because this was going to be by far the biggest assault of his life so far. According to a secretly circulated communiqué, one group was to assault and destroy the airport and telecommunications tower at Phaplu, a distance of half an hour's walk from the town to the north, and the main group was to subdivide and attack the army barrack, police station, the office and residence of the Chief District Officer and other government buildings in the town. For this purpose, hundreds of unwilling men and women from the nearby villages had been coerced at gunpoint to act as human shields. They would form the vanguard of the attack. This was a coldly calculated strategy – when the enemy ran out of ammunition after slaughtering the human shields, the guerillas at the rear would move in for the kill. As darkness swallowed the hills, the rebels made their way noisily towards the town from different directions, shepherding their human shields, beating drums and shouting slogans.

Ratna's unit was led by Comrade Jeevan, a battle-hardened guerilla fighter who was a *Magar* man of twenty-eight. Magars are the largest and most widespread of the Mongloid ethnic groups in the country. This short but stout, fair-complexioned man, whose real name was Jai Bahadur Pun, hailed from a poverty-stricken village in mid-western Nepal, the heartland of the rebellion, where the hostilities had first begun with a few muskets. Despite his poverty Comrade Jeevan had managed to go to college in Kathmandu and graduate with a bachelor's degree. There, deeply angered by rampant corruption, social injustice and exploitation of the poor he had seen all around him, he had educated himself on the political philosophy of Marx, Lenin and Mao, and also found the time to get involved in student politics. After completing his studies he had worked as a teacher in a private school, and when the rebellion had started he had seized the opportunity and promptly joined the guerilla outfit and gone *underground*. This had been a natural step for him. As a student he had been arrested a number of times by the police while taking part in violent demonstrations against the government. After five years as a guerrilla commander, he had become a veteran of the people's war with a fierce reputation and his name was known to the police. Ratna had been with this taciturn but fearless and reckless fighter since the day he had joined the outfit, and considered the older man his guru, mentor, friend, commander and father-figure all rolled into one. Comrade Jeevan, however, was not without faults. He was hot-tempered, impatient and reckless to the point of being foolish at times, but so far he had come out unscathed every time. Since theirs was a mobile unit, traveling from one part of the country to another throughout the year to take part in assaults, Ratna had been all over the place with Comrade Jeevan, who had personally selected him because of his physical tenacity, loyalty and zeal for the revolution.

"Now, listen to me carefully, comrades," Comrade Jeevan said to the young men and women under his command, whose unquestioned loyalty and awed respect he enjoyed, "As you have been told earlier, the objective of our unit is to attack and destroy the police station and capture as many weapons as we can. Do you understand?"
They shouted an affirmative answer in unison. They had reached the outskirts of the town by this time.

While the rebels and their human shields began to encircle the town, beating drums and chanting shrill slogans, the outnumbered soldiers and policemen in their respective positions hastily prepared to defend themselves, and the terrified townspeople began to hunt for holes inside their houses. The guerillas, however, took their time to attack. They had a well laid-out plan and they didn't make haste. They went about it slowly and deliberately, chanting ear-splitting slogans all the time and making a great show of force. Sheer number and surprise (the army and the police had not expected the attack) was on their side and they were confident of victory. They divided into different groups and each group headed resolutely towards its designated objective. One group of guerillas headed for the army barracks, one for the district administration office, one to the bank, one for the land revenue office, and Ratna's unit headed for the police station. His hand ready on the trigger and his whole body tense and sweaty with excitement, he walked alongside his comrades with a grim and determined expression on his face. *Ratna, you will probably not survive this night,* he said to himself. *But you will kill as many enemies as you can before you die. So have no fear. Have no fear because tonight you will die a glorious death for your motherland. You will become a martyr and your comrades will cover your body with a red flag and bury you with full military honour.*

The battle started at approximately an hour before midnight. Before the assault the rebels cut off the electricity supply and telephone lines. The town plunged into darkness and all external communication lines to and from it became dead simultaneously. At the same time, near the police station, Comrade Jeevan bawled at the top of his voice, "Comrades, Charge!" Suddenly the area exploded into a frenzy of gunfire and explosions as the guerillas went on the attack and the policemen returned fire. There were incessant 'rat-rat-tat' of guns and deafening explosions of grenades accompanied by the shouts and cries of men and women, some encouraging others to move forward, some shouting hoarsely in sheer excitement while some, the more unfortunate ones, whining in sheer pain and terror. At the same instant the whole town exploded into a fury of battle as the other units attacked their respective targets simultaneously - the army barrack, government offices and banks. Scores of combatants on both sides fell - their bodies riddled with bullets and soaked in the warm and invisible blood in the dark - their own blood - never to rise again. The whines of the wounded filled the gap between the noise of the guns and explosions. '*Move forward, keep moving forward*', Ratna told himself as he ran towards his objective, '*Do not fear death because sooner or later one has to die.*' The policemen put up a stiff resistance and their incessant bullets mowed down many of his comrades, but he didn't stop to watch them fall; he didn't stop to lend them a hand; he didn't stop to tend to their wounds. There was no time for that. This was not the time to stop for anything. This was the time to fight and kill. '*Kill, kill, kill,*' he chanted as he fired at the dark shapes that were the policemen, the hated enemies. "*Kill the dogs. Destroy them all.*" On several occasions he felt hot bullets whiz and whoosh past his ears. Unafraid, he kept running towards his objective, shooting all the time.

But in spite of their sheer number, it took the guerillas almost an hour to break into the police station, and it cost them dearly to do so. Scores of Ratna's comrades were killed and wounded in the process. Finally, the firing petered out from the other side, and Ratna and his comrades stormed into the burning building. Inside, illuminated by the reddish glow of fire, several policemen lay dead and dying. Seeing the guerillas the remaining promptly threw down their guns and held their hands above their heads.
"Don't shoot. We surrender. We have run out of ammunition." One of them shouted in a frightened voice through a haze of smoke. Some of them were coughing.
"Comrades, Stop! Don't shoot. It looks like they have run out of ammunition," the first rebel to enter the compound cautioned his comrades.
"On your knees! Quick!" He screamed hoarsely. The frightened policemen sank down on their knees, raising both hands above their heads, as the victorious guerillas surrounded them triumphantly.

"What shall we do with them? Take them prisoners? Or shall we kill them all?" Ratna turned to Comrade Jeevan, who was a step behind him.

Comrade Jeevan looked at the cowering policemen with his eyes filled with hatred. With dark blotches of blood splattered all over his face and clothes, he looked a fearsome sight in the flickering red glow. "Kill them all," he spat out cold-bloodedly.

"But we can't kill those who have surrendered. It is against the ...." One of the educated guerillas in the group started.

"Against what?"

"Against the Geneva Convention."

"What's that? I don't care. That's a law made by the capitalist-imperialists to protect themselves. I don't give a damn about it. These dogs deserve to die. Shoot them all."

"What if human rights groups find out?"

"Fuck the human rights groups. They are nothing more than tools of the imperialists."

"Spare our lives. Please! We have surrendered. We can't harm you," a frightened young policeman pleaded in a last ditch effort to save himself, "I've got a young wife and a little daughter."

Comrade Jeevan, his face contorting with hatred (and it's surprising how much a man can 'hate'), threw a disdainful look at the cowering policeman and without bothering to reply shot him point blank in the right eye. The dying man's eye became a dark hole and thick, dark blood squirted out of it – at first in trickles and then in a torrent. He convulsed and tumbled like a log to the floor - face down, dead. Comrade Jeevan kicked the dead body and said, "Die, you dog!"

Then he scanned the uncertain faces of his sub-ordinates. "What are you waiting for? Shoot the motherfuckers. Kill them all," he screamed. At this command from his superior,

Ratna galvanized into action. In a quick succession he shot two of the nearest policemen point blank in the head, splitting their skulls into several fragments and scattering their brains on the floor. When the dying men fell, he kicked their corpses in the same manner his commander had done. He didn't feel anything at that time – no fear, no pity, no compassion and no remorse. *These are the hated enemies of the people and they must be killed. All class enemies and their guard dogs must be slaughtered.* He didn't realize it at the time but that day his transformation into a cold blooded killing machine had become complete. He was, like the luckless policemen he had so cold-bloodedly murdered, a victim of the people's war – damaged for ever, incapable of anything else but slaughter. The other guerillas quickly followed suit and finished the job. Within a minute a dozen policemen lay dead beside their fallen colleagues, in their own dark and ominous-looking pool of blood.

Comrade Jeevan spat at the prostrate corpse of a dead policeman and shouted, "Comrades, we've won a great victory. Nothing can stop us now. Congratulations to you all. Now, grab all the weapons and ammunition you can find and follow me. We are going to help our comrades assaulting the army barrack." He needn't have given the order. By this time, the other rebels numbering in their hundreds had already ransacked the place, taking whatever they could lay their hands on and putting to fire everything they didn't need.

The victorious guerillas made their way towards the army barracks where a fierce battle was raging. Despite being grossly outnumbered the soldiers were putting up a ferocious fight, and the guerillas had not been able to gain any significant ground. Ratna's unit took up positions about a hundred meters from the army barrack and joined the battle. From the other side, a soldier with a loud hailer was calling upon the rebels to surrender over the staccato report of rifle-fire, continuous rat-tat-tat of machineguns and the intermittent explosion of grenades and improvised bombs.

"Surrender? Us?" sneered the Maoist commander derisively. "It's they who should surrender; we have them under siege."
The others attempted a derisive laugh. The battle raged on.
After exchanging fire for about half an hour, Comrade Jeevan, frustrated by the lack of progress, shouted to another commander over the noise of the battle, "It can't go on like this. We must charge."
"That will be suicide. They have automatic rifles and machine guns. We have already lost a large number of comrades." The other commander shouted back. His unit had been at it since the beginning.
"If it is suicide then let it be so. The way I see it there is simply no other way. You give us cover, I'll lead my men," Comrade Jeevan shouted back.
"No. Let's continue to put a steady fire on them and wait. They are bound to run out of ammunition sooner or later," the other commander shouted back. Comrade Jeevan did not insist; he was not in charge here. The other commander was. And the battle raged on, both sides taking heavy casualties.

But when the battle still raged on after two fruitless hours, with the guerillas still pinned down to their initial position, Comrade Jeevan, who had by now lost a quarter of his men and women, lost whatever little patience he had left.
"Comrades, we can't wait any longer. We must charge," he shouted over the noise to his men. "Prepare yourselves. We'll charge and capture the barracks, or we'll die trying."

"What about the other units?" someone asked.

"They can follow us if they like. Now get ready," comrade Jeevan said.

"We are ready to die if we must," replied Ratna who as always stuck loyally by his commander's side and had become by now as frustrated as his commander by the lack of progress. The others quietly braced themselves for the assault.

"Comrade," Comrade Jeevan called out to the other commander over the head of his subordinates, "Give us cover. We are going in."

"Go ahead, comrade," came the reply, "We'll be right behind you."

He waited for half a minute, took a deep and long breath and then screamed at the top of the voice, "Charge!" At the same time he picked himself up and ran forward at his top speed, firing constantly. His subordinates followed him repeating his battle cry. He had run only a short distance when a hail of bullets caught him squarely in the chest and threw him back several feet. He landed on his back, limp and dead, instantly, his body riddled with bullets and covered in blood. Several others fell with him; some of them had their heads blown off by the torrent of machinegun fire. The survivors threw themselves on the ground. "Comrade Jeevan has been hit," Ratna cried in panic, "Everybody down, Comrade Jeevan has been hit."

"Keep your heads down and crawl back," a female voice yelled at the top of her voice. But a few guerillas who failed to hear or obey her got up and started to run. That proved to be a foolish move as they were immediately mowed down by another burst of machinegun fire.

We must crawl back to our previous position, Ratna thought, and he screeched: "Crawl back, everybody, don't stand up, just crawl back." He pulled himself to his dead commander's body lying several feet on his right, and dragging the corpse by the collar slowly crawled backward as red hot bullets whizzed dangerously above his head.

By four o'clock in the morning the tide of the battle had begun to turn on the rebels. Instead of them gaining ground, the soldiers were putting heavy and concentrated fire on them and pushing them back inch by inch. To Ratna the situation was beginning to look hopeless. *It's time to call it quits and scatter,* he thought, *we have achieved our objectives today. There'll always be another day and another place for more fights.*

As dawn broke over the hills, the guerillas began to retreat. "Retreat! Retreat. Our objectives have been achieved. There's nothing more to do now. Let's go back and regroup," weary commanders urged their remaining comrades. Ratna took a long sorrowful look at the cold, lifeless and blood-coated corpse of his commander. Even in the heat of the battle he hadn't left the dead man's side. Now he put down his gun and took out his khukuri. "Please forgive me, Comrade," he said softly, almost sentimentally, "I had always hoped that I wouldn't have to see this day, but now that I have, I've got to do what needs to be done. It's what you instructed me to do to protect your identity." Holding the corpse by the hair he hacked at the stiff neck and severed the head from the torso. "Farewell, comrade. You have achieved martyrdom. Your sacrifice will not be in vain. Thousands of others will take inspiration from your sacrifice and follow your example. We'll take this fight to every corner of this country. We will fight to the last drop of our blood. We won't stop until we achieve victory." He didn't cry when he said that. After a night of continuous fighting he was too numb and drained of emotions to shed tears of grief. Taking the severed head in his hand and not daring to look at it, he ran alongside his comrades as the soldiers advanced.

By early morning, as the white mist that had blanketed the hills that cool November morning dissipated to reveal a shattered and smoking town, the guerillas had already scattered into the neighbouring villages, forests and ravines in small numbers, with the army in hot pursuit. The battle had taken a heavy toll on both sides. The rebels had managed to destroy completely the district administration office, district police office and the district jail. They had killed the Chief District Officer, the highest ranking government officer to have been killed so far, and dozens of soldiers and policemen. Before retreating they had made off with a large cache of rifles and ammunition, and a large sum of cash from the local banks. But in terms of human cost, they had paid far more dearly than the government forces. Two hundred of them had been killed in the eight-hour battle and their blood-splattered and bullet-riddled bodies, many of them headless, littered the trails and terraces. In the streets of the town, bodies, bones and brains lay scattered everywhere and a noisy caucus of quick-witted crows, the ever-present scavenger of the hills, darted here and there happily to peck at them.

In a small forest two hours walk north-west from the devastated town, Ratna and his small band of guerilla dug a deep hole on the ground and laid the severed head of their dead commander to rest.

"Comrade Jeevan, you have become a martyr. You are an inspiration to all of us. You have given your life for the liberation of the downtrodden people. There can be no sacrifice greater than this. The war will go on until we achieve victory. We'll avenge your murder; we'll defeat our enemies;

we'll fight to the end," Comrade Suchitra said for everybody in the most solemn tone of voice. After Comrade Jeevan's death this petite but daring young woman of twenty-five had immediately taken charge. She had run away from home to join the outfit three years earlier after her abusive in-laws had forced her uncaring husband to take another wife owing to reasons of dowry. In these three years she had proved her mettle and emerged as one of the fiercest and most dedicated of fighters. Of course, she had to be endorsed by the high command, but that was as good as certain.

That attack was the last straw for the government. The very next day, the government put the terrorist tag on the Maoists and imposed a nationwide state of emergency, suspending a number of fundamental pillars of human rights guaranteed by the constitution.

The imposition of the nationwide state of emergency and the mobilization of the army had the desired effect on the moderate Maoists. Hundreds of rebels and rebel-installed members of village local governments and area commanders surrendered to the army all over the country within a few days. Most of them were released after interrogation. But it had practically no effect on the hardcore rebels like Ratna who vowed to fight on. In fact, those who had surrendered now became the target of their former comrades and refused to return to their villages out of fear for their lives.

In the village of Khewang, Dil Bahadur and his uncle Jit Bahadur, the unwilling chairman of the village people's government, suddenly found themselves in a dilemma. *To surrender or not to surrender*; that was the question on each frightened man's mind. When the army arrived - it was not a question of 'if' but 'when' as they were bound to come marching sooner or later - they would be caught and killed. But if they took the initiative and went to the army to surrender voluntarily, the Maoists would certainly kill them – and in the most gruesome manner. Taking lives was routine work for them, as simple as swatting a fly dead. Thus, these two reluctant members of the village local government began to live in constant terror. They had wanted no part in the rebellion; yet they had found themselves smack in the middle of it, and through no fault of theirs either.

Two weeks after the imposition of the state of emergency, Jit Bahadur quietly sneaked out of the village early one morning, much before the rooster crowed, while the hills and the village and the river below were still covered by an all encompassing blanket of darkness. He took his wife and two adolescent children, and made straight for the district headquarters in Taplejung Bazaar. He didn't confide in anyone, not even his nephew and confidante Dil Bahadur. His eldest son and daughter-in-law remained behind to look after the house. Upon arrival in the town, he went straight to the office of the Chief District Officer where he surrendered unceremoniously.

The place was filled with many others like him - pinched and frightened faces, constantly shifting eyes. They threw furtive glances at any new arrival – suspicious and terrified. It seemed that they were afraid of even their own shadows. The army took them into custody for interrogation and after they signed a statement promising to forfeit all links with the rebels, they were released, free to go anywhere they liked, but the problem was that they had nowhere to go now. During the interrogation, Jit Bahadur willingly provided his interrogators all the information they needed pertaining to the activities of the rebels in his village. Then the very next day he caught a bus to the city of Dharan where his second son, a soldier serving in the British army, had settled down. He was extremely fortunate in this. He had somewhere safe to go to. Many others had nowhere to go and took asylum in the town. Although his son was away on service in England, his daughter-in-law lived there with her three teenaged children in their two-storey brick house. And although he knew that she would grumble privately at having to provide food and shelter to so many people for an indefinite period of time, he also knew that she would welcome them warmly and make them feel at home.

When Comrade Prakash learnt of Jit Bahadur's desertion, he was livid. He ordered the whole village to gather at the usual place and threatened the remaining village government members with dire consequences if any one of them ever thought of deserting. Everyone implicitly understood what the term 'dire consequences' meant. He also warned all that he and his comrades would keep a hawk's eye on them and anybody found to be collaborating with the government forces in anyway would be immediately executed. This had the desired effect. It struck mortal fear into the hearts and minds of the remaining members, some of whom had, as a matter of fact, been secretly toying with the idea of defecting.

Dil Bahadur, as usual, resigned himself to fate. He had contemplated surrendering but had been too timid to do so. He was, rightly, more afraid of the Maoists than the army. *The soldiers will only get me if they come looking for me, which is not very likely, but the Maoists are everywhere. There is no escape from them.* "It's all in the hands of the gods," he declared with resignation, "Whatever happens in life, one has to accept it and go along with it. A person is a slave to circumstances; there's simply nothing one can do to change one's fate." That was his enduring philosophy on life, handed down through generations of his forefathers. He wasn't surprised when he learnt that his uncle had fled ("*It was his destiny to leave the village.*"), nor was he surprised at his own inability to do so ("*It is my destiny to remain behind.*").

Milan advised him to surrender. "Father, the army is sure to arrive sooner or later and they're sure to come looking for you. You know as surely as I do that the soldiers can be as brutal as the Maoists," he said to his father.

"I'll tell them that I am innocent, that I have done nothing wrong, that I was forced to sit on the committee against my will," Dil Bahadur replied.

"Do you think they will believe you? They'll say 'if you are innocent then why didn't you surrender when you were given the chance?' What will you do then?" Milan asked of his father.

The old man pondered for a long moment and said, "If I surrender now I will never be able to come back home, you know. The Maoists will kill me."

"You and mother can go to uncles' house in Kathmandu and take refuge there until this war blows over."

"No," Dil Bahadur replied. "I can't. I can't be dependent upon anybody. I'd sooner die than live a life like that."

As far as Dil Bahadur was concerned the conversation was closed. He didn't want to talk about it. Understanding his father's sentiment Milan didn't raise the topic again, though he was concerned for the old man. The following days were spent in dreadful anticipation. As for the question regarding the arrival of the army the Maoists were of two minds. Some of them believed that the army's arrival was imminent, but others argued that it wasn't. "This village is too remote and the trail is too treacherous," they said, "They would not dare to attack us here."

In spite of the logic of the nay-sayers the army did arrive. They arrived one sunny and lazy afternoon two weeks after Jit Bahadur's flight. The rebels had taken some precautions, just in case, and laid booby traps along the trail in the forests and streams. One had even died when his improvised pipe-bomb had exploded in his hand. But mines and booby traps aren't enough to stop professional soldiers, and man to man the rebels could match neither their skill nor their firepower. In an encounter near a stream a few kilometers from the village, three rebels were shot dead; one was captured and executed on the spot after a cursory interrogation while the remaining ran back to the village as fast as their feet could carry them.

"The army! The army!" they shrieked shrilly, "The army has arrived. Some of our brave comrades have already been martyred. We are outnumbered. Everybody run for the forest." Frantic Maoist cadres ran up and down the village screeching at the top of their voice. Immediately, all the guerillas picked up their firearms and ran uphill to hide in their camp in the forest. In spite of their boast, they had no stomach for direct confrontation with the army.

Both Dil Bahadur and Milan were outside in the courtyard at the time, along with the children. A frightened Kamala shooed the children into the house. Then she urged her husband to follow the rebels to save himself, but Dil Bahadur refused. "They will not harm me, I am innocent. They cannot harm me. I am innocent. I have done nothing wrong," he kept repeating.

"But they will not know that you are innocent," she implored.

"There is God looking down upon me, and he knows everything. He will save me," Dil Bahadur said calmly, with conviction.

Kamala had never been so frightened in her life. She pleaded with her husband, argued with him and yelled at him, but he still refused to budge. He sat on his bamboo stool, calmly lit a khosela and blew wisps of smoke that curled lazily upward as he waited for the soldiers. "They will not harm me," he said, "I am innocent." He looked utterly calm and unafraid, and this disturbed Kamala even more. *He is crazy. He's lost his mind.* She thought sadly.

A young rebel came running and screeched in a frightened voice, "The army will be here any minute. Come on, let's run!"
But Dil Bahadur stared at the young man calmly, almost sympathetically, without blinking his eyes and said, "I am not going to run."
"You'll face the army alone? By yourself?" The young rebel asked incredulously.
"Maybe, I don't know. I'll do whatever needs to be done, but I won't run. I've never run away from anything, so why must I run now?" Dil Bahadur replied. But the fact of the matter was that he really didn't know what to do; his senses had become too numb to react. The young rebel gave him a curious look and ran off shaking his head.

"Why are you running away? Why aren't you fighting back? Didn't you people used to boast that you could take on the army anytime, anywhere?" Dil Bahadur yelled after the rebel.

The young rebel stopped abruptly, did an about turn and gave him an uncertain look. Then he turned back and jogged a few steps. Then he stopped again, turned around and said, "Because they are too numerous and there are too few of us. We have to save ourselves for future battles. In any case, they won't stay here for more than a day or two. We'll return after they go back."

Giving up on her obstinate husband, Kamala gave her son a pleading look and said, "What about you? You are not safe here either."
"Mother, they will not bother me, I am not *with* the Maoists," Milan replied.
"How will they know that you are not with them?" she asked him.
"I'll tell them," he replied.
"And do you think they'll believe you?" she asked.
"Maybe. Maybe not. I don't know, but let's hope they will," he was as calm and serene as his father.

Perplexed at this strange and apparently foolish behaviour of her husband and son, Kamala dejectedly said, "Do whatever you like, but don't blame me if anything happens to you."

She called out to Narmaya, "Mother, mother! Come out and talk some sense into the thick ears of your son and grandson."
"Why? What's the matter with those two?" the old woman limped out stooping a little, with her right hand on her waist. She was still in the dark as to what was going on outside.

Kamala quickly explained to her the situation. Narmaya, too, persuaded her son and grandson to go into hiding, but both men refused. At length she too gave up and, shaking her head, said, "You have both gone mad."
"You two women go inside," Dil Bahadur said to his mother and wife. But they didn't budge.

"If you are staying out here, then we are doing the same," replied Kamala.

A short while later the soldiers entered the village. They spread out in groups of four or five and barged into each house along the way, conducting house-to-house searches. They dragged a man out of Man Bahadur's house, which was a short distance away, and after kicking and beating him, shot him point blank in the head, execution style. When the man fell dead, a soldier kicked the dead body. Man Bahadur was an active member of the village local government. He had taken to the Maoist cause with a gusto rarely seen in middle-aged men. He often urged Dil Bahadur and the others to do the same and become more involved, to put their hearts into the cause. But it was not Man Bahadur who lay dead because he had already run away. The dead man was his innocent nephew who had come to visit him from the plain.

As the four watched and waited, the same group of soldiers arrived at their nearest neighbour Khem Bahadur's house, kicked the door open and entered the house. They shepherded old Khem Bahadur and his family out into the courtyard at gunpoint and interrogated them. Apparently satisfied that they were telling the truth, the soldiers left them and headed for Dil Bahadur's house.

When the soldiers saw the four men and women watching them, they dropped their speed and came slowly and cautiously, pointing the muzzle of their guns at the four. They stopped at a distance of ten feet from the frightened family, and the sergeant barked, "You people there, put your hands above your heads." They did as they were told to do. The soldiers, there were six of them, converged around them, one cautious step after another, leveling their guns at them, their fingers ready to squeeze the trigger at a moment's notice. One suspicious move and they'd all squeeze the trigger simultaneously. There was no doubt about that.

"Please don't shoot," Dil Bahadur said to the sergeant, "We are unarmed and innocent."

"We'll find that out in a moment," barked the sergeant. He was a swarthy man with heavy-set features. "Search the bodies of the men and tie them up," he barked an order to his subordinates. Two soldiers slung their guns down, searched the father and son, pushed them down roughly, tied their hands at the back deftly with a rope, and made them stand on their knees.

"What about the women, sir?" one of the soldiers asked.

"Search them as well, but no need to tie them up if they are unarmed."

The soldiers searched Narmaya and Kamala. One of them fondled Kamala's breast and she winced in pain and shame.

"Who's inside the house?" the sergeant asked.

"Only my daughter-in-law and grandchildren," Dil Bahadur replied.

"Are you sure there's no one else inside?"

"There's no one else. You can go inside and take a look for yourself if you don't believe me."

"Don't talk back to me, or else I'll turn you into a corpse," barked the sergeant. He ordered two of his men to guard the captives, two to search the main house and one to follow him to the other house.

Ten minutes later all members of the family were lined up in the courtyard where Dil Bahadur and Milan stood uncomfortably on their knees, with their hands tied behind their back. Laxmi stood with her head bowed in shame. She had been searched, manhandled and her private parts fondled by the eager hands of the soldiers. The utterly terrified children were sobbing. The sergeant gave a contemptuous look at the red flag fluttering in the wind above the roof and ordered his subordinates to pull it down. Two of the soldiers promptly climbed on the roof and tore it up into little pieces.

Looking at Dil Bahadur, the sergeant said sardonically, "You old man, look at me. Let me take a good look at your revolutionary face."

"I am not a Maoist," protested Dil Bahadur. "We've got nothing to do with the Maoists. We are innocent."

"If you are not a Maoist, then how come that red flag was fluttering proudly above your roof?"

"We didn't put it up there, it was put by them," Milan said.

"Who asked you to speak?" the sergeant roared angrily and landed a kick in his chest. Milan staggered and fell on his back with a cry of pain.

"Bloody Maoist," the sergeant spat out. Laxmi quickly moved to help Milan up, but the sergeant yelled, "Woman, you stay where you are." She froze in fear. The muzzle of his rifle was leveled at her face. Milan twisted and turned and got up on his own, spitting out a blob of muddy saliva from his mouth. Half his face was painted with dust.

"So you say that you are not a Maoist?" The sergeant asked in a cold, mocking, voice.

"That's the truth, sir," Dil Bahadur replied in a frightened voice. "We are not Maoists. We've got nothing to do with them. We are innocent," he added.

"You think we are fools, eh? Do you? You think we don't know that you are a member of the so-called village people's government?"

"I am but I was nominated against my will, sir," the old man replied, almost in tears now.

"Do you think I am here of my free will? Do you think I enjoy doing this? Do you think you will not kill me if you got the chance just because I am here against my better judgment?"
"No, I won't. I won't kill you because I am not a Maoist," Dil Bahadur replied boldly.
"If that is the case, then why didn't you come to us to surrender?"
Dil Bahadur had no reply for that. Yes, why didn't he surrender while there was still time? But life is full of post-event questions like that. *How on earth didn't I see that? Why the hell didn't I do that? What made me make that choice?*
"Why didn't you surrender when you were given the chance?" the sergeant repeated his question.
"Because I was afraid ….." His voice faltered.
"Afraid of what? Afraid of who? The army?"
"No, the Maoists. They'd have killed me."
"Don't lie to me." The sergeant cried. In a swift and powerful motion he pulled the old man by the hair with his left hand and slapped him four times on both cheeks with both sides of his right hand. "Liar. Bloody motherfucker Maoist son of a whore," he exploded, "I will kill you this instant."

"Shall I shoot him, sir?" one of the soldiers asked. The sergeant pondered for a quarter of a minute.
"No," he said watching the blood trickling out of the old man's mouth. "The captain wouldn't like that. We'll take these two into custody. They might be more useful to us alive than dead."

The women were too scared to speak. The children hid behind the women tugging at their wrappers and sobbed as the soldiers shepherded the two men away.

That whole day the soldiers conducted house-to-house search from the bottom to the top of the village and back. They demolished the house where the area commander lived, set fire to an abandoned hut, made five more arrests and dragged out and executed one more man at the upper end of the village. This one was indeed a Maoist who had taken shelter in the attic of old Tanka Prasad, a half-blind octogenarian Bahun priest. But the soldiers didn't go into the forest, although they knew perfectly well that that was where the rebels were hiding. They didn't dare take the risk, same as the Maoists didn't dare fight them on open ground. As sunset approached they set up base in the local people's government office, formerly the Village Development Committee office, and stayed the following day and night. They pulled down and tore to shreds all the Maoist flags from the offices and houses. They confiscated the papers and pamphlets, and whatever arms and ammunition they could find belonging to the Maoists. Among the firearms captured were several muskets, three self-loading rifles (which the rebels are looted from the army earlier), and some improvised pipe-bombs and one kettle-bomb.

The detainees were leashed to wooden pillars outside the office, with their hands tied behind their back. Among them were two Bahun men from the upper end of the village. One of them was a well-known Maoist sympathiser. The other was innocent and he cried all night. Two soldiers stood guard over them. Some of the more curious and intrepid villagers came to have a look but the soldiers shooed them away. Early in the morning of the third day, the soldiers left with the detainees, all five of them chained to one another. As soon as they were sure that the soldiers were gone for good, the Maoists returned triumphantly and declared victory.

It was the most harrowing journey any of the detainees had ever made to Taplejung Bazaar. Walking to the town used to be fun. Well, at least not as uncomfortable as this. But this was sheer torture. Two of the prisoners had been beaten and severely bruised, and they dragged themselves along as the soldiers prodded them to walk faster, sometimes striking them with the butt of their rifles. On top of that there was the constant fear of ambush along the way. But fortunately, that didn't happen.

Upon arriving at the army headquarters in the evening, the five detainees were thrown into a dark, damp cell that reeked of urine and faeces. They spent an uncomfortable night lying and turning on the cold, hard earthen floor.

The next morning, they were taken for interrogation – separately, one after another. When Dil Bahadur entered the captain's office, he noted with a mild surprise that the man who was going to interrogate him was about the same age as his son. But there was a cold and unfriendly look in the young man's aristocratic visage. Despite his frosty look, the captain cut a very handsome figure with fair and unblemished skin and slick black hair. He was obviously a scion of an aristocratic family, the sort that usually has a long dark history.

The captain scrutinized the frightened old man from head to toe with cold, unwavering eyes. "Now I am going to ask you some questions. Answer as truthfully as you can and I'll let you go unharmed, but if you lie my men will be more than willing to beat you to pulps. Do you understand?" the captain said softly but threateningly.
"Yes," Dil Bahadur replied. "I'll tell you the truth."
"Good. I hope you will, because I'd sure hate to use violence against an old man like you. You see, my own father is almost

the same age as you, perhaps a few years older but not much. Now, to begin with, tell me your name," the captain started the interrogation.

"Dil Bahadur Limbu," the old man replied.

"I have been here for the past one year and I have learnt a lot about Limbu clans. What clan are you from?"

"Sambiu."

"Must have heard of it, but I am not quite sure. What's the name of your village?"

"Khewang."

"Yes, obviously. How long have you been living there?"

"All my life. I was born there. It's my ancestral village."

After asking Dil Bahadur after his home and family details, the captain started asking questions relating to his association with the Maoists.

"Look into my eyes and answer honestly. Are you a Maoist?"

"No, sir."

"Tell me the truth."

"That's the truth, sir."

"No, it's not. You are not telling the truth."

"Yes, I am, sir."

"If you answer honestly and truthfully, I'll let you walk out of here a free man. If not, then you will rot in jail for many years. Now, tell me, are you or are you not a Maoist?"

"No, sir. I am not a Maoist. I am telling the truth."

"Really? Aren't you a member of the so-called people's government in your village?"

"Yes, I am, sir."

"So how can you claim that you are not a Maoist?"

"Because I was nominated against my will, sir. I had no choice. If I had refused they'd have killed me."

"Then what about your son? I've got information here that he is a guerilla fighter."

"It is true that he is with the guerillas. But honestly, sir, I didn't know anything about it until he left home suddenly one day. If I had known I'd have stopped him, sir," Dil Bahadur said.

"You are lying to me. I've got a report here which states that you voluntarily sent your son to the Maoists."

"No, sir. That's not true, sir."

"The charges against you are very serious, old man. We have got information here that you regularly gave shelter to the Maoists even before they took over your village."

"No, sir. Yes, sir. But that, too, was against my will. They came and stayed at will. I was helpless to do anything." Dil Bahadur replied trembling.

"But did you ever take the trouble to report that to the police?"

"No, sir."

"Why not?"

"Because I was afraid, sir. They'd have killed me."

"Tell me about the rebels in your village. Everything that you know."

The frightened man quickly gave away the names and details of the rebels in the village. At the end the captain produced a typed statement and read it out to Dil Bahadur. It was a confession by the accused confirming his association with the Maoists and his admission of guilt. "Sign here," the captain said pointing at a position at the bottom of the page.

"I can't sign, sir," Dil Bahadur.

"Why can't you sign?" The captain asked sternly, with a cold and ruthless edge in his voice.

"I can't read and write, sir."

"You can't? Oh, of course not. How can you? You are illiterate," the captain said mockingly. "In that case, you can put your thumb-print on the paper, the old way," he added and pushed a stamp pad towards Dil Bahadur and waited. Dil Bahadur didn't move.

"I am waiting, old man," the captain said after a minute.

"I cannot sign, sir," Dil Bahadur said, "I am not a Maoist, sir. I am an innocent man."

"Shut up, and stop lying to me. Do you think I am a fool? If you value your life just put your thumb-print on the paper and I'll let you go." The captain said coldly.

But still Dil Bahadur didn't move. *I am innocent. I am innocent. I am innocent. I am innocent.* He kept repeating to himself silently.

"You refuse to obey my order?" the captain asked angrily.

"I am not a Maoist, sir," replied Dil Bahadur, "I am just a poor farmer caught in the middle. I have nothing to do with the Maoists and their people's war. All I want is to live in peace. That's all I want. Please let me go." Dil Bahadur, though a quiet man, was also an obstinate man when it came to that.

The captain gestured to a soldier with his eyes. The soldier lifted his rifle and struck Dil Bahadur squarely on the back with its butt, sending the old man crashing down to the cold and hard earth floor. As he tried to pick himself up, the soldier added a swift kick and the old man doubled up in pain.

"Pick him up," the captain ordered, "and make him put his thumb-print on the paper."

Two soldiers pulled him up roughly by the arms and made him stand straight, but the old man swayed and nearly fell. A small rivulet of blood trickled out of his left nostril.

"This is just the beginning, old man. Now you will do what I tell you to do," the captain said. "Press your thumb on the stamp pad and make an imprint on the paper."

Before Dil Bahadur could do anything, the soldiers caught his right hand forcefully, pressed his right thumb on the stamp pad and then pressed it on the paper.

"Good. That will suffice for now. Now take him away!" the captain barked.

When Milan's turn came for the interrogation, he was as surprised to see his interrogator as the young captain was to see him. The two stared at each other for half a minute and the one in uniform broke into a broad smile on his handsome aristocratic face.

"I think we have met before, haven't we? If I remember correctly your name is Milan and we went to the same college," the captain said.

"Yes," Milan replied with an uncertain smile, "and you are Sameer. Sameer Rana." Captain Sameer Rana was a scion of a wealthy aristocratic family in Kathmandu – a family with a history. He was a direct descendent of one of the hereditary Rana prime ministers who had ruled the country with an iron fist in his time. Milan had met Sameer Rana in college, and though they had not become friends, owing to their vastly different stations in life, they were well acquainted. Tall, fair-complexioned, good-looking, debonair and rich, with an unashamedly hedonistic lifestyle, he was the epitome of aristocratic breeding. The young man used to alternately drive a shiny Japanese car and a big Japanese motorcycle, and he had been a ladies' man thorough and thorough. There was always a beautiful girl by his side, on his motorcycle, inside his car, different girls at different times - svelte and sexy, with a pert nose, delicate skin, small breasts trying to push their way out of their tight T-shirt, slender waist and round buttocks squeezed tightly inside stretch jeans – the sort that Milan used to dream of before he had met Lalita. Sameer spoke fluent English; it was said that they spoke English as the first language in his house. Milan remembered that like many other less fortunate young men of lesser birth, he used to look at the flamboyant young man with a mixture of awe and envy.

But that had been many years ago. Now here he was again, face to face with the young man he had envied and sometimes idolised. Captain Sameer Rana was a well-placed army officer now, with a promising future. These days he went by his full aristocratic name, Captain Sameer Shumsher Junga Bahadur Rana, a substantial name in Nepal because of its historical association. Just as his family name was enough to lure the girls into his arms (and to a room in a sleazy hotel or a tourist resort outside the city, owned by businessmen friends, where it inevitably led to wild romps on the bed), the same was enough to propel him to higher ranks. *Give him some more years and he'll be wearing the stars of a general*, Milan thought enviously. *But did he complete his college education?* Milan wondered. It was well known that many dissipated young men from aristocratic families - who wasted their time in pursuit of hedonistic pleasure - bought counterfeit certificates from India to enter the commission.

Forgetting for a minute that this was an interrogation, Captain Sameer exchanged pleasantries with him and reminisced the good old college days. Finally, he asked: "What are you doing here?"

Milan explained to him the situation, and told him about him and his father. The captain listened to him without interrupting and said, "Since there is nothing against you, I may be able to secure your release. But as for your father, I am sorry there's nothing I can do. The charges against him are too serious to let him go."

Milan told the captain everything he knew and the officer was satisfied. At least, it appeared to be that way. But despite the assurance from his friend, it took Milan five more days to be free from captivity. On the sixth day, after he was made to sign a statement to the effect that he'd refrain from getting involved in any activities contrary to the constitution of the country, they let him go. Captain Sameer Rana was there himself to see to it that he was released honourably. He bade his father goodbye and gave the old man assurance that he would do everything possible to secure his release. Of course, he didn't know what that meant, but hope is always better than despair because that's what keeps one going in times of difficulties. He bought a packet of cigarette and walked back home alone, chain-smoking all the way.

When Milan arrived back home, he noticed that the Maoists had reasserted full control over the village. As he stepped into the courtyard of his house, fatigued and downcast, tears suddenly welled up in his eyes almost blocking his sight. *Milan, you are a man; you mustn't cry. Grown up men do not cry.* He chided himself. Narmaya, Kamala, Laxmi and his children were inside. They had not seen him coming. The past six days had been very difficult for them. They had waited for the return of the two men with now-rising, now-falling hope, but always worrying, always afraid. *Are they going to come back at all? Are they still alive? What will happen to us now?* The once peaceful hills had changed forever. There was no guarantee to one's life any more. But they had hoped and waited, hoped and waited; there was little else to do.

"Father, father, my father is back," Kalpana came out running delightedly. She had spied him from the window. She threw herself at him and he lifted her up and kissed her. Hearing the little girl's joyful cry, Kamala and Laxmi rushed out, followed by Narmaya and the children who, like their elder sister, threw themselves upon him. But the happy smile on Kamala's face subsided when she failed to see her husband.

"Son, you have come back?" she asked. It was more of a statement than a question.
"Yes, mother. They let me go," he answered.
"But where's your father?" she asked fearfully. "Has anything happened to him?"
"He's not been released, mother, but he is all right," Milan replied. Dil Bahadur had asked him not to tell his mother that he had been beaten.
"When are they going to release him?"
"I don't know, mother. Very soon, I guess."
"They have not hurt him, have they?"
"No, mother, they have not," he replied trying to keep a straight face. *I must not tell her. She must not know the truth, because it will be too painful for her to bear.* But it's always difficult to keep a straight face when lying to a loved one.

"I have been worried sick since the two of you were taken. I have not slept well. When I do fall asleep out of sheer exhaustion, I have terrible nightmares. It's the same with daughter-in-law. Why do we have to suffer so much? Why don't the merciless gods have pity on us?" Kamala began to sob. Laxmi sat quietly beside her with a gloomy expression on her face.

Milan gave his mother a long, sympathetic look and said, "Mother, don't cry. I'll get father out of there. I promise I will. I will do whatever it takes to free him."

"For the past six days, we – mother, daughter-in-law and myself – have stretched our eyes until they hurt, waiting for you, looking out for you. Now that you have arrived I am happy. It feels like an enormous weight has partially lifted off my head. But I am worried sick for your father. He is a good man, a simple and honest man. He has no malice towards anyone; he wouldn't hurt anyone. He is not clever like other men."

She sobbed long and hard. She hid her face in the palms of her hands and sobbed. Sorrow, like happiness, is contagious and the kind-hearted Laxmi was quickly affected. Her eyes became wet and she too broke into a sob. But a moment later she wiped her eyes and said, "Mother, don't cry. We are here for you. Milan will do everything in his capacity to get father out."
"Yes, mother. I'll go back to secure my father's release. I'll beg the army captain to help me. He is my friend."
"Then take me along with you," Kamala said between sobs.
"We'll go together, mother," he said.

That night after supper Milan lay on his bed on the floor staring at the ceiling doing a *walk through* of the recent events in his tangled mind, while Laxmi lay on the bed with the child, she too staring at the ceiling lost in her own train of thoughts. She had learnt long ago to take refuse in the cozy world of fantasy to escape the grim reality of life. A world which is perfect, where there is only happiness, where things always go according to plan and where one always gets what one wants. That was her secret world – a world sheltered from the drudgery of life.

Nine months into their marriage, they still slept separately by an unspoken, mutual accord. Usually, when Milan went to bed at night Laxmi would already be sound asleep, and when he woke up in the morning she would already be up and about – sweeping the courtyard, feeding the chicken or making tea in the kitchen, the rural woman's lot.

That night, however, both twisted and turned and sighed in their respective places, unable to fall asleep. Recent events had been too traumatic to push away from their thoughts. But grief sometimes does wonderful things to human relationship. It brings people closer. Estranged husband and wife, father and son, mother and daughter, brother and brother, sister and sister, and brother and sister reconsider and re-examine their relationship to find a common ground for reconciliation. Since their marriage, Milan had felt the growing urge to touch Laxmi, lie beside her, take her in his arms, kiss her and make love to her. He hadn't touched any woman since Lalita's death and the urge had been rising inside him. His mind and body were hungering for a taste of the female body. Over the nine months the hunger had steadily grown, and reached to a point where every waking hour he secretly yearned to hold her and pour himself into her, tenderly, lovingly. But something had held him back, something inexplicable, something he could not fully understand. Perhaps it was that lingering feeling of guilt, or fear of rejection, or both, he was not sure. As he now twisted and turned in discomfort he realized that during his detention by the army, the one person he had constantly thought of was Laxmi. He had longed to see her, hold her in his eyes, take her in his arms, lie beside her and make love to her every night. And on the way back after his release his feet had carried him briskly because reaching home had gained a newfound urgency. At that time he had been too preoccupied to dwell on the reason for that, but as he now immersed himself in his thoughts he knew exactly why. It was Laxmi. He had been anxious to see her. He had married her for two reasons, one, for the sake of his children, and two, he had taken pity on her miserable existence. Love, real passionate man-to-woman love, like it had been with Lalita, had never been a part of the plan. Real love comes but only once in a lifetime and it happens with only one person, he had firmly believed. But something he believed impossible had happened. So here he was again, falling in love, real love – the kind that throbs like a sweet pain somewhere deep inside the subconscious mind. He had fallen in love with Laxmi, with due apology to his dear departed wife. Amidst the trouble in his life, Laxmi had been a mountain of stability – steady, rock solid, dependable, always there for him. Did she love him? He knew that she did care for him, deeply. But love? He didn't know. *I must find out. We cannot go on living separate lives forever. And since I am a man I must make the first move. She won't because she is a woman. So I must do it. But is she ready? Will she accept me with an open heart?* He wasn't sure.

Laxmi, on her part, had felt much the same way. But she had not understood her own feelings; or rather she had been too timid to explore it with an open mind. Every time she tried, the memories of her dead husband had stood in the way. She had loved him. He was a simple, good, honest and caring man, but he had never been passionate in his love. Theirs was not a passionate, sexual love. He was a practical man, not a lover, and certainly not a dreamer. He used to go to bed early at night and wake up early in the morning (by which time she was also awake), nudge her and ask, "Shall we?" If her answer was "Yes," then he made a quick love to her and it was "Not today," then he quietly got up and went outside. With him she had found sex mildly enjoyable – she neither looked forward to it nor detested it. But Milan was different. He was not practical but he had dreams in his eyes, and she had found herself drawn to him in a way that she had never been drawn to any man before. She was not a student of psychology to try to unravel the mysterious ways that her mind worked. Before their marriage she hadn't for even a moment looked at him that way. He was her younger brother-in-law and would always be, that was the way she had thought. But fate had thrown them together, intertwined their lives, given them a common ground and a common purpose. At least that's how she now looked at it now. *Perhaps it was destined to happen this way, like Amrita used to say*, she thought. So, as the days had changed into weeks and weeks into months, her affection for him had changed into a sexual yearning which pulsated with increasing intensity inside her, and no matter what she did it refused to go away. She had fallen in love. She hadn't realized how much until the day Milan had been taken away by the soldiers. Sometimes she thought she saw that look in his eyes which gave her hope, but then it quickly faded away. She was too shy to make the move. But now she longed to touch him, to wrap him in her arms, to kiss him and take him into her, forcefully, passionately, in complete abandon. *Women of good character do not throw themselves at men; they always play the passive role.* She had been brought up to believe. But now she doubted the wisdom of that dictum. "In this world it's the bold and the determined who get what they want; the rest have to make do with what they get with the least effort," Lalita had once told her. *We cannot go on like this day after day while life just passes us by*, she concluded. *If he is unable to make the first move for reasons of his own, then I will. Had Lalita been in my place, she'd have done it a long time ago.*

"Milan," Laxmi spoke breaking the silence of the night. It was almost midnight.
"Huh," Milan said.
"Are you still awake?"
"Yes!"

A long silence ensued.
"You can come up if you want to," she said.
"Can I?" he asked uncertainly, his heart racing.
"Yes," she replied, "if you want to."
Milan didn't answer her. He quietly got up and climbed on the bed. There was not enough space for the three of them on the narrow bed, so he lifted the little boy gently and laid him on his own bed on the floor. The boy was in such a deep slumber that he didn't even move.

The two lay side by side without speaking for sometime. Laxmi hadn't touched a man in the past five years, and Milan hadn't touched a woman in the past three years. As their warm bodies pressed into each other, gently and self-consciously, they both felt an electrifying sensation pass through their bodies. And their breathing became faster and audible in the small moonlit room. Milan ran his hand over her warm breasts and fiddled with the nipples that seemed to become erect at his touch. When she didn't object, he ran his hands slowly down her abdomen to the valley between her thighs and to his mild surprise found it already wide apart and wet with desire.

They made love three times that night, passionately, with complete abandon. And for once Milan did not think of his dead wife, neither did Laxmi think of her dead husband. The dead are dead, consigned to the past where they belong, to be remembered occasionally but never to be resurrected. The 'living' are the present and the future, and as long as death doesn't cheat one of one's life one must go on living, no matter what, for life is precious. To each individual life happens only once. Each individual exists for a brief moment in the vast span of eternity. There is no past birth. There is no rebirth. There is no Heaven. There is no Hell. There is only this earth and maybe some other planets in the future. Birth is the beginning of life and death is the end of everything associated with it. In between the two is the time to 'live' – to eat, drink, laugh, cry, quarrel, fight, make friends, procreate, make war, to create, to destroy and to make love. Therefore, life should not be a preparation for death; rather it should be a celebration of itself while it lasts.

The army held Dil Bahadur without formally charging him. Soon after Milan's return Comrade Prakash summoned him to his office and interrogated him for close to an hour, and let him go when he found his answers to satisfactory. After that, with the kind permission of Comrade Prakash, who was rather nice and civil to him, as compared to Comrade Kishor, the former school teacher, he made several journeys to seek his father's release, but without any success. He went twice in the company of his mother and once with Laxmi. But every time a young boy of twelve (who looked not more than nine) accompanied him. Comrade Prakash had assigned this boy to keep a close watch on him with strict instructions for both of them not to lose sight of eath other. This boy, who was a nephew in relation, also spied on the activities of the army along the way and reported back to his superiors giving them every little detail he observed with his sharp little eyes. Though Milan was at first annoyed at this intrusion into his private life, it was to save his life afterwards. And although the soldiers had their own suspicion about him, they never suspected the frail looking little boy.

Milan made it a point to meet his friend, Captain Sameer Rana, on each visit. The officer kindly allowed him to see his father, and tried to extract information on the rebels. But because of the presence of the boy, Milan only gave him vague answers – general things that the captain already knew. When

Milan asked his friend the Captain what the army was planning to do with his father, the latter replied that they were still working on that, without being specific. But he did tell Milan that the charges against the old man were quite serious, enough to warrant at least a few years' jail term. Milan took care not to tell his mother as he knew she would be further distressed by this unsettling news.

Three months into Dil Bahadur's detention, two incidents that were to have a profound and tragic impact on Milan's life took place. First, two rebels stationed in Khewang were arrested by an army patrol near Tellok Bazaar while on a routine patrol. A week later the army came back to Khewang and in a skirmish near the village killed the area commander, Comrade Prakash, and Comrade Kishor, the former school teacher. It was evident that they had come specifically after the two. After the army went back, the guerillas quickly reasserted control with a new area commander in charge, a ruthless little fighter named Comrade Raktim.

Now this Comrade Raktim, his *nom de guerre* meant 'painted with blood' or something to that effect, a shifty-eyed wiry little man, was as ruthless as he was skinny. To a much higher degree than his predecessor, he was a man blinded by ideology - an ideology that sees humans in only two roles – the exploiters and the exploited. Anyone who didn't share his view was an immediate suspect as a possible class enemy. And he immediately set about finding and punishing the informer, as he firmly believed that this was the work of one, and his suspicious eyes fell on Milan, naturally. As soon as he took over command, he summoned Milan to his office and interrogated him for an hour. But luckily for Milan, the little boy swore that Milan had told the army nothing of importance. So, after failing to implicate his prime suspect he let him go reluctantly, but not before threatening to pull the trigger personally on his head if evidence ever turned up to prove that he (Milan) had in any way been involved in the capture of his comrades and the murder of his predecessor. "Be careful," the ruthless little man growled, "I'll be watching your every move, like a hawk."

Milan knew that for some reason Comrade Raktim didn't like him and was looking for an excuse to slit his throat. Even the slightest offence would be enough to kill him. This was the right time for him to leave; there was nothing here for him except death and despair. But he couldn't just up and run away. In the absence of his father, he was now the head of the family, whether he liked it or not. He had to take care of his family members and protect them. It was his filial duty to do so and being a conscientious man he was not going to run from that duty under any circumstances.

Two weeks after the above incident Milan saw his father for the last time. The next time he visited the old man, which was a week after that; the old man was not there. Captain Sameer told him that he had been moved to another, more secure place, but refused to elaborate or dwell on the specifics. "I am sorry," the captain said with a look of genuine sympathy, for he had come to like Milan, "It's beyond my power."
"My father is innocent," Milan said.
"I believe you," said the captain, "and I wish I could do something to help you, but my hands are tied. I am unable to do anything."
"What are they going to do with my father?" he asked anxiously.
"I don't know," the captain replied.
"Is there nothing you can do to help me?"

"I wish I could but I am sorry the answer is no. I am just a mid-ranking officer, you know," Captain Rana replied in a sympathetic voice. It never occurred to Milan than it was the same Captain Sameer Rana, his friend, who had recommended indefinite imprisonment for his father.

As a parting shot Captain Sameer said, "Milan, it's a pity that we didn't have time to get close in college. We could have really hit it off, you know. You and I." Milan agreed. Yes, he said to himself afterwards, him and I. In college he had wanted to be Sameer Rana – the young man with everything - family name, disarming good looks, pretty girls, and plenty of money to blow away. Only a precious few in this impoverished land are so fortunate.

Before returning home he handed a packet of dark-brown, dry tobacco leaves to the captain.
"What is it?" asked the captain.
"Tobacco leaves. I brought these for my father, but you can have them now."
"I don't chew tobacco; I only smoke cigarettes," the captain replied with a smile. He smoked only foreign brands.
"You can give it to your soldiers," Milan said.

The captain accepted it. "Thank you. I'll hand it to one of my soldiers then," he said and bade Milan farewell. On every visit Milan brought his father dried tobacco and maize leaves. The old man used to spend his time in detention preparing and smoking his beloved *khosela*. First, he carefully cut the dry maize leaf into neat rectangles (he had been allowed a small pair of scissors, by courtesy of Captain Sameer Rana) and put them in neat little stacks. Then he cut the tobacco leaves into fine pieces on a sheet of paper, coughing and sneezing in the process as the fine dust wafted into his nostrils. Then he spread the tobacco in a single line across the length of a maize leaf which he had earlier prepared. Finally, he rolled the maize leaf into a cylindrical shape, and tied it at one end with a small string made of maize leaf. He always tucked one neatly above his right ear and put the rest in the pocket of his *daura*, the traditional Nepali shirt with laces instead of buttons to fasten the two sides.

As he walked back home, dejectedly, he thought of his father. *Where is the poor old man now? Where have they taken him? What have they done to him? Is he still alive? Who's going to give him tobacco for his khosela?* He walked briskly without looking left or right. He walked without speaking to or waiting for the boy, who struggled to keep pace with him. He walked without stopping to greet fellow travelers who looked at him curiously.

It's a cruel world out there, he said to himself. *This is what happens to good and honest men. The really 'bad' always manage to get away and the 'good' get trampled by all and sundry.* He pondered on the injustices of life all the way. *Why? Oh, Why? Why do good and honest men have to suffer?* At length he himself provided the answer to his question. *They suffer because their goodness makes them weak, and there is no place for the 'weak' in nature.*

The Maoists claim to represent the grassroot. They talk as if they have a monopoly on the word 'grassroot', as if a poor man is by birth a communist. And then they go around destroying with impunity the very things that are designed to uplift the life of the poor. *Grassroot*, he smiled sarcastically as he spat out the English word so dear to the communists. The government on its part claims to represents the people and then its armed forces go about killing and imprisoning the same people at random. *Why don't they - the army and the*

Maoists - go somewhere else and fight it out in the open and stop bothering innocent people? Why can't we live in peace in our own land?

By the time he had reached within a kilometer of his home, it was approaching midnight and he was almost running along the deserted trail that twisted and turned like a ribbon of white under the moonlight, with the boy trailing behind him, panting. He hadn't eaten anything along the way; he hadn't been hungry, but he had bought the boy a packet of biscuits along the way. Normally, he would have been wary of the ghosts and malicious spirits, even though he had doubts as to their existence, that were said to lurk in the bamboo groves and the branches of trees to haunt the passersby, but today he was too preoccupied to think of such things. The dogs along the way barked and howled but quickly wagged their tails when they recognized him. Two armed Maoists youths on night patrol appeared out of the darkness and accosted him, but when they recognized him they let him go after a brief interview. No one could enter and leave the villages without the knowledge (and permission) of the Maoists. When he reached home he saw a dim yellow light flickering in his mother's room. He knew that she was still awake.

A few days later, the Maoists accused a man of collaborating with the army. This man, Hemraj by name, was his father's distant cousin-brother and therefore an uncle. Maoist spies had noticed him loitering near the army camp in Taplejung Bazaar. Since Comrade Raktim was firmly of the view that 'the accused is guilty until proven innocent', he didn't give the man any opportunity to clear his name. He needed to make an example to strike terror into the hearts of would be informers and collaborators. He had tried that with Milan and having failed to implicate him, he had even thought of making false accusations. But the thought of Milan's younger brother Ratna, whose reputation among the rebel ranks was rapidly rising, had prevented him from doing so. Nevertheless, his eyes were still set on Milan. "One wrong move, just one wrong move, and the motherfucker is a dead man," he had told his overly-submissive subordinates. Even *comrades* are not equal, for theirs is a greater illusion. And when absolute power is concentrated in the hands of a few individuals driven to the extreme by their political ideology then they are bound to commit the greatest injustices of all, for no human is infallible. In the luckless Hemraj, a man who had been heard denouncing the Maoists privately, Comrade Raktim had found the perfect example. It didn't matter whether he was guilty or not.

Two days later the whole village gathered at the school ground at three o'clock in the afternoon. Everyone was there, the old and the young, the able and the disabled. There was a somber mood among the crowd, for they knew what was about to take place. Comrade Raktim had given his verdict and his was the last word in the village. There was no one superior to him; nobody dared raise a squeak of objection.

As usual the red flags of the Maoists fluttered proudly in every conceivable space, and young guerillas in green uniform flaunted their might to the beat of drums. After the customary speech by the area commander which was followed by a thunderous applause as usual, the ashen-faced accused, his hands bound behind his back, his face swollen and bruised, was paraded in full view of the spectators. "Informer, collaborator, public enemy, ..." – a rebel read the numerous charges against him. The verdict: he was to be flogged and executed. This was followed by another round of applause. The people had given their consent. The frightened man hung his head in shame and humiliation, and most of all terror. Then there was complete silence. Narmaya, Kamala, Milan and Laxmi sat on the grass at the front row of crowd. Somewhere nearby sat the family of the condemned man – to watch him suffer pain, humiliation and death.

"Barbarians," Milan hissed under his breath, "This is not people's rule; it's the rule of barbarians. Look at the poor man. They've already beaten and tortured him. It could as easily have been me, you know," Milan whispered to Laxmi indignantly. He had a lot of affection for the condemned man who was his uncle and friend.

"Shh.... Keep your voice down. They might hear," Kamala whispered with terror in her wet, sunken, reddish eyes. She had cried herself to sleep many nights. She looked older than her years. Recurrent visitation by ill fortune had taken its toll on her.
"I don't care," Milan replied, "It's my uncle and an innocent man they are parading like a criminal."

Hemraj was dragged to the middle of the ground and made to stand facing the crowd. Then Comrade Raktim's sharp and cold voice tore through the silence, "Fathers, mothers, brothers and sisters, and my dear comrades! You all know this man very well, and you also know why we have brought him before you today. To those of you who are still in the dark, let me enlighten you. This man who stands before the people's court today is a traitor. He was caught red-handed liaising with the army. He has betrayed our glorious revolution by collaborating with the army of the reactionary and feudalistic government, which is but a mere stooge of Western capitalist-imperialists and Indian expansionists. Therefore, in your presence today, this criminal will be flogged and executed. And lest anyone think that it is too harsh a punishment, let him remember that even this punishment is not sufficient for the crime he has committed."

He turned to the big and swarthy guerilla standing near the frightened man and said: "Flog the son-of-a-bitch."

The big, swarthy man examined his intended victim with scornful eyes. He already had a meter long, fresh-green bamboo staff in his hand. He gripped it tightly with both hands and raised it above his head.

"Wait," the area commander said, "I think we should give the first chance to his eldest son. Errant parents should be punished by the hands of their own children. No humiliation can be as total as this. Don't you think so, comrade?"
The swarthy man stopped, looking confused at first, and then broke into a broad gleeful smile. "Sure, comrade, let the boy have fun."

At a signal from their commander, four young rebels briskly made their way towards the spot where the condemned man's wife and children were sitting. They dragged out a wiry little boy of fifteen, who followed them meekly, like a sacrificial goat. The swarthy man handed the boy his bamboo staff and said, "Look at your father, boy. Take a good look at his face. Can you see his real face? He is not your father; he is a traitor and he needs to be punished. Strike him with this."

The shaking boy made no move to obey the order. He stood mutely, with an utterly bewildered and anguished expression, his hands and legs trembling with fright.

"Hurry up, boy. We don't have all the time in the world," the big swarthy man bawled.

But the boy did not move. Instead, he began to sob.

"Hurry up, boy, do it," Comrade Raktim shouted impatiently, "or you will also end up like you father."

When the boy still refused to budge, Hemraj said to his son, "Do it, son. Strike me. These murderers will kill you too if you don't obey them. I am a doomed man; nothing can save me. Save yourself, for me and your mother."

With trembling hands, the boy lifted the staff it over his head, hesitantly. "I am sorry father. Please forgive me," he whispered.

"Don't be sorry, son, it's not your fault. Everyone knows that you were forced to do it," said Hemraj to his son.

The boy brought the staff down on his father's back, softly.

"That's not good enough. Hit harder. Aim at the legs," the swarthy man shouted. The boy looked hesitant.

"Do as he says, son," Hemraj said to his tearful son.

The boy swung the staff above his head once again to strike his father. At that instant, watching the spectacle from the periphery with mounting anger, something snapped inside Milan's head. The anger that had built up inside him over the past three months exploded in all its fury, sweeping everything in its path. Nothing mattered anymore, not even his own life. In a flash he had made up his mind to stand up against this blatant act of injustice being perpetrated in the name of justice. *Evil people win and keep winning when good people are not prepared to stop them.* Milan was prepared to risk his life to stand against these evil men.

"No. Stop!" Milan suddenly stood up and cried angrily, pointing a finger at Comrade Raktim. "That's enough. I won't allow this madness to continue anymore."
The crowd gasped in astonishment. All eyes turned towards him. It was as if a single large eye was watching him, scrutinizing him from every direction incredulously. *What's the bloody fool doing? Has he gone insane? This is suicide. Doesn't the idiot know that Comrade Raktim will have him shot right here at this very instance?*

Comrade Raktim glared at Milan with eyes livid with fury. Fire smouldered in his eyes - fire fueled by hatred. He was filled with such a rage that for a long moment he was unable to utter even a single word. *How dare he? How dare the son-of-a-bitch? How dare the mother-fucking son-of-a-bitch challenge my authority?* His anger simmered and boiled, and then exploded with a fury of a volcano. "What did you say? What is it exactly that you said? How dare you say it? I'll have you shot right now, right here," he screamed at the top of his voice, scattering invisible droplets of saliva from his mouth. At this outburst even the earth and the sky seemed to tremble. A dozen guns were suddenly leveled at Milan, fingers ready to squeeze the trigger. The commander had only to say 'Kill the son-of-a-whore' and it would be over in less than a minute.

But Milan did not flinch. He wasn't afraid anymore. He didn't care what was going to happen to him; he was past caring. Occasionally, life presents one with such an opportunity, and only the really bold have the guts to make their stand. Milan had decided to do that.
"I said stop this madness right now," he yelled back.
Laxmi jumped up to pull him down, begging in a whisper to back down, but he pushed her away.
"Stop this madness right now," he yelled again.

"Bring him to me," Comrade Raktim ordered his subordinates, who complied hastily, dragging Milan by his collars, sleeves, hair and whatever they could lay their hands on, and not forgetting a land a few kicks and punches on him.

"You will apologize or I'll have you shot this instant," the enraged commander screamed.

"No," said Milan defiantly, "I won't." He didn't care anymore because he had given up hope of getting out of this alive. He had made up his mind to die with dignity, not whimpering like a coward. He unbuttoned his shirt to reveal his chest and said, "Shoot me if that is you want. I am not afraid. I am not afraid to die. I am ready to die laughing than live the life of a coward. Since you have only hatred in your poisoned mind, that's the only thing that you can give me. Kill me. Now. Right now. You can take my life, but you cannot take my dignity."

"Kill him. Kill the insolent son-of-a-whore," Comrade Raktim yelled. Milan turned defiantly to face his would-be murderers. There was no fear in his eyes as the guerillas lifted their guns - a dozen of them simultaneously. But they hesitated.

"What are you waiting for?" Comrade Raktim shouted, "Shoot the son of a bitch. No. Don't shoot. Wait. Why waste precious bullets on this scum? Just slit his throat with a knife."

The rebels with the guns looked confused, but they didn't lower their guns. Then the big, swarthy man pulled out a shiny khukuri that shone like silver in the sun and sauntered towards Milan. He was going to do the killing.

Suddenly there was a commotion in the crowd and Laxmi ran out screaming as the crowd gasped in yet another bout of astonishment. She ran as fast as her little feet could carry her.

She ran like the wind. She overtook the swarthy man and flung herself upon her husband and shielded him.

"Spare my husband's life," she shrieked. "Don't kill him. Have mercy on him. He is innocent. He has done no wrong."

"Move away from him, woman," the swarthy man shouted.

"No," she shouted back, "I won't."

Milan tried to push her away. "Go back to your place," he said to her. "Let them kill me. I am not afraid to die."

But she hugged him tighter and cried, "I have already been widowed once. Please don't make me a widow again. I can't live without him. If you kill him then you'll have to kill me along with him."

At this heart-rending cry, a sympathetic murmur arose from the crowd. She continued, "I don't understand politics, I am just a simple woman. But even I know what justice means. You Maoists say that you are fighting for justice. You claim to have brought the people's rule in the village. But how can that be true when innocent people are beaten up and murdered for the smallest of offences? How can there be 'people's rule' when people can't even voice their objections? Aren't we *the people*? Don't we have the right to express our views?"

Comrade Raktim stood with his mouth open with an expression of utter amazement on his face. He hadn't expected this quiet and timid-looking woman to be so fearless, so selfless and so eloquent. He knew her well. He knew her history. He had always thought her to be a rural typical housewife – quiet, timid and submissive. But here she was – defending her husband with her life. For once he didn't know what to do.

He thought for some time. "All right," he spoke at last, slowly, "I will spare your husband's life, although he doesn't deserve to live. But I have a condition and that is this. He will not go unpunished. He will be flogged, and then tied to that wooden post over there for three days and three nights, without food and water. If he survives at the end of three days, then I'll let him go."

"Have mercy on him, don't do that to him. Let him go now," Laxmi pleaded. But the comrade was adamant.

Milan's attitude wasn't helpful either. "Let him do what he likes, I don't care," he said loudly.

"Send her back to her place," Comrade Raktim barked an order to his subordinates who grabbed Laxmi by the arm and dragged her back to her place.

Then the beating began. The big swarthy man put away his khukuri, looking genuinely sorry at having to do that. From the expression of disappointment on his face it was clear that he would have loved to slit Milan's throat. *But there'll always be another day for that. As long as the war lasts there will be plenty of opportunities to slit throats.* After putting away the khukuri, he examined his palms carefully, as if there was something there, and spit on each of them and then rubbed them together. Then he picked up a bamboo staff, swung it up and down a number of times in the air, "swiiiish, swiish", as if he were practising. Then he suddenly brought it down at a lightning speed on the back of Milan's legs. Milan wasn't expecting it. A sharp and loud report filled the air, and he buckled under the impact. He sprawled on the dusty ground, grabbing his legs in pain. Immediately, two young rebels ran to him, propped him up and retreated as quickly as they had come. The swarthy man repeated his action with undiminished vehemence.

At the fifteenth stroke Milan started crying out in pain. So far he had remained silent. He had gritted his teeth and held his mouth tightly shut. After the twenty-fifth stroke he stopped screaming. The blow came again and again, on his legs, on his arms, on his back. But strangely it didn't seem to hurt anymore. He was slipping into unconsciousness, into the realm beyond pain. By the thirty-fifth stroke, he had fallen unconscious. His body lay limp on the ground, covered in blood. Then he was dragged away and tied to a wooden post.

"Leave him there for three days and three nights without food and water," Comrade Raktim said with satisfaction, "We'll see if he can survive."

After that the commander turned his attention back to the accused and his son. He said to the boy, "Now, let's go through it again."
The frightened boy had seen enough. He was too scared to defy the commander. He lifted the staff and struck on his father's legs. Hemraj's face contorted in pain, but he didn't cry.
"Again. Five more times," Comrade Raktim said.
The boy complied.
"Bravo," said the commander, "You have proved that you are a true patriot. Now go back to your place."

The boy stumbled back to his place, his head hanging in shame, his heart filled with disgust and pain. He squatted beside his mother with his head between his knees and sobbed. This day would forever haunt him – the day he had struck his father and become a patriot. After that some of the young rebels took turns to beat the screaming man senseless. When the beating was over, the unconscious man was dragged to where Milan was tethered and left with two young guerillas to watch him.

After the badly shaken villagers had been ordered home, the guerillas surrounded Hemraj (he had regained some consciousness by that time). They tied his hands and legs with a rope, covered his eyes with a scarf, and pushed another scarf into his mouth. The condemned man, who had resigned himself to fate, did not put up any resistance. As it was, he was already half-dead anyway. The big, swarthy man (who was the designated 'butcher' of the group) took out his shiny khukuri, examined its cutting edge with his fingers and apparently satisfied, squatted near the bound and blind-folded man and calmly slit half of his throat. Thick red blood spurted out like a fountain from the incision and painted the killer's hands and clothes in red. A series of ghastly sound emanated from the dying man's throat. It required two more slashes to separate the head from the torso. The swarthy man lifted the severed head and handed it to his comrades, who held it in their hands one by one and examined it. Then he took it back and lifting it by the hair looked at it for an extended moment. There was a quirky smile of satisfaction on his lips and a strange look in his eyes.

They hung the corpse on a pole at a crossroad near the village for the benefit of all passersby. A sign with a bad handwriting was scrawled on a piece of paper using the dead man's blood: 'This is what happens to traitors, informers, collaborators and other enemies of the people!'

Milan, tied to a post nearby, slipping in and out of consciousness and in excruciating pain, closed his eyes and tried to shut the world out. Though he was able to shut his eyes, he wasn't able to shut his ears and mind. He was conscious when they had slit Hemraj's throat; he had heard the ghastly gargled sound that had escaped from the dying man's throat. Then he had drifted into unconsciousness. Now a huge inferno suddenly broke out and engulfed him in flames. A hideous face, burnt and macabre, lunged at him with an evil grin. Then a hand appeared holding a khukuri dripping with blood. He screamed in terror but no sound came out. He tried to run but his feet wouldn't carry him. He tried to crawl but his hands wouldn't move. It was horrible, horrible. And he came back to consciousness again. In this way he drifted in and out of consciousness.

Early the next morning, Laxmi came with food and water. She had been ordered to stay away the whole night. "You go home, nobody will be allowed near him," the rebels had said. She had begged them to let her stay with him, but they had shooed her away. She hadn't slept a wink all night, crying, and as soon as the first rooster had crowed, she had run to the kitchen and prepared tea and food for Milan. Her eyes were red and she looked small, frail and haggard. She sat by Milan's side and gave him food and water, but the young rebels on guard prevented her. "You can't give him food; not even water," they told her. Laxmi pleaded and begged, but they didn't relent. "We have strict orders, sister. Our lives also depend upon it," they told her.

She sat beside Milan throughout the day. As Milan wasn't allowed to eat, she also didn't touch the food that she had brought. She didn't even drink the water. Even when Milan scolded her to have the food and water, she refused. When the sun reached its zenith at midday and it became too hot to bear, she covered his face with her shawl. When the flies buzzed about him to scavenge on the wounds on his exposed flesh, she chased them away. Narmaya and Kamala came and stayed for two hours and went back reluctantly. They didn't bring the children. "It will be too traumatic for them see their father in this condition," Kamala said and Laxmi agreed. An hour before dusk Comrade Raktim came. He looked at Milan with mocking eyes and said "Humm..." with a satisfied smile and left.

Laxmi sat by Milan's side all night and fell asleep with her head leaning against his chest. She was hungry and thirsty but she didn't care. Milan's badly bruised legs, arms, face and cheeks were swollen and he groaned in pain and babbled incoherently in delirium as he slipped in and out of consciousness. At midday on the second day the young guerillas relented a little and said, "You may throw a bucket of water on him, but that's all. Do not give him any to drink." Weak as she was, with thirst, hunger and grief, she hurried to the nearest house. The man of the house volunteered to carry the water for her and she threw it upon Milan, who feebly licked the drops that flowed down his lips. Then she drank some herself. Kamala came with food and water and stayed for two hours, but she had to go back. She urged Laxmi to have the food, but she refused. An hour before dusk Comrade Raktim came again. "Still alive, is he? But I don't think he'll last this night," he said and went away.

The days were hot and the nights were cold. During the day curious people came continuously to take a look at the condemned man. They shook their head sympathetically from a distance and went away without uttering so much as a word. The third day was not any different from the first and second, except that Milan's condition had worsened. "Water, water ...," he mumbled every time he became conscious. But then he slipped back into the dark world of nightmares again. He was at the top of a high and steep cliff and Purna was calling out to him from the bottom with outstretched arms, "Jump, Milan, jump!" He wanted to jump but he was afraid. He was weak, thirsty, hungry and in terrible pain. A gust of wind hit his face and it was so hot that he felt like he was in the middle of an inferno. He moved closer to the edge and peered down. It was a sheer drop of over a hundred meters. "No, I can't. I am afraid," he shouted back. Then suddenly he was falling, falling, falling .... And he screamed. But only a hoarse, muffled sound came out of his throat. And he suddenly woke up. His head was hot with fever and he was shivering even under the intense heat of the glaring sun. "Laxmi, I am dying ...." he whispered. "No, you are not. You are not dying. I am not going to let you die on me. Hang on a few more hours and it will be over. Hang on there, you'll be all right," Laxmi reassured him. At midday the rebels allowed a bucket of water to be thrown upon him again. "Don't worry, he'll be out of his misery soon enough," one of them said with a smile.

But Milan didn't die. Through an extraordinary reserve of strength in his body and spirit, he survived the ordeal. When Comrade Raktim arrived again in the evening he asked, "Is he still alive?" His face fell visibly when he got the answer. "Why did I let myself listen to a woman? I should have had him shot there and then," he muttered in a dismayed voice. "But a promise is a promise. Cut him loose," he said. "But he cannot stay here. He he must leave this village as soon as he recovers," the guerilla commander added as if as an afterthought before goin away. There was no arguing against that.

A month after the ordeal, which Milan preferred to call '*the incident*', he fully recovered and prepared to leave for

Kathmandu. The physical wound had healed easily enough, but the psychological wound inflicted upon him was too deep to be healed and he still had nightmares. While he was recuperating, both his mother and wife had pleaded with Comrade Raktim to let him stay, but the guerilla commander had been adamant. "My decision is final and irreversible," he had told them, "He is a troublemaker. There is no place for him here. He can't stay. As soon as he recovers send him away." Pleading with him was like hitting one's head against the wall - the only thing that comes out worse from the experience is one's own head.

When he was recuperating Milan mused at the irony of life. When he had desperately wanted to leave, circumstance had forced to stay. Now when he wanted to stay, he was being forced to leave. So he had decided to leave of his own accord as soon as he got better. He had decided to go alone. He couldn't take his wife and children with him because he had nowhere to take them. And though Laxmi was overwhelmed by sadness at having to part with him, she herself decided that she would stay back to take care of her mother-in-law, grandmother-in-law and the children. And although Milan was overcome with sadness at having to leave his wife and children behind, he didn't insist. After all, he had nowhere to take them even if they were to follow him. He had decided to go to Kathmandu and seek refuse at his uncle's house once again. Hopefully, his uncle and aunt would help him to go abroad for employment.

"I'll try to go abroad once again with my uncle's help. And when I have made enough money I'll come back and take you away from here - all of you, including mother and grandma. Will you come with me then?"

"I will. I don't want to stay here forever without you," Laxmi said with tearful eyes, wondering if she would ever see him again. As long as Comrade Raktim remained in the village, he'd never allow Milan back. He had made it very clear to her. "And I'll write to you every week. Will you also do the same?"
"Yes, I will," she replied with tears in her eyes.

So, thirty-seven days after his ordeal, Milan bid a tearful farewell to his grandmother, mother, wife and children.
"Don't cry for me. I'll come back as soon as I can," he told his tearful mother and grandmother.
"Daddy will be back to take you away from here," he said to his children.

One sunny morning a month after Milan's departure Laxmi was washing clothes by herself. When she was alone she mostly thought of Milan wondering when they'd be together again. The thought always filled her with melancholy and she felt helpless against the unending trials of life. Milan had kept his promise and written to her every week and this was the only thing that her given her comfort. Kamala came holding a few pieces of clothes and said, "Daughter-in-law, could you please wash these as well?"

She had become a shadow of her former self. Her waist-length hair had lost its shine. Her eyes had lost their glow. Lines of sorrow were etched on her cheeks. And there was a permanent sadness in her voice.

"Give them to me, mother," Laxmi replied. Kamala handed her the clothes. Laxmi put them in the bowl along with the other clothes and began to stroke them together. After watching the younger woman for a minute, the she headed for the vegetable garden, where she usually spent many brooding hours each day. Laxmi watched her mother-in-law's emaciated figure and felt sorry for her. A year had passed since the detention of her father-in-law and there was still no trace of his whereabouts. No news, no rumours, nothing. He had simply vanished. And then to add to her woes her son had been beaten up and expelled.

All of a sudden she felt a strange sensation in her abdomen, as if it were filled up, and then she felt her inside rise up her throat. Greatly alarmed, she walked a short distance to a nearby tree and holding onto a low branch and bending down she vomited. It was so unexpected. She didn't know what had happened to her.

Kamala heard her and made an about turn to give her a curious look. She eyed her daughter-in-law incredulously.
"Did you just throw up, daughter-in-law? Is there anything wrong with you?"
"I don't know mother," she replied with the bitter taste still on her tongue. "I was all right and then suddenly this happened."
The older woman scrutinized the younger woman with her eyes and said, "Oh, my god. Can it be?"
"What mother?" she asked.
"Are you having your periods?"
Laxmi thought for a moment and said, "I missed it this month. But I miss it from time to time, so it's quite normal."
"But you don't normally feel like throwing up when that happens, do you?"
"No, mother"
"Then if my suspicion is correct, you are with a child. This is the most amazing thing," Kamala said, a hundred watt smile lighting up her face. For the first time since the arrest of her husband, there was real happiness on her face. "The gods have looked upon you at last," she added delightedly. She then

closed her eyes, joined the palms of her hands in a Namaste in front of her face - ten joined fingers pointing upwards - and standing in that posture murmured softly, but loud enough for Laxmi to hear, "All you gods, goddesses and spirits that roam the hills, forests, rivers and valleys, thank you for looking after my daughter-in-law. Thank you for listening to our prayers. Thank you, thank you so much for fulfilling her most fervent wish. And thank you for fulfilling my most fervent wish." Then she turned to Laxmi and said, "It seem that the goddess of good fortune had finally begun to smile upon you."

Laxmi couldn't believe that she was pregnant. It was simply incredible. Truly incredible! It was like a miracle. *I am pregnant. Look, I am pregnant. Look all of you nay-sayers, I am pregnant. Look at my belly. There's a child in it. It's going to grow and grow and grow .... And out of it will come the most beautiful baby.* She wanted to shout at the top of her voice. A happy smile - a truly, pristinely happy smile, not diluted by sorrow - broke upon her face, and lit up her eyes. *Yes, I am pregnant. I am with a child at last. I am going to give birth. Oh, God! Why did you make me wait for so many years for this day? Why?*

I must tell Milan. I must write to him. He will be so... happy. And I am so happy. I am so happy that .... that I just cannot describe how happy I am. I am that much happy. In fact, I must be the happiest woman in the world at this moment. I have not known this much happiness since....... Since when? Since the carefree days of my childhood. God, let it be real. Let this not be a false pregnancy. I'll give anything, anything, even my own life for this chance at motherhood. That's the thing about happiness. When one feels truly happy, one believes that it's the first time in a long, long time.

She ran her fingers tenderly over her belly, and noticed that her mother-in-law's eyes were fixed there as well. Overcome with self-consciousness, she quickly removed her hand.
"It doesn't show yet," said the older woman with a smile, "but I am positive that you are pregnant."

When Kamala went back into the house, Laxmi called out to the little girls who were playing nearby and asked, "What would you like? A little brother or a little sister?"
Kalpana, the older of the two, thought for a moment and replied, "I want a little brother."
Samjhana, her little sister, cried out, "I want a little sister."
"But there are already two of you, and you have only one brother," said Laxmi giggling like a girl.
"Yes, but I am my elder sister's little sister. I want my own little sister," replied the little girl sweetly. Laxmi scooped her up in her arms and kissed her.
"I'll give you a little brother, sweetie," she said laughing out loud.
"But I don't want a brother, I want a sister," the little girl sulked.
"Where do babies come from, mother?" Kalpana asked.
"They fall from the sky, like you did," Laxmi replied.
"Do babies really fall from the sky like everybody says, mother?" Samjhana asked innocently.
"Yes, they do," Laxmi replied with a happy smile.

Two weeks later in Kathmandu, Milan tore open the envelope and read the letter Laxmi had sent. At first he couldn't believe what he was reading. It was so unexpected. So incredible! Then he broke into a smile as the full meaning of the message sank in. He didn't really care for another child. In fact, he had decided that it was wrong to add any more children to this already overpopulated world. But he was happy for Laxmi. It was her fervent wish, the only one ambition she had in life, in fact. It was the only one thing that would make her feel a complete woman. He immediately sat down to write a long letter to Laxmi. "Although I am unemployed at present and dependent upon my aunt and uncle, you must come to Kathmandu to have the child in the hospital here. I know that Amrita will be more than happy to see you and help us," he wrote.

A month later, after missing another period and observing some changes in her physiognomy, Laxmi confirmed that she was truly pregnant. Her unexpected pregnancy quickly turned into fodder for village gossip. Neighbours and relatives dropped by citing one or another reason to confirm for themselves what they had heard and went back satisfied.

Inevitably, many theories sprung up to explain her past inability to conceive and most fingers pointed at her long dead husband. Perhaps it was merciful that he was already dead.

"It was her dead husband's fault after all," an old man said to other old men over a cup of tea, "he was impotent". The others quietly agreed.
"Did you hear that Purna had a missing ball?" a young woman whispered to her giggling friends at the village spring.
"So I've heard," quipped another.
"Is it true that a man cannot impregnate a woman if he has a ball missing?" another added mischievously and they all laughed.

"I bet poor old Purna had a very small penis," one young man said to his friends, "If I remember correctly even as a boy he hardly ever talked of sex and never showed us his penis. You know, he was never known to masturbate."

"Perhaps he was incapable of having sex," another added.
"But how is it that his wife never left him? They say that women can't live with husbands who cannot satisfy them sexually," a third added, "I have heard that once they get a taste of it, they need it more than us, you know."
"Perhaps, she is just too nice and kind to do such a thing."
"Or perhaps she never got the first taste in the first place."

In the villages, people do not need the supposedly corrupting influence of television and films to talk dirty. It comes to them naturally, and they use dirty words liberally. Men of all ages and many older women intersperse every sentence they utter with vulgar words and although people may vehemently deny it, sex is the favourite topic of discussion anywhere in the world, among both the male and female gender.

All of the malicious rumours circulating about Purna were, of course, untrue. Only Laxmi knew the truth. True, Purna was a man of shy disposition, but he had been sexually active. It has taken some tacit encouragement from her in the beginning, but after that he had taken to it. He had never been as passionate, virile and exciting as his younger brother, but he was capable of it. But, of course, Laxmi never got to hear the rumours herself. Even if she had, she wouldn't have refuted the allegations. There was no point in that.

A month later Laxmi received a hand-carried letter from her sister-in-law Amrita.

Dearest Elder Sister-in-law,

Lots and lots of love and sweet remembrance! It's been a long time since I last wrote to you. To think of it, I realize now that I haven't written to you since we were in England, and that was almost a year ago. But I hope I will be excused for my laziness considering that I haven't heard from you since the last time you wrote to me at about the same time. It's going to be a long letter and I hope I will not bore you to death.

First of all, I pray from the bottom of my heart that the gods and goddesses are keeping you in good health and that the baby inside your womb is growing well. When I heard the good news from my brother Milan I was so happy (for you) that I just cannot express in words how happy I was. I hope that you are taking good care of yourself. But my happiness is tempered by our poor father's disappearance. I worry about him every day. Deep inside my heart I know that he is still alive and hope he'll return home one day. I pray for him every day. That's all we can do in these difficult times, pray. This cruel and senseless war that they call the 'people's war' has affected the lives of all of us. It breaks my heart to think that my father's whereabouts is unknown, my older brother was beaten senseless and left to die, and my younger brother is fighting somewhere putting his life at risk every day. Sometimes dream of Ratna, and I see him lying dead in his own pool of blood, killed by the army. But I hope he is still alive. The injustice of it all infuriates me and saddens me. Sometimes I feel depressed thinking how utterly helpless we are in the face of the insurmountable odds stacked against us.

Sister-in-law, beside my parents and grandma, it's you that I miss and long to see the most. I was but a little girl when you came to become a part of our family, and you know that I have always looked upon you as my own elder sister. Now that I have become older, I realize that you were not much more than a child yourself at that time. I don't remember you ever saying an unkind word to me, not even when I threw tantrum, the silly little girl that I was, and let slip out of my tongue words that I shouldn't have uttered. Remember sister-in-law, how we used to go to the woods together to cut grass and gather firewood, and you used to carry some of my load, too. Remember how once when it rained so heavily that the two of us had to take shelter in an abandoned cowshed for two hours, and the roof leaked so profusely that it made us all wet anyway. There are so many beautiful memories I have of you. When I heard the news of my eldest brother's death I cried for many nights, not so much for him as for you. He was quiet and distant, and never talked much to me, but you have a special place in my heart. And when you got married to my second brother, I found myself shedding tears of joy once again. Believe me, if I were to be given a choice, I would ask to be born as your little sister in my next life. I can't wait to see you and share my feelings with you. I've got so much to tell you, and so much to hear from you. So much water has flowed in the river of time since we were last together that it seems like ages ago. But what can we mere mortals do when the almighty gods and goddesses themselves wish otherwise? The daily deteriorating law and order situation in the country does not allow us to visit you. My in-laws have sent a message from the village that the Maoists are waiting to collect a huge sum (running into hundreds of thousands of rupees) as 'donation' from my husband if he were to ever set foot there.

    We have finally decided to settle for good in Kathmandu. The older children do not want to live in Dharan, let alone return to the village. The life that I used to live in the village is alien to them. But one day, when the situation improves, I hope to bring them along with me to Khewang to meet their grandparents. We have sold our house in Dharan and moved all our belongings to Kathmandu. Life in the city comes with its own problems. There is chronic shortage of water and we have to save every drop of it. Kathmandu is dusty, congested and crowded, and everywhere you go there are people. They say that the population of the city has exploded because of the Maoist problem. Here everything has to be bought and that at exorbitant prices, even things like vegetables, oranges, lemons and bananas. This is not to say that things are entirely bad. There are lots of good things, too, which one can never hope to get in the village. Life in the city affects one in more ways than one can think. I myself am amazed when I realize how I have transformed into a city woman. I do miss the village life, once in a while, but I also know deep inside my heart that I can't live there any more because this life of comfort has spoilt me.

My son and daughter are growing up fast. Bibek, who is now five, and Sumnima, who is now three, are quite a handful and take up all my time. Bibek has started going to an English medium school nearby. I walk him to and from school every morning and afternoon. We are thinking of sending Sumnima to the same school next year. Everybody says that Bibek looks like me and Sumnima looks like her father. It is said that if a son resembles his mother and a daughter her father, then they will be very fortunate. I hope the saying is true. Sister-in-law, marriage and motherhood have changed me a lot. You can see from the photographs that I have sent that I have gained weight. I am not the same naïve little girl any more. I know that you still remember me as the frivolous girl who used get into trouble. And believe me when I say this, in spite of the age difference I have found happiness with my husband Rajkumar. He is gentle and caring, and a good husband to me and a good father to his children.

Rajkumar is thinking of going to a place called Afghanistan. There was recently a big war in that country after the terrorists killed all those people in America. We watched it on television. Now that the war has ended, former British Gurkhas are in great demand to keep the security. He is not going for the money. He is going because he has found it difficult to adjust to civilian life after so long in the British army. You see, he's been in the army all his adult life. Since his retirement he's got practically nothing to do except to sit on the sofa, drink beer and watch television. Initially, he was happy to be free at last, but now I can feel his restlessness. People say that the situation is still dangerous in that country, but his mind is set and he is determined to go. This idle and sedentary life style, he says, will kill him faster than the war. Many of his colleagues have already left.

Gorimaya has been a great help to me ever since she came to live with us. She has turned into a proper city girl and wears jeans, T-shirts and miniskirts like the other girls. She's become very pretty, too. But I have told her very strictly not to make any boyfriends. Young men here are not trustworthy. All they want to do is get into a girl's skirts. So far as I know she hasn't, but she does receive a few bluff calls every week. She has recently completed her first year in nursing college. She hopes to become a staff nurse, and in this I support her. We didn't get the chance to further our education but we must provide opportunity to those who come after us. This reminds me of my second sister-in-law Lalita who used to tell me that her dream as a young girl was to become a nurse. Poor woman, she died so young. She was such a beautiful, lively and strong-willed person. Although I had misgivings about her initially, I was won over by her liveliness and had grown fond of her, and she towards me.

Sister-in-law, I am upset at you for not writing to me personally about your pregnancy. Anyway, it is the most amazing news I have heard in a long time, and I am so happy for you. Please take good care of yourself. Do not work too hard. Do not carry heavy loads. Do not cut firewood. Do not run and do not travel too far. You need a lot of rest for the child to grow properly. In the village we never give importance to such things and that's why so many women lose their babies and their lives during and after delivery. And in these modern times, you must deliver the baby in a hospital. Therefore, it is my fervent wish that you come to Kathmandu. My brother agrees with me. I have plenty of space in my house. I'll take good care of you. Please do come. Don't say no. If you decline I'll feel terribly hurt thinking that you don't care for me.

Sister-in-law, please take good care of our mother and grandma. I know that I don't have to tell you this because you are much more mature and wiser than me. I hear that my mother has become emaciated and looks older than her age. And as for my poor old grandma, who has seen so much in her long life, I think of her a lot, too.

This is all for today. I hope I did not bore you with my endless monologue. I'll write to you again when I am free. Please do write back to me. I am so anxious to hear about the people I have been out of touch for so long. I'll be waiting. I hope to see you in Kathmandu soon. My regards to all and love to the children (I want to see them so much).

> With lots of love,
> Your loving sister-in-law,
> Amrita

After reading the letter once again, slowly so that she could digest every word, Laxmi put it back carefully in its enveloped, pulled the painted tin box that was under her bed, and deposited it along with the other older letters. She kept all her valuables in the tin box. There was a smile on her face. She had made up her mind to go to Kathmandu.

In the midst of the monsoon season, there was an abrupt change in the ongoing political drama in the country, though much of the rural area (under the firm grip of the Maoists) remained unaffected. After being unable to muster the support of his own fractious party to extend the state of emergency, the prime minister dissolved the bickering parliament and called for fresh general elections. The common man in the street shook his head in a gesture of denial and remarked, "This is ridiculous. How can general elections be held when much of the countryside is in the hands of the rebels?"

That year's monsoon was particularly harsh for the eastern hills. In Taplejung district, landslides caused by incessant rain swept several houses to the swollen river down below in a number of villages. Several people lost their property and lives, and the tragedy made headline news in the national media. But they were quickly forgotten, for the world must move on. Nothing and nobody can stop the endless march of time.

At the end of monsoon, Laxmi made the long-awaited journey to Kathmandu. First she travelled to the town of Phidim with a male escort, a cousin. Milan was waiting for her there. Everytime he passed through the town, it reminded him of Lalita and filled him with sadness. It was where she had died, and down below it flowed the river where she was cremated. From there they took the bus to Kathmandu.

Milan considered the city of Kathmandu practically his home, and every time the bus entered the valley through the smoke-filled narrow street with unpainted two-storey brick houses lining the sides, it felt like homecoming. He had spent his formative years in this city and truly felt at home here. He inhaled the black smoke spewing out of the exhaust pipe of the packed buses and enjoyed the ordour; every time was like the old times all over again and feeling of nostalgia overwhelmed his senses. Now that he couldn't go back to Khewang, the city had become his permanent home. Since coming to Kathmandu six months ago, he had stayed at his uncle's house plotting his future. There was practically no work for him in the city as its streets were full of young men like him, displaced by the people's war. He was hoping to go abroad and his uncle and aunt had promised to help.

Laxmi covered her nose with a handkerchief and coughed. "What a horrible smell!" she said. "How can people live in such a place?"
"You'll get used to it," Milan replied as she wrinkled her nose in disgust.

It was the first time in Kathmandu for Laxmi and though she had heard so much about the fabled city, she still felt awed by its sheer size. She had never been anywhere near a city as large as this. "I don't think I'd be able to find my way if I were to get lost here," she confided to Milan as the bus weaved its way along the Chinese-built Ring Road that was meant to encircle the city at the time it was built but has now been completely swallowed up by the ever-expanding urban sprawl. Milan smiled knowingly and said, "I remember feeling the same way when I first came here as a little boy. But now I know every nook and corner of the city. It's actually not that big compared to foreign cities like Bangkok and Kuala Lumpur."

When they alighted from the bus at the large and modern bus park in Gongobu (built with Japanese aid), they found that Amrita was waiting for them with her eldest son – her husband's eldest son by his first wife – with a taxi. The two women stared at each other in awe for close to a minute and then they both broke into an effusive laughter simultaneously and fell into each other's open arms.

"Sister-in-law, I had almost given hope of ever seeing you again," Amrita said happily, "Oh, I am so happy."

"Me, too. But here I am," Laxmi replied, laughing.

"Sister-in-law, you are as pretty as ever," Amrita said.

"You, too, Amrita," Laxmi returned the compliment.

"You must be tired," Amrita said. "This is Prabin, my eldest son," Amrita pointed at the boy. The tall and slim young man greeted Milan and Laxmi shyly with a *Namaste* and picked up Laxmi's bag.

Amrita's three-storey house was in a place called Baluwatar, a posh locality near the prime minister's official residence. She lived alone with her children since Rajkumar had left for Afghanistan. Gorimaya lived in the hostel in her nursing campus and came home during the weekends only. Laxmi marveled at the sheer size and beauty of the house. The floor and staircase were covered with expensive-looking cold, hard and shiny marbles of different colours and patterns. The windows were made of tinted glass where one could see one's reflection from outside but nothing of the inside. After a breakfast of tea and bread with butter and fried eggs, Amrita took Laxmi on a guided tour of the inside of her house. Every corner of the house mesmerized her. There were more rooms than its inhabitants could fill. The immaculately furnished living room was filled with expensive-looking sofas that were a delight to sit on - warm, soft and cozy. She introduced Laxmi to her children who were watching a cartoon film on the television, comfortably sprawled on the sofa. Laxmi touched the multi-coloured flowers and fruits on the glass table and realized that they were made of plastic. Amrita's bedroom had a double-sized bed covered with a beautifully patterned quilt and a life-size mirror with a dressing table attached to it. The kitchen had a gas oven, a squeaky clean wash basin, a microwave oven and a large refrigerator among other things. Amrita showed her how to operate them. Beside the kitchen was the dining room where they had earlier had their breakfast. The bathrooms were spotlessly clean and fragrant. Laxmi knew that in the cities there were stool-like toilets, but she didn't know that they could be this clean and shiny. Amrita showed her how to flush the toilet. Pointing to the automatic washing machine Amrita told her that she never used it because of the chronic shortage of water.

Luckily for Laxmi, Milan had instructed her on many of the things on the way and though she had never laid her eyes on them before she recognized many of the objects without much difficulty. She had formed some idea about Amrita's life in the city (from the latter's letters), but she had never imagined that her sister-in-law lived in such luxury. "Fate! This is all according to one's fate," she murmured inaudibly as she her eyes darted from one object to another in marvel. Not everyone who has a dream gets to live that dream.

This was the kind of life Milan had dreamt of. He had even suffered for it. Then he had given up that dream until he had been forced out of his village. On the way to Kathmandu, Milan had talked effusively. After his ordeal at the hands of Maoists he had acquired a more philosophical outlook on life.

"There are some things in life that are beyond one's control. But time is the greatest force in the universe. The Maoists seem all-powerful today, with their guns and terror-tactics, but there will come a day when they will become nothing more than distant memories. When that day comes where will Comrade Raktim be? He'll probably be running for his life hiding his tail between his thighs, repenting the crimes he has committed in the name of the people," he had said as Laxmi had listened quietly.

He had also told her of his hope for his country: "People see only corruption, death and destruction everywhere, but I see hope. This war will not last forever and our country will not always remain impoverished. When this rebellion blows over, as it certainly will for there is no place for dictatorship of any kind in today's world, even in the name of the people, we will rise up and rebuild our lives. We Nepalese have a place in the world and one day we'll take that place. We'll stand tall and proud as a free people of a free nation among all the other free and democratic nations of the world." Laxmi hadn't understood it in its entirety, but she had nodded her head quietly.

"Make yourself at home," Amrita said to her older brother and sister-in-law. Milan temporarily moved to his sister's house. Amrita was a generous hostess. She fed them sumptuous meals every day, and every night Milan sat on the sofa with a jar of *tongba* with his nephews and nieces to watch television. Sometimes the *tongba* was replaced by a bottle of ice cold beer. During the days he visited old friends to catch up on their latest news. And every few days Laxmi visited Milan's uncle's house, sometimes with Milan and sometimes with Amrita.

In Kathmandu, the Maoists seemed few and far away. If one were to shut oneself in one's house and refrain from reading the newspapers and following the news on television then it was as if they didn't exist. But to shut the world out would be to live a life of illusion, because the streets were full of people - displaced, unemployed and desperate. Refugees in their own land. Some had been driven out by the rebels, like Milan, and others had run away to avoid joining the militia. Since there were no employment opportunities for them there, all of them were desperate to go abroad – to East Asia, South East Asia, the Middle East, Australia, Europe and North America, anywhere they could go, it didn't matter where. They just wanted to get the hell out of this Hell in the making. Every day Milan saw thousands of young men like him in the clogged streets of Kathmandu, semi-educated, unskilled and unemployed, with shattered dreams and unattainable goals. The rebellion had destroyed everything for them – their lives, their future, their hopes and their aspirations. There was nothing left for them. Some of these same men and women, once they ran out of all options, would be forced to go back to the villages and join the ranks of the rebels to wreak more destruction.

Laxmi insisted on helping Amrita in the kitchen, but the latter wouldn't let her. When Amrita finally relented, she let her do only the lightest chores. Thus, by the time her delivery date arrived Laxmi had gone soft and gained considerable weight. A few days after arrival Amrita had taken her to the Japanese built Teaching Hospital, built with Japanese aid, for check up and after that they had continued the visit regularly for follow-up.

One day at the dinner table Amrita said to Milan, "Older brother, my neighbour was saying that the South Korean government is giving work permits to thousands of Nepalese workers. Is that true?"

"It might be true. All of my friends have been talking about it," he replied.
"If it is true and if you got the chance, will you go?" she asked.
"Of course, I will," he replied, "That's what I have been trying to do for the past one year. I would have already gone to Saudi Arabia if your sister-in-law hadn't got pregnant."
"They say it's a lot better to go to South Korea money-wise. But they also say that the agents charge an exorbitant sum."
"That's true."
"Have you got the money, older brother?"
"Uncle has promised to help me," Milan replied dubiously.
"You've never asked me, but you can take it from me," Amrita said.
"I can't take any money from my younger sister." It was his pride speaking.
"You will not be taking it from me. It will be a loan from your brother-in-law. Free of interest, of course."
"I'll pay you the amount as well as the interest," he said and was surprised that he had already decided to grab the offer.
He turned to Laxmi and said, "If I go I might be away for many years. Will you wait for me?"
"Yes," she said, "I will. I will always wait for you."
"And when I come back, you'll come with the children to live with me in the city?"
"I will. I'll also bring mother and grandma. I'll talk to them. I'm sure they'll agree."
"And when I am away will you take care of my mother and grandma?"
"Of course, I will. What kind of question is that? Haven't I until now? You know I love them much more than you do." Laxmi replied and Milan knew that what she said was true.

Milan gave her a fond look and said, "If you don't like living in the city, we can return to the village some day. There will come a day when the people will get sick of this so-called people's war and the mindless violence that goes in its name. That day the wind will change course and blow the Maoists away into oblivion. Sometimes, the forces of extremism win by brute force, as the Maoists seem to be doing now, but their victory won't last long. No one can stop mankind's march towards freedom, not even in the name of the people, for it's every man's destiny to be free."

Three months after her arrival, Laxmi was admitted at the same hospital. Milan and his nephew Prabin accompanied the women this time. As the two men paced up and down the floors of the sprawling hospital complex, Prabin, Amrita's guitar-strumming eldest son by her husband's first wife, observed sarcastically, "Everything in this country is built with foreign aid."
Milan agreed with a resigned smile, "Yes, in the past half a century we have turned into a nation of beggars."
"I wonder where all the money goes."
"That's no secret. Our politicians and bureaucrats have to maintain an expensive life style and send their children to universities in Australia, Europe and North America. How do you think they manage to do that?"

The following day, after a labour pain of nearly four hours, Laxmi gave birth to a healthy baby. Milan was not allowed to witness the birth. He did not want to. He spent anxious hours pacing the hospital's cold, hard floor with his sister and nephew, oblivious to the hundreds of people coming in and going out – half of them ill and the other half accompanying the ill. When a nurse finally came out and told him that his wife had given birth to a healthy child, he was immensely relieved.

Laxmi spent three more months in Kathmandu on Amrita's insistence. Amrita fed her chicken soup and laid her out in the sun on the attic every morning and massaged her body with liberal quantities of mustard oil. During her stay another political drama played itself out in Kathmandu. When the beleaguered prime minister postponed the elections citing security reasons, the King dismissed him accusing him of incompetence. Immediately after that, using an article of the constitution, the King assumed the executive powers of the state in his own hands and installed a loyal royalist as prime minister. Now suddenly there were three sides to the war – the King and his royalist followers (who called themselves nationalists) on one side, the hardline communist Maoists on the other side and the 'constitutional-monarchist' parliamentary parties hemmed in the middle. The parliamentarians were the only ones who didn't have guns in their hands.

In winter it take the whole morning for the thick white mist that covers the hills and riverbeds to dissipate to reveal a mild sun, and the white frost that covers the barren fields, trees and roofs of houses take even longer to thaw and disappear. Then after a few hours of warmth the sun disappears behind the western hills giving way to a dark and frosty cold night. It was one such biting cold January day when Laxmi arrived back home with her newborn child hidden under several layers of cloths in the company of a male escort. He was the same cousin who had accompanied her before. Milan had accompanied her to as far as the town of Phidim and returned.

Kamala was overjoyed to see her daughter-in-law once again. As soon as Laxmi set foot into the courtyard she scooped up the baby in her hands and stared at it in wonder, smiling happily, as if it was the first time she was seeing a baby.

"What is it? It's a daughter, isn't it?" she asked excitedly, answering her own question. She already knew the sex of the baby, but wanted to make doubly sure.

"Yes, mother, it's a daughter," Laxmi replied shyly.

"I thought you were going to have a boy. But never mind. Look how beautiful she is. She looks just like her father, doesn't she? She'll be very fortunate," Kamala cooed. "What have you named her?"

"Anjali," Laxmi replied, "Milan gave her that name."

"What a beautiful name!" Kamala said as she took the baby in her arms and planted several kisses on its cheeks.

The children ran to Laxmi squealing in delight and threw themselves at the two. "Mother, where have you been for so long?" they cried as they leapt into her arms.

"Mother had gone to bring you a little sister, my little darlings. But I have now come back to you," Laxmi said in the most endearing voice.

"Don't leave me like that again, mother, or I'll be angry with you," cried Santosh, now a lively little boy of three.

"No, I won't. I won't ever leave my son again," Laxmi said as she took the boy in her arms and showered his cheeks with kisses.

A month later the government and the Maoists announced another truce. This time it was to last for a full eight months before it was to be broken abruptly by the rebels again. This time, in spite of Kamala's prayers, Ratna didn't come home. He didn't even send a message. Later one of the local Maoist leaders told them that he had made a name for himself as a feared and respected fighter in a mobile unit somewhere in central Nepal.

Five months after Laxmi had returned to Khewang, Milan left for South Korea to work for a private company, with perfectly legal papers this time. As he made himself comfortable in his seat on the Royal Nepal Airlines Boeing 757, he smiled smugly. *My dream is finally taking shape. And this time it's for real. I hope in three years I'll be able to save enough money to build or buy a modest house in Kathmandu. Then I'll be united with my family.*

In Kathmandu the royalist prime minister installed by the king was replaced by yet another royalist prime minister, though to a lesser degree. Both men were ghosts from the past; each had served several years in that capacity during the thirty-year Panchayat system. They possessed neither the ability nor the credibility to solve the country's problems and propel the country into the brave new world of the 21st century. The streets of Kathmandu and other urban areas were wracked by violent strikes, *chakka-jam* (jam the wheels) and *Nepal Bandh* (Close Nepal) that took place almost every day.

Meanwhile, the village of Khewang, like the rest of the rural area, was peacefully under the tight grip of the Maoists. In spite of there being a people's government, real power lay in the hand of Comrade Raktim because he was the one with the gun. He saw to it that those who said or did anything contrary to the spirit of the revolution were swiftly dealt with. After the initial thrusts the army never returned to the village. Undermanned and over-stretched, the soldiers were too busy protecting the towns and bazaars.

Kamala spent most of her time in the vegetable garden – digging, planting, watering, picking and weeding the plants – and constantly worrying about her missing husband. The octogenarian Narmaya spent her days playing with her four great-grandchildren as she patiently awaited death which she knew was not very far in the future. "I dreamt of your great-grandfather last night. He was calling me to go to him. He was on the other side of the river and I was wading across the river towards him. But when I had reached halfway I suddenly woke up," she mumbled to the two girls who were not big enough to understand the meaning of her words.

When the Maoists came to discover six months later that Milan was employed abroad, they promptly arrived with a request for 'donation' presenting Laxmi with a bill of a hundred thousand rupees. They had come up with the figure without bothering to consult anybody. Frightened, Laxmi wrote to Milan the very next day. When Milan got the letter three weeks later he became very angry and fumed the whole day. But realizing that he was powerless to do anything he borrowed the requisite amount from his friends and sent it to Laxmi which she promptly *donated* to the rebels and got a receipt with a 'thank you' note in exchange.

Early one morning exactly a year after the birth of Laxmi's daughter, Kamala walked out of the kitchen into the courtyard with a broom and abruptly froze in her tracks. She stared and stared at the emaciated figure of the man who was her husband sitting quietly on his favourite stool, smoking *khosela* and gazing at the slope of the hill across the River Tawa. She pinched her arm to ascertain that she was awake. Yes, it was for real; it was not a dream. The apparition was indeed her long lost husband in flesh and blood. Dil Bahadur took a long sip from his khosela and slowly turned to face her. Their eyes met – hers utterly astonished, and his sad and sunken but glad to see her at last. He had become as thin as a stick and every line on his gaunt face betrayed the suffering he had been through.

"They let you go?" was all she could say.

"Yes," he replied but did not elaborate. He turned towards the slope across the River Tawa and said: "Purna's mother, when my eyes were still good, I could clearly see the houses on the opposite slope, like little match-boxes. I could even make out the tiny human figures going into and coming out of those houses."

Then turning to her he said, "Are you all right?"

"I am," she replied with tearful eyes.

"How's mother?"

"She is fine."

"And daughter-in-law and the children?"

"They are also fine."

"Is Milan still at home?"

"No, he's gone abroad," she replied.

"Good. I was hoping that he had left. This is no place for a young man like him anymore," he said, shaking his head slowly.

Kamala was overcome with emotions - surprise, shock, disbelief, relief, joy and a host of other feelings that mere words cannot express. As she stood gazing at him with a stream of tears trickling down her cheeks, a joyful smile broke on her face like the full moon, for these were tears of joy. He looked into her eyes and smiled, creasing his forehead into several folds and revealing his gapped and smoke-stained teeth.

"Mother, Laxmi," she cried out at the top of her voice, "Purna's father is back. He's come back. Come out, quick. He's come back to us." He was truly back, in flesh and blood, and nothing else mattered anymore.

And thus life goes on, like the river, twisting and turning and overcoming all obstacles, but always on course to its final destination. For what is life? It's a journey, as they say. But words cannot sufficiently describe it, for to each person it has a different meaning. But one thing is true, and that is life is too short to cry over spilt milk and shattered dreams. The hills and the mountains have been there for millions of years; they will be there for millions and millions of years to come. A person's life is but for two days only, as the Nepalese are fond of saying, one a sunny day and the other a rainy day. Another truth is this: pain and suffering recur constantly in life in their many guises, but they do not last forever. They are interrupted by periods of happiness – some brief and some extended. This is what makes life so sweet and worth living.

The End